Supernatural Beings

from Japanese Noh Plays of the Fifth Group

Supernatural Beings
from Japanese Noh Plays of the Fifth Group

Parallel Translations
with Running Commentary

Chifumi Shimazaki & Stephen Comee

The Cornell East Asia Series is published by the Cornell University East Asia Program (distinct from Cornell University Press). We publish affordably priced books on a variety of scholarly topics relating to East Asia as a service to the academic community and the general public. Address submission inquiries to CEAS Editorial Board, East Asia Program, Cornell University, Ithaca, New York 14853-7601.

Publication of this volume was made possible through the generous assistance of the late Dr. Howard B. Hamilton.

Cover illustrations: *Front*—Tsukioka Kōgyo, "Adachigahara" (from the series *Pictures from Noh Performances* [*Nōgaku-zue*], woodblock print, 1898). Coll. Stephen B. Comee (ex Coll. Howard B. Hamilton). *Back*—Manzaburō Umewaka III as the *Nochi-shite* of *Adachigahara* (Tokyo, 1999). Photograph by the Maejima Photo Studio, courtesy the Umewaka Kennōkai Foundation.

Illustrations used on title pages of each play: Taken from *Yōkyoku Taikan*, published by Meiji Shoin (Tokyo, 1931–39), and used here with the kind permission of the publisher. Illustration on p. 291: Dr. Howard Hamilton as the *Mae-shite* of *Nue* (Itsukushima Shrine, Miyajima, ca. 1974). Photo courtesy Dr. Howard B. Hamilton.

Book design and typography by Stephen Comee, with great thanks to his best friend, Aisin Gioro Pu T'ien-pao, for constant support and dedicated companionship.
Proofread by Terrance Swanson.

Number 161 in the Cornell East Asia Series

ISSN 1050-2955
ISBN: 978-1-933947-31-0 hc
ISBN: 978-1-933947-61-7 pb
Library of Congress Control Number: 2012949605
Printed in the United States of America

∞ The paper in this book meets the requirements for permanence of ISO 9706:1994.

If not unto you,
To whom, then, can I show the
Blossoms of the plum—
For I know that you well know
Their fragrance and their splendor.

—Ki no Tomomori, *Kokin-shū* 38

In Memoriam

Chifumi Shimazaki
(May 15, 1910–October 14, 1998)

✧

Howard B. Hamilton
(December 14, 1918–April 27, 2007)

✧

Karen Brazell
(April 25, 1938–January 18, 2012)

✧

Madalyn L. Comee
(May 16, 1927–June 29, 2012)

Contents

Prefaces & Acknowledgments

THE FIFTY or so plays that are classified as *gobanme-mono* (fifth-on-the-program pieces), with their great variety, can be further divided into sub-groups. A large part of the general introduction to the fifth-group Noh is devoted to analysis and classification of this group. My classification differs slightly from those of other writers, as it is based strictly upon the structural characteristics of individual Noh plays themselves, while other systems are more or less traditional and are therefore not always logical.

The publication of this book owes much to the assistance and encouragement of many friends, to whom I would like to express my deepest thanks. For their devoted assistance and great encouragement over the last twenty-five years, I am especially grateful to Dr. Howard Hamilton, a Noh expert of the Kita school, and my co-author for this volume, Mr. Stephen Comee, a Noh actor of the Kanze school who also serves as special consultant to the Japan Foundation and teaches Japanese classics at Meiji Gakuin University. Continuing from the preceding book (*Troubled Souls*), Dr. Hamilton has undertaken the heavy responsibility of serving as general coordinator, generously offering his time and energy for the task; and Mr. Comee, who had originally translated three of the plays and given me his manuscripts to work with, placed his expertise as both a professional editor and a Noh actor at my disposal, spending untold hours discussing various aspects of the plays and their translations with me, and helping me in the chores of writing the introductions and annotations. I am also much indebted to him for donating countless hours formatting the manuscript for the publisher.

I would also like to express my sincere thanks to Professor Haruo Nishino of Hōsei University and the Nogami Kinen Hōsei Daigaku Nōgaku Kenkyūjo (Nogami Memorial Noh Research Institute, Hōsei University), for his personal advice over the years; I have consulted his many scholarly works, including "Nō genkō kyoku ichiran" [List of Currently Performed Noh], which appears in *Nōgaku Zensho* [Compendium of Noh Drama], vol. 6 (Tokyo: Sōgensha, 1979), in formulating my own classification.

The overall plan for the full series of translations titled *The Noh* by Chifumi Shimazaki includes (previously published titles are marked with an asterisk):

Shimazaki, Chifumi, ed. and trans. 1972–. *The Noh.* 5 vols., 11 books planned. Tokyo: Hinoki Shoten (HS); Ithaca: East Asia Program, Cornell University (CEAS).

*Vol. 1: *God Noh* (1972); translations of: *Ema, Kamo, Ōimatsu, Seiōbo, Takasago, Yōrō;* with a general introduction to Noh and an introduction to *kami* (god)-Noh. HS.

*Vol. 2: *Battle Noh,* Book 1 (1987); translations of: *Atsumori, Kiyotsune, Tadanori, Tomonaga, Tsunemasa;* with an introduction to *shura* (battle)-Noh. HS; CEAS 91 (1998).

*Vol. 2: *Battle Noh,* Book 2 (1993); translations of: *Kanehira, Michimori, Tomoakira, Tomoe, Yashima, Yorimasa.* Published as: *Warrior Ghost Plays from the Japanese Noh Theater.* CEAS 60.

*Vol. 3: *Woman Noh,* Book 1 (1976); translations of: *Hajitomi, Kochō, No-no-Miya, Yūgao;* with an introduction to woman-Noh. HS.

*Vol. 3: *Woman Noh,* Book 2 (1977); translations of: *Eguchi, Izutsu, Kakitsubata, Matsukaze, Obasute.* HS.

*Vol. 3: *Woman Noh,* Book 3 (1981); translations of: *Futari Shizuka, Hotoke no Hara, Ohara gokō, Senju, Yuya.* HS.

*Vol. 4: Fourth-group Noh, Book 1 (1994); translations of: *Funabashi, Kazuraki, Saigyō-zakura, Tenko;* with an introduction to fourth-group Noh. Published as: *Restless Spirits from the Japanese Noh Plays of the Fourth Group.* CEAS 76.

*Vol. 4: Fourth-group Noh, Book 2 (1998); translations of: *Aoi no Ue, Jinen Koji, Kagekiyo, Kogō, Semimaru.* Published as: *Troubled Souls from the Japanese Noh Plays of the Fourth Group.* CEAS 95.

Vol. 4: Fourth-group Noh, Book 3 (planned); with Stephen Comee; translations of: *Fujito, Hyakuman, Ikkaku Sennin, Koi no Omoni, Matsumushi, Tsurukame, Uta-ura* (planned).

Vol. 5: Fifth-group Noh, Book 1 (this volume); with Stephen Comee; translations of: *Adachigahara, Kumasaka, Kurama Tengu, Kuruma-zō, Kuzu, Matsuyama Tengu, Nue, Shōkun;* with an introduction to fifth-group Noh. Published as: *Supernatural Beings from the Japanese Noh Plays of the Fifth Group.* CEAS 161.

Vol. 5: Fifth-group Noh, Book 2 (planned); with Stephen Comee; translations of *deus-ex-machina* plays and other outstanding pieces (planned).

—Chifumi Shimazaki
Tokyo; May 14, 1998

I FIRST MET Mrs. Chifumi Shimazaki at a performance given at the Suidōbashi Noh Theatre on December 1, 1974. I had been purchasing the *utaibon* (script) for the day's feature plays, and the owner of Hinoki Shoten, the late Mr. Tsunetarō Hinoki, was kind enough to introduce us. The day marked my first attendance of a formal Noh performance, and the plays were *Sumidagawa* (Fusao Hōshō) and *Dōjōji* (Hisao Kanze). Mrs. Shimazaki was very eager to tell me all about the plays, so that I would appreciate the performances all the better.

She even told me of how she had once escorted Leonard Bernstein to a performance of *Sumidagawa.* When the hip-drum player began—with plaintive, piercing cries and a loud strike of the drum—Bernstein just gasped and said, "How tragic!" She assumed that his innate musical sense was keen enough to understand the emotion packed into that one drumbeat. She added that I was lucky to be experiencing the play performed by the same drummer, Living National Treasure Haruo Yasufuku. She guided me through the tale of a mother crazed with longing for her lost son, who searches all over for him, only to find his grave and his ghost.

She also explained the Kyogen play (*Kane no Ne* [Manzō Nomura VI]), and then tried to prepare me for *Dōjōji.* She told me the outline of the story, and very carefully explained all about the *ranbyōshi.* Again, she said I was lucky to be seeing the play performed by the best actor of the time, and to hear the *ranbyōshi* played by one of the leading shoulder-drum players, Hisashi Uzawa. Her kind guidance—coupled with what many have since called "the ideal Noh program"—insured that I was to become enamored of Noh forevermore. I was happy to have found—at last—someone who knew so much about Noh and who loved Noh so much. In a manner of speaking, it was love at first sight.

We saw each other many times after that, sometimes at one of the Noh theatres, sometimes at her home, where she would help me understand the meaning of the texts I was learning to chant. The following May saw both of our birthdays, and Chifumi very generously gave me copies of the Shōgaku-kan and Iwanami books (*see* Bibliography) to facilitate my study. She also suggested that if I really wanted to understand Noh, I had to gain a good grasp of the *Tale of Genji* as well as court poetry. She invited me to visit her whenever I had the time, and we first read *Genji* in its entirety, taking about 20 years, with her very carefully explaining the language and the grammar, but more importantly, the meaning of, and the heart infused in, the text. Even in the midst of studying *Genji,* we moved on to study sections of the *Man'yōshū,* the *Kokinshū,* the *Shin Kokinshū,* the *Hyakunin Isshū,* the *Heike Monogatari,* the *Taiheiki,* and the *Kojiki.* Under her excellent tutelage and expert guidance, I gradually formed a solid base upon which to base my appreciation and study of Japanese classical literature—and drama, for all the while, we were also studying and translating and analyzing various Noh plays and aesthetic treatises.

I began studying Noh as an amateur performer under Makio Umewaka (as of October 2001, he has taken the name Manzaburō III) in early 1975 and was later promoted to *uchi-deshi* (professional actor in apprenticeship) under both Makio and his father, the great Manzaburō Umewaka II. As a semi-professional, I not only had to study and understand the texts, but also had to take lessons in all four Noh instruments, a knowledge of which is essential for a *shite* (main character) actor. Chifumi was a godsend in this regard also, since she had been studying the *ko-tsuzumi* and *ō-tsuzumi.* She helped me immensely with my study of those instruments, and encouraged me to go on to try the *nō-kan* (Noh flute) and *taiko* as well. I was fortunate in being able to study all four instruments under great teachers. But in addition, I was blessed by having Mrs. Shimazaki not only explain the different techniques and how they were used in different plays to indicate different actions or create different moods, but also bring together the whole of Noh—its music, chant, acting, text, costuming—into one great gestalt.

Whoever invented the word "walking encyclopedia" must have had Chifumi in mind. As a youth, she had memorized all 100 poems of the *Hyakunin Isshū,* as well as the major poems of the *Man'yōshū, Kokinshū,* and *Shin Kokinshū;* she also knew many passages of *Genji*—and myriads of its poems—as well as the major sections of numerous Noh plays by heart. One day I called her and said: "Chifumi, isn't there a poem in *Genji* that is based on the *Wen Hsüan* tale about a goddess appearing as mist and rain?" She replied: "I'm surprised you don't remember that one. Tō no Chūjō recalled it at the death of Lady Aoi. It's about two-thirds of the way through the "Aoi" chapter, and if you have the Shinchō version, you'll find it on about page 100." So I was not at all surprised when I found it on page 101! To think that such a treasure-house of knowledge is now lost forever. . . .

Chifumi Shimazaki was stricken with great pain in the late summer of 1997, but, being a strong and proud Meiji woman, she bore it silently. During all that time, while we were working to tie up loose ends in *Troubled Souls* (CEAS 95, 1998), she involved me more and more in the making of Volume 5. Saying that she wanted me to work on this volume as her co-author, she gave me a list of the plays she wanted to do, and asked if I had already translated any, so I gave her copies of the translations of *Adachigahara, Nue,* and *Shōkun* that I had earlier done for the Umewaka Kennōkai's monthly performances. She re-worked all à la Shimazaki, and then I re-wrote them, had her re-do them, and then edited them. They are now, as much as possible, truly her own translations, in her own, distinctive style.

Gradually, however, as the pain became worse and worse, her condition rapidly deteriorated, requiring hospitalization for a full barrage of tests. During the testing, she celebrated her eighty-eighth birthday. As it is a special occasion in China and Japan, I brought her a piece of her favorite cake and a chalcedony seal I had carved for her that said: "May you be protected from all disease, be free from all danger, and enjoy a long and peaceful life." She was a strong woman, but, alas, no prayers or force of will could hold her back. On that birthday, she told me that she knew it was the "Will of Heaven" (*tenmei*) that she would soon depart, and she made me promise to finish Volume 5 for her, so that her series could be complete. Without finishing the series, she feared that, like the restless spirits and troubled souls of the fourth-group plays, she would be forced to forego salvation, held back by her attachment to this world because of the unfinished work. She bade me work very closely with Dr. Howard Hamilton, whose generosity and encouragement had been a source of solace and great help to her. When she told me it would take over ten years for me to finish the work, I did not believe her, but now more than a decade has passed since her demise.

Five other plays—including the introductions, the translations, and the notes—were all done entirely by Mrs. Shimazaki, except for *Kurama Tengu,* which she translated—much to the amazement of her doctors—literally on her deathbed. A few days after finishing her rough draft of the play (she had not yet done the introduction or notes), she suffered a serious stroke. A short time later, she was gone.

This whole series—and especially this volume—was from the start a work of pure love. Here I would like to offer the last lines of the play *Tōru,* for the repose of Chifumi's soul. As they are often sung at the end of a funeral service, I thought it would be an appropriate way to end the series. Also, as that play contains more poetic allusions than any other work in the fifth group, I thought that it would be a fitting tribute to her great love of classic poetry as well.

Invited by the play of light and dark,
[She] seems to enter the Lunar Realm.
Ah! Only a vestige of her glory remains,
There lingers only a memory.

In terms of mechanics, I have planned this book to follow the others in the series in style. Where I have differed is in these four major points:

1) Whenever Chinese names—both those of individuals and works—are given in the text, I have rendered them in Chinese, rather than keeping them in Japanese, since even in Japanese they are so foreign looking. I have used the modified Wade-Giles romanization of Mathews' *Chinese–English Dic-*

tionary, since these names are, for the most part, a millennium or more removed from our times, and the *pinyin* style seemed too modern.

2) Works quoted from Chinese sources—including the Chinese poems in the *Wakan Rōei-shū*—are given first in their Chinese reading, followed by the authoritative traditional Japanese reading in square brackets.

3) I have included the *ai-kyōgen* sections of all plays, to which Mrs. Shimazaki agreed, so that readers may compare the ways the tales are told in the Noh proper and by the Kyogen actor. Mrs. Shimazaki herself began this trend with her inclusion of the *ai-kyōgen* for *Eboshi-ori* in *Troubled Souls.* For reasons of space, however, we decided to omit the Japanese texts of the *ai-kyōgen* scripts.

4) I have not included her excellent appendixes, since she did not work on them, and they would, perforce, be all of my own conception and not accurately reflect Mrs. Shimazaki's thought; I have, however, included a glossary, basing it on those included in the two books of Volume 4 previously published by the Cornell East Asia Program.

✧

My deepest thanks and appreciation must be expressed to the following people, without whose great assistance this book could never have been completed: Mr. Keiichi Shimazaki, Chifumi's nephew, whom she raised as her own son, for freely making all of her writings and computer files available, for lending me many important and invaluable works from her extensive library on Noh and court poetry; Mr. Naoto Shimazaki, his son, for his help in computer matters; the late Dr. Howard Hamilton, for his great encouragement and unceasing efforts in doing all he could to insure the publication of this volume, including proofreading the manuscript in many stages and lending a photograph of himself performing *Nue;* Mr. John Dunbar, Howard's good friend, and Mr. Terrance Swanson, mine, for their help in media transfer and proofreading, respectively; Mr. Don Kenny, for graciously supplying the *ai-kyōgen* texts; Mr. Mitsuo Kakinuma and the late Mrs. Yaeko Nukada, for their patience and ingenuity in helping me to unravel difficult passages in ancient texts and explaining them in modern-day terms; the staff of the library of the Japan Foundation Library, especially Ms. Chieko Okuizumi, for so cheerfully helping me to track down hard-to-find materials; and the staff of the East Asia Program of Cornell University, for agreeing to do this volume and thus bring out Mrs. Shimazaki's first volume on the fifth-group plays of the Noh theatre—especially Karen Brazell and her love of Noh. To all of them, I am eternally grateful. Needless to say, I am solely responsible for any errors that might remain.

—*Stephen Comee*
Tokyo; May 5, 2012

Notes on the Pronunciation of Noh Language

The Japanese version of the Noh libretti in this series is romanized according to the system used in *Kenkyusha's New Japanese Dictionary* (4th ed.).

Unless marked by a macron, the vowels are all short:

a as *a* in st**a**r: *hana* (flower), *yama* (mountain), *mata* (again);
e as *e* in n**e**st: *take* (bamboo), *tera* (temple), *ware* (I);
i as *e* in b**e**low: *ima* (now), *aki* (autumn), *kami* (deity);
o as *o* in **o**bey: *hito* (person), *kono* (this), *tokoro* (place);
u as *u* in r**u**de: *uta* (song/poem), *mizu* (water), *yuki* (snow).

All long vowels, which are pronounced by doubling the length of the short vowels, are indicated by macrons (*mōsu* [to speak].

There are no diphthongs, and all vowels are pronounced:

mai (dance) = *má-i; tae* (exquisite) = *tá-e; shite* (protagonist) = *shi-té.*

Consonants are pronounced approximately as in English, but:

ch as in **ch**urch; *fu* as *foo* in **foo**t, but shorter;
g as in **g**ood (hard) at the beginning of a word; elsewhere as *ng* in si**ng**er (sometimes also soft initially: as in *kimi* ***ga*** *yo* [my lord's reign]).

Because Noh language was mostly based upon the literary language of the Muromachi period (1336–1573), there are certain words with pronunciations peculiar to those times, such as literary or colloquial words, or philosophical or Buddhist terms (for more detail, see "Notes on the Pronunciation of Noh Language" in *The Noh,* Vol. 1: *God Noh,* pp. xv–xviii). In brief, when followed by an *m/n,* the letter *u* is pronounced like an *n: ume* (plum)→ *nme; yamauba* (mountain hag) → *yamanba.* There are times when the *n* is omitted, as in: *ho**n**zon* (main object of worship) → *hozon;* or added, as in Urin'in (the name of a temple) → U**n**rin'in. In some cases, there is also liaison on the *n: kon'ya* (tonight) → *ko**nn**ya;* in some cases, there is a reduction of *tsu* to *'n: butsu* (buddha) → bu'**n.** In addition, ***~n*** often adds an *n-* to the next word *(on ide = on-**n**ide;* even *~n wa = ~n **n**a*).

Also, compounds containing the elements *yō* or *yū* are pronounced as two syllables: *iu/yū* (to say/evening) → *i-u; mōshū* (attachment) → *mo-o-shi-u; kyūjo* (court lady) → *ki-u-jo; ryūsui* (running water) → *ri-u-su-i.* Also, *ha* is often pronounced as *wa,* as in: *haha* (mother) → *ha**wa**; ha-hakigi* (broom tree) → *ha**wa**kigi;* or *Yahata* (an alternate reading of Hachiman) → *Ya**wa**ta.* The use of hyphens in *The Noh* series is not always consistent. Often, especially in notes, they are used to clarify the meaning of elements of words or to point out plays on words. As in the earlier volumes of this series, Ze-ami and Kan-ami are given in a hyphenated form.

The romanizations of the libretti in this volume are based upon the texts and pronunciation of the Kanze school.

Plan of a Noh Stage

(based upon the Kanze Noh Theatre, Tokyo)

The main stage area, defined by four large pillars, is about 19 ft square (361 ft^2). The *hashi-gakari* (bridgeway) is about 25 ft long. The stage floor is made of long thick planks of unpainted but highly polished *hinoki* cypress. Many stages have large earthenware jars buried or suspended beneath the floor to add reverberation to the stamping action performed in many dances.

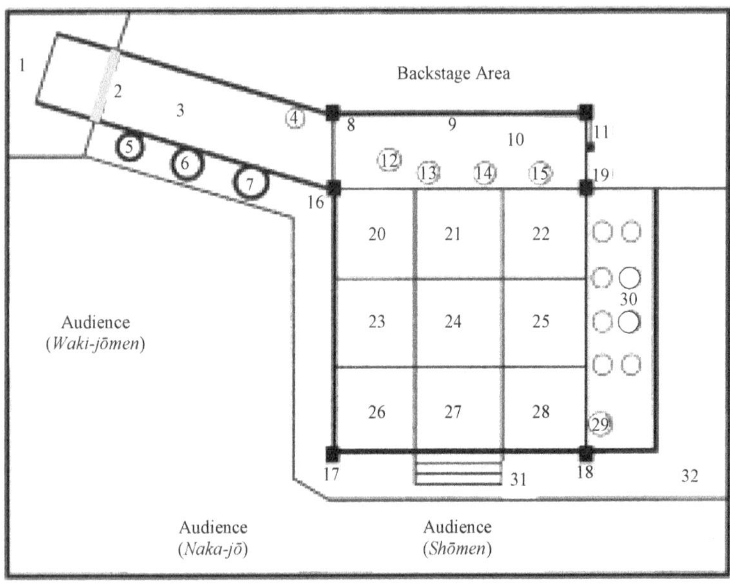

1. *Kagami no ma:* mirror room
2. *Age-maku:* curtain (raised with long poles)
3. *Hashi-gakari:* bridgeway
4. *Kyōgen-za: ai-kyōgen* spot
5. *San no matsu:* third pine
6. *Ni no matsu:* second pine
7. *Ichi no matsu:* first pine (near the *shite-bashira*)
8. *Kōken-za:* stage-assistant spot
9. *Kagami-ita:* sound board (with a painting of the "Manifestation Pine" of the Grand Shrine of Kasuga)
10. *Ato-za:* rear stage area
11. *Kiri-do:* upstage left sliding door
12–15. Musician's seats: (from left) *taiko, ō-tsuzumi, ko-tsuzumi,* flute
16. *Shite-bashira*: the *shite* pillar
17. *Metsuke-bashira:* the sighting pillar
18. *Waki-bashira:* the *waki* pillar
19. *Fue-bashira:* the flute-player pillar
20. *Jō-za:* the *shite* spot; also *nanori-za* (naming spot); upstage right
21. *Dai-shō–mae:* upstage center
22. *Fue-za–mae:* upstage left
23. *Waki-shō:* center stage right
24. *Shōnaka:* center stage
25. *Ji-utai–mae:* center stage left
26. *Sumi:* downstage right
27. *Shōsaki:* downstage center
28. *Waki-za–mae:* downstage left
29. *Waki-za: waki* spot
30. *Jiutai-za:* chorus spot
31. *Shirasu-bashigo:* staircase to the *shirasu* at downstage center
32. *Shirasu:* white stones separating the acting area from the audience.

Introduction to Fifth-Group Noh

PART I
Five-Group Classification of Noh and *Jo-Ha-Kyū*

WELL OVER two hundred plays in the current repertoires of the five schools of Noh are classified into five groups according to their prescribed positions in a formal five-Noh program. The five groups are named: *ichibanme* (*shobanme*)-*mono* (first-on-the-program-pieces), *nibanme-mono* (second-on-the-program pieces), and so on. An explanation of the origin and meaning of this classification and descriptions of the five different groups have been given in the four preceding volumes of *The Noh* series, and can be summed up as follows.

Plays for a formal five-Noh program are selected on the principle of *jo-ha-kyū,* governing the spirit and form of individual plays. (*Jo-ha-kyū* is the term used for the three stages of development—*jo:* beginning / slow / simple and straightforward; *ha:* developing / quickening / breaking out into variation; *kyū:* finale; quick; free and active. Borrowing it from Gagaku, classical court music, Ze-ami applied *jo-ha-kyū* to Noh as the basic principle governing all the phases of the art—from the composition of a play, to the utterance of a single sound.) A first-on-the-program Noh is a god-Noh, also named *waki*-Noh,[1] divine and congratulatory in spirit, dignified, formal and straight-forward in structure; the second piece, *shura*- or battle-Noh, about a warrior ghost from the Ashura hell, is bathetic and romantic in mood, less formal in style. A graceful mood against a background of quiet lyricism characterizes a third-on-the-program Noh, whose typical leading character is an elegant woman, often a ghost. Compared with the first two groups, this group is of greater variety in the types of characters and stories told. While the first three are homogenous groups, each classified under one name, such as "god Noh," "*shura* (warrior ghost)-Noh," or "woman Noh," the fourth and fifth groups are heterogeneous, not easy to unify under one name, and are thus referred to as *zatsu* (miscellaneous)-Noh.

---

[1] *Waki* means "next to." A god-Noh is called *waki-nō* because it comes "next" to *Okina* (Old Man), a ceremonial piece performed first before the five other plays in a formal program.

Table 1. The Five Groups of Noh with Respect to *Jo-ha-kyū*

Jo–ha–kyū	Noh Group	The *Shite* (leading role)
1. *Jo*	*Sho(Ichi)banme-mono* (First piece)	Deity (except for *Tsurukame* and *Uchito-mōde*, structurally fourth-group plays)
2. *Ha-no-jo*	*Nibanme-mono* (Second piece)	Warrior ghost from the Ashura hell
3. *Ha-no-ha*	*Sanbanme-mono* (Third piece)	Typically, but not always, a woman, either a ghost or a living person
4. *Ha-no-kyū*	*Yobanme-mono* (Fourth piece)	Miscellaneous characters
5. *Kyū*	*Gobanme-mono* (Fifth piece)	Miscellaneous characters

True to the principle of *jo–ha–kyū,* while the first three homogenous groups with their standardized structures constitute the basic groups, the miscellaneous plays in the fourth and fifth groups are more or less variants of the three basic groups. Compared with the basic groups, in the miscellaneous groups there is greater variation in the types of characters, greater freedom in dramatic structure, and a quickness of tempo, and this trend becomes more conspicuous as the *jo-ha-kyū* develops from the last stage of the tripartite *ha* section, in which a fourth-group Noh is performed, to the final *kyū* stage, in which a fifth-group Noh is presented.

One of the most distinctive features of *gobanme-mono,* the play in the final *kyū* position, concerns the type of main character. In addition to *shite* that are similar to those of other groups, such as deities, ghosts, or living humans, the fifth group has types unknown in the preceding groups, and in greater variety. They include supernatural beings such as *tengu* (strange, winged, long-nosed creatures), monstrous animals, demons, and fiends. The fifth-group Noh with such *shite* are all supernatural or visional. None of them is totally realistic. These ghosts, deities, and monsters appear just to tell their stories, to attack men, or sometimes even to help them. Another characteristic concerns their dance and dance action. There is a predominance of two types of instrumental dance action named *mai-bataraki* (dance action) and *uchiai-bataraki* (fighting action). Over half of the fifth-group Noh have one or the other. Both types are short and quick. The first represents some active movement, and is also performed in some god-Noh (e.g., *Iwafune, Enoshima,* and *Kamo;* see *God Noh,* p. 99) and in one fourth-group Noh (*Ikkaku Sennin*); the second, which represents fighting, typically between a monster and its conqueror, is unique to the fifth group. A quick and longer instrumental dance called *haya-mai* (quick dance) is exclusive to *gobanme-mono* and is performed in two subgroups, namely, in six *haya-mai* pieces and in one *reiken-mono* (miracle play). *Shishi* (lion dance), which is performed in two fourth-group Noh, *Uchito-mōde* and *Mochizuki,* only in a make-shift costume as an entertainment for a guest, is performed in full costume in the fifth-group piece *Shakkyō,* as a dance by a real beast, a sacred lion.

Another characteristic of the fifth group is its structure. Placed at the last stage of *jo-ha-kyū, gobanme-mono* plays have great structural freedom and quickness of tempo. For example, the *kuse,* a long thematic song in a slow tempo, which constitutes the most important part of many Noh, is absent in about fifty percent of *gobanme-mono,* a ratio far higher than in the other groups. In many plays, a large number of characters, often including *ai-kyōgen,* freely enter and exit as in ordinary realistic plays. This is particularly true with some miracle plays that are realistic until a miracle occurs in the final part. In spite of this freedom of structure, there is one feature common to *gobanme-mono* with few exceptions, and that is, they are in two acts. Usually, a supernatural being appears as an ordinary human in the first act, then reveals its true form in the second. Exceptionally in some miracle plays, the *mae-shite* and *nochi-shite* are different beings, an ordinary person in the first act, and a deity in the second, who appears as a *deus ex machina* at the end of the drama.

The plays of the fifth group, with their great variety, can be divided into a number of subgroups, like those of the fourth group. However, because of the above-mentioned structural freedom, it is often difficult to draw clear-cut lines between groups. In the case of the fourth group, the subgroup can to some extent be determined by the type of *shite.* Similarly, the type of *mai* to be performed can be determined from the subgroup in which it appears; for example, the typical dance in a mad-person Noh is a *kakeri,* and that in a musical-entertainment piece is a *kakko.* This is not the case with most *gobanme-mono.* The same type of dance and action are performed, and similar types of *shite* appear in different subgroups, so that, when the plays are divided into different groups, they are like creatures with different heads but with similar bodies, or vice versa. Thus, classifications differ from school to school, and from one scholar to another. The classification attempted in this book differs from those given by others not only for this reason, but also because it is based strictly on the dramatic and structural characteristics of the individual plays, while the other classifications are more or less conventional. Also, for the sake of clarity, the classification here is made on the principle of including each play in only one of the five main groups, whereas in conventional classifications, one play is often included in two subgroups in order to allow more freedom in the making of a program.

PART II
Fifth-Group Noh Classified into Seven Subgroups

According to their structural characteristics, fifth-group Noh, fifty in number, can be divided into seven subgroups as in Table 2 below.

Table 2. Seven Types of Fifth-Group Noh

The plays are all in two acts, except:

1. *Shōjō,* which was originally in two acts but is in one act now; and
2. *Matsuyama Kagami,* which is structurally in one act, but is treated as if it were in two acts by the Kanze school.

Unless otherwise specified, *mai* and special actions are those by the *nochi-shite.*
For technical terms in Japanese, see the Glossary.
All Chinese personal and geographical names are given in modified Wade-Giles romanization.

Note: (V) = visional; (S) = supernatural; (VS) = visional-supernatural; (RS) = realistic-supernatural.

1. *Haya-mai–mono* (Quick-dance pieces)
The *nochi-shite* performs a *haya-mai.*

a. Male Pieces
The *Shite* are deified persons of high status, such as an emperor or great lord.

Title	*Shite*	*Mai* and special action
1. *Tōru* (V) (Lord Tōru)	Act 1. Lord Tōru's ghost as an old man.	———
	Act 2. The same, deified.	*Haya-mai*
2. *Suma Genji* (V) (Genji at Suma)	Act 1. Lord Genji's ghost as an old man.	———
	Act 2. The same, deified.	*Haya-mai*
3. *Matsuyama Tengu* (VS) (Goblins of Matsuyama)	Act 1. Emp. Sutoku's ghost as a man.	———
	Act 2. Emperor Sutoku's ghost.	*Haya-mai; mai-bataraki* by *Tsure tengu*
4. *Raiden*–B (V) (Thunder and Lightning)	Act 1. Lord Michizane's ghost.	———
	Act 2. The same, deified.	*Haya-mai*

b. Female Pieces
The *nochi-shite* are deified women.

Title	*Shite*	*Mai* and special action
1. *Ama* (VS) (The Diver)	Act 1. A woman diver's ghost.	———
	Act 2. The same, as a dragon goddess.	*Haya-mai*

2. *Taema* (V) (Taema Temple)	Act 1. Buddha in a nun's form.	———
	Act 2. Lady Chūjō, deified.	*Haya-mai*

2. *Tōjō-mono* (Warring-Ghost Pieces)
A historically well-known warrior's ghost tells his story and describes his fighting. *Kusanagi* tells a victorious story; all others tell of defeat.

Title	*Shite*	*Mai* and special action
1. *Ikari-kazuki* (V) (Drowning with an Anchor)	Act 1. Heike general Noritsune's ghost as an old man.	———
	Act 2. Heike general Tomomori's ghost.	*Mai-bataraki*
2. *Kō-u* (V) (Hsiang Yü)	Act 1. Hsiang Yü's ghost as an old boatman.	———
	Act 2. The same, as himself.	*Mai-bataraki*
3. *Kumasaka* (V)	Act 1. Highwayman Kumasaka's ghost as a monk.	———
	Act 2. The same, as himself.	———
4. *Kusanagi* (V)	Act 1. Prince Yamato Takeru's ghost as a grass cutter.	———
	Act 2. The same, as himself.	———

3. *Oni-mono* (Demonic-Apparition Pieces)
A demonic human ghost, or a demonic deity from hell appears. In 3 and 4 under a, the demonic being comes to attack men.

a. Demonic-ghost pieces (demons who were once human)

Title	*Shite*	*Mai* and special action
1. *Shōki* (V) (Chung K'uei)	Act 1. Chung K'uei's ghost as a villager.	———
	Act 2. The same, deified.	*Mai-bataraki*-like action
2. *Shōkun* (RV) (Lady Chao-chün)	Act 1. Chao-chün's father.	———
	Act 2. Chao-chün's husband, a demonic ghost.	*Mai-bataraki* in most schools
3. *Raiden-A* (VS) (Thunder and Lightning)	Act 1. Lord Michizane's ghost.	———
	Act 2. The same, as the thunder god.	*Inori*-like action.
4. *Funa-Benkei* (RS) (Benkei on Board)	Act 1. The dancer Shizuka.	*Chū no mai*
	Act 2. Heike general Tomomori, a vengeful ghost	*Mai-bataraki*

b. Demonic-Deity Pieces (true demons)

Title	*Shite*	*Mai* and special action
1. *Ukai* (V) (The Cormorant Fisher)	Act 1. A fisherman's ghost.	———
	Act 2. A demon god from hell.	*Mai-bataraki*-like action

2. *Nomori* (V) (Game Keeper)	Act 1. A demon god from hell as an old man.	———
	Act 2. The same, as himself.	*Mai-bataraki*

4. *Tengu-mono* (Goblin pieces)

The goblin of *Kurama Tengu* is a benevolent one. In the rest, *tengu* approach men to work mischief on them, but are defeated by a deity or by prayer. As a rule they first appear as *yamabushi* priests. Their interim exit and second entrance are accompanied by the dignified *raijo* and *ō-beshi* music, respectively.

Title	*Shite*	*Mai* and special action
1. *Kurama Tengu* (S) (The Goblin of Mt. Kurama)	Act 1. A *tengu* as a *yamabushi.*	———
	Act 2. The same, as himself.	*Mai-bataraki*
2. *Zegai* (S) (Goblin Shih Chieh)	Act 1. Zegai, a *tengu* from China, as a *yamabushi.*	*Tachimawari*
	Act 2. The same, as himself.	———
3. *Kuruma-zō* (S) (Priest on a Flying Couch)	Act 1. Tarōbō, the *tengu,* as a *yamabushi.*	
	Act 2. The same, as himself.	———
4. *Dai-e* (S) (A Great Mass)	Act 1. A *tengu,* as a *yamabushi.*	———
	Act 2. The same as Buddha, and then as himself.	*Tachimawari; Uchiai-bataraki* with *Tsure* god.
5. *Dairoku-ten* (VS) (The Sixth Heaven)	Act 1. A goddess, as a village woman.	———
	Act 2. *Tengu* = Demon of the Sixth Heaven	*Tachimawari; Uchiai-bataraki* with *Tsure* god.

5. *Igyō-mono* (Strange-Apparition Pieces)

Strange creatures perform dances or tell their stories.

a. Mai-mono (Dance Pieces)

Title	*Shite*	*Mai* and special action
1. *Shakkyō* (V)	Act 1. A deity as boy.	———
(The Stone Bridge)	Act 2. A sacred lion.	*Shishi* (Lion Dance)
2. *Shōjō* (S) (The Tipster Imp)	A *shōjō.* (The play is in one act.)	*Chū no mai.*
3. *Taihei Shōjō* (S)	Act 1. A *shōjō* as a boy.	———
(The Tipster Imp and the Wine Jug)	Act 2. The same, as itself.	*Chū no mai* by a group of *shōjō.*
4. *Yamanba* (S) (The Old Woman of the Mountains)	Act 1. A strange mountain woman as a village woman.	———
	Act 2. The same, as herself.	*Tachimawari*

b. Non-Dance Pieces

Title	*Shite*	*Mai* and special action
1. *Kappo* (S) (Kappo Bay)	Act 1. A strange-looking fish-man	———
	Act 2. The same, as itself.	———
2. *Sesshōseki* (S) (The Death Stone)	Act 1. A monster-fox spirit, as a woman.	———
	Act 2. The same in its own form.	———
3. *Nue* (V) (The Chimera)	Act 1. A ghost of the monster Nue, as a strange person.	———
	Act 2. The same in its own form.	———
4. *Ryōko* (V) (The Dragon and the Tiger)	Act 1. The supernatural tiger in a man's form.	———
	Act 2. The same in its own form.	*Uchiai-bataraki* with *Nochi-tsure*, the dragon.

6. *Akki-mono* (Evil-Fiend Pieces)

a. Plays in which a fiend is conquered by a deity or by prayer

Title	*Shite*	*Mai* and special action
1. *Adachigahara* (S) (Adachi Moor) (*Kurozuka* in other schools)	Act 1. A fiend, as a village woman.	———
	Act 2. The same in its own form.	*Inori* ("prayer") with *Waki* and *Waki-tsure* monks
2. *Hiun* (S) (Hiun the Fiend)	Act 1. The fiend Hiun as a man.	———
	Act 2. The same in its own form.	*Inori-bataraki* (prayer action) or *inori* with *Waki*
3. *Shari* (S) (The Sacred Relic)	Act 1. The fiend, as a man.	———
	Act 2. The same in its own form.	*Uchiai-bataraki* with *Tsure*.

b. Plays in which a fiend is conquered by warriors

Title	*Shite*	*Mai* and special action
1. *Orochi* (S) (The Dragon)	Act 1. An old man whose daughter is about to be taken by a dragon.	———
	Act 2. The dragon.	*Uchiai-bataraki* with *Waki*, the deity Susano-o
2. *Ōe-yama* (S) (Mt. Ōe)	Act 1. The fiend of Mt. Ōe as a boy.	———
	Act 2. The same in its own form.	*Uchiai-bataraki* with *Waki* and *Waki-tsure*
3. *Rashōmon* (S) (The Rashō Gate)	Appears in Act 2 only, as a fiend.	*Mai-bataraki*
4. *Tsuchigumo* (S) (The Monstrous Spider)	Act.1. A monster spider, as a monk.	*Uchiai-bataraki* with *Waki* and *Waki-tsure*
	Act 2. The same in its own form.	
5. *Momiji-gari* (S) (The Maple-Viewing Party)	Act 1. A fiend, as a lady.	*Chū no mai*
	Act 2. The same in its own form.	*Mai-bataraki*

7. *Reiken-mono* (Miracle Pieces)

a. Waki-Noh*–type plays*

As a rule, the *mae-shite* and *nochi-shite* are the same supernatural being and a miracle is wrought for a cause other than human relations. These plays are more formal and dignified, as well as more fantastic, with more dance actions, than those in the other subgroup (human-interest group). Because of the dignified nature of these plays, any of them can take the place of a *waki*-Noh in a formal program.

Title	*Shite*	*Mai* and special action
1. *Genjō* (VS) (The Lute "Genjō")	Act 1. Emperor Murakami's ghost, as an old man.	
	Act 2. The same, deified.	*Haya-mai*
2. *Kasuga Ryūjin* (VS) (The Dragon God of Kasuga Shrine)	Act 1. A supernatural being as a man working at a shrine.	
	Act 2. A dragon god (= Avalokiteśvara).	*Mai-bataraki*
3. *Taisanpukun* (VS) (Taishanfuchün)	Act 1. A heavenly maiden (the Tsure in Act 2).	
	Act 2. The deity Taishanfuchün.	*Mai-bataraki; Tennyo-mai** by *Tsure* goddess
4. *Kuzu* (S)	Act 1. An old man; may be the incarnation of a mountain god (optional).	
	Act 2. Mountain god.	*Gaku* by *Tsure* goddess
5. *Kokaji* (S) (Kokaji the Swordsmith)	Act 1. Tutelary god, as a boy.	
	Act 2. The same in its own form.	*Mai-bataraki*
6. *Chōryō* (S) (Chang Liang)	Act 1. The supernatural hermit Huang Shih Kung, as an old man.	
	Act 2. The same, as himself.	*Mai-bataraki* by *Tsure* dragon
7. *Kōtei* (S) (The Emperor)	Act 1. The immortal Chung K'uei, as an old man.	
	Act 2. The same, as himself.	*Uchiai-bataraki* with *Nochi-tsure* fiend

**Tennyo-mai* = heavenly maiden's dance (*see* Glossary).

---

b. Human-interest (ninjō-mono)*–type Noh*

In this group of Noh, the *mae-shite* is an ordinary person and the drama develops realistically until the appearance of the *nochi-shite* as a *deus ex machina* in the finale. A miracle is wrought for the solution of a conflict that involves a family relationship. All the plays have a *kokata.* Most of the Noh have no dance action.

Title	*Shite*	*Mai* and special action
1. *Chōbuku Soga* (RS) (The Incantation Story of the Soga Brothers)	Act 1. A young boy's enemy. Act 2. The deity Acala, who destroys the enemy's effigy.	———

2. *Danpū* (RS) (The Propitious Wind)	Appears in Act 2 only. The god of Mt. Kumano, who helps a boy to escape.	———
3. *Tanikō* (RS) (The Valley Rites)	Act 1. A boy's mother. Act 2. A god, who resurrects the boy.	——— ———
4. *Matsuyama Kagami* (RS) (The Mirror of Matsuyama)	In one act. A demon from hell (= the ghost of a girl [*Tsure*]'s mother), who is transformed into a bodhisattva.	*Mai-bataraki*
5. *Aisome-gawa* (RS) (The Aisome River)	Act 1. A boy's mother. Act 2. The shrine god who resurrects a boy's drowned mother.	——— ———
6. *Take no Yuki* (RS) (Snow-laden Bamboo)	Acts 1 and 2. A mother, who has her frozen son resurrected by the Seven Immortals of the Bamboo Grove.	———

PART III
Characteristics of the Seven Subgroups Of Fifth-Group Noh

Following are brief descriptions of the seven subgroups of *gobanme-mono* and the plays contained within them.

1. *Haya-mai–mono* (Quick-Dance Pieces)

a. Four male pieces: *Tōru, Suma Genji* (Lord Genji at Suma), *Matsuyama Tengu* (Goblins of Matsuyama), *Raiden–B.*
b. Two female pieces: *Ama* (The Diver), *Taema* (Taema Temple).

The most distinctive feature of this group is the *haya-mai* (quick dance). This dance is of the same musical and choreographic pattern as *kami-mai, kyū no mai, otoko-mai, jo no mai,* and *chū no mai,* and, like *kami-mai,* is always accompanied by the *taiko. Haya-mai* is exclusive to this subgroup, with one exception: *Genjō,* which also has a *haya-mai,* but is included among *reiken-mono* (miracle plays), explained below, because of its other similarities to that group. In quickness of tempo, *haya-mai* is next to *kyū no mai* and *kami-mai. Haya-mai–mono* can be divided into two subgroups, one whose *shite* is male, and the other whose *shite* is female.

a. Otoko haya-mai–mono (Male quick-dance pieces)

The *Shite* of all four plays in this subgroup are the ghosts of noble personages, and include an emperor, a royal prince, and a grand minister of state.

In each of them, the spirit first appears to a traveler as a humble old man and tells the story of the place, and, revealing that he is the ghost of the hero in the tale, disappears. Then, in the second act, he appears in his true form, in full princely attire, and performs a *haya-mai.* Of the four male *haya-mai* pieces, *Tōru* and *Suma Genji,* the authorship of which is attributed to Ze-ami,[2] are purely visional, while *Matsuyama Tengu* and *Raiden-B* are visional-supernatural.

Tōru: Minamoto no Tōru (822–95), the *Shite* in the title role, was Emperor Saga's son, who assumed the status of a subject, and was granted a new family name, Minamoto (= Genji, like the hero of the *Genji Monogatari*). He was Grand Minister of the Left for twenty years and led a life of luxury and elegance, building gorgeous palaces, remnants of which still exist today. The garden of one of his palaces in Kyoto, known as Kawara no In, was modeled after the seascape of Shiogama ("Salt Kilns") in the northern provinces, famous in poetry for its salt kilns. He had sea water carried from the sea and had it boiled in the salt kilns in his garden. Half a century after his death, the poet Ki no Tsurayuki, who visited the place, composed the following poem, included in the *Kokin-shū* (16: 852): *Kimi masade / Kemuri taenishi / Shiogama no / Ura-samishiku mo / Mie-wataru kana* (Bereft of my Lord, / The smoke has long ceased to rise / At Shiogama / Bay. How lonesome and barren / The sight that spreads before me.) (In the above poem, Shiogama no **Ura** [Shiogama Bay] blends into ***ura-****samishi* [heartfelt loneliness]).

In the play, which is based on the above poem, and the stories about Tōru in the *Konjaku Monogatari* and other old tales, a traveling monk who has come to the ancient palace meets an old fisherman, who tells the story of the late Grand Minister and his salt kilns, quoting the thematic poem by Tsurayuki. The fisherman also shows the monk all the famous sights surrounding the garden, quoting old poems associated with the place. This part, referred to as *meisho oshie* (telling a traveler about the celebrated places in view) occurs in the first act of some visional Noh, beginning with *mondō* (questions and answers) and *kakeai* (alternate singing in free rhythm), and ending in a song in rhythm. (For examples, see *Yorimasa* and *Kanehira,* translated in *Warrior-Ghost Plays from the Japanese Noh Theatre.*) Suddenly he remembers his task of drawing salt water, and is about to

[2] Unless otherwise stated, the authorship of the plays discussed in this introduction is according to Haruo Nishino's "Nō Genkō-kyoku Ichiran" [List of Currently Performed Noh] in *Nōgaku Zensho,* vol. 6. No mention of the author means that the author of the play in question is not known with any certainty.

set off to get seawater for the kilns, but his form fades out of sight. In the second act, the monk, resting on the beach stones and waiting for a further miracle, sees a noble figure appear before him who announces himself as Grand Minister Tōru. In songs he reminisces about the past when he used to hold banquets on the beach, enjoying music and dance in the moonlight. He then performs a *haya-mai,* continues to dance, until the moon sinks, and as dawn approaches, the monk sees the noble figure disappear into the moon.

Suma Genji (Lord Genji at Suma): This Noh is based on the *Genji Monogatari.* The scene is Suma Beach, where Lord Genji lived three years in self-exile. A traveling Shinto priest comes to Suma Beach, meets an old man, and asks him about the Young Cherry Tree, made famous by the Suma-chapter story in the *Genji Monogatari.* (The tree is fictitious, but is treated like a real tree, a common practice of Noh writers. For that matter, Genji himself is presented as a historical person.) In answer to the priest's question, the old man tells the life story of Lord Genji, rendered in songs with quotations from the original story, and disappears with a hint that Lord Genji himself will appear, descending from his palace on the moon. In the second act, Lord Genji appears in a splendid costume, and performs a *haya-mai* against the background of moonlit Suma Beach.

While *Tōru* and *Suma Genji* are genuinely visional music-and-dance pieces with more or less standard structure similar to that of the three basic groups, there are some dramatic conflicts in the remaining two *haya-mai* pieces. We may say that the heroes of the first two plays as well are not entirely free from emotional conflicts and frustration.

According to the *Ōkagami,* when the successor to Emperor Yōzei was being elected, Tōru recommended himself, saying, "Here I am." However, he was rejected by the Grand Minister of State, Fujiwara no Mototsune, who said that a person who had assumed the status of a subject could not become an emperor. Some old story books tell how Tōru's spirit harassed the Retired Emperor Uda and his consort. Many scholars consider that there was an older version of the Noh *Tōru* (perhaps called *Shiogama*), in which the *Shite* Tōru appeared as an evil spirit.

Lord Genji lived at Suma as an exile, bereft of all the worldly glory that had surrounded him. In spite of this, both plays present only the bright side of their heroes, elevating them to the status of divinity. In contrast, the heroes of the other two plays are persons of noble status who died in exile, and whose bitter feelings toward their enemies remain as worldly attachment.

Matsuyama Tengu (Goblins of Matsuyama): The *Shite* of this play is Emperor Sutoku, who, after his abdication, later decided to revolt against his brother and successor to the throne, was sorely defeated, and died in exile. In the Noh, the ghost of Sutoku appears to the itinerant poet-monk Saigyō, who has come to visit his grave, and, pleased with a poem that Saigyō had dedicated to him, holds a banquet and performs a *haya-mai.* For further details, see the introduction to the translation of the play included in this book.

Raiden–B: The last of the male *haya-mai* pieces, *Raiden–B* is a new version of another Noh that is also named *Raiden,* which is written in different Chinese characters and belongs to a different subgroup. To avoid confusion, we refer to the original play as *Raiden–A,* and this new one as *Raiden–B.* The older *Raiden–A* belongs to a group classified as "demonic-apparition Noh," and it does not have a *haya-mai. Raiden–B* is placed among the *haya-mai* group, because it does have this dance, as well as some characteristics common to the group, explained below.

In this Noh, the *Shite* is the ghost of Sugawara no Michizane (845–903), the Grand Minister of the Right, who was exiled to Kyushu and died there. In the Noh, Michizane's ghost appears to his teacher, a high priest, and tells him that he will appear at the Imperial Palace to avenge himself on those who wronged him. In the second act of the original version, the ghost of Michizane become a thunder god comes to attack people at the Imperial palace, but is driven away by the priest's prayer. In *Raiden–B,* the ghost, pacified by the Imperial indemnities bestowed on him, performs a *haya-mai* and then disappears. Thus, the play ends in a spirit of congratulation. (*Raiden–B,* which was originally written as a play of different type, is left out of further discussion on the structural characteristics of *haya-mai-mono.*)

As described above, the *Nochi-shite* of the male *haya-mai* pieces is the ghost of a man of high status, such as an emperor or a royal prince. With the exception of *Matsuyama Tengu,* these *Nochi-shite* wear a handsome young male mask such as a *chūjō* or *imawaka,* an elegant cap called *ui-kanmuri,* and noble clothes. This combination of the mask and costume is exclusive to only a few handsome noblemen, including the ghost of Ariwara no Narihira in two male *jo-no-mai* pieces of the fourth group, *Unrin-in* and *Oshio;* and the ghost of Emperor Murakami, who performs a *haya-mai* in *Genjō,* a miracle play explained below. Lord Genji, the *Tsure* in *Sumiyoshi-mōde,* a realistic *sanbanme-mono,* performs a *jo-no-mai* in this costume without a mask.

b. Onna haya-mai–mono (Female Quick-Dance Pieces)

The difference between the a and b types of *haya-mai–mono* is not merely that the *shite* is a male in the one, and a female in the other; they also tell different kinds of stories, and the dance originally performed in the female pieces was not really a *haya-mai,* as is explained below.

Ama (The Diver): The source of one of the two female *haya-mai–mono, Ama,* is a story about the origin of Shido Temple in Sanuki Province, present-day Kagawa Prefecture, in Shikoku. According to this story, Fujiwara no Fuhito (659–720), Grand Minister of State, had a sister married to a Chinese Emperor, who sent some wonderful jewels to his brother-in-law. One of the jewels was lost on its way to Japan, taken by the Dragon King of the sea. In order to retrieve the jewel, Fuhito went to the seaside and lived with a woman diver, who bore him a son, later Minister of State, Fusasaki (681–737). At Fuhito's wish, the woman dove into the sea to steal back the jewel. Attacked by the dragons who guarded it, she cut open her breast, put the jewel inside the wound, and floated up. Thus, Fuhito obtained the jewel, but the diver died and was buried on the beach. When Fusasaki was twelve years old, he visited his mother's burial place and had a temple dedicated to her built there. In the Noh, the son, Fusasaki, who has come to visit his mother's burial place, meets a fisher woman, who is actually the ghost of the diver of old. At Fusasaki's request, the woman tells how the diver retrieved the jewel at the sacrifice of her life. Then, with a hint that she is actually the boy's mother, the woman disappears. In the second act, the diver appears in the form of the sacred Dragon Woman,[3] sings in praise of the Lotus Sutra, gives a scroll of the sutra to Fusasaki, and performs a *haya-mai.* The section where the ghost of the diver dances, describing how she retrieved the jewel, is a highlight named *Tama no dan* (Jewel Section).

Taema (Taema Temple): Taema is the name of an ancient temple in present-day Nara Prefecture, famous for an enormous mandala kept there, woven of lotus-root fibers. According to old stories and records, Chūjō-hime, a young daughter of the Grand Minister of the Right, Fujiwara no Toyonari (704–65), became a nun at Taema Temple in 763. She wished to see Amitābha, and, as she was ardently praying to Buddha to grant her wish, two women appeared before her. One of them spun thread from the

---

[3] According to the tale told in the Lotus Sutra (Ch. 12, "Devadatta), the Dragon Woman, who was the Dragon King's daughter, attained Buddhahood, which was denied to women, by first being transformed into a man.

fibers of lotus roots and dyed it in the well water. The other wove the thread into a huge mandala, which depicted Buddha's Paradise in all its splendor. The women were actually the buddha Amitābha and the bodhisattva Avalokiteśvara in disguise. In the Noh *Taema,* a traveling monk who has come to Taema Temple meets an aged nun accompanied by a young woman, and they tell him the story of the famous mandala. Then they reveal themselves as the two women of yore and disappear. In the second act, the spirit of Chūjō-hime appears as the Bodhisattva of Music and Dance, sings in praise of the Pure-Land sutra, gives the sutra to the monk, and performs a *haya-mai.*

Besides the performance of *haya-mai,* these two Noh are similar in many respects: both are based on stories and records about the origin of ancient temples with their miraculous episodes, and the *Shite* are both women who are actually incarnations of Buddhist deities. In the second act, the *Shite* in both Noh appear as those divine beings, one, the diver woman in her true form as the Dragon Woman, the other, Lady Chūjō as the Bodhisattva of Music. Both of them sing in praise of the Lotus Sutra, and give the scroll to those praying before them. Except for their crowns, the two *Nochi-shite* are in exactly the same costume, including the *deigan* mask with its gilt eyes, symbolizing an unearthly being.

The author of *Taema* is Ze-ami. It is said that *Ama* was originally in the Konparu repertory, and that Ze-ami rewrote it, adding a *mai* that was not in the original version. In Ze-ami's time, the *mai* in these two plays was not a *haya-mai,* but one named *tennyo* (*no*) *mai* (heavenly woman's dance), which no longer exists. This dance was quite different from the modern type of *tennyo-mai* with the same name, which is basically a variation of a *chū no mai.* The *tennyo-mai* we now have is performed by a *tsure-tennyo,* whereas the defunct *tennyo no mai* was performed by a *shite*-deity, not only in the two Noh under discussion, but also by *shite* goddesses in some female god-Noh in the first group. As it is, these female *haya-mai–mono* are basically different from the male pieces. While they are eulogies of Buddhism, there is nothing especially Buddhistic in the male *haya-mai–mono.* (Unlike in most visional Noh, the Waki in *Suma Genji* is not a Buddhist monk but a Shinto priest.) Regarding the two female plays, *Taema* is written according to the dramatic structure of a visional Noh, while in the first part of *Ama* there is greater deviation from standard form. Both Noh can take the place of *waki*-Noh.

✧ ✧ ✧

2. *Tōjō-mono* (Warring-Ghost Pieces)
Four plays: *Ikari-Kazuki* (Drowning with an Anchor), *Kō-u* (Hsiang Yü), *Kumasaka, Kusanagi*

Unlike *haya-mai–mono,* and like some other subgroups of fifth-group Noh, the second subgroup has no established group name. It is named differently by different scholars, and the grouping itself of these Noh is different among them. For example, Haruo Nishino names this group *mōshō-mono* (fierce-general pieces), and Mario Yokomichi, *bujin-mono* (warrior pieces). The traditional Kanze-school classification even includes *Ikari-Kazuki,* which is exclusive to that school, among the second-group *shura*-Noh. Nishino includes *Funa-Benkei* in this group, which this book includes among *oni-mono* (demonic-apparition pieces), as explained below. In the name adapted here, *tōjō* (fighting) is often used with the word *shura* (< Skt. *asura,* warrior ghost), and connotes the fighting of god-like titans (warriors) in hell.

The Noh in this group are all visional and are written more or less in the style of such Noh. Their *Shite* is the ghost of a warrior, who first appears to a traveler or a local man in the form of an ordinary person, tells his story, and disappears. In the second act, he reveals himself as a brave warrior, and tells in active dance action the story of the battle he fought. Exceptionally, the *Shite* of *Kumasaka* is not a warrior, but a highwayman, the same character as the *Nochi-shite* of *Eboshi-ori* (The Eboshi Maker), a *kiriai-mono* (sword-fighting piece) in the fourth group (published in *Troubled Souls*). *Kusanagi* tells a victorious story, the remaining three are tales of defeat. In *Ikari-Kazuki* and *Kō-u,* the *Shite* performs a *mai-bataraki,* an instrumental dance action.

The *mai-bataraki* is a short and quick series of dance-like movements, and it usually either describes some action, or is a sort of self-demonstration. It is performed not only by the warrior ghosts of this group, but also by many other types of characters, including deities and supernatural creatures, in many fifth-group Noh. It is also performed in some god-Noh, as well as in *Ikkaku Sennin,* a fourth-group Noh.

Ikari-Kazuki (Drowning with an Anchor): In *Ikari-Kazuki,* a traveling monk takes a ferry boat and comes to the bay known as Dan no Ura, where the Heike clan was destroyed by the Genji in 1185. At the monk's request, an aged ferryman tells the story of the battle and the Heike general, Taira no Noritsune, the Lord of Noto, who, having fought bravely, threw himself into the sea, taking two enemy warriors in his arms. The old man asks the monk to pray for his salvation and disappears. While the monk is praying, the *Nochi-shite,* the ghost of Taira no Tomomori, another Heike general (and Noritsune's cousin), appears in full battle attire, describes the battle scene, and performs a *mai-bataraki.* In the final dance action, he tells how, after fighting bravely, he sank into the sea, carrying armor and an anchor with him. There is a variant performance of this Noh, entitled *Funade no Narai* (Embarking), in which the second act begins with a moon-viewing ceremony on the Imperial ship. The battle breaks out in the midst of the ceremony and Kenreimon'in (herself the *Shite* of *Ohara Gokō* and the grandmother of the boy Emperor Antoku) throws herself into the sea with her Imperial grandson. The remaining part, which tells about the fighting of Tomomori and his death, is the same as in the standard version.

Kō-u (Hsiang Yü): The *Shite* in the title role of *Kō-u,* Hsiang Yü, was a Chinese general (232–202 BC) who killed himself when he was defeated by Liu Pang, the first Emperor of the Former Han dynasty. His consort killed herself. It is said that from the ground soaked with her blood, a flower of deep crimson grew, and people called it after the lady's name, Yü Mei-jen (Jpn. Gu Bijin), or "poppy." In the first act, the *Shite* appears as an old ferryman and takes two grass-cutters on his boat. For the fare the boatman asks for some poppies the grass-cutters have among the grass they have cut, and tells them about Hsiang Yü and his lady. Then with a hint at his identity he disappears, begging the grass-cutters to pray for him. In the second act the ghosts of *Kō-u* and his lady tell about the battle and their deaths, and the *Shite* performs a *mai-bataraki,* which describes his emotional agitation. The tale is also immortalized in the popular Peking Opera favorite, *Pa-wang Pieh Chi* (usually translated as *Farewell, My Concubine*).

Kumasaka: The *Shite* of *Kumasaka* is the highwayman by that name who was killed by the boy Ushiwaka, later Minamoto no Yoshitsune (1159–89), as he attacked the inn where Ushiwaka was staying with the goldmonger Kichiji. For details, see the introduction to *Kumasaka,* translated in this book. Kumasaka is also the *Nochi-shite* in *Eboshi-ori,* a sword-fighting piece, translated in *Troubled Souls* in the Noh Series.

Kusanagi: Kusanagi is the name of the sacred sword that was originally found by the deity Susano-o no Mikoto in the tail of the great snake he killed (as described in the Noh *Orochi;* see below), and which was originally named Muragumo ("Gathering of Clouds"). Now reputedly kept at Atsuta Shrine in Nagoya, it is told in the *Nihon Shoki* and *Kojiki* that when Prince Yamato Takeru no Mikoto, son of Keikō, the twelfth Emperor of

Japan, was attacked by rebellious folk who set fire to the field where the Prince was, he cut the grass with the holy sword, and the fire spread toward the enemy and destroyed them. Thus, the sword's name was changed to Kusanagi (*kusa* means "grass," and *nagi* means "to cut down"). In the Noh, the *Shite* and *Tsure,* the ghosts of the Prince and his consort, appear to a traveling priest as flower vendors and sing about various flowers, and then disappear with a hint at their identity. In the second act, the Prince and Princess in their true form tell about the military prowess of the Prince. *Kusanagi* is now in the repertoire of the Hōshō school only.

In the above description of the four warring-ghost plays, we notice many points that are similar to the *shura* (battle)-Noh of the second group. Both types of Noh are all visional: The *Shite,* a ghost, appears to the *Waki,* first assuming the form of a humble person, only revealing his own form in the second act. In both groups the major theme is a battle, and the *Shite* is the ghost of a warrior who fought in the battle. Generally, the play ends with a description of the fighting and the hero's death. In spite of this, there are a number of features that fundamentally distinguish the two groups. A discussion on this subject leads us to Ze-ami, who says: "*Shura* [-Noh] has its own style. Even when well-performed, there is not much appeal in it. You should not do it too often. . . . And yet, if you take a famous Genji or Heike person and associate him with *ka-chō-fu-getsu,*[4] and if it is a good Noh, then it will be more interesting than anything else" (*Fūshi Kaden,* Chap. 2, *Shura*). He wrote a number of *shura*-Noh according to his theory. Before his re-structuring of the canon, *shura*-Noh had been simply plays about warrior ghosts, the ruling spirit of which had been valor and strength. Ze-ami transformed them into plays of deep pathos, rich in *yūgen,* by presenting their heroes as they are depicted in the *Heike Monogatari* and narrating their tragic stories in songs of great lyrical beauty. Compared with the elegant and pathetic warrior ghosts in Ze-ami's *shura*-Noh, the ghosts of the primitive *shura*-Noh were fiercer beings that Ze-ami referred to as *oni* (demonic beings, including human ghosts). It is possible that, because of this, the new type of *shura*-Noh came to be performed in the second place, and the primitive type in the fifth place by the time the standard five-Noh program was introduced. Although the dates of the four warring-ghost plays under discussion are probably more recent than Ze-ami's time, by dramatic structure they belong to the primitive type of battle Noh.

---

[4] Literally, "flower–birds–wind–moon," this phrase refers to the ever-changing beauty of nature, which moves a sensitive soul.

When we look at the four Noh in the light of the above discussion, we see that the basic sources of three out of the four Noh are other than the *Heike Monogatari,* and the *Shite* of these three are not members of the Heike or Genji clans. The lack of poetic and romantic elements in these plays is related to the scarcity of references to classical Japanese and Chinese poems in their libretti. Such references are absent in the standard version of *Ikari-Kazuki,* and the average number of quotations or allusions for the four plays is 2.0, whereas the average for the sixteen *shura*-Noh in the second group is 6.6 (*see* the "List of Poems Quoted in Fifth-Group Noh" in Appendix 2). Like the fifth-group Noh in general, the warring-ghost Noh are short, with the frequent absence of structural elements essential to the standard form. For example, the *kuri–sashi–kuse,* which constitutes an essential part of most Noh, is absent in three of the four Noh included in this category, and only a *kuse* is sung in *Kumasaka.* In contrast, all sixteen *shura*-Noh have the *kuse* section, albeit some only partially. Another difference between the two groups is also found in the types of dance actions. The type performed in the *shura*-Noh is called *kakeri,* which is accompanied only by the off-rhythm quiet beats of the two hand drums, which suddenly quicken with a sharp, stretched-out cry by the shoulder-drum player, followed by sharp, staccato alternating beats of the two drums, and by the dancer's heavy and slow stamping of the feet. This shift from slow to quick, which occurs twice, describes the emotional agitation of the dancer.

In contrast, the dance action in the fifth-group Noh, called *mai-bataraki,* is, as the term *bataraki* (from *hataraki,* meaning "action") suggests, is quick and active, and in rhythm; it is accompanied by all four instruments, including the *taiko,* the effect of which is exciting, in contrast to the *kakeri,* which is more subdued. The two types of warrior-ghost Noh also have differences in their choreographic patterns, or *kata.* When a *shura*-Noh ends with a fighting scene, which it does in most cases, the dancer executes a series of *kata* exclusive to such a scene, and often having specific names, such as *tate-ōgi* ("shield fan"), a gesture of holding out a shield, made with an open fan. The choreographic differences between the two groups are inevitable, since the types of weapons used by the *shite* differ between them. With the exception of *Tomoe,* a female Noh that employs a halberd, an ordinary sword is used in the *shura*-Noh, while different types of weapons, including a halberd, are used in the fifth-group Noh.

Another important element of difference is the costume, including the mask. While the *shura*-Noh ghosts wear human masks, some young and elegant, others more mature and brave, or venerable, warring-ghosts in the fifth group wear demonic masks with angry expressions. This is true even with *Ikari-Kazuki,* which is very similar to a *shura*-Noh, and is classified as such by the Kanze school. Its *Shite,* in the second act, wears a weird mask unknown among *shura*-Noh, and his head, covered with long black hair, is crowned with a helmet instead of the elegant cap worn by other *shura*-Noh heroes. Moreover, the dramatic structure of *Ikari-Kazuki* is quite different from that of *shura*-Noh, in that the *Shite* in the first and second acts are different characters. The former is the ghost of a Heike general, Taira no Noritsune, in the form of a humble old man; the latter, the ghost of Taira no Tomomori as a brave general. Both tell the unrelated stories of their own military prowess and heroic deaths. Thus, the play has similar battle stories in the first and second acts, told by different characters, and, unlike the standard *shura*-Noh, there is no reference or allusion that adds poetic or romantic touches to the play. All these features distinguish the warring-ghost Noh of the fifth group from the *shura*-Noh of the second group.

3. Oni-mono (Demonic-Apparition Pieces)

a. Four demonic-ghost pieces: *Shōki* (Chung K'uei), *Shōkun* (Wang Chao-chün), *Raiden–A* (Thunder and Lightning), *Funa-Benkei* (Benkei on Board)
b. Two demonic-deity pieces: *Ukai* (The Cormorant Fisher), *Nomori* (The Gamekeeper)

The word *oni* has many meanings, such as fiend, devil, demon, spirit, ghost, or the dead. It is often used in such phrases as: *ikoku no oni* (foreign-land *oni* = one who died in a foreign country), *fukushū no oni* (avenging *oni* = a person bent on vengeance), or *shigoto no oni* (working *oni* = one who works too hard). The Japanese word *konpaku* (soul, spirit) is made up of two characters, *kon* and *haku,* and these two characters are in their turn made up of two parts: the right-hand part of each character is *oni;* the left-hand part of *kon* is a character meaning "cloud," and the left-side of *haku,* "white," is symbolic of "bones." It is believed that when a man dies, his *kon* ascends to heaven (represented by the character "cloud") while his *haku* remains on earth and is buried under the ground. The expression, "to join the *oni* family" means "to die." In the world of Noh, a ghost in an attachment-play of fourth-group Noh, which is denied nirvana because of its worldly attachment, is considered a kind of *oni.* The King of Hell, Emma (Skt. Yama), is also considered an *oni.* Haruo Nishino also includes under *oni-mono* such plays as *Nue* or *Ryōko,* whose *Shite* are monstrous animals.

In regard to *oni,* Ze-ami explains that there are two types: 1) one who is an *oni* in appearance, but who has a human heart; and 2) one who is both an *oni* in appearance and who has the heart of an *oni.* He further explains how to perform the parts of these two types of *oni.* Also, he says that the part of an angry god can be performed in the manner similar to that for an *oni* (*see* Omote, pp. 25, 128–29). The ghosts of *shura*-Noh in the second-group, of attachment pieces in the fourth group, and of *haya-mai* and warring-ghost pieces in the fifth group can be considered more or less as *oni.*

Of the six *oni-mono* in this category, the *Shite* of *Shōki* (Chung K'uei), *Shōkun* (Wang Chao-chün), *Raiden–A,* and *Funa-Benkei* (Benkei on Board) are *oni* with a human heart, that is, they were originally human beings, and those of *Ukai* and *Nomori* are demons from hell.

The second acts of these *oni* plays are very active, with the *shite* demonstrating his power, or fighting. He performs a *mai-bataraki* or some action similar to it in all Noh except *Raiden–A.* Also, in all Noh except *Raiden–A,* his entrance is accompanied by the exciting *haya-fue* (quick flute) music. The *Nochi-shite* in these plays wear demon masks, such as a *ko-beshimi* for benign beings, a *shikami* for the angry human demon of *Raiden–A,* and an *ayakashi* ("weird ghost" mask) in *Funa-Benkei.*

a. Demonic-Ghost Pieces

Among the four demonic-ghost plays, in *Shōki* and *Shōkun,* the demonic ghosts simply make their appearance, but in *Raiden–A* and *Funa-Benkei,* they appear to attack men.

Shōki (Chung K'uei): Chung K'uei is a legendary Chinese who committed suicide when he failed in an examination, success in which meant a post as a government official. The Emperor took pity on him, and buried him duly, according him an official rank. After his death, he became a being of supernatural power, and to this day he is worshiped by people as their protector from evil spirits. In popular folklore, he is revered as a "Demon Queller." In the Noh *Shōki,* the ghost of Chung K'uei appears to a traveler and asks him to tell the Emperor that His Majesty has no cause to worry about his country, which will be protected by Chung K'uei. In the second act, Chung K'uei appears in his demonic form and performs a *mai-bataraki,* demonstrating his power. The author of *Shōki* is Konparu Zenchiku, Ze-ami's son-in-law.

Shōkun ([Wang] Chao-chün): Chao-chün (fl. first century BC), a consort in the court of the Han Emperor Hsüan-ti (91–49 BC), was made to marry the Hun leader, Hu-han-yeh Khan (Kokan'ya Zennu), and died in the alien land. In the first act of the Noh, Chao-chün's aged parents, the *Shite* and *Tsure,* who grieve over Chao-chün's being taken to the remote Hun lands, sweep their yard and tend a willow tree, a keepsake of their daughter. They hang a mirror on a peach tree, believing an old story about a man who saw the image of his lover in a mirror that reflected peach blossoms. In the second act, the ghost of Chao-chün, the *Kokata,* enters, to show her parents her image reflected in the mirror. She is followed by the ghost of her husband, the *Nochi-shite,* who enters accompanied by *haya-fue* music, which is normally performed at the entrance of a Dragon King or an active supernatural being. Seeing people terrified by his appearance, he looks at his demonic image in the mirror, is shocked, and disappears. In some schools, the *Nochi-shite* performs a *mai-bataraki.* The first act of *Shōkun* is realistic, while the second act is visional, and the *Mae-shite* and *Nochi-shite* are different characters. For details, see the introduction to the translation of *Shōkun* in this book.

Raiden–A: *Raiden–A* (Thunder and Lightning), an *oni-mono,* is the original version of *Raiden–B,* a *haya-mai–mono.* Its source is a story told in the *Taiheiki* about Sugawara no Michizane (845–903), the Grand Minister of the Right, who, due to the calumny of his rival, was exiled to Kyushu, where he died. According to the *Taiheiki,* Michizane, who had prayed to the gods that he might avenge himself on his enemies, became a thunder god after his death, and appeared at the Imperial palace and killed his enemies. In the first act of both versions of the Noh *Raiden,* the spirit of Michizane, the *Shite,* appears to his priest-teacher, the *Waki,* and tells him his intention to take revenge and asks him not to pray to pacify him, even if the Emperor orders him to do so. As the priest refuses, the spirit gets angry and disappears amid burning fire. In the second act of version A, the spirit of Michizane appears in the form of the dreadful thunder god and attacks his enemies, but is placated by the priest's prayers. The second act of version B is entirely different: It depicts a felicitous banquet scene in which the pacified spirit of Michizane performs a *haya-mai* in honor of the Imperial reign.

Funa-Benkei (Benkei on Board): This Noh by Kanze Kojirō Nobumitsu (1435–1516) is based upon a story about the Genji hero, Minamoto no Yoshitsune, told in the *Gikeiki.* However, a large part of the play is fiction. In the first act, Yoshitsune, who has made himself an enemy of his brother Yoritomo, is about to make his escape from a seaport. At the advice of his retainer Benkei, the *Waki,* Yoshitsune tells his mistress, Shizuka, the *Mae-shite,* to return home. At the farewell party, Shizuka performs a dance, a *chū no mai,* and in tears takes leave of her lord. In the second act, Yoshitsune and his followers are attacked at sea by the ghost of their enemy, Taira no Tomomori, a Heike general, the *Nochi-shite.* Benkei drives the ghost away with his prayers. The *Nochi-shite* performs a *mai-bataraki* as he comes to attack.

Funa-Benkei is different from the other *oni-mono* in that, while all the rest are totally or partly visional, with the interval between the acts joined by the narration of an *ai-kyōgen* and a waiting song (*machi-utai*) by the *Waki, Funa-Benkei* is a drama in which a supernatural phenomenon occurs before the eyes of many people. In a visional Noh, the same story is presented continuously from the first to the second act. In *Shōkun,* although the *Shite* in the first and second acts are different characters, it is supposed that the *Mae-shite* remains—invisible—on stage (similar example: *Tomonaga,* a *shura*-Noh in *Battle Noh*). In *Funa-Benkei,* the *Shite* in the two scenes are different characters—Shizuka in the first act, and Tomomori's ghost in the second—and the first and second acts tell different stories: the first, about the parting of Yoshitsune with Shizuka; the second, about Tomomori's ghost, who attacks Yoshitsune. The two acts are joined, not by a narration by an *ai-kyōgen,* but by the action of an *ai-kyōgen,* a boatman who battles with the rising waves. *Funa-Benkei* is a difficult play to classify. It is grouped among "prayer pieces" (plays in which evil spirits are placated by prayer) by Mario Yokomichi, and among "fierce-warrior Noh" (= the warring-ghost pieces in this book) by Haruo Nishino. However, the play is different from the warring-ghost pieces in which the ghost appears as a vision, since in *Funa-Benkei* the ghost actually appears to attack its enemy.

b. Demonic-deity-pieces

The major difference between the four *oni-mono* discussed above, and the remaining two, *Ukai* and *Nomori,* is that the demons in the first group are all human, whereas those in the second group are what Ze-ami refers to as *makoto no meido no oni* ("real demons from hell"). In each of the following two plays a demon deity appears to demonstrate his power.

Ukai (The Cormorant Fisher): Two traveling monks, the *Waki* (Nichiren) and *Waki-tsure,* pass the night in an old cormorant fisher's hut. One of the monks says that years ago, on a night like this, he was offered a night's lodging by a cormorant fisher. At this, the fisher says that the fisherman is dead, having been drowned in the sea as punishment for catching fish in a forbidden place. Then he reveals himself as that fisher's ghost. Upon the monk's wish, the ghost tells them how he caught fish using cormorants, forgetting the sinfulness of the act and retribution thereof. Then the ghost returns to the land of darkness. Nichiren writes the mantra of the Lotus Sutra, *Namu myōhō renge kyō* ("Praised be the wonderful law of the sutra of the lotus blossom") on some rocks and throws them into the river. Then, while the monks are reading the sutra and praying for the fisherman's soul, the *Nochi-shite,* the Demon King of Hell, appears and sings in praise of the sutra, saying that the fisherman, who once did a good deed, that is, giving hospitality to monks, will be saved by virtue of the Lotus Sutra.

The scene in which the old fisher dances, describing his fishing with cormorants, which dive and catch fish in the bright torchlight, until the moon rises high and the game has to come to an end, is a highlight named *U no Dan* (Cormorant Section). The song beginning, "What a fascinating sight!" and ending, "Now it is all moonlight. What a pity!" was crystalized into a haiku by Bashō in 1688: *Omoshirōte / Yagate kanashiki / Ubune kana* (Fascinating at first, / Then it comes to a sad end, / The cormorant-fishing boat!) *Ukai* is a revision by Ze-ami of an older play.

Nomori (The Gamekeeper): This Noh is based on various legendary stories about a *nomori* (gamekeeper), as well as a poem in the *Shin Kokin-shū* (15: 1431) about a "gamekeeper's mirror." One of the stories tells that when one of the Emperor's hawks became lost, the gamekeeper saw its image reflected in a pool of water, which enabled him to catch it and return it to the Emperor. Since then, the pool came to be known as "the gamekeeper's mirror," in which one could see what one wished. The poem goes: *Hashitaka no / Nomori no kagami / Eteshigana / Omoi omowazu / Yosonagara min* (Where they hunt with hawks, / The gamekeeper has a mirror. / I wish it were mine! / Whether you love me or not, / I'd see you reflected there.) Also, the word *nomori* came to be closely associated with Kasugano (Kasuga Moor) and Tobuhino (Tobuhi Moor) in Nara, the scene of the play, through an anonymous poem in the *Kokin-shū* (1: 18): *Kasugano no / Tobuhi no nomori / Idete miyo / Ima ikuka arite / Wakana tsumiten* (On Kasuga Moor / And Tobuhi Moor, Keeper, / Pray, go out and see / How many days we must wait / Ere we may gather young herbs.) The phrase *nomori no kagami* has become a poetic stock-phrase. It is also said that in the gamekeeper's mirror one can see heaven and hell reflected, and that the owner is actually a demon from hell.

In the first act of the Noh, a traveling *yamabushi,* the *Waki,* who has come to Kasuga Moor in Nara, meets an old man, the *Shite,* who tells him the legend about the gamekeeper's mirror. Then the old man reveals himself as the gamekeeper and disappears into a grave-mound. In the second act, the demon deity, the *Nochi-shite,* appears with a large mirror, and demonstrates how heaven and hell are seen reflected in it. He performs a *maibataraki,* and then, striking the ground with his feet, he returns to hell. The author of *Nomori* is Ze-ami.

4. *Tengu-mono* (Goblin-plays)

Five plays: *Kurama Tengu* (The Goblin of Mt. Kurama), *Zegai* (Goblin Shih Chieh), *Kuruma-zō* (Priest on a Flying Couch), *Dai-e* (A Great Mass), *Dairoku-ten* (The Sixth Heaven)

In Buddhist mythology, the word *tengu* originally meant "heavenly fox." The word is also found in ancient Chinese literature, including sutras, used in the sense of "a crying meteor," or "a monstrous mountain beast." The following examples from the Japanese classics indicate that the meaning of the word changed with time. "It must be the doing of a *tengu*" (*Utsubo Monogatari,* ca. 970); "Something like a *tengu* or a tree spirit may have cheated and taken her away" (*Genji Monogatari,* ca. 1000); "The saintly priest in exile died of grief and became a *tengu.* He made himself the head of many other *tengu*" (*Konjaku Monogatari,* ca. 1100); "Indeed, there must have been many *tengu* here. We see a great number of dirty footprints of beasts on the floor mats" (*Taiheiki,* late 14th cent.); "At this time a *tengu* monk (= *yamabushi*), who was three meters in height, walked about the Capital City and took away peoples' swords" (*Gikeiki,* mid-15th cent.). In the Noh *Kagetsu,* there is this passage: "When I was seven years old, I was kidnapped by a *tengu.* The mountains I passed, caught by the *tengu*—oh, how sad to remember them!"

The *tengu* in Noh plays reflects the contemporary idea of a *tengu:* In appearance it is like a *yamabushi* priest, with a grotesquely long nose shaped like a pipe, or a beak like that of a crow, and is able to fly with its large wings. It was endowed with supernatural powers, and could freely change its form. There were several types of *tengu.* For example, mountain deities who "encourage good people and punish bad ones," and who protected Buddhism; monks and priests who became *tengu* because of their great conceit, which is symbolized by their long nose; or those who sank to the state of *tengu* because of their worldly anger or jealousy. Among the five *tengu* pieces, *Kurama Tengu* belongs to the first type; *Kuruma-zō* and *Zegai* present their *tengu* as creatures of great conceit; *Dairoku-ten,* as an enemy of Buddhism; and *Dai-e,* as a mischievous devil. They are all closely related to Buddhism. With the exception of *Dairoku-ten,* whose *Mae-shite* and *Nochi-shite* are different characters, the *Shite tengu* first appears in the form of an ordinary *yamabushi,* and then in the second act as a "great *tengu*" in a gorgeous costume, which is fundamentally that of a *yamabushi,* symbolized by the *tokin,* a small cylinder-shaped head-piece made of folded cloth.

Kurama Tengu (The Goblin of Mt. Kurama): This is the only *tengu* piece in the entire repertoire in which a goblin is presented as a sympathetic being. In this play, the *tengu* appears in order to help the young Ushiwakamaru, the future Genji hero Yoshitsune. For further details, see the introduction to the translation of the Noh in this book.

Zegai: Shih Chieh (Jpn. Zegai; also Shan Chiai, written in different characters) is a Chinese *tengu,* and the Noh *Zegai* is based on a story about this *tengu* told in the *Konjaku Monogatari.* In the first act, the *Shite* comes to Japan with the intention of corrupting the priests of the holy Mt. Hiei and driving them to the kingdom of *tengu.* So he calls on a Japanese *tengu* named Tarō-bō, the *Tsure,* and tells him of his intention. In the second act, led by Tarō-bō, Shih Chieh goes to Mt. Hiei and approaches the high priest, but is driven back by Buddhist deities who have appeared at the invocation of the priest. Like all *tengu-mono,* the Shite's interval exit is accompanied by solemn *raijo* music, which is usually played at the exit of deities and emperors, performed by the three drums; the music then changes to *kyōgen raijo,* accompanying the entrance of an *ai-kyōgen,* a temple servant or a lesser *tengu,* who delivers a comical speech. The *Shite's* entrance in the second act is accompanied by the slow and dignified *ō-beshi,* special to the entrance of a *tengu,* performed by all four instruments. The *Nochi-shite* of *Zegai* performs an *iroe* (= going slowly about the stage to a quiet instrumental accompaniment) as he tries to approach the Hiei priest; then to represent his struggle with the Buddhist deities, he performs a *mai-bataraki.* (The deities do not actually appear; they are only described in the song.) The author of *Zegai* is Takeda Hōin.

Kuruma-zō (Priest on a Flying Couch): *Kuruma-zō* is similar to *Zegai* in that its *Shite tengu,* also named Tarō-bō, a common name for a *tengu,* is also an incarnation of self-conceit, and approaches the priest-on-a-flying-couch, the *Waki,* to defeat him, but fails and disappears in awed veneration. For details, see the introduction to the translation of the Noh in this book.

Dai-e (A Great Mass): *Dai-e* tells a story different from the other *tengu-mono.* It is about a *tengu* who tried to do a good turn for his benefactor. A monk who took pity on a hawk about to be beaten to death by a group of youngsters exchanged the hawk for his fan and set the bird free. In the Noh, a *yamabushi,* the *Shite,* comes to this monk, the *Waki,* and, saying that he is the bird that was rescued by the monk, tells him that he will fulfill any wish for him. The monk answers that he would like to see Śākyamuni Buddha preaching. The strange *yamabushi,* who is actually a *tengu* in disguise, leaves, warning the monk not to be moved to the feeling of worship by what he will see, since that would lead to a grievous end. In the second act, the monk witnesses the scene of Śākyamuni's sermon, and, forgetting the *tengu's* warning, prays in worship. At this, the Vedic deity Indra, a mighty protector of Buddhism, the *Tsure,* descends from Heaven, accompanied by *haya-fue* music, and beats the *tengu,* who escapes to his mountain cave. The scene in which the *tengu* is being driven away by the deity is presented by an active dance named *uchiai-bataraki* (beating action). In the second act of this Noh, the *Nochi-shite* first appears as Śākyamuni, then, preceding the appearance of the heavenly deity, changes his costume on the stage to that of a *tengu.*

Dairoku-ten (The Sixth Heaven): The Sixth Heaven is the highest of the six spheres bound with blind desires (*see* "Six Realms" in the Glossary). It is also the abode of demons. The play is unique among the *tengu-mono* in that the *Shite* in the two acts are different characters. The *Mae-shite* is a village woman, who is actually a goddess, who is accompanied by a *tsure*-woman. In the first act, the venerable priest Gedatsu (1155–1213), the *Waki,* who has come to the Great Shrine of Ise, meets the goddess in the form of an ordinary woman, who tells him the story of the shrine, and disappears, accompanied by *raijo* music, with a hint at some monstrous beings attempting to do harm to the rightful religion. While the priest is praying, the head of evil spirits of the Sixth Heaven appears in the form of a great *tengu,* accompanied by *ō-beshi* music, and approaches the priest, but is driven back by the *Nochi-tsure,* Susano-o no Mikoto, the brother of the Sun Goddess, who enters accompanied by *haya-fue* music. The fighting between the *Shite,* the King of the Sixth Heaven, and Susano-o is presented by an *uchiai-bataraki.* (Susano-o is also the *Waki* in *Orochi,* an evil-fiend piece explained below.)

The above description of four *tengu-mono* points to some characteristics common to them. The *Shite* is presented as a monstrous creature of great self-conceit, whose attempt to attack the rightful religion is defeated by a priest's prayers or by a heavenly deity. There are two types of dance actions to describe this scene, *mai-bataraki* and *uchiai-bataraki.* (These actions are performed in other types of fifth-group Noh also.)

One significant feature of the Noh of this genre is its leading character, the *tengu,* in his huge, grotesque mask and gorgeous, ostentatious costume, with an enormous black-and-white feather fan in his hand, whose interim exit and second entrance are respectively accompanied by solemn *raijo* and *ō-beshi* music. *Ō-beshi* is used almost exclusively for *tengu.* This, and the fact that the *tengu* is a familiar folklore figure, make him a being of strong impact unique among Noh characters.

5. *Igyō-mono* (Strange-Apparition Pieces)

a. Four *mai-mono* (Dance Pieces): *Shakkyō* (The Stone Bridge), *Shōjō* (Hsing-hsing), *Taihei Shōjō* (Hsing-hsing and the Large Vat), *Yamanba* (The Old Woman of the Mountains)

b. Four non-dance pieces: *Kappo* (Kappo Bay), *Sesshōseki* (The Death Stone), *Nue* (The Chimera), *Ryōko* (The Dragon and the Tiger)

The word *igyō* (literally,"'strange figure") means a strange creature that is unlike a human. In *Nue* and *Kappo,* the *Waki* says to the strange figure that has appeared, "To all appearances you do not look like a human. What are you?" The apparitions in this group of Noh include supernatural beasts such as a lion, tiger, dragon, and fox; strange creatures such as a *shōjō* (an orangutan-like creature), *a kōjin* (shark-man), and a *nue* (chimera); and a demonic mountain hag. Although some of them attacked men in the past, they all appear as harmless beings. Some appear as friends of man and their benefactors (Examples: *Taihei Shōjō, Shōjō, Kappo*), or simply for self-demonstration (Example: *Ryōko*). Some appear to a priest, from whom they seek prayers for their salvation. What is hindering them from attaining nirvana is their worldly attachment, which has its root in their thwarted ambition or jealousy (Examples: *Nue, Sesshōseki*). This is true of *Yamanba,* also. In this play, the demonic mountain hag appears to a dancer traveling along a mountain path. Yamanba is jealous of this woman, who has become famous for her song about a mountain hag wandering through the mountains. In a long narrative song, Yamanba tells what meritorious things she does, invisibly, for men. Then she wonders whether it is her blind attachment that makes her say these things. The *igyō-mono* can be divided into two groups: those whose major feature is music and dance, and those without such a special feature.

a. Mai-mono (Dance Pieces)

Shakkyō (The Stone Bridge): This Noh takes place in the Ch'ing-liang (Jpn. Seiryō/Shōryō) Mountains, in Shanhsi Province, China, on a holy mountain upon which resides Mañjuśrī, the Bodhisattva of Wisdom. In the first act, the *Shite,* a boy, appears to the *Waki,* Monk Jakushō (962–1034) from Japan, who wants to enter the holy land of Mañjuśrī beyond a stone bridge that spans a deep valley. The boy warns the monk of the danger of crossing the narrow, slippery, moss-grown bridge, and describes for the monk the splendor of Buddha's land, which, he says, the monk will see if he waits where he is. In the second act, the monk sees a lion, the sacred beast on which Mañjuśrī rides, dancing among Chinese peonies. The dance it performs, named *shishi* (lion), is unique.[5] The lion, the *Nochi-shite,* first appears accompanied by special entrance music called *ranjo* (wild introduction), which consists of three parts: a prelude, played slowly and solemnly in rhythm by the three drums, accompanied by sharp cries, with the flute playing *ashirai* (off-rhythm accompaniment); the second part, called *tsuyu no hyōshi* (dew-drop beats), played by the shoulder and stick drums, beaten quietly at long intervals, which is said to describe the quietness of the mountain fastness, in which the dripping of the dew drops can be heard; and the third part, played by the four instruments in a gradually quickening tempo, during which the lion enters the main stage and begins the *shishi* dance. It is a spectacular dance by an actor in a gorgeous lion costume and a golden lion mask, his long red hair tossed about as he hops up and down the two platforms on which stand Chinese peony trees, one with red, the other with white, flowers in full bloom. In a variation named *Ōjishi,* two lions appear, parent and child, one in a white (father), the other in a red (son), wig. Besides *Shakkyō,* two fourth-group Noh, *Uchito-Mōde* and *Mochizuki,* musical entertainment pieces, have a *shishi* dance, performed, not by a lion, but by a man as impromptu entertainment in make-shift costumes, without any special accompaniment such as *tsuyu no hyōshi.*

Shōjō (Hsing-hsing): A *hsing-hsing* (Jpn. *shōjō*) is an imaginary beast of Chinese origin, which is said to speak human words and is fond of rice wine. *Shōjō* was originally in two acts but has been reduced to one act. It is similar to *Taihei Shōjō,* but there is only one *hsing-hsing. Shōjō* was probably written first, and was the model for *Taihei Shōjō.* In the variation of *Shōjō* named *Midare,* there is special movement of the feet during the *chū no mai,* to represent dancing on water. In another variation, two *hsing-hsing* appear. The *shōjō* mask, depicting a red-faced, smiling, tipsy youth, is one of the most charming Noh masks. This Noh, in which a *hsing-hsing* enters wearing this mask, accompanied by the rhythmical music called *sagariha,* and dances as the reed leaves play the flute, the waves beat drums, and the autumn wind sings in a clear voice, is like a scene from a fairy tale.

---

[5] The correct name of the lion dance in Noh is *shishi.* A similar term, *shishi-mai,* is used to describe the lion dance performed by street artists, familiar from Chinatown parades around the world.

Taihei Shōjō (Hsing-hsing and the Large Vat): In *Taihei Shōjō,* as in *Shakkyō,* the scene is China. A *hsing-hsing* appears to a wine vendor and drinks rice wine. He disappears with a promise that the merchant will be made a rich man in reward for his devotion to his parents. In the second act, as the wine vendor is waiting by the seashore, several *hsing-hsing* appear out of the water, drink the merchant's wine out of his huge crockery vat, and together perform a *chū no mai.* The special feature of this Noh is the dance performed by as many as five to seven dancers. (Similar examples are found in a variation of *Yoshino Tennin* [Heavenly Maiden on Mt. Yoshino], a third-group Noh, in which four to eight heavenly maidens perform a *chū no mai,* and *Momiji-gari* [Maple Viewing] explained below, in which five fiends perform a *mai-bataraki.*) The word *taihei* in the Noh title means "peaceful reign," as well as "large vat." In the play, the group of *hsing-hsing* drink wine from an enormous vat formed of brocade that is placed at center stage. *Taihei Shōjō* is exclusive to the Kanze school.

Shakkyō, Shōjō, and *Taihei Shōjō* are among the few *kiri-* (final) Noh, that is, congratulatory Noh, that can be additionally performed after a formal five-Noh program.

Yamanba (The Old Woman of the Mountaina): In the word *yamanba* (= *yama-uba*), *yama* means "mountain." The character *uba* is made up of two characters, one meaning "woman" and the other, "old." In spite of this, the word *uba* does not necessarily mean an old woman. It is often applied to much younger women, and a wet nurse, who can be quite young, is also called *uba.* In the Noh *Yamanba,* there is no allusion to Yamanba's age. However, her hair is described as "snow-white." The *yamanba* mask depicts a woman in her sixties, vigorous and fierce, but not angry or fiendish. In the mountainous districts of Japan, all sorts of stories have been told about *yamanba,* the supernatural women who live on the mountains. The Noh *Yamanba* is based on a *kuse-mai* song about Yamanba wandering through the mountains. (A *kuse-mai* is a type of popular song that was in vogue in Ze-ami's time.) In the Noh, a *kuse-mai* singer celebrated for her *yamanba* song, on her way to the temple Zenkōji, meets a woman in the deep mountains, and passes a night at her cottage. The woman is actually Yamanba. She chides the singer, whom the *yamanba* song has made famous, for her failure to remember her benefactor. Later, in the second act, Yamanba appears in her true form and tells her story. This is presented in a special type of *kuse* named *nidan-guse* (a three-part *kuse* with two dividing lines).

Usually a *kuse* is sung all through by the chorus, with one or two lines in the middle sung by an actor. This solo singing, called *ageha,* divides the *kuse* into two parts. The *kuse* in Yamanba has two *ageha,* which divide the *kuse* into three parts. As a rule, an ordinary *kuse* is preceded by a *kuri* and *sashi;* a *nidan-guse* has in addition a *shidai* song by the chorus before the *kuri* and *sashi,* and the *kuse* ends with a repetition of the lines sung in the *shidai.* Only a few Noh have a *nidan-guse. Yamanba* is unique among the fifth-group Noh, not only in having this type of *kuse,* but also in that it comes in the second act. The long and slow *kuse* should have no place in the second act of a fifth-group Noh performed in the final *kyū* stage. It is the long *kuse* with a dance that ranks *Yamanba,* which has no instrumental dance except a short and simple *tachimawari* (going about the stage), among dance-and-music plays. Still, it ends quickly, with Yamanba going swiftly up and down the mountains till she vanishes.

In the first act, the Noh poses us a question: what is a *yamanba?* Then in the second act, Yamanba sings: "Dust accumulates to form a mountain woman." There is a Japanese saying that goes: "Dust accumulates to form a mountain." Man is dust—so is a *yamanba,* the accumulated dust of worldly attachments, obsessions, feelings, karma-bound destiny, and so on that bind man. The *kuse* song portrays the "human" Yamanba, seeking the society of men, or in solitary contemplation under an autumn moon, in dignified, poetic language with an undertone of Zen philosophy that regards buddhas, men, and *yamanba* all as one. It is no wonder that this play (probably by Kan-ami, and re-written by Ze-ami) has been attributed to some great Zen priests, such as Ikkyū (1394–1481).

b. Non-Dance Pieces

Kappo (Kappo Bay): *Kappo* tells a story about a strange creature of the sea called *chiao-jen* (Jpn. *kōjin* [merman; lit., "shark man"]), whose tears are said to turn into pearls. A man who lives in Ho-p'u (Jpn. Kappo) in China, famous for its pearls, buys a fish from a fisherman and puts it back into the sea. The fish appears to the man, thanks him, and disappears, saying that he will give him pearls in return for his kindness. His interim exit is accompanied by solemn *raijo* music, which duly changes to *kyōgen raijo* to accompany the entrance of two *ai-kyōgen* as spirits of fish. In the second act, the *chiao-jen* appears with some pearls, performs a *mai-bataraki,* and offers the jewels to his benefactor. Many young children perform this as their first *shite* role.

Sesshōseki (The Death Stone): This Noh is based on a legendary story about a huge stone in Nasu Moor in present Tochigi Prefecture, named Sesshōseki (Death Stone) because the vapor it emitted killed whomever approached it. In the Noh, a woman appears to the priest Gennō (died in 1396, aged 71) near the stone and tells him that the stone was originally a fox, who, changing itself into a beautiful woman, wrought mischief in India, China, and Japan, until it was killed in this field, whereupon it turned into a huge stone. Then the woman tells the priest that she is the spirit of that stone, and disappears into the stone, a stage prop set at center stage. As the priest is praying before the stone, it breaks into two, revealing the monstrous figure of the fox. In dance and song it describes how two warriors hunted it down with their dogs, until they killed it with their arrows. The figure vanishes into the stone, with a stone-hard pledge that it will never work mischief again.

The highlight of this Noh is the final long song and dance, which describe the hunting of the fox. The author of this play is probably Sa-ami (dates uncertain).

Nue (The Chimera): *Nue* is the name of a strange animal whose voice was like that of a bird of the same name. A *nue* was thought to have the head of a monkey, the body of a badger, the legs of a tiger, and a snake as a tail. Due to its appearance, it is sometimes referred to as a Japanese chimera. In legend, a *nue* could fly by transforming itself into a black cloud, and was thought to bring misfortune. The play is translated in this book with a detailed explanation in the introduction.

Ryōko (The Dragon and the Tiger): Like most of the plays in this group, the scene of this Noh is in China. A monk from Japan meets two woodsmen on a mountain and exchanges words with them. In the peaceful spring landscape, the monk sees bamboo bushes suddenly covered with black clouds and being blown by a violent wind. The elder woodsman tells the monk about the fighting of a tiger and a dragon that often takes place there. Then songs are sung in praise of the tiger, who waits on great saints, and of the dragon, whose image adorns the Imperial robes and vehicles. Then telling him that if he waits in hiding, he will see their fight, they exit, accompanied by the solemn *raijo* music played at the interim exit of deities, emperors, as well as *tengu.* In the second act, the monk witnesses the fierce fighting of the tiger and dragon, who strike at each other with sticks, rendered in a fighting action named *uchiai-bataraki.* The eternal battle between the tiger and dragon has been a popular theme of painting on scrolls and sliding screens, likely sources of this play. This play in praise of the strength of the tiger and dragon, written in a dignified style, can be performed informally as a *waki*-Noh. The author of this Noh is Kanze Kojirō Nobumitsu.

6. *Akki-mono* (Evil-Fiend Pieces)

a. Three Noh in which the fiend is conquered by prayer or by a deity: *Adachigahara* (Adachi Moor), *Hiun* (Hiun the Fiend), *Shari* (The Sacred Relic). Note that Adachigahara is the Kanze name of the play known as *Kurozuka* (Black Mound) in the other schools, as well as in Kabuki.

b. Five Noh in which the fiend is conquered by warrior(s): *Ōe-yama* (Mt. Ōe), *Orochi* (The Dragon), *Rashōmon* (The Rashō Gate), *Tsuchigumo* (The Monstrous Spider), *Momiji-gari* (The Maple-Viewing Party).

In this group of Noh, an evil fiend is conquered by a deity or by prayer, or killed by warriors. These warriors are all well known in history. The warriors in *Ōe-yama, Rashōmon,* and *Tsuchigumo* belong to the Genji clan. The warrior in *Momiji-gari* is a Heike general. In *Orochi,* Susano-o, the *Waki,* who kills the dragon, is a deity, being the younger brother of the Sun Goddess, Amaterasu, but he is presented as a human hero. In most Noh, the fiend first appears in a human form, and then reveals his own form in the second act. In four out of eight Noh in this group, namely, *Hiun, Orochi, Rashōmon* and *Momiji-gari,* the *Nochi-shite* has no lines to speak or sing. The fight between the fiend and man is presented by *mai-bataraki, uchiai-bataraki* (fighting action), or *inori* (prayer). As a rule, the *Nochi-shite* wears a mask with an angry, inhuman expression, called *shikami* (frown). In *Adachigahara,* a *hannya* mask is worn by the female fiend, and in *Orochi* the monster dragon wears a *kurohige,* a mask for dragons. For further details about the Noh in this group, see the introduction to the translation of *Adachigahara.*

a. Plays in which a fiend is conquered by prayer or by a deity.

Adachigahara (Adachi Moor): This Noh is about a demoness who is conquered by the prayers of two *yamabushi.* The fight between the devil and the priests is presented by an *inori* (prayer), a dance action that is performed only in this play and two fourth-group Noh, *Aoi no Ue* and *Dōjōji* (as well as in *Hiun* in the Hōshō and Kongō schools). For more details, see the introduction to the play, which is translated in this book.

Hiun (Hiun the Fiend): In this Noh, a traveling *yamabushi* meets a woodsman on a mountain, and together they look at the beautiful landscape in autumn colors, until it grows dark and the woodsman makes his exit, accompanied by *raijo* music. In the second act, the woodsman reappears in his real form as the devil Hiun, but is driven away by the *yamabushi's* prayer. The fighting scene is presented by a special type of *mai-bataraki* named *inori-bataraki* (prayer action), or, in the Hōshō and Kongō schools, by *inori* (prayer), which, apart from this Noh, is exclusive to *Aoi no Ue, Dōjōji,* and *Adachigahara.* The source and authorship of this Noh are unknown.

Shari (The Sacred Relic): In this Noh, which is based on a story told in the *Taiheiki,* the *rākṣasa* (Jpn. *rasetsu*, originally a kind of demon with supernatural power said to bewitch and eat men; later, guardians of Buddhism) called "Swift-footed Devil" appears at the temple Sennyūji in Kyoto in the form of a strange ghostly person, and talks with a traveling monk about the holy ashes of Buddha celebrated in the temple. Then he reveals his identity, snatches the relic from the altar, and escapes. In the second act, Skanda (Jpn. Idaten), the swift-footed Buddhist deity, the *Tsure,* appears, runs after the devil, beats it, and takes back the relic. The fight is represented by an *uchiai-bataraki.* After this, the *rākṣasa* performs an *iroe* (slow walking about the stage to an instrumental accompaniment), to represent the beaten fiend trying to escape. In this group, this Noh is unique in that it is a deity who conquers the devil.

b. Plays in which a fiend is conquered by warrior well known in history.

Orochi (The Dragon): The Noh is based on an episode told in the *Kojiki* and *Nihon Shoki* about a monstrous dragon with eight heads and tails. The Sun Goddess's brother Susano-o no Mikoto, the *Waki,* who was driven from the High Heavenly Field because of his offensive deeds, in his wanderings meets an aged couple, the *Mae-shite* and the *Tsure,* and their daughter, the *Kokata,* in deep grief. He is told how the couple's seven daughters were eaten by a monstrous dragon, who is now coming to get the last one. Susano-o changes the daughter into a comb, which he puts in his hair, and then tells the couple to fill eight large vats with saké. In the second act, the monstrous dragon, the *Nochi-shite,* appears, sees the girl's image reflected in the vats, into which it lowers its eight heads and drinks the saké. When it becomes intoxicated, Susano-o cuts it to pieces and finds a magnificent sword in its tail. (Later this sword, Muragumo, was renamed Kusanagi [see the description of *Kusanagi* on p. 16] and became one of the Three Imperial Regalia.) The fight between the dragon and Susano-o is represented by an *uchiai-bataraki.* Although the Sun Goddess Amaterasu's brother, Susano-o, is a deity, he is treated here as a human hero. In *Dairoku-ten,* a *tengu* piece, he appears as the *Nochi-tsure* deity. The author of this Noh is Kanze Kojirō Nobumitsu.

Ōe-yama (Mt. Ōe): Minamoto no Yorimitsu, also pronounced Raikō, a Genji general (d. 1021), the *Waki,* and his retainers, the *Waki-tsure,* disguise themselves as *yamabushi* and go to Mt. Ōe to kill the fiend Shuten Dōji. By a river they meet a woman, an *ai-kyōgen,* washing the bloodstained clothes of those who were eaten by the fiend. The woman takes the warriors to the fiend's abode, where the fiend appears in the form of a young boy, and entertains the warriors with saké. The fiend, whose name means "saké drinker," gets tipsy and performs a dance, singing about the autumn flowers of the mountain. Then he withdraws into the bedchamber. In the second act, the warriors attack the fiend where it is sleeping. The fiend appears, revealing its dreadful form. The ensuing *uchiai-bataraki* represents the fight between the fiend and the warriors, at the end of which they kill the fiend. The source of this Noh is unknown.

Rashōmon (The Rashō Gate): This Noh is based on a tale in the *Heike Monogatari,* and as in *Ōe-yama,* the *Waki* and *Waki-tsure* are Raikō and his retainers. On a long spring day of rain, as they are killing time, drinking saké, and chatting, one of them mentions a rumor that the Rashō Gate is now the abode of a devil. (The gate, which stood at the southern end of Kyoto's central street, was immortalized in Kurosawa's film of the same name.) Another retainer, Watanabe no Tsuna, the *Waki,* does not believe it, and says that he will go to the gate in the depth of night, to find out if the rumor is true. In the second act, Tsuna, who has arrived at the gate, is attacked by the fiend, the *Shite.* Tsuna fights with the fiend and cuts off its arm, and the monster disappears into the sky. An *uchiai-bataraki* represents the fighting action. The *Shite* appears only in the second act, and has no line to speak or sing. The interim exit of Tsuna, followed by all the other characters, is accompanied by *haya-tsuzumi* (quick drum), which is continued until an *ai-kyōgen* enters as a messenger. This music, played when all the characters exit at the advent of some impending event, followed by the entrance of an *ai-kyōgen* as an urgent messenger, is performed by two hand drums, started first by the small drum, and soon joined on and off by the large drum, alternately beating short, stacatto beats, and it occurs in a few Noh. We have examples in *Tsuchigumo* and in some miracle plays explained below, and in such fourth-group Noh as *Kanawa* and *Eboshi-ori* (both in *Troubled Souls*). This Noh is by Kanze Kojirō Nobumitsu.

Tsuchigumo (The Monstrous Spider): This is another tale of bravery of Raikō and his retainers told in the *Heike Monogatari.* A strange monk appears to Raikō, the *Tsure,* who is ill in bed, and throws what looks like a spider's thread, trying to catch Raikō. When Raikō strikes him with his sword, the stranger disappears. Hearing Raiko's voice, his retainer Hitori Musha ("Single Warrior"), the *Waki,* rushes to the scene and sees traces of blood on the floor. Hitori Musha goes in chase of the monster, following the traces of blood. The entrance of Hitori Musha and his interim exit with Raikō are accompanied by a *haya-tsuzumi,* which continues to accompany the entrance of an *ai-kyōgen,* a servant, who describes the incident. In the second act, Hitori Musha and several other retainers of Raikō trace the monster to where it is hiding in his cave and attack it. A monstrous spider, the *Nochi-shite,* comes out of the cave and throws webs of white thread at the warriors, who finally kill it. An *uchiai-bataraki,* which represents the fight, is the highlight of the play. During this action the monster spider throws little balls of white paper cut into long, fine threads, which spread out like white-flaming fireworks all over the stage, enmeshing the swords the warriors brandish.

Momiji-gari (The Maple-Viewing Party): The source of *Momiji-gari* is unknown. Its *Waki* is a Heike general, Taira no Koremochi, a legendary hero of the mid-Heian period. The play begins with the entrance of the *Shite* in the form of a beautiful lady accompanied by some ladies-in-waiting. They sing songs describing the lovely autumn landscape they see as they stroll about the mountain. Koremochi, while hunting, comes upon the ladies holding a maple-viewing party. As he dismounts, and is about to pass on, a beautiful lady, the *Shite,* invites him to join the banquet. He declines at first, but finally lets himself be invited and drinks saké. The lady performs a *kuse* dance and a *chū no mai.* As Koremochi falls asleep, the dance quickens into a *kyū no mai,* the quickest dance of the *chū-no-mai* type, and the lady disappears into a stage prop representing a cave, accompanied by *raijo* music, which changes to *kyōgen raijo.* An *ai-kyōgen,* a minor deity, enters and tells the sleeping Koremochi that the lady is actually a devil, and that Koremochi should kill it with a divine sword. Koremochi awakes and finds the divine sword placed before him. As he waits, the devil in its real form appears, performs a *mai-bataraki,* and fights with Koremochi, who kills it.

In a *kogaki* version named *Oni-zoroe* (an array of *oni*), the *kuse* dance and the first part of the *chū no mai* are performed by the ladies-in-waiting, the *Tsure,* and the *Shite* dances the last part of the *mai.* In the second act, a *mai-bataraki* is performed by five devils, and the *Shite*-devil performs a *tachimawari* in the finale. Like *Orochi* and *Rashōmon,* the authorship of this play is attributed to Kanze Kojirō Nobumitsu.

✧ ✧ ✧

7. *Reiken-mono* (Miracle Plays)

a. Seven *waki* (god)-Noh–type plays: *Genjō, Kasuga Ryūjin* (Dragon God of Kasuga Shrine), *Taisanpukun* (Taishanfuchün), *Kuzu, Kokaji* (Kokaji the Swordsmith), *Chōryō* (Chang Liang), *Kōtei* (The Emperor)

b. Six human-interest-(*ninjō-mono*)–type plays: *Chōbuku Soga* (The Incantation Story of the Soga Brothers), *Danpū* (The Propitious Wind), *Tanikō* (The Valley Rites), *Matsuyama Kagami* (The Mirror of Matsuyama), *Aisome-gawa* (The Aisome River), *Take no Yuki* (The Snow-Laden Bamboo). (Note that there is also a subgroup among the fourth-group Noh called *ninjō-mono.*)

The *reiken-mono,* thirteen in number, are plays about miracles wrought by supernatural beings to help men. They can be divided into two subgroups: a) *waki* (god)-Noh type, seven in number; and b) human-interest (*ninjō-mono*) type, six in number. In the *waki*-Noh–type Noh, *Kōtei* (The Emperor) excepted, the cause of the miracle is something other than human life or human relationship, while in the human-interest Noh, as well as in *Kōtei,* a miracle saves a human life, or helps to solve a conflict that concerns a family relationship, particularly the parent–child relationship. In some plays both issues are involved. There are also other features that distinguish the two groups. *Kōtei,* in which a miracle saves the life of the emperor's favorite lady, is included among the *waki*-Noh–type plays rather than the other group, because of its other dramatic features, which are common to the first group. The characteristics of the two groups, as well as the differences between them are discussed below, following brief descriptions of individual plays in the two groups.

a. Waki-*Noh–type plays*

Genjō: In *Genjō,* the scene is Suma Beach. Fujiwara no Moronaga (1138–92), Grand Minister of State, a celebrated player of the *biwa* (a musical instrument similar to a lute), is on his way to China, where he wants to learn the secret of *biwa* music. He comes to Suma Beach and spends a night at a fisherman's cottage. The old fisherman and his wife beg the celebrated player to play on his *biwa.* While Moronaga is playing, he is disturbed by the sound of rain beating the roof. The old man spreads straw mats on the roof and says that now the sounds of the *biwa* and rain are harmonious. Much impressed by the old man's words, Moronaga asks him to play on the *biwa,* which the old man does, and the old woman accompanies him with her *koto.* Deeply moved by their playing, Moronaga realizes that his wish to go to China was a mistake, when there are such excellent players in his own country, and he decides to return. The old man stops him to say that he is actually Emperor Murakami (reigned 926–67), the owner of the sacred *biwa* named Genjō,[6] and the old woman is his imperial consort, who have appeared to detain Moronaga. With these words the couple fades out of sight. Their interim exit is accompanied by solemn *raijo* music.

In the second act, the deified Emperor Murakami appears and orders a dragon god, the *Nochi-tsure,* to bring the sacred *biwa* Shishi-maru from the Dragon King's palace in the sea and bestow it on Moronaga. The dragon enters, accompanied by *haya-fue* (quick flute), and gives the *biwa* to Moronaga. While Moronaga plays the *biwa,* the Emperor performs a *haya-mai,* and disappears in a coach drawn by flying horses. The *Shite* of this Noh is Emperor Murakami, and the old woman and Moronaga are the *Tsure.* Moronaga is accompanied by an attendant, the *Waki,* and by some servants, the *Waki-tsure.* The first act, which ends with the old man's words, "To detain you from going to China, I have appeared in your dream," is visional in a way, and yet it is unusual in that the dream is seen by the *Tsure* instead of the *Waki.* (We have a similar example in *Kiyotsune,* a *shura*-Noh, in which the ghost of a warrior appears to his wife, the *Tsure.*) The second act, in which a dragon god bestows the musical instrument on Moronaga, can be considered miraculous and supernatural. The source of inspiration of this Noh may be an episode in the *Heike Monogatari* about Emperor Murakami and his miraculous *biwa.* The story about Grand Minister Moronaga is fiction, although he is a historical person and is known to have been a celebrated *biwa* player.

Kasuga Ryūjin (Dragon God of Kasuga Shrine): The saintly priest Myōe (1173–1232), who is said to be greatly favored by the god of Kasuga Shrine in Nara, "as if he were one of the god's eyes," is going to China and India to study Buddhism. He comes to Kasuga Shrine to bid farewell to the god. An old man meets him and tells him about the superb power of the Buddhist deities in Japan. The priest therefore gives up the thought of leaving the country, and the old man disappears.

In the four Noh schools other than Kanze, the exit of the old man is accompanied by *raijo* music, which is performed in *waki*-Noh at the exit of the *mae-shite,* a deity in the form of an old man. In the second act, accompanied by *haya-fue* music, the dragon god, the *Nochi-shite,* who is actually

---

[6] Genjō is one of the three sacred *biwas* sent to the Emperor from China, but one of them, named Shishi-maru, was seized by the Dragon King and brought to his palace beneath the sea.

the bodhisattva Avalokiteśvara, appears and asks the priest twice about his decision to go abroad. As the priest replies twice in the negative, the dragon god performs a *mai-bataraki* in praise of the shrine. (It is to be imagined that the Dragon King is followed by numerous other dragon deities, who are described only in the song.) The sources of inspiration of the play are the writings of the priest Myōe himself, and other stories based on them.

Kasuga Ryūjin and *Genjō* are similar in that the exodus of a celebrated person is detained by a divine power.

Taisanpukun (< Ch. Taishanfuchün): The Noh is based on a story in the *Genpei Jōsuiki.* Fujiwara no Shigenori (1135–87), who was nicknamed Sakuramachi no Chūnagon (Cherry-Garden Middle Councillor)[7] because he loved cherry blossoms and planted many cherry trees in his garden, is the *Waki,* and he prays to Taisanpukun, the deity of fertility and one of the gods of hell, to let the cherry blossoms in his garden bloom for three weeks instead of just a week. At night a heavenly maiden, the *Mae-shite,* descends to the cherry garden, admires the flowers, plucks a branch, and flies back to heaven. In the second act, Taisanpukun, the *Nochi-shite,* appears and discovers that a heavenly maiden has plucked a cherry branch. The maiden, the *Nochi-tsure,* reappears with the cherry branch in hand and performs a *tennyo-mai* (heavenly maiden's dance). The *Nochi-shite* performs a *mai-bataraki,* and causes the cherry blossoms to last for three weeks.

Kokaji (Kokaji the Swordsmith): This Noh relates a miraculous story about a sword, the source of which is unknown. The swordsmith Sanjō no Kokaji Munechika (fl. mid-Heian period), the *Waki,* is ordered by the Emperor to make a sword for him. He goes to the Inari Shrine, the tutelary shrine of his family, and prays that he might be enabled to make a good sword. A boy (an old man in a variant version) appears to Munechika, tells him various miraculous stories about swords, and disappears with a hint at his identity as Munechika's family god, and with a promise that he will come and help him make a worthy sword. In the second act, while the swordsmith is praying to the gods for their assistance, the *Nochi-shite,* the fox-deity of Inari Shrine, appears, accompanied by *haya-fue* music, performs a *mai-bataraki,* and together with Munechika beats and forges the iron until the sword is made. The god then offers it to the imperial envoy.

---

[7] The nobleman Sakuramachi is the father of Kogō, the heroine of the Noh *Kogō,* an *otoko-mai–mono,* translated in *Troubled Souls* in *The Noh* series.

Munechika's chanting of prayer is accompanied by special music called *notto* (incantation). There are other examples of *notto* in two fourth-group plays: *Makiginu,* a female quasi-*waki*-Noh, and *Kanawa,* a fiendish-woman Noh, which is translated in *Troubled Souls.*

Kuzu: Kuzu is the name of a river at the foot of Mt. Yoshino, famous for its sweetfish, also named *kuzu.* In the Noh, which is based on a tale in the *Genpei Jōsuiki,* Emperor Tenmu (631–86), played by a *kokata,* and his followers come to Mt. Yoshino as refugees of war and rest at the cottage of an old montaineer and his wife. They protect him from his enemies, and then become deities who bestow their blessing upon the Emperor and his reign. For further details, see the introduction to the translation of the Noh included in this book.

Chōryō (Chang Liang): This play is about an episode told in Ssu-ma Ch'ien's *Records of the Historian.* Chang Liang (Chōryō), a Chinese general (d. 168 BC), the *Waki,* tells in his introductory speech about a strange dream he had: On a river bridge he met an old man on horseback, who dropped one of his shoes and told Chang Liang to pick it up and put it back on his foot. Chang Liang did as he was told out of respect for the man's old age. Much impressed, the old man promised to give Chang Liang the secret writings on military arts and told him to come to the same bridge in five days. After his speech, Chang Liang hastens and arrives at the designated place. The old man of the dream, the *Mae-shite,* appears, scolds Chang Liang for his late arrival, tells him to come again in five days, and disappears. Chang Liang expresses his decision to obey the old man in order to obtain the secrets of military arts, and makes the interim exit, accompanied by *haya-tsuzumi* (quick drum) music.

In the second act, the old man reappears to Chang Liang in his magnificent form as the mysterious hermit Huang Shih Kung (Jpn. Kō Sekikō), accompanied by solemn *ō-beshi* music, which is usually played at the entrance of a *tengu.* The hermit drops one of his shoes into the river, and tells Chang Liang to pick it up. As he jumps into the river and tries to retrieve the shoe, a dragon, the *Tsure,* appears, takes the shoe, and attacks Chang Liang. The dragon performs a *mai-bataraki.* Then the Chorus describes the fight between Chang Liang and the dragon, who dance to the song, until the dragon offers the shoe to Chang Liang, who puts it on Huang Shih Kung's foot. The hermit gives Chang Liang the secret writings on military arts, and the dragon, who is actually Avalokiteśvara, becomes Chang Liang's protector deity. The highlight of this play is the fight between the dragon and Chang Liang. It is one of the rare Noh in which a *waki* performs a dance action describing a scene. This Noh is also by Kanze Kojirō Nobumitsu, an accomplished Noh playwright as well as an able *waki* actor.

Kōtei (The Emperor): The *Shite* of *Kōtei* is the same character as the *Shite* in the title role of *Shōki* (Chung K'uei), an *oni-mono* (demonic-apparition piece). In the Noh *Kōtei,* a strange old man, the *Shite,* appears to the Emperor Hsüan-tsung (Jpn. Gensō, 685–762), the *Waki,* by the sickbed of his favorite consort, Yang Kuei-fei (Yōkihi, herself the *Shite* in a third-group play of her name), the *Kokata.* The old man says that he is the spirit of Chung K'uei, who killed himself when he failed in the national examination, but was accorded posthumous honors by the Emperor. In return for the Emperor's kindness, he is going to save the lady's life with his magic power. The old man disappears, telling the Emperor to place a bright mirror by the lady's bed.

In the second act the Emperor places a mirror near his lady's bed. As it grows dark, he sees in the mirror the image of a frightful devil, the *Tsure,* whose entrance is accompanied by *haya-fue* (quick flute) music. As the Emperor strikes at it with his sword, its form becomes invisible. Then, accompanied by solemn *ō-beshi* music, Chung K'uei reveals his magnificent form, and fights with the devil, until the devil is cut into pieces and the lady is cured. The fighting scene is represented as an *uchiai-bataraki.*

The play begins with a *kyōgen kuchiake* (an opening speech by an *ai-kyōgen* delivered as a prologue), followed by the entrance of the Emperor, accompanied by solemn *shin no raijo* music played at the entrance of an emperor. This Noh is similar to the human-interest plays in that the miracle is wrought to save a person's life; and, as in them, there is a *kokata.* However, it has many other features common to the *waki*-Noh–type plays, namely: the *Mae-shite* and the *Nochi-shite* are the same character; its characters are people of high status; and it has a dignified structure, beginning with a *kyōgen kuchiake* and *shin no raijo.* There is also dance action, an *uchiai-bataraki,* rare among the plays of other groups/subgroups.

As for the *Kokata* in this play, the child plays not a child's role, but an adult's, as in *Kuzu, Funa-Benkei,* and numerous other plays. The author of this Noh also is Kanze Kojirō Nobumitsu.

b. Human-interest-(ninjō-mono)*–type plays.*

Chōbuku Soga (Incantation Story of the Soga Brothers): The source of inspiration of *Chōbuku Soga* is the *Soga Monogatari* (*The Tale of the Soga Brothers*), which tells how the Soga brothers killed (in 1193) their enemy, who had murdered their father eighteen years before, when the brothers were young children of five and three. The scene of the Noh is Hakone Gongen Shrine, where the younger Soga brother, the boy Hako-ō, lives under the care of the head priest. The Noh begins with the entrance of the Shōgun, Minamoto no Yoritomo, who has come to visit the shrine. Hako-ō asks the priest the names of the Shōgun's numerous attendants. At the boy's reaction when his enemy Kudō no Suketsune's name is mentioned, the priest, the *Waki,* is about to take the boy away. Suketsune, the *Shite,* detains him and teases the boy before leaving with the others. The boy steals a priest's sword and runs after Suketsune, but is stopped by the head priest. In the second act the head priest places on the altar an effigy representing Suketsune, and together with his fellow-priests (not actually present on the stage) prays to the deity Fudō (Skt. Acala, or Acalanātha) to destroy Hako-ō's enemy. The deity, the *Nochi-shite,* appears, followed by his attendant deities, described only in the song. They all attack at the effigy, until finally Acala cuts its head off.

The author of this Noh is Miyamasu, an enigmatic figure about whom almost nothing is known, except that he flourished in the late Muromachi period.

Danpū (The Propitious Wind): This play by an unknown author is the only Noh (with the exception of *Shari* and *Raiden–A*—as well as one modern work, *Kusu no Tsuyu,* an *otoko-mai–mono*) that is based on an episode in the *Taiheiki.* This book tells the tale of Mibu no Suketomo (1290–1332), a royalist, who was caught and exiled to Sado Island. His son Kumawaka, a young boy, traveled to Sado, hoping to see his father before his execution, but his wish was not granted. Having ordered his servant to take his father's ashes to the holy Mt. Kōya, Kumawaka stole into the executioner's house, killed him, and escaped. An old *yamabushi* priest took him to the harbor, and called to a ship about to embark, asking the captain to take them on board. When this was refused, the *yamabushi* caused the ship to return to the shore through his prayers and thus they made their escape. In the Noh, the boy's name is changed to Umewaka. The boy is accompanied by an elderly *yamabushi* priest, Sochi no Ajari (the Ācārya), the *Waki,* from the beginning. Honma, the *Waki-tsure,* the executioner in the original story, is presented as a sympathetic warrior who lets the boy meet his father, the *Tsure.* The father is executed not by Honma, but by one of his men. Umewaka steals into Honma's house and kills him with the priest's help. The Noh ends with the appearance of the deities worshiped by the *yamabushi* sect (represented by one, the *Nochi-shite*), who cause a strong wind to blow a ship that has already set sail back to the harbor and take Umewaka and the priest on board. The *Shite* appears only briefly in the second act.

Danpū is a play of a free structure, with many characters, including two *ai-kyōgen,* making their entrances and exits freely while the scenes shift one after another as swiftly as if in a movie. This is one of the characteristics of some human-interest–type miracle plays, such as *Take no Yuki,* or *Aisome-gawa.*

Tanikō (The Valley Rites): *Tanikō* is the practice among *yamabushi* priests of throwing to the bottom of a valley anybody who became ill during a pilgrimage on a mountain. In the Noh *Tanikō,* an elderly *yamabushi* priest, Sotsu no Ajari, the *Waki,* comes to see his young disciple Matsuwaka, who nurses his sick mother. When the boy learns that his teacher is going on a pilgrimage over the holy mountains, he begs him to let him accompany him, so that he may pray for his sick mother. He takes leave of his mother, the *Mae-shite,* and departs with his master and other priests. The scene in the second act is on the mountain. Matsuwaka tells his master that he has a cold. The elder priest lets him rest on his knees. The other priests find out about the boy's illness and the boy is subjected to the rites of *tanikō.* Then the elder tells his followers to execute the same rites on him, since his deep grief, he says, is the same as an illness. The other priests decide that they should pray to the mountain deity in order to restore the boy to life. So they all pray together, begging En no Gyōja (also, En no Ozuno), the immortalized founder of the *yamabushi* sect, to send his messenger Gigaku Kijin ("Music Demon"), the *Nochi-shite.* At the order of En no Gyōja, the deity comes flying, accompanied by *haya-fue* music, restores the boy to life, and brings him to En no Gyōja, who caresses the boy's hair, and praises the boy for his devotion to his mother. Then, accompanied by the music demon, Gyōja disappears into the sky. (En no Gyōja does not appear actually. His presence is described only by the chorus.) The source of this Noh is not known.

Matsuyama Kagami (The Mirror of Matsuyama): In ancient times a mirror was a rare object unknown to the common people, and there are stories about naïve people being mystified by the images reflected in a mirror. *Matsuyama Kagami* must be based on such a story. A man, the *Waki,* goes to the altar room to pray for his recently deceased wife, and finds there his daughter, the *Kokata,* who hides something at her father's approach. The father, who has heard a rumor that his daughter prays to gods for the death of her stepmother, suspects that she has hidden an effigy representing the stepmother, to which she was trying to draw the gods' curse by prayer. Scolded by her father, the girl tells him that what she has hidden is a mirror her mother had left her, telling her that, when she should miss her mother, she could see her image in the mirror. The father recalls that the mirror was his gift to his late wife, who, having lived where a mirror was unknown, was very pleased with the gift. He explains to his daughter how a mirror reflects images of things, and the girl gazes dearly at her own image, which looks so much like her mother. The ghost of the girl's mother, the *Tsure,* enters, and sings songs about mirrors. Accompanied by *haya-fue* music, Gushō-shin, a demon from hell, the *Shite,* enters, to drive the woman back to hell. In the mirror, which has now become the mirror in Hell that reflects the good and bad deeds of men, the demon sees the image of the woman transformed into a bodhisattva, whereupon the demon breaks the earth open by stamping his feet and sinks into Hell. Uniquely, this Noh is in one act, and the *Shite* appears only at the end. Another unique feature is that it is not a *deus ex machina,* but an invisible power which, moved by the girl's devotion to her mother, rescues the mother from Hell, transforming her into a divine being.

Aisome-gawa (Aisome River): Aisome-gawa is the name of the river that flows by the Tenman-gū, a shrine in Dazaifu, in the northern part of Kyūshū. The shrine celebrates Sugawara no Michizane (845–903), the Grand Minister of the Right, who was exiled and died there. (He is the *Shite* of *Raiden–A* and *–B.*) *Ai-some* means: 1) to dye blue, and 2) to meet for the first time, alluding to the beginning of a romance. In the Noh, a woman, the *Mae-shite,* and her son, Umechiyo, travel from Kyoto to Dazaifu, to see the woman's lover and the boy's father, who is the head priest of the Tenman Shrine. They take lodging at an inn. The landlord, the *Waki-tsure,* who is the head priest's retainer, takes the woman's letter to the head priest's house. The priest is absent and his wife, the *Ai-kyōgen,* reads the letter and writes a cruel answer in her husband's name. She also tells the landlord not to let the woman and her son stay at his place. The woman reads the letter and in despair throws herself into the Aisome River and dies. In the second act, a folded robe is placed in downstage center (as in *Aoi no Ue*), to represent the woman's body. Umechiyo is told about his mother's death by the landlord and is about to throw himself into the river, but is stopped by the landlord, who gives the boy a letter the mother has left him. The head priest comes back and sees a crowd gathered by the river. The landlord brings Umechiyo and his mother's letter to his lord. Thus, the father and son meet for the first time. The priest goes to where the woman's body lies and is stricken with grief. (The robe is removed, and a stage prop representing a shrine is placed center stage.) The priest prays ardently to the deities, to let the woman come to life again. The *Nochi-shite* Tenman Tenjin, the deified spirit of Sugawara no Michizane, appears from the shrine, says that the woman shall be resurrected, and returns to heaven. The source of this Noh is unknown.

Take no Yuki (The Snow-laden Bamboo): The scene in *Take no Yuki* is the snowy northern province of Echigo, the present Niigata Prefecture. A man, the *Waki,* who has divorced his wife, leaves his home for a while, telling his new wife, the *Ai-kyōgen,* to take good care of her stepson, Tsukiwaka, during his absence. He also tells her to have a servant brush off the snow that has fallen on the bamboo bushes. The new wife calls the boy and scolds him, saying that he must have told his father false stories about her. The boy makes up his mind to leave home, and goes where his mother, the *Shite,* and his sister, the *Tsure,* live, to take leave of them. Together mother and son lament their sad fate. The stepmother, finding that the boy is not at home, sends a servant, an *Ai-kyōgen,* to bring the boy back. The woman scolds the boy for going to his mother's in his father's absence, and tells him that his father wants him to brush the snow off of the bamboo bushes. She takes off the boy's robe and makes an exit. The boy, too cold to work, in vain knocks on the door, begging her to let him in, till he freezes to death. In the second act, informed by the servant, the boy's mother and sister come, and while songs of lament are sung, they rake the snow until they find his body. At this moment the father comes home, and as the three of them are sunk in grief, they hear a voice in the sky, telling them that the Seven Sages of the Bamboo Grove[8] take pity of them and will restore the dead boy back to life. Thus, Tsukiwaka is resurrected and they live happy together ever after. Unlike the rest of plays in this group, the *Shite* in the first and second acts of this play is the same living person, the boy's mother, and there is no appearance of the *Nochi-shite* as the *deus ex machina.* The source and authorship of the Noh are unknown.

In the above outlines of thirteen miracle plays we find certain differences between the two subgroups. While most plays in the first group involve historically well-known people of higher social status, such as an emperor, nobleman, general, or high priest, and their dramatic conflict concerns something other than human relationships, the characters in the second group are in most cases common people, and their dramatic sources are

[8] The Seven Sages of the Bamboo Grove are seven legendary Chinese immortals who had once been sages living in about the third century, who lived away from the worldly life, hidden in bamboo groves, enjoying music, saké, and "metaphysical talks."

often obscure. Further, their dramatic conflicts are based on family relationships, particularly the relationship between child and parent, often man and wife and their child.

The *waki*-Noh–type plays with their noble characters are more formal and dignified in their dramatic structure than those in the second subgroup. One indication of this is the presence or absence of the *kuse,* the thematic song. While four out of seven *waki*-Noh–type plays have a *kuse,* two of them complete with *kuri* and *sashi,* only two out of six human-interest–type plays have a *kuse,* and none of them in the complete form. The dignified characters of the first subgroup make their entrance accompanied by music appropriate to their status, such as *shin no raijo,* performed at the entrance of an emperor, or *ō-beshi.* This is not so with the second-group plays. Moreover, in the *waki*-Noh–type plays, true to the standard form, the *mae-shite* and *nochi-shite* are the same character, a supernatural being, who appears in the form of an ordinary person in the first act. Even when they are different beings, they are both supernatural, with some relationship between them. Because of this, the audience feels a mysterious mood pervading the whole play. They are more fantastic and spectacular than human-interest–type plays, with different types of dance actions performed. A *mai-bataraki* is performed in five plays. Often more than one deity appears in the second act as the *nochi-shite* and the *nochi-tsure,* and they perform an *uchiai-bataraki,* or a *tsure* goddess performs a *mai.* In contrast, the *mai-bataraki* in *Matsuyama Kagami* is the only example of a dance action that occurs in the Noh in the second subgroup. The plays in the first subgroup, whose *Shite* are deities and immortals, have some similarity with *waki*-Noh, and all of them can be performed in place of such in a formal program; but, according to Haruo Nishino, among the Noh in the second subgroup, only one play, *Aisome-gawa,* can take the place of a *waki*-Noh, although the late Gakudō Yamazaki (1885–1944), an authority on Noh, did not include this play among those that can be performed in place of a god-Noh.

In contrast with the Noh in the first subgroup, in which the *Shite* is the same supernatural being both in the first and second acts, the Noh in the other group feature a *mae-shite* who is an ordinary human, and the drama develops realistically until the climax in the second act, where the *nochi-shite* appears as a *deus ex machina.* In *Take no Yuki,* the immortals who work a miracle do not even appear in person, but are only sung about by the chorus.

In the Noh of the second subgroup, whose dramatic conflict involves parent–child relationships, a *kokata* is essential; whereas among the Noh in the first subgroup, *kokata* appear only in two plays, *Kuzu* and *Kōtei,* in which they play adult roles. Two human-interest–type plays, *Danpū* and *Chōbuku Soga,* are about a boy whose father was killed by an enemy. In one, the boy wants to kill the enemy; in the other, the boy actually kills him. In *Tanikō* a boy joins a party of *yamabushi* and climbs a steep mountain in order to pray for his sick mother. *Matsuyama Kagami, Aisome-gawa,* and *Take no Yuki* present the dramatic conflicts involving the parents, child, and the father's new wife. In two plays, *Aisome-gawa* and *Take no Yuki,* the *ai-kyōgen* play active parts as the father's new wife, adding to the plays, even if superficially, the realistic touches of a human-interest drama.

國栖

KUZU

あの祖父が、伏せ屋の上に。紫雲の靉いたるを、拝まい給うたか。

Above this old man's humble cottage there,
Lies a stretch of purple cloud. Do you not see it?

Introduction

Kuzu is based on an episode related to the Jinshin no Ran (Jinshin Civil War [672]). Prince Ōama, the Crown Prince of his elder brother, Emperor Tenchi (626–71; r. 662–71), renounced life and left the Capital in 671, when Tenchi's son, Prince Ōtomo, was made Prime Minister and then Crown Prince, replacing Ōama. After the death of Emperor Tenchi in the same year, Ōtomo succeeded his father. The next year, Prince Ōama raised an army at Yoshino, a mountainous district in the present Nara Prefecture, and attacked his nephew, who, defeated, hanged himself. Prince Ōama then became the Emperor now known as Emperor Tenmu (631–86; r. 673–86). (The Imperial reign of Prince Ōtomo was recognized for the first time during the seventeenth century, when the *Dainihon-shi* [Great History of Japan, in 397 scrolls], edited by Tokugawa Mitsukuni [popularized in the TV program about him, known as *Mito Kōmon*], included him in the Imperial lineage. In 1870, he was officially made the thirty-ninth Emperor and was posthumously named Kōbun [648–72; r. 671–72].)

While the exact circumstances of the incident are not known, in literature, Prince Ōama is often presented as the one who was attacked first. Legendary tales are told of how he wandered about the Yoshino mountains[1] as a refugee, being helped by humble people who hid him from the enemy and of-

[1] Yoshino is a mountainous district in the southern half of the Yamato area (present-day Nara prefecture). The scenery around the area has been immortalized in countless poems, and the five principal peaks of what is known collectively as Mt. Yoshino are Misen, Sakagatake, Ōmine, Inamura, and Shichimen (*see also* Note 21 to the play). The area sheltered numerous refugees, such as Prince Ōama (Emperor Tenmu, preparing to attack Prince Ōtomo, in 672), Minamoto no Yoshitsune (fleeing from his brother Yoritomo, in 1185), and Prince Morinaga (fleeing from the Hōjō, in 1333). Also, Emperor Go-Daigo (r. 1319–38), expelled from Kyoto, fled to Yoshino, where he established the Southern Court. His son, Emperor Go-Murakami (r. 1339–68), driven out in 1348 by Kō no Moronao, fled to Kawachi, and the Yoshino Palace used by the Southern Court was burned to the ground.

fered him food and shelter. This constitutes the theme of the Noh *Kuzu,* its direct source being the *Genpei Jōsuiki,* one of many different versions of the *Heike Monogatari.* The following is a rough translation of the passage concerned in Volume 14: "The Emperor Tenchi made his brother Prince Ōama his successor to the throne. After the Emperor Tenchi's death, his son, Prince Ōtomo, raised an army and attacked the new Emperor, who fled and hid himself on Mt. Yoshino. A heavenly deity took pity on him and sent heavenly maidens, who performed dances to comfort and encourage him. As he wandered on, he was helped by an aged couple who sheltered him."

Kuzu is the name of a river in the Yoshino mountains that is famous for its sweetfish, also named *kuzu* (but more popularly known now as *ayu*). In the Noh, Emperor Tenmu, played by a *kokata,* and his followers come to Mt. Yoshino as refugees of war and rest at the cottage of an old mountaineer and his wife, the *Shite* and *Tsure,* who serve the sweetfish to the Emperor. When the old man throws the remains of the fish into the river, it comes to life and swims away. The old man, hearing the enemies approaching, hides the emperor beneath his overturned boat. (The approach of the enemy is preceded by *haya-tsuzumi,* which continues, accompanying their entrance.)

There follows an exchange between the enemies, played by two *ai-kyōgen,* and the old man, who gets rid of the enemies with his witty speech. As it grows dark, the sound of music is heard in the air. While *gaku* dance music is performed, the elderly couple makes the interim exit and a heavenly maiden, the *Nochi-tsure,* enters and performs a *gaku* dance. The maiden then greets the mountain deity, the *Nochi-shite,* who appears and dances, giving blessings to the Imperial rule.

The section in which the *Mae-shite* dances, describing the remains of the fish coming to life and swimming away, is a highlight, and is named *Ayu no dan* (Sweetfish Section). It is not clear whether the old man in the first act is actually the mountain god of the second act, or just an ordinary mountaineer. There is a close association in the legend and folklore between Emperor Tenmu and the villagers of the Kuzu district, which may have lent a supernatural power to the old man.

The following is an outline of the Noh:

Act 1

1) Accompanied by *issei* music, the Emperor Tenmu, played by a *kokata,* enters with two palanquin bearers, the *Waki-tsure,* and a courtier, the *Waki.* In a *sashi* and *sage-uta,* the *Waki* and *Waki-tsure* tell that their lord was attacked by his enemy and is now wandering about as a refugee.

2) A stage prop representing a boat is placed on the *hashi-gakari.* Accompanied by *ashirai* music, an aged couple, the *Shite* and *Tsure,* enter and get into the boat. One carries a fishing rod; the other, an oar. They see purple

clouds above their cottage and wonder if that is an omen telling the presence of a noble person there. On arriving home they are stricken with awe to discover that what they thought to be the case had actually proven to be true.

3) The *Waki* tells the couple that his lord has not eaten anything for two or three days. Whereupon the old woman offers him some parsley root and the old man roasts a sweetfish for him. The old man, saying how the Empress Jingū (regent, 201–69) divined the future by fishing for sweetfish, throws the remains of the roasted fish into the Yoshino River. The fish swims as if it were alive again, a happy omen.[2]

4) *Haya-tsuzumi* music announces the approach of enemy pursuers. The couple hide the Emperor beneath the boat. Two pursuers, *Ai-kyōgen,* arrive, armed with bows and arrows, and ask the old man about the refugee. After a comic exchange, the old man threatens the pursuers, saying that he is an influential person with many strong men at his beck and call. The pursuers take fright and flee.

5) The Emperor thanks his benefactors, who are moved to tears. This is rendered in a *sashi* and then an *age-uta* by the Chorus.

6) A short half-*kuse* announces a musical entertainment by heavenly maidens[3] to comfort the Emperor. Accompanied by *sagari-ha* music, the *Shite* and *Tsure* make an interim exit. In the Ai-kyogen, two enemies have a humorous exchange with the *Shite* before they leave.

Act 2

7) The *Nochi-tsure,* a heavenly maiden, enters.

8) The heavenly maiden performs either a *sagari-ha* or *gaku* dance, and continues to dance to the Chorus, which describes lovely maidens dancing, sparkling with gems. Then the goddess greets the arrival of the mountain god, Zaō Gongen, the *Nochi-shite.*

9) The *Nochi-shite,* Zaō Gongen, appears and dances to the end, demonstrating his power, and bestowing blessings upon the Emperor and the land.

According to the above outline, based on the current Kanze text, this Noh presents Prince Ōama as an Emperor escaping from the enemy, whereas actually, it was his nephew, Prince Ōtomo, who was the reigning Emperor at the time of the civil war, and it was Ōama who had raised an army at Yoshino and who attacked Ōtomo. The Kanze text is based on the text published during the Genroku era, toward the end of the seventeenth century. However, unlike in the four other schools, the Kanze text neutralizes all names and words that would betray the identity of princes Ōama and Ōtomo,

---

[2] For more on Empress Jingū, *see* Note 22 to the play.

[3] A similar example is found in the *kuse* of *Futari Shizuka.* See the translation of this Noh in Vol. 3, *Woman Noh,* Book 3 of the *Noh* series.

a common practice of the time when improper references to royalty and the authorities were avoided. The following are a couple of examples:

Line 9.
Genroku text: This is the Emperor Kiyomibara (= Tenmu).
Kanze text: This person [is] a being of divine status.

Line 12.
Genroku text: My Lord (= Emperor) was attacked by his uncle, Prince Ōtomo.
Kanze text: The Prince was attacked by his uncle, a certain Muraji.

Muraji is one of a number of titles affixed to the family name in order to indicate the family status. Other similar deviations from the Genroku version are indicated in the notes.

In connection with the identity of characters, we have seen that the *reiken-mono* (miracle Noh) are divided into two subgroups: 1) Those in which the deity who works miracle appears as an ordinary human in the first act, revealing his true form in the miracle scene in the second act. As a rule, the characters other than the *shite* in this group of plays are people of high rank. 2) Those in which the first act develops realistically, and the dramatic conflict is dissolved by a supernatural being in the second act. In these plays, the *mae-shite* and *nochi-shite* are different charcters, the first, an ordinary person, and the second a supernatural being. (*See* the Introduction to Fifth-Group Noh.) The Noh *Kuzu* belongs to the first group. As it is, although there is no hint to indicate that the *Mae-shite* old man is an incarnation of a supernatural being, he should be considered as one, perhaps the deity Zaō Gongen in disguise.

We see in the above outline that, excluding the occurrence of the miraculous phenomenon about the sweetfish, the first part of the Noh develops naturally like a realistic play. For example, the *Shite* and *Tsure* after their first entrance, begin to talk with each other, instead of singing some preliminary song. There is a scene in which the *Shite,* who has concealed the Emperor under his boat, confronts the enemies and with his clever speech frightens them away. This exchange with the *Ai-kyōgen* in spoken lines adds to the realism of the play, which heightens the dramatic effect instead of making it prosaic. There is one thing in *Kuzu* that will strike an uninitiated audience as unrealistic: the part of the Emperor, an adult, is played by a *ko-kata,* a boy actor. This is a common practice in both realistic and visional Noh, aimed at the effect of decreasing the importance of the character, so as not to overshadow the part of the *Shite.*

The contribution of the realistic elements to the dramatic effect is achieved in combination with other elements, mainly the dramatic background, Mt. Yoshino, a place rich in historic and poetic associations. Yoshino is situated in modern-day Nara Prefecture, the site of the Imperial palaces beginning with Jinmu, the first Emperor of Japan. From ancient times Emperors had their detached palaces at Yoshino. People went on excursions there. Poems they made at Yoshino are included in anthologies and historical records. The eighth-century *Man'yō-shū,* Japan's oldest anthology, includes a few poems that Emperor Tenmu composed at Yoshino. Here is an example: *Yoki hito no / Yoshi to yoku mite / Yoshi to iishi / Yoshino yoku miyo / Yoki hito yoku mi* (A good person took / A good look and thought, "How good!" / And said, "This is good, / This Good Field [Yoshino]! " Take a good look, / You good man, take a good look.) The *Nihon Shoki* records the Emperor's excursion to Yoshino in the eighth year of his reign. The *Genpei Jōsuiki* twice mentions Emperor Tenmu in the Yoshino mountains: 1) when Emperor Tenmu made an excursion to the Yoshino River and played the koto, five heavenly maidens appeared and danced and sang the jewel song, sparkling in the jewel light. This is the beginning of the *Go-sechi* ("5 Melodies") Dance, so named because the dance is performed by five dancers, each with a different melody (vol. 1);[4] 2) the passage quoted at the beginning of this introduction, telling how the heavenly deities took pity on the Emperor wandering in the mountains and made heavenly maidens descend and perform a dance to comfort him (vol. 14). In the Noh *Kuzu,* these two episodes are combined together in lines 188 through 192, the last part of the *kuse* at the end of the first act, and the first song in the second act, telling how heavenly maidens sparkling in jewel-like light dance to comfort the Emperor, this being the beginning of the *Go-sechi* Dance.

Yoshino is the site of the Zaō-dō, a hall that is dedicated to Zaō Gongen, the mighty deity who appeared at the invocation of the founder of the *yamabushi* sect of Buddhism, En no Gyōja.[5] This deity is the *Nochi-shite* of *Kuzu,* who dances, blessing the Emperor and the land. Kuzu is the name of a place at Yoshino, as well as of the indigenous people there, who were closely related to the Imperial court. For example, on certain ceremonial occasions, the Kuzu people used to come to the Imperial Palace and perform a congratulatory dance, *Kuzu no sō* (Kuzu performance), a practice continued until the time of the Emperor Hirohito (d. 1989). Yoshino is famous for its sweetfish, which they call *kuzu-uo* (*kuzu* fish). With all of these historical and traditional features of the Yoshino mountains in the background, *Kuzu* is a play of unusual dramatic appeal.

---

[4] *Go-sechi* Dance: Dance performed at the Imperial court at the time of the *Daijō-e* (enthronement ceremony) and *Shinjō-e* (thanksgiving ceremony).

[5] En no Gyōja: Also known as En no Ozuno (b. 634), he was active at the time of Emperor Monmu (r. 697–707), Emperor Tenmu's grandson (*see* the Introduction [p. 119] and Note 42 to *Kurama Tengu; see also* the Introduction [p. 79] and Note 32 to *Kazuraki* in *Restless Spirits*).

Scene: Kuzu, in the Yoshino mountains, Yamato Province, now Nara Prefecture.

Season: March by the lunar calendar.

Characters and costumes: *

Kokata The Emperor Tenmu, a prince in the Kanze text, wearing an Emperor's costume consisting of an *ui-kamuri* crown, a red *nui-haku kitsuke,* a scarlet *ōkuchi* divided skirt, with or without a *sashi-nuki* divided skirt over it, and an unlined *kariginu* robe.

Waki A courtier, wearing an *atsuita kitsuke,* a white *ōkuchi* divided skirt, and a *happi* robe.

Waki-tsure Two palanquin bearers, wearing an *atsuita kitsuke* and white *ō-kuchi* divided skirt.

Mae-shite An old fisherman, wearing an old man mask such as an *Asakura-jō* and a plain *noshime* or plaid *atsuita kitsuke* under a *mizugoromo* robe. The *Mae-shite* should be considered a manifestation of the deity Zaō Gongen, the *Nochi-shite,* even though there is no indication to that effect in the text.

Mae-tsure An old woman, wearing an *uba* mask, a plain *noshime kitsuke,* a *karaori* in subdued colors, and an opaque *mizugoromo* robe.

Nochi-tsure A heavenly maiden, wearing a *tsure* mask, a long black wig, a heavenly maiden's crown, a *surihaku kitsuke,* a white or colored *ōkuchi* divided skirt, and a *chōken* or *maiginu* robe.

Nochi-shite The God Zaō Gongen, wearing an *ō-tobide* mask, an *aka-gashira* (a wig of long red hair hanging down along the back), a *rinkan* (small headgear in the shape of a pill box, with a short horizontal stick on the left and right), a *dan-atsuita kitsuke,* a *hangire* divided skirt, and a lined *kariginu.*

Ai-kyōgen Two enemy pursuers.

Mai: *Sagari-ha* or *gaku* by the *Nochi-tsure,* the Heavenly Maiden.

Author: Unknown.

Kogaki:

Shiro-gashira (White Wig) in the Kanze, Hōshō, Konparu, and Kongō schools. The *Nochi-shite* deity wears a white-haired wig instead of a red-haired one, and wears a *Fudō* or *Zaō* mask instead of the usual *ō-tobide.* He begins to sing before the curtain is raised. The performance becomes more deliberate, and there are some changes in the action patterns. There are other variations similar to the *Shiro-gashira* version.

Tenchi no Koe (The Voice of Heaven and Earth) in the Kanze (Umewaka) school. The *Shite* begins to sing before the curtain is raised, and enters running.[6]

* *For technical Japanese terms concerning costumes, see the Glossary.*

---

[6] Some have noted that the name of this variant performance reflects that of the former Emperor, Tenchi, Ōama's brother and Ōtomo's father. Could it be possible that this name gives some indication of the identity of the old man—the spirit of Emperor Tenchi?

Kuzu

—ACT 1—

ISSEI *The* Kokata, *Emperor Tenmu, enters, walking between the* Waki-tsure, *two palanquin bearers, who hold over the* Kokata's *head a roof-like* tsukurimono *representing a palanquin. They are followed by the* Waki, *a courtier. The* Kokata *and* Waki-tsure *stand at center stage, the* Waki *to their right, facing front.*

Issei, *awazu*

WAKI & WAKI-TSURE

Who ever dreamed this?
Leaving behind the abode of cloud this spring night,[1]
The moonlit Capital
We are loath to part.

WAKI

If the Way runs straight and true, then to Throne Mountain[2]

WAKI & WAKI-TSURE

It will lead without fail. Placing our trust in God, we pray.

Sashi, *awazu*

WAKI

From the divine-wind–blown Isuzu River in ancient times[3] having sprung,
The Mimosuso River as his source descends[4]
This person, a being of divine status,

WAKI & WAKI-TSURE

As the heir to the throne, this Prince
Should have succeeded the late Emperor. However,
The Prince was attacked by his uncle, a certain Muraji,[5]
And away from the Capital, in the remote country,

---

[1] Abode of cloud (*kumoi,* "cloud[-bound] abode"): Means "heaven" and "Imperial palace." "Leaving behind" is related both to the moon, which is emerging from the clouds, and "we," who are leaving the Capital. *Tsuki no Miyako* ("moonlit Capital") is a set phrase.

[2] Kurai-yama ("Rank Mountain," with "rank" meaning the rank of the emperor) is in the present Gifu Prefecture. *Kurai* also means "dark," which offers a nice contrast.

[3] Lines 7–9: *Kami-kaze* ("divine wind"): pillow word for Ise, the site of the Great Shrine of Ise, dedicated to the Sun Goddess, Amaterasu Ōmikami. Here, it is a pillow-word for Mimosuso River (= the Isuzu River), which flows by the shrine. "To have the Mimosuso River for a source" means that one is a "descendant of Amaterasu." The man described as *yagotonaki on-*

Omowazu mo.
Kumoi o izuru haru no yo no.[1]
Tsuki no miyako no
Nagori kana.

Michi-michi tachiba Kurai-yama.[2]

Noborazarame ya. Tada tanome.

Kami-kaze ya Isuzu no furuki sue o ukuru.[3]

Mimosuso-gawa no on-nagare.[4]
Yagotonaki on-kata ni te owashimasu.

Kono kimi to mōsu ni on-(n)yuzuri toshite.
Amatsu hi tsuki o ukubeki tokoro ni.
Hakubu nanigashi no Muraji ni osoware tamai.[5]

Miyako no sakai mo tō-inaka no.

---

kata (one of divine status) is "The Emperor Kiyomibara (= Ōama)" in the Genroku version, published in the Genroku 8 (1695.)

[4] The double meaning hidden in these lines is: "The Mimosuso River . . . descends" and "From . . . the Mimosuso River [= Amaterasu] descends this person."

[5] Muraji is one of a number of status titles given by the emperor to his subjects, to be used affixed to the family name. In the schools other than the Kanze, the real name of the enemy, Ōama's nephew Prince Ōtomo, is used. In actual fact, it was Ōama who attacked his nephew. See the introduction.

Crossing unknown mountains and fields, through trees and grasses dripping dew,
We make our way endless long, and yet
Hopeful in the thought that this is a royal outing.[6]

Sage-uta, *au*

The weary Autumn Mountain, and alike, this life,[7]
Sadly named Uda's hunting field we go passing by,

Age-uta, *au*

On the hart-haunted mountain, Kasuga-yama,
On the hart-haunted mountain, Kasuga-yama,
The water having risen high in the spring rains,
The sound comes, but where is Yoshino River?[8]
Even if but for a little while
The flower may be veiled in mist on this spring night,
The moon will return home to its cloud-bound abode.[9]
Trust in God and let the royal carriage go quickly,
Trust in God and let the royal carriage go quickly.

Tsuki-zerifu, *spoken*
The Waki *faces front.*

WAKI

You have traveled in haste
And now have arrived here on an unknown mountain.
Please be seated here for a while.

The Kokata *sits on a stool at the* Waki-za; *the* Waki, *to his right. The* Waki-tsure *exit.*

A tsukurimono *representing a boat is placed near the first pine (or on the stage, between the* metsuke-bashira *and the* jō-za*).*

ASHIRAI *The* Tsure, *an old woman, and after the* Tsure, *the* Shite, *an old man, enter. The* Tsure *carries a fishing rod. They get into the boat. A Stage Assistant hands a rowing pole to the* Shite.

Spoken

SHITE

I say, Old Woman, look at that.

TSURE

What is it?

SHITE

Above this old man's humble cottage there,[10]

---

[6] A royal visit was considered a blessing to the subjects. The Chinese character *yuki* in *mi-yuki,* the Japanese word for "royal visit or outing," means "bliss."

[7] Lines 17–21: *Mi o* ***aki*** (Of one's being to be **weary, to get tired of** oneself) → **Aki-**yama in the present Kyoto. *Yo no naka no* ***u*** (this life's sadness) → ***U****da no mi-kariba* (Uda Hunting Field). "Hunting Field" leads to "hart" in the next line, which in turn leads to Kasuga-yama,

Narenu san(n)ya no kusaki no tsuyu.

Wake-yuku michi no hate made mo.
Mi-yuki to omoeba tanomoshi ya.[6]
Mi o Aki-yama ya yo no naka no[7]
Uda no mi-kariba yoso ni mite.
Ojika fusu naru Kasuga-yama,
Ojika fusu naru Kasuga-yama.
Mikasa zo masaru harusame no.
Oto wa izuku zo Yoshino-gawa.[8]
Yoshi ya shibashi koso.
Hana-gumori nare haru no yo no
Tsuki wa kumoi ni kaeru beshi[9]

Tanomi o kake yo tama no koshi,
Tanomi o kake yo tama no koshi.

On-isogi sōrō hodo ni.
Izuku tomo shiranu sanchiu ni on-tsuki nite sōrō.
Mazu kono tokoro ni goza wo, nasaryōzuru nite sōrō.

Nba ya, mi-tamae.

Nani-goto nite sōrō zo.

Ano ōji ga fuseya no ue ni[10]

---

where they make their home, their "haunt," which itself leads to *mikasa* which means: 1) water level; 2) Mt. Mikasa, another name for Kasuga-yama.

[8] **Yoshi**no-gawa (**Yoshi**no River) → **Yoshi**ya (**even if**).

[9] *See* Note 1 to line 2.

[10] Note that the *Shite* often refers to himself in the third person.

Lies a stretch of purple cloud. Don't you see it?

TSURE

Indeed, I see purple clouds lying in a long stretch,[11]
And there is an extraordinary sign in the sky .

SHITE

Yes, indeed, there is something quite extraordinary.

Kakaru

Since long ago it is said that, where the Emperor is present,
One sees purple cloud rising up above.

Spoken

Could it be that by some strange chance, at this old man's hut,

Kakaru

TSURE

We might find such a noble person?

The Shite *makes a* kata *of rowing.*

SHITE

Rowing the boat we come home and see.

TSURE

Spoken

Oh, how strange! Just as we have thought.

SHITE

Here is one in a bejeweled crown, in a long sleeved robe,

TSURE

Though wet with dew and frost,

Kakaru

SHITE

There is no mistaking the noble attire.

Age-uta, *au*

CHORUS

This must be a person of supreme majesty[12]
Without doubt, 't is as clear as the white thread

The Shite *and* Tsure *get out of the boat, enter the stage, and sit, the* Shite *at center, the* Tsure *to his right.*

Of their fishing rods, which they lay aside.[13]
But this is all most strange, indeed! What does this mean?
A humble place as this within a brushwood door,[14]
Though for a brief while into a royal seat
Is transformed. . . . We are at a loss what to do,
Our hearts filled with awe at the honor accorded us,
Our hearts filled with awe at the honor accorded us.

---

[11] Purple clouds were considered an omen of some miraculous phenomenon. This is due to the belief that Amida (Amitābha) Buddha would come upon a purple cloud (*shiun*) to take believers to the Western Pure Land at the time of death.

[12] Lines 47–49: *Samo yagotonaki on-kata to wa* = This must be a [lofty] person of supreme majesty. This line appears as "This must be the Emperor Kiyomibara" in the Genroku version.

Shiun no tanabiitaru o ogamai tamōta ka

Geni geni atari ni shiun tanabiki.[11]

Tada naranu sora no keshiki ya na.

Ou tada naranu keshiki zōrō yo.
Mukashi yori tenshi no goza-dokoro ni koso

Shiun na (= wa) tatsu to mōse.
Moshi mo fushigi ni jō ga sumika ni

Sayō no kinin (n)ya owasuran to

Fune sashi-yosete waga ya ni kaeri

Mireba fushigi ya sareba koso

Tama no kōmuri (= kanmuri), nōshi no sode

Tsuyu shimo ni shiore tamaedomo

Sasuga magirenu on-(n)yosōi

Samo yagotonaki on-kata to wa[12]
Utagai mo naku shira-ito no
Tsurizao o sashi-okite[13]
Somo ya ikanaru on-koto zo.

Kahodo iyashiki shiba no to no[14]
Shibashi ga hodo no o-mashi ni mo
Narikeru koto yo ika ni sen
Ara, katajikena no on-koto ya,
Ara, katajikena no on-koto ya.

Utagai mo naku ***shira*** (doubtlessly **known**) → ***shira****ito* (*white* thread) → *tsurizao* (fishing rod) in the next line.

[13] In *tsurizao o sashi-oki* (the fishing rods they lay aside), the verb *sashi-oki* (to put aside, forget) is used in two ways, such that the phrase means, "**forgetting about** their fishing rods, which they **lay aside**."

[14] ***shiba*** *no to* (**brushwood** door) → ***shiba****shi ga hodo* (**brief** while).

Spoken

SHITE

Pray, tell me what all this means.

WAKI

You are in the presence of a person of high status.[15]
Attacked by his kinsman
He has secretly made his escape as far as this place.
He is relying on whatever assistance you, old man, can offer.

SHITE

So this is a person of high status.
This place happens to be the cottage of this old man,
So I beg you to rest here at your ease.

WAKI

Old Man,
I hesitate to tell you that
For the last two or three days, my lord has had no access to the table.
Serve him whatever you can.

SHITE

I will talk with my old woman.

The Shite *turns to the* Tsure.

Old Woman, have you heard?
I am told that for the last two or three days, His Lordship has had no access to the table.
Serve him whatever you can.

TSURE

It happens that there are some parsley roots I have gathered.

SHITE

That is the best thing under the sun.
And I have some *kuzu* fish here.[16]
Let us serve these on the table.

Kakaru

TSURE

The old woman, who is deeply moved,
With her heart beating fast, what she has gathered,
Parsley roots, she washes; in her aged body,

[15] *Kore wa yoshiaru on-kata nite gozasōrō ga / Majikaki hito ni osoware-tamai* (You are in the presence of a person of high status. Attacked by his kinsman, . . .) In the Genroku version, these lines are given as: "You are in the presence of the Emperor Kiyomibara [Tenmu]. Attacked by Prince Ōtomo, . . ."

Kore wa somo nani to mōshitaru on-koto nite sōrō zo.

Kore wa yoshi aru on-kata nite goza sōrō ga[15]
Majikaki hito ni osoware tamai.
Kore made on-shinobi nite sōrō.
Nanigoto mo jō o tanomi oboshimesaruru to no on-koto nite sōrō.

Sate wa yoshi aru on-kata nite goza sōrō ga
Saiwai kore wa kono jō ga io nite sōrō hodo ni
On-kokoro yasuku on-(n)yasumi arōzuru nite sōrō.

Ika ni jō.
Menboku mo naki mōshi-goto nite sōraedomo
Kono Kimi ni-san nichi ga hodo gugo o chikazuke tamawazu sōrō.

Nani nite mo gugo ni sonae sōrae.

Sono yoshi nba ni mōsōzuru nite sōrō.
Ika ni nba, kiite aru ka.
Kono ni-san nichi ga hodo gugo o chikazuke tamawazu sōrō to no on-koto nari.
Nani nite mo gugo ni tatematsuri tamae.

Orifushi kore ni tsumitaru nezeri no sōrō.

Sore koso Nippon-ichi no koto.
Ware-ra mo kore ni kuzu-uo no sōrō.[16]
Kore o gugo ni sonae mōsōzuru nite sōrō

Nba wa amari no katajikenasa ni
Mune uchi-sawagi tsumi-okeru
Nezeri araite oi ga mi mo

---

[16] *kuzu* fish = a type of sweetfish (also called *ayu*), so called after the name of the place that is most famous for this type of fish.

Feeling her heart grow young, the green herbs she cooks[17]

The Tsure *turns to the* Waki.

And offers them to the royal table.
This is the origin how Mi-Yoshino's
River came to be called "Herb-Gathering Stream."[18]

Spoken

SHITE

The old man, too, in the wood burning maple branches in deep autumn colors,[19]
Roasts the sweetfish caught in the Kuzu River

Kakaru

And also serves the fish to the royal table.

During the above, the Shite *opens his fan, and, holding it like a dish, goes before the* Waki, *makes a gesture of giving him the dish, and then resumes his seat. The* Waki *mimes serving the dish to the* Kokata.

Age-uta *au*

CHORUS

The tradition named the *kuzu* of Yoshino[20]
Has its origin in this incident, 't is said.
Even soup with water shield inside, or a dish of perch,[21]
Could never be better than what they have offered.

The Waki *calls the* Shite.

I say, come nearer here, you venerable man,
I say, come nearer here, you venerable man.

Mondō *spoken*

WAKI

I say, old man,
My lord wills that you shall have the remains of the royal table.

SHITE

The Shite *makes a* kata *of receiving the dish in front of the* Waki.

Oh, blessed be his gracious heart!
Then let me receive them, turning them over.

WAKI

You said that you would receive the remains, turning them over.
What do you mean?

---

[17] *kokoro* ***waka*** (heart **young**) → ***waka****na* (**young** herbs).

[18] Mi-Yoshino is an elegant variation of the place name, and is found especially in classical poetry. Written numerous ways (here, as "Triple Yoshino," "August Yoshino," "Beautiful Yoshino," etc.), many have conjectured that it means simply "Beautiful Yoshino" (where *mi* = *utsukushii*), but we have rendered it as Mi-Yoshino here. In the name of the Natsumi River, *na* means "herbs" and *tsumi* means "to gather." The statement is an invention of the author.

[19] From the following poem by Po Chü-i (772–846) in the *Wakan Rōei-shū* (221): ***Lin-chien*** *nuan chiao* ***shao heng ye*** / *Shih-shang ti shih fu lu-t'ai* [***Rinkan ni*** *sake o atatamuru,* ***kōyō o taki*** / *Sekijō ni shi o teisuru, ryokutai o harau*] (I warm saké **in the woods, burning red leaves**;

Kokoro wakana o soroe-tsutsu[17]

Gugo ni sonae tatematsuru.
Sore yori shite zo Mi-Yoshino no
Natsumi no kawa to mōsu nari.[18]

Ôji mo iro koki momiji o rinkan ni taki

Kuzu-gawa nite tsuritaru ayu o yaki
Onajiku gugo ni sonaekeri.

Yoshino no Kuzu to iu koto mo[20]
Kono toki yori no koto to ka ya.
Junsai no atsumono rogyo totemo.[21]

Kore ni wa ikade masaru beki
Majikaku maire oibito yo,
Majikaku maire oibito.

Ika ni jō.
Gugo no on-nokori o jō ni tamaware to no on-koto nite sōrō.

Ara, arigataya-zōrō.
Saraba uchi-kaeshite tamawarōzuru nite sōrō.

Somo uchi-kaeshite tamawarōzuru to wa

Nani to mōshitaru koto nite aru zo.

I write a poem on a stone, brushing away green moss). In the Noh text, *kōyō* is pronounced *momiji*.

[20] The *kuzu* of Yoshino: *See* the introduction. Yoshino is also famous for its arrowroot (*kuzu*).

[21] Soup of water shield and a dish of perch have become symbols of delicacies from an episode about Chang Han of Chin, a government official, who, when he remembered the taste of the water shield and perch in his hometown, wanted so much to taste them that he resigned from his office and went home. The story is told in the *Chin-shu*, the orthodox history of Eastern Chin dynasty of China (317–419).

SHITE
I said I would receive the remains, turning them over.
We can say thus only for the *kuzu* fish.
I say, my old woman,
His lordship wills that this old man should have
the remains of the royal table. However,
This fish looks so fresh, as if it is alive.

TSURE
Yes, indeed, it still looks fresh as if it is alive.

SHITE
Let me release it in the Yoshino River here.

TSURE
Don't speak senselessly like that.
Even if you release it,
How will it come to life again?

SHITE
But we have such an example in the past.
When the Empress Jingū fought and defeated
Silla,[22] she divined the outcome of the war
By catching *kuzu* fish in the Tamashima River.

Ayu no dan (111–20)
The Shite *dances.*
Kakaru
Age-uta, *au*

In the same way, this lord, too,
If he were to return to the Capital again,
Then this fish, why wouldn't it live again—saying thus,

CHORUS
Into the rushing water he puts the fish,
Into the rushing water he puts the fish
Where the river is flowing in quick cataracts.
But, oh, look, at Mi-Yoshino a miracle[23]
Is revealed to us by the fish, which by itself
Comes to life again. Your fortune is told thus.
Trust the omen, and rest assured of your luck.

The Shite *sits at center.*
Haya-tsuzumi
Spoken

WAKI
I say, old man,
The enemy warriors are coming in pursuit.

---

[22] Empress Jingū (170–269): Emperor Chūai's Empress, she was the regent for her son, Emperor Ōjin (201–310) for about 70 years after the Chūai's death in 200. The *Kojiki* and the *Nihon Shoki* record that, when the Empress was sailing to attack Korea, she tried to divine the

Uchi-kaeshite tamawarōzuru to wa, mōsu koso
Kuzu-uo no shirushi nite sōrae.
Ika ni nba.
Gugo no nokori o jō ni tamaware to no on-koto nite sōrō ga

Kono uo wa imada iki-iki to miete sōrō.

Geni kono uo wa imada iki-iki to miete sōrō.

Iza kono Yoshino-gawa ni hanaite myō

Suji naki koto na, notamaiso.
Hanaitareba tote
Iki-kaeru beki ka wa

Iya, iya mukashi mo saru tameshi ari.
Jingū Kōgō Shinra o shitagae tamaishi ura-kata ni[22]

Tamashima-gawa no ayu o tsurase tamō

Sono gotoku kono Kimi mo
Futatabi miyako ni kankō naraba
Kono uo mo nado ka ikizaran to

Iwa kiru mizu ni hanaseba
Iwa kiru mizu ni hanaseba
Sashimo hayase no takigawa ni
Are Mi-Yoshino ya kichizui o[23]
Arawasu uo no onozukara
Iki-kaeru. Kono uta-kata
Tanomoshiku oboshimesare yo

Ika ni jō.
Oi-te ga kakarite sōrō.

---

future by fishing at Tamashima in Kyushu and inspecting the sweetfish that she caught. Silla (J. Shinra) was an ancient kingdom on the southeastern portion of the Korean peninsula.

[23] *Are* ***miyo*** (Oh, look!) → **Mi-Y**oshino.

SHITE
Leave it to me.
I say, my old woman,
Let us bring the boat here.
TSURE
With all my heart.

The Shite *and* Tsure *bring the boat to the* waki-za, *place it there upside down, and hide the* Kokata *under it. The* Shite *sits by the boat, and the* Tsure *near him. The* Waki *withdraws behind the musicians.*

Accompanied by haya-tsuzumi, *which has quickened its tempo, two* ai-kyōgen, *the pursuers, enter, one with a bow and arrow, the other with a halberd, calling out, "You shall not escape!" They ask the* Shite *if he knows whereabouts of the Emperor of Kiyomibara, meaning Emperor Tenmu.*

AI 1& 2
You'll not escape, you'll not escape!
AI 1
By the Three Treasures,[24] we've lost him.
AI 2
It is as you say, indeed.
AI 1
It is due to the thick mountain forest. Now, let's go this way.
AI 2
With all my heart.
AI 1 (*Seeing the* Shite:)
He must indeed know something. Let's go question him.
AI 2
That is a fine idea.
AI 1 (*Speaking to the* Shite:)
I say, old man, I have some questions to ask you.
Do you know the whereabouts of Emperor Kiyomibara?

Spoken SHITE
What did you say?
Ablution rites? If it's ablution rites, go further
down the river.[25]

[24] Three Treasures: The Three Treasures were the three things that all Buddhists were taught to revere: the Buddha, the Law (Skt. *Dharma*), and the Priesthood (Skt. *Saðgha*). The *Ai* are using them much as we might say "By all the Saints!" or "By the Holy Trinity!" or some similar expression.

Konata e on-makase sōrae.
Ika ni nba.
Ano fune kaite kō.

Kokoroe mōshi sōrō.

(*In the interest of saving space, the original Japanese text of the* Ai-kyōgen *dialogue is omitted here.*)

[25] Emperor Tenmu is called Kiyomibara, which is the name of the place where he had his palace. The *Shite,* pretending that he is hard of hearing, answers as if the pursuer asked about *kiyomi-barae* (ablution rites), and not Kiyomibara.

Thinking that the Shite *is hard of hearing, they repeat the same question.*

AI 1

What is this? It appears that he is so aged that he is deaf.

AI 2

Since he is deaf, try speaking a bit louder.

AI 1

With all my heart. (*To the* Shite:) I say, old man,
do you know the whereabouts of Emperor
Kiyomibara.

SHITE

I see, Kiyomibara is someone's name.
That is an unfamiliar name, indeed.
Moreover, this mountain
Is compared to the inner temple of Tuÿita.[26]
Also called Mt. Wu-t'ai or Mt. Ch'ing-liang,[27]
As far as China continues this Mt. Yoshino,
With many hiding places on it.
How are you going to search such a place as this?
You had better return quickly.

The Ai *are about to leave, then see the boat, and go to search it.*

AI 1

It is just as the old man says. So, let's go back there. Come this way. (*They start to leave, but notice the boat:*) Hey! What's this? Here's an overturned boat. Let's ask the old man about it. (*To the* Shite:) I say, old man, why is that boat overturned? I have my suspicions about what it might contain. Let's go investigate it.

SHITE

What? Do you say that that boat is suspicious?
It is being dried there.

AI 1

It does not matter that it is overturned to dry out,
we must investigate it.

---

[26]Tuṣita: The sacred land on the top of Mt. Sumeru, the high mountain at the center of Universe. The inner temple there is the residence of bodhisattvas, where Śākyamuni lived before attaining Buddhahood, and where the Bodhisattva Maitreya (Jpn. Miroku) now dwells.

[27] Lines 133–34: Wu-t'ai (Jpn. Godai) and Ch'ing-liang (Jpn. Seiryō/Shōryō) are two names for the same high mountain with five peaks in China, the sites of great Buddhist temples. Be-

Sate wa Kiyomibara to wa hito no na yo na.
Ara, kiki-narezu no hito no na ya.
Sono ue kono yama wa
Toso'n no nai'in ni mo tatoe.[26]
Mada Godai-san, Shōryō-sen tote[27]
Morokoshi made mo tōku tsuzukeru Yoshino-yama
Kakushiga ōki tokoro naru o
Izuku made tazune tamō beki
Sumiyaka ni kaeri tamae.

Nani to fune ga ayashii to ya.
Kore wa hosu fune zo to yo.

---

lieved to be the sacred abode of the Bodhisattva Mañjuśrī (Jpn. Monju), Mt. Wu-t'ai is mentioned in the Noh *Shirahige, Kanehira* (in *Warrior Ghost Plays*), and *Kazuraki* (in *Restless Spirits*); Mt. Ch'ing-liang is the setting of *Shakkyō.* It is said that a piece broke off of Mt. Sumeru and came flying to Japan, where it became Mt. Yoshino.

SHITE

Oh, do you want to search the boat?
For a fisherman, to have his boat searched is like having his house searched.
Though I am a lowly being,

The Shite *rises.*

Around this place, this old man is a powerful man.
I have grandsons and great-grandsons.
You people of the mountains and valleys, come hither
And beat these rogues, beat these rogues.

AI 1

What a ruffian!

AI 2

How strong he is!

AI 1

Even if we had a whole gang to help us, we would not be able to beat him. Let's just get out of here while there is still breath enough in our bodies to do so.

AI 2

That is a fine idea.

The Ai *in a fright take to their heels.*

AI 1

Come with me, oh, come with me.

AI 2

With all my heart, with all my heart.

The Tsure *rises.*

Kakaru.

TSURE

Have you heard? The enemy warriors have gone.

SHITE

We are safe now. The old man and woman

TSURE

In joy, together strain themselves,

The Shite *and* Tsure *lift the boat.*

SHITE

Heave, ho!

SHITE & TSURE

Heave, ho!

During the next song, the Kokata *and* Waki *return to their seats and sit down.*

Age-uta, *au*

CHORUS

Then they lift the boat and find the royal being,
Then they lift the boat and find the royal being

Nani to fune o sagasō to ya.
Ryōshi no mi nite wa fune o sagasaretaru mo ie o sagasaretaru mo onaji koto zo ka shi.
Mi koso iyashiku omou to mo
Kono tokoro nite wa okina mo nikkuki mono zo ka shi.
Mago mo ari, hi-mago mo ari.
Yama-yama, tani-tani no mono-domo ide-aite

Ano rōzeki-bito o uchi-tome sōrae, uchi-tome sōrae.

Nō, kikoshimese oi-te no bushi wa kaeritari

Ima wa kō yo to ōji, nba wa

Ureshi ya chikara o

Ei, ya! Ei, to!

Fune hiki-okoshi sontai no
Fune hiki-okoshi sontai no

Without harm, hidden underneath the river boat,[28]
Which has oared the most worthy life to
Safety. Oh, how our hearts fill with joy and
gratitude!

During the kuri, *the* Shite *and* Tsure *place the boat near the* shite-*pillar. The* Tsure *sits before the* fue-za; *the* Shite, *at center. The boat is removed by the Stage Assistants.*

Kuri, *awazu* CHORUS

'T is said, "The Lord is the ship and the subjects are the
water;[29]
The water makes the ship float." This saying is
Exemplified in the loyalty of this couple.

Sashi, *awazu* WAKI

Oh, how deeply impressive! A humble mountaineer to all
appearances,

CHORUS

To be endowed with a mind superb in strategy. . . .
Indeed, it depends not on being gentle or simple.

WAKI

The reward for long-accumulated good deeds
being boundless,[30]

CHORUS

Ceaselessly flows the River Mimosuso,
In this polluted world, 't is hard to live a clean life.

KOKATA

As it is so, it is a sovereign

---

[28] Lines 153–55: *kawabune no* ***kai*** (river boat's **oar**), related to *fune* (boat) in the previous line, used solely to introduce the word ***kai****aru* (**worth**y).

[29] From the *Hsun-tzu* chapter on ruling by the Chinese philosopher Hsun-tzu (315–ca. 230 BC): *Chün che ch'uan ye, hsu jen zhe sui ye; sui tse tai ch'uan, sui ze fu ch'uan* [***Kimi wa fune*** *nari, chōnin* ***wa mizu*** *nari;* ***mizu*** *sunawachi* ***fune o*** *noseru, mizu sunawachi fune o ou*] (**The Lord is the boat, the** people **are the water; the water** thus supports **the boat,** the water also engulfs the boat). The Japanese text (lines 165–57) has: *Sore* ***Kimi wa fune,*** *shin* ***wa mizu. Mizu*** *yoku* ***fune o*** *ukamu* ('T is said, :**The Lord is the ship and the subjects are the water;** / **The water** makes **the ship** float). Note that where the original has "people" the Noh text says "subjects," using a character often reserved to mean court officials.

[30] From the *I Ching,* one of the Five Classics of ancient China: *Chi-shan chih chia pi yu yü-ch'ing, chi-pushan chia pi yu yü-yang [***Shakuzen no*** *ie, kanarazu* ***yōkei*** *ari; shakufuzen {no} ie, kanarazu yōou ari*] ("A family of long-accumulated good deeds is blessed through generations; a family of long-accumulated evil deeds suffers through generations"). The lines appear as the Wen Yen commentary for the bottom line of Hexagram 2 and are translated by John Blofeld (p.

On-tsutsuga naku kawabune no[28]
Kaiaru on-(n)inochi
Tasukari tamō zo arigataki.

Sore kimi wa fune shin wa mizu.[29]

Mizu yoku fune o ukamu to wa
Kono chūkin no tatoe nari.

Arigataya sashimo sugata wa yamagatsu no

Kokoro wa takaki hakari koto.
Geni kisen ni wa yorazarikeri.

Shakuzen no yokei kagiri naku[30]

Nagare taesenu Mimosuso-gawa
Nigoreru yo ni wa sumi-gatashi

Sareba Kimi toshite koso

---

91) as: "A household which accumulates good deeds will enjoy blessings in abundance, while one which piles up evils will inevitably face a host of sufferings." Here the line is related to the phrase, *jūzen no tenshi* (the ten-good-deeds Emperor), referring to a Buddhist belief that becoming an emperor is the result of not having committed any of the ten carnal crimes in a former life. The ten good deeds are: 1) not killing living beings; 2) not stealing; 3) not committing adultery; 4) not lying; 5) not uttering harsh words; 6) not uttering words causing enmity among others; 7) not engaging in idle chatter; 8) not being greedy; 9) not being angry; and 10) not having wrong views. The phrase *jūzen no tenshi* can also be seen in the *Taiheiki* (3, 17).

Thus, lines 162–63 mean: "Thanks to the good deeds piled up by a succession of emperors, the River Mimosuso (= the Imperial family [*see* Note 3]) flows ceaselessly." In the Genroku version, *shakuzen* (accumulated good deeds) is used instead of *jūzen,* which refers to an emperor. The same correction from *jūzen* to *shakuzen* also occurs in line 168. *Nigoreru* (polluted), an *engo* of *Mimosuso-gawa → sumi (clear, clean)→ sumi-gatashi* ("to be clean is hard"; also, "to live is hard," or "it is hard to live," with *sumi* meaning both "clean" and "to live." The world is "polluted" because of the civil disturbance over the Imperial succession.

Who has always helped his subjects in trouble. But now
They, on the contrary, have so kindly helped us.

Age-uta *au* — CHORUS

All former life's good deeds were in vain, an oarless,[31]
All former life's good deeds were in vain, an oarless,
Small leaf of a boat, with destination unknown,
Where the great dragon dwells, the cloud-
bound heaven,[32]
At last, why does it not arrive? To the Capital
When we have returned, and in this Dragonfly Land,[33]
Should his peaceful reign prosper like thick-
growing reeds,
We would pay for our life that has been thus
rescued.
The royal words penetrate deep into the hearts
The Shite *and* Tsure *weep.* — Of the venerable man and wife,
Whom his lordship's graciousness has moved to tears.

Kuse *au* — As time passes on,
It has grown late; in deep stillness awesome reigns
the night.
What can we do for him who for some time past has
So deeply troubled his soul? How can we comfort him?
But this is a place renowned for the moon and snow,[34]
The Shite *and* Tsure *rise.* — Mi-Yoshino, where flowers and birds in diverse[35]
Colors and voices sweet perform dance and music,

---

[31] For *shakuzen,* see note 30. In *mi wa shakuzen,* the word *mi* means body, and thus, by extension, this physical life, so we have translated the phrase as "life's good deeds"; but it refers to the good karma accumulated in past lives; in *kai zo naki,* the word *kai* means: 1) good result, 2) oar; *zo* is an emphatic particle; and *naki* means "without," so that the phrase means: 1) in vain, 2) without an oar.

[32] The Genroku version of line 171, *Banjō no kurai* (the rank of generalissimo = Emperor) has been changed in the Kanze version to: *Banryō no kumoi* (Where the great dragon dwells, the cloud-bound heaven = the Imperial Palace). Thus, the phrase carries a double meaning: "Why can we not return to the Capital?" as well as "Why does not our Lord attain the rank of emperor?"

[33] Lines 173–74: *Akitsu-su* (Dragonfly Isle): A poetic name for Japan, from the shape of the main island, which appeared to the ancient people like a dragonfly (*akitsu*) spreading its wings.

Tami o hagokumu narai naru ni
Kaette tasukuru kokorozashi.

Mi wa shakuzen no kai zo naki[31]
Mi wa shakuzen no kai zo naki
Ichiyō no fune no yukusue
Banryō no kumoi tsui ni nado[32]

Itarazarame ya. Miyako-ji ni
Tachi-kaeri-tsutsu Akitsu-su no[33]
Yoshi ya yo no naka osamaraba

Inochi no on (n)o hōzen to

Ringen kimo ni meiji-tsutsu
Fūfu no rōjin na (= wa)
Katajikenasa ni naki itari.

Saru hodo ni
Fuke shizumarite monosugoshi

Ika ni toshite ka kono hodo no
On-kokoro. Nagusame mōsu beki.
Shikamo tokoro wa tsuki-yuki no[34]
Mi-Yoshino nare ya hana-tori no[35]
Iro-ne ni yorite ongaku no

Akitsu-su in the sense of Japan is an introductory word (*jo-kotoba*) for *ashi* (reed), the beginning of another ancient name of Japan, **Ashi**wara no Mizuho no Kuni (Reed-Marsh-and-Fresh-Rice-Ear Land). *Ashi* (reed) is homonymous with "bad," so that people often call the plant *yoshi,* which means "good." This explains the sudden appearance of the word ***yoshi**ya* (even if) here.

[34] *Tsuki* (the moon), *yuki* (snow), and *hana* (flower) in the next line form a trio that represents natural beauty. The combination of these three expressions of natural beauty appears in numerous classical poems, and can be found in several Noh, including *Kazuraki* (in *Restless Spirits,* lines 11–14). In Mi-Yoshino in the following line, *mi* is used to mean "beautiful" as well as "triple."

[35] *Hanatori* (flowers and birds): A *jo-kotoba* for *iro-ne* (colors and sounds).

The Shite *listens to the music.*

With the sounds of *koto* music pitched high and low[36]
Mingles with pine wind from the mountain top
coming down;
Heavenly maidens wave their long-streaming sleeves,
This should be the origin of the Quintuple Dance.[37]

SAGARI-HA, NAKAIRI *Accompanied by* sagari-ha *music, the* Shite *and* Tsure *exit. Immediately, during the same music, the* Nochi-tsure, *a Heavenly Maiden, enters.*

—ACT 2—

SAGARI-HA *dance by the* Nochi-tsure, *a Heavenly Maiden. At the end of the dance, the* Nochi-tsure *continues to dance to the chanting.*

Watari-byōshi
The Nochi-tsure *dances.*

CHORUS

Heavenly maidens— Heavenly maidens[38]
In sparkling gems, by the gem-inlaid *koto's* strings
Drawn hither, perform music and dances, until
Celestial Beings make their appearance,
Katsute and other Eight Mountain Gods,
Once hidden with Komori no Gozen, Zaō now
appears[39]—

Toward the end of the above song, the Nochi-tsure *stands by the* shite-pillar, *facing the curtain, lifts an open fan held in the right hand, greeting the arrival of the god, Zaō Gongen, and then sits before the Chorus. The* Nochi-shite, *Zaō Gongen, enters and stands by the first pine. His head and the upper part of his body are covered with a dark robe.*

---

[36] Lines 186–88: From a poem by Saigū no Nyōgo (Imperial Consort and Former Head Priestess of Ise Shrine), Princess Kishi (d. 985), in the *Shūi-shū* (No. 451): *Koto no ne ni / Mine no matsukaze / Kayōrashi / Izure no o yori / Shirabe-someken* (With the *koto's* sound / The wind from the mountain ridge / Appears to mingle. / I wonder which *o* it was / That had started playing first?). The poem is prized for the pun on the word *o* in the fourth line, *izure no o* (which "o") , with *o* meaning both "mountain ridge" and "string." The poem is also quoted in the Noh *Senju* (in *Woman Noh,* Book 3: lines 219–21 and the note to those lines [pp. 96–97]) and *Kogō* (in *Troubled Souls:* see the introduction, p. 92, lines 55–56 [Note 10], 84–85 [Note 20]).

Kayoi-kuru ("repeatedly come") is related both to *matsukaze* ("pine wind") and *amatsu otome* (heavenly maidens) in the next line. *Koto* here and in line 191 alludes to the story about the heavenly maidens who came descending from heaven and danced to the *koto* music played by Emperor Tenmu (*see* the introduction). *Ryo-ritsu* ("high-low"): Two contrasting modes popular

Ryo-rit'n no shirame koto no ne ni[36]
Mine no matsukaze kayoi kuru

Amatsu otome no kaesu sode
Go-set'n no hajime kore nare ya.[37]

Otome-go ga. Otome-go ga.[38]
Sono Kara tama no koto no ito
Hikare kanazuru ongaku ni
Kami-gami mo rairin shi
Katsute hat'n-sho kono yama ni
Komori no gozen Zaō to wa[39]

---

in ancient Chinese and Japanese music. *Ryo* was lower and minor, while *ritsu* was higher and major.

[37] *Go-sechi* (Quintuple ["Five-Melodies"] Dance Ceremony): *See* the introduction.

[38] Lines 190–91: From an ancient poem quoted in the *Genpei Jōsuiki: **Otome-go ga** / Otome sabisu mo / Kara tama o / Otome sabisu mo /**Sono Kara tama o*** (**Heavenly maidens**— / How the maidens do long for / The bright sparkling gem! / How the maidens do long for / Naught but **that bright sparkling gem**!); *see also* the introduction. *Koto no ito* (*koto* strings) leads to: *Hikare* (to be drawn [an *engo* of *ito*], to be played) → *ongaku* (music).

[39] Lines 194–95: Katsute, Komori: Shrines to these deities on Mt. Yoshino. For Zaō, *see* the introduction. These deities are also mentioned in the finale (*kiri*) of the Noh *Arashiyama: Shujō o mamoru chikai o arawashi. **Komori, Katsute. Zaō Gongen** dōtai imyō no sugata o misete* (Protecting all living things, living proof of my holy vow—[As] **Komori, Katsute, Zaō Gongen**—The same form but diff'rent name, in that form I now appear).

Awazu

NOCHI-SHITE

To hide a monarch, here at Yoshino Mountain[40]

Noru. *The* Shite *drops the robe, enters the stage and dances to the song.*

CHORUS

In an instant the godly form reveals itself,
In an instant the godly form, having revealed itself,

SHITE

One of his hands points heavenward to Taizō,[41]

CHORUS

The other hand points downward

SHITE

To Kongō, on whose adamantine ground standing,

CHORUS

With one foot lifted high,[42]
Over the numberless realms in all directions universal,
The deity goes flying through the air.
In all places under heaven, in remotest lands,
Nobody should make light of the Imperial power,
Says the divine being, who, using his mighty power,
Brings in a new order and peace to the land governed by
Tenmu, the sacred Emperor of mercy most profound,
An example miraculous and divine indeed!

The Shite *stamps the* tome-byōshi.

---

[40] In Zaō, the deity's name, *za* means "to preserve" or "to hide" and *ō* means "monarch." Thus, his very name indicates that he has come in order to protect the monarch by hiding him. *Kakusu* (to hide) → *arawasu* (to reveal) in the next line.

[41] *Taizō* (line 199) and *Kongō* (line 201): In esoteric Buddhism, *Taizō-kai* (Skt. *garbha-kośa-dhātu;* the "matrix-storehouse" [or "womb"] realm) represents the womb of compassion of Dainichi Nyorai (Skt. Mahā-Vairocana, the Great Sun Buddha), likened to the mysterious power of an infant growing in its mother's womb. It is the home of the Five Wisdom Kings. *Kongō-kai* (Skt. *vajra-dhātu;* the diamond realm) represents this Buddha's Perfect Wisdom, so

Ō o kakusu ya Yoshino-yama[40]

Sunawachi sugata o arawashite
Sunawachi sugata o arawashi tamaite

Ten (n)o sasu te wa Taizō[41]

Ta o mata sasu wa

Kongō hōseki no ue ni tatte

Issoku o hissage[42]
Tōzai-nanboku jippō sekai no
Kokū ni higyō shite
Futen no shita Sot'ndo no uchi ni
Ô-i o ikade ka karonzen to
Tai seiriki no chikara o idashi
Kokudo o aratame osamuru miyo no
Tenmu no seitai kashikoki megumi
Arata narikeru tameshi kana.

---

powerful as to be able to crush even an adamantine diamond. Zaō Gongen dwells in this Diamond Realm. (*See also* the following note.)

[42] In Buddhist iconography, Zaō Gongen is always represented lifting one leg up high. The *kiri* of *Arashiyama* also contains this line: *Kon-Tai ryōbu no issoku o hissage* (The Diamond and Womb Worlds are both One, with a single step, I lead them forth). *Ryōbu no [hitotsu]* indicates that both realms (*see* Note 41) are but different manifestations of a single unity. *Issoku no hissage* could also mean "with one leg raised up high," a verbal depiction of the accepted iconography for Zaō Gongen.

松山天狗

MATSUYAMA TENGU

誠に妙なる玉體の。花の顔ばせたをやかに。
ここも雲居の都の空の。夜遊の舞楽は面白や。

Truly the Imperial form so graceful and noble,
With features exquisite as sweet-smelling flowers,
Here too, like the cloud-bound sky of the Capital City,
The moon casts her light on the sparkling dancing sleeves.

Introduction

The *Shite* of *Matsuyama Tengu* is the ghost of Retired Emperor Sutoku (1119–64), who was enthroned at the age of four. In 1141, his father, Retired Emperor Toba (1103–56), forced him to abdicate and then placed his favorite son, the three-year-old Konoe, on the throne. When Emperor Konoe (1139–55) died at the age of seventeen, Sutoku hoped that, if not himself, at least his son, Prince Shigehito, might be made Emperor. However, contrary to his expectation, Toba established Sutoku's younger brother, Go-Shirakawa (1127–92), as the new Emperor. This increased his bitter feelings toward his father.[1]

At that time, Fujiwara no Yorinaga (1120–56), the Grand Minister of the Left, was vying for power with his elder brother, the Prime Minister Tadamichi (1097–64). When Sutoku's father, the Retired Emperor Toba, died in 1156, Sutoku and Yorinaga revolted against the new Emperor (Go-

[1] It is said that in actual fact Sutoku was not Toba's real son, but the child born to Toba's consort of his grandfather, the Retired Emperor Shirakawa (1053–29). Because of this, Toba hated Sutoku, calling him "Uncle Son." It was Shirakawa who enthroned the child Sutoku. The confusing succession of emperors (with the regnal years [followed by birth and death dates]) in this era was as follows:

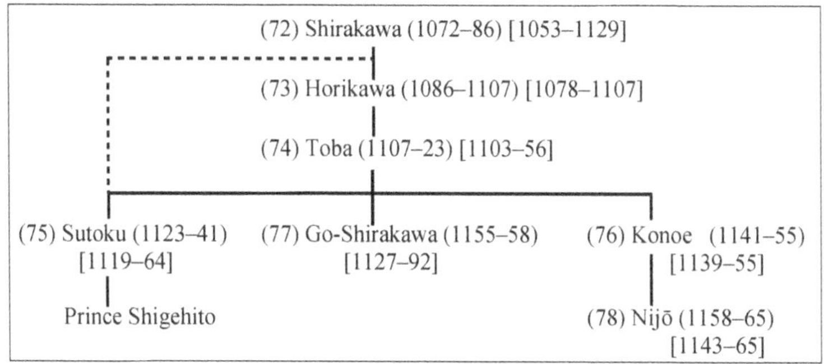

Shirakawa). They were defeated. Yorinaga was wounded and died; Sutoku was caught and exiled to Sanuki Province in Shikoku, dying there in 1164. This uprising is known as the Hōgen no Ran.[2] During his exile, Sutoku copied out five major Buddhist sutras. It was his wish to have the sutras placed at a temple in Kyoto and thus to attain salvation. He wrote a letter to his younger brother Kakushō, the Abbot of the temple Ninnaji, expressing his wish in elaborate poetic language. At the end of the letter, Sutoku wrote this poem, one of the thematic poems of this Noh: *Hama-chidori / Ato wa miyako ni / Kayoedomo / Mi wa Matsuyama ni / Ne o nomi zo naku* (Though the beach plover's / Footprints in the Capital / Leave traces behind, / I shall at Matsuyama / Remain, crying bitterly.) "Beachplover's footprints" in the poem means the letter. *Matsu* in Matsuyama means "to wait for," as well as "pine tree," so that the word conveys the feeling of anxious waiting—pining—for a favorable answer. Moved to tears, Abbot Kakushō appealed to the Imperial Court to grant Sutoku's wish, but in vain. Enraged and in despair, Sutoku was transformed into a *tengu.*[3]

When the sutras were copied out, he swore that he would turn the benign power of the sutras into an evil one, so that he might become a great evil power and overthrow the Imperial throne. Biting off the tip of his tongue, with the blood from the wound he wrote at the end of the sutras the words of pledge, and a prayer to the immortals in the universe to help him to attain his wish. Then he cast the sutras into the sea. After nine years of exile, he died at the age of forty-five. In 1166 the poet-monk Saigyō visited the grave of Sutoku, which he found neglected and run wild with weeds. He stayed for hours there, addressing words of consolation to the departed soul, and dedicated this poem, another thematic poem, to the departed soul: *Yoshi ya Kimi, / Mukashi no tama no / Yuka totemo / Kakaran nochi wa / Nani ni kawasen* (Even though, my Lord, / In days gone by, jewel-bright / Were your palace floors, / After all has come to this, / What can be the use of it?). It is said that when Saigyō recited this poem, the tomb trembled and shook three times, a sign that the Imperial wrath was appeased by this poem. The above story about Sutoku is told in the *Hōgen Monogatari* ("Tale of the Hōgen Era"); the *Senjū-shō,* a collection of short poetic stories by Saigyō; and a number of other books.

The Noh *Matsuyama Tengu* is, despite its name, not a *tengu-mono* (*tengu*

---

[2] Hōgen is the name of the era from April 1156 to April 1159, and *ran* means rebellion. For more detailed information on the rebellion, see Wilson (trans.), *Hōgen monogatari: Tale of Disorder in Hōgen* (1971).

[3] For more on *tengu,* see the explanation on the *tengu* pieces in the Introduction to Fifth-Group Noh, as well as the section on *tengu* in the introduction to *Kurama Tengu.*

piece); rather, it is one of the four male *haya-mai* pieces, in which the ghost of a noble person performs a *haya-mai* (quick dance). The scene is the tomb of the Retired Emperor Sutoku at Shiramine ("White Peak") on Mt. Matsuyama in Sanuki Province.

In Act 1, the poet-monk Saigyō, the *Waki,* comes to Sanuki to visit Sutoku's tomb. He meets an old man, and asks him the whereabouts of the Imperial grave. The old man, much impressed to hear the stranger's name, takes him to the grave. Soon they are talking like old friends, and Saigyō on his part is much impressed by the old man, a simple rustic, but one whose speech betrays a heart sensitive to beauty. So they go together, climbing rocky mountain ways and arrive at Matsuyama. Saigyō is shocked at the miserable state of the grave, and in tears composes the thematic poem cited above. The old man, though a humble person, is deeply moved by the poem. He tells Saigyō how the *tengu* named Sagami-bō and his followers used to come from Shiramine to comfort the Retired Emperor who had no visitors save these *tengu.* Then, telling how he himself used to come to console the Retired Emperor, the old man recites the beach-plover poem and fades out of sight, making an interim exit into the *tsukurimono,* accompanied by solemn *raijo* music, which is performed at the entrance and exit of a dignified character, such as a deity or an emperor, as well as at the exit of a *tengu.*

When an actor has made his exit accompanied by *raijo,* the music changes to *kyōgen raijo,* accompanying the entrance of an *ai-kyōgen* as a minor god or, in this case, a minor *tengu.* Usually the minor deity or *tengu* performs a soliloquy, delivering a message or making a proclamation. In this play, he announces an Imperial banquet in honor of Saigyō, and tells the *tengu* in the district to attend the party.

In Act 2, a voice is heard singing from within the grave, and Sutoku appears in his Imperial splendor, expresses his appreciation of Saigyō's visit, and performs a *haya-mai* to entertain the monk. While he dances, remembrance of his past causes anger to mount in his heart. At this moment, the music changes to *haya-fue* ("quick flute"), which is performed at the entrance of a supernatural character, such as a divine dragon, who performs a *mai-bataraki.* Sagami-bō, a *tengu,* and his followers, represented by a single *tengu,* come flying in, and together they perform a *mai-bataraki* to console the Retired Emperor. The group of subordinate *tengu* who come to attend the Emperor used to be represented by two or four *tsure* accompanying Sagami-bō, but currently only one accompanies him. As a rule, the entrance of a *tengu* is accompanied by the solemn *ō-beshi* music performed almost exclusively for this character. In this Noh, *haya-fue* is played in place of *ō-beshi,* because the chief *tengu* is only a *tsure.* The dance continues until daybreak, and the *tengu,* still dancing, make their exit.

Matsuyama Tengu is different from two other male *haya-mai* pieces, *Tōru* and *Suma Genji,* and similar to another *haya-mai* piece, *Raiden-B,* in this respect: while *Tōru* and *Suma Genji* are pure visional dramas featuring music and dance, there is some dramatic conflict in the latter two: the *Shite's* anger at his enemies, presented in the first act in *Raiden-B,* and in the second act in *Matsuyama Tengu.* These two Noh have a dramatic atmosphere quite different from that of the other two. In *Matsuyama Tengu,* this feeling is intensified by the appearance of monstrous beings, *tengu,* who wait on the Emperor, who has himself become one of them. *Matsuyama Tengu* is a good example of legendary people who are said to have become *tengu* because of their conceit or frustration, and who attracted to them many *tengu* who became their followers.

Matsuyama Tengu is currently performed only by the Kongō school. Their text does not indicate the identity of the Mae-shite, the old man. According to Sanari Kentarō, the old man is Sagami-bō, the leader of the *tengu,* who appears in the second act as the major *Tsure* (*Yōkyoku Taikan,* 5: 2884). On the other hand, according to the *Kaichū Yōkyoku Zenshū,* edited by Nogami Toyoichirō, the old man is Sutoku (*Matsuyama Tengu,* 6: 355). There are passages in the text that indicate that the old man should be the ghost of Sutoku:

1) In the *Yōkyoku Taikan* text, there is this passage spoken by the *Mae-shite* old man toward the end of the first act, and which is not in the current Kongō text: "The words of the poem Saigyō has recited just now have moved my heart so very deeply." It is more appropriate to attribute this speech to Sutoku than to the *tengu.* The fact that lines almost identical to these, found both in the Kongō and Sanari texts, are spoken by Sutoku in the second act confirms this (*see* the translation of this Noh, lines 94–95).

2) In the first act of the Kongō text, the old man disappears into the tomb, having recited the thematic beach-plover poem composed by Sutoku. This indicates that the old man is Sutoku's ghost. Sanari's version does not have this poem, and the words in this section are slightly different from the Kongō version.

3) The old man is described as an elegant person, rare in the remote countryside, who appreciates poetry. Example: "This man here—though a humble rustic, one can see / The nobleness of his heart under the waves of age, / Even in his rising or moving, / One perceives an air of elegant gracefulness" (lines 73–76). This fits with the image of Sutoku, who was an accomplished poet, whose poems are included in Imperial anthologies and quoted in a number of Noh plays. The *Shika Waka-shū,* the sixth Imperial anthology, was compiled at his order. The *Gyokuyō Waka-shū,* an Imperial anthology compiled in 1312, about a hundred and fifty years after Sutoku's death, includes the following poem by him, made on his death bed: *Yume*

no yo ni / Narekoshi chigiri / Kuchizushite / Samen ashita ni / Ō koto mogana (In this dream-like life / The tie that bound us closely / Not rotting away, / Awaking in the morning, / Would I might see you once more). In the poem, *samen* (future tense of *sameru* = to awaken) is an *engo* (associated word) of *yume* (dream) and means "to leave this dream-like life and attain enlightenment." He wanted this poem to be shown to Fujiwara no Toshinari (= Shunzei) in Kyoto, a great poet and the compiler of the Imperial anthology *Senzai-shū.* It is hard to associate this poem, which is philosophical and affectionate, with the image of Sutoku in the Noh *Matsuyama Tengu.* This pathetic poem is free from the anger or bitter feelings expected of its author as presented in the Noh. As it is, the play is not solely motivated by the sinister elements. There are glimpses of the hero as a sensitive and refined man of letters. The charm of this demonic drama is deepened by the counterpoint created by such contradictory features.

Finally, in confirmation of this hypothesis, the text of the *Ai-kyōgen* states without a doubt that "the soul of Retired Emperor Sutoku appeared to Saigyō in the form of an aged man."

Matsuyama Tengu can be performed first in a program as a *waki*-Noh. In that case, the *Nochi-shite* performs a *gaku* dance, instead of a *haya-mai,* and line 115 immediately preceding the *mai* changes as follows:

Original: *Koko mo kumoi no Miyako no sora no*
Tsuki mo terisō mai no sode.
(Here at this place, now turned into the cloud-bound Capital,
The moon casts light on the sparkling dancing sleeves.)

Variation: *Koko mo kumoi no Miyako no sora no*
Yaiu no bugaku wa omoshiro ya.
(Here at this place, now turned into the cloud-bound Capital,
The dancing at this night party, how fascinating!)

Until the Kongō school restored this play to their repertory during the 1880s, *Matsuyama Tengu* had remained for a long time excluded from the repertories of all five Noh schools, perhaps because it presents such a cruel story about a former emperor. A new version of *Matsuyama Tengu* was written by Haruo Nishino, set to music by Rokurō Umewaka, and performed by Kanze-school actors belonging to Noh-geki no Za (Noh-Drama Company) for the first time in 1994. In this new version, the *Nochi-shite,* Sutoku's ghost, performs a *gaku* dance instead of *haya-mai.* A *gaku* is a long and dignified dance that is performed, with a few exceptions, exclusively in the *gaku*-dance pieces among the *waki*-Noh and in the Chinese fourth-group *gaku*-dance pieces. No traditional fifth-group Noh has a *gaku.*

(In *Kuzu,* however, the *Nochi-tsure,* the heavenly maiden, performs a *chū no mai,* during which the *taiko* plays *gaku* music.) A *gaku* is performed by the Kongō school in *Matsuyama Tengu* only when this Noh is played as a *waki*-Noh. A fifth-group Noh with a long and heavy *gaku* dance goes against the principle of *jo-ha-kyū.* However, it may be permissible at the present time, when a day's program has usually only one or two Noh instead of five or more.

The text, stage directions, and costumes are mainly based on the current version of the Kongō school.[4]

Scene: Near Shiramine in Matsuyama, Sanuki Province, Shikoku (present-day Kagawa Prefecture).

Season: Spring, during the Nin'an Era (1166–68).

*Characters and costumes:**

Waki Poet-monk Saigyō, wearing a typical monk's costume consisting of *sumi-bōshi* head gear and a plain *noshime kitsuke* under a *mizugoromo* robe, carrying prayer beads in hand.

Mae-shite The ghost of Retired Emperor Sutoku in the form of an old man, in the typical costume of a humble old man, consisting of an old-man mask such as *Sankō-jō* or *Asakura-jō* and a plain *noshime kitsuke* under a *mizugoromo* robe, carrying a walking stick in hand.

Nochi-shite The ghost of Retired Emperor Sutoku, in the typical costume of a nobleman who performs a *haya-mai,* consisting of a handsome *chūjō* mask, an *ui-kamuri* court cap bound with a colored headband, a *nuihaku kitsuke* under an unlined *kariginu* robe, and a *sashinuki* divided skirt, with an *ōkuchi* divided skirt under it.

Nochi-tsure A *tengu* named Sagami-bō, in the typical *tengu* costume, including an *ō-beshimi* mask, a great *tokin* head piece, a long red-haired wig, an *atsuita kitsuke* under a lined *kariginu* robe, and a *hangire* divided skirt, carrying a large feather fan in hand.

Nochi-tsure A *tengu* who accompanies Sagami-bō, attired like Sagami-

---

[4] The authors are indebted to Ms. Rebecca Teele and the popular actor Kunzō Teshima (elder son of the legendary Yazaemon), both of the Kongō school, for their advice and instruction concerning the present-day performance practices of this play.

bō, except for his robe, which is a *happi,* instead of a *kariginu.*

Ai-kyōgen A minor *tengu.*

Mai: *Haya-mai* by the *Nochi-shite. Mai-bataraki* by the two *Nochi-tsure.*

The author: Unknown.

Variation: *Matsuyama Tengu* can be performed as a *waki*-Noh (see the last part of the introduction above).

* *For technical Japanese terms concerning costumes, see the Glossary.*

Matsuyama Tengu

松山天狗

—ACT 1—

A tsukurimono *draped in a dark cloth, which represents a grave mound, is placed before the* daishō *at upstage center.*

SHIDAI *The* Waki, *the monk Saigyō, enters and, pausing at the* nanori-za, *turns around to face the pine tree painted on the back panel.*

Shidai *au*

WAKI

Following the way in which the wind is blowing,
Following the way in which the wind is blowing,
To Matsuyama let me travel then in haste.[1]

Jidori, *awazu*
The Waki *faces front.*

CHORUS

Following the way in which the wind is blowing,
To Matsuyama let me travel then in haste.

Nanori, *spoken*

WAKI

I am the monk Saigyō, who lives in a remote corner of Saga Moor.[2]
Now, there was a quarrel for the throne between the Emperor and the Newly Retired Emperor.[3]
At a place named Matsuyama in Sanuki Province,[4]
The Newly Retired Emperor passed away not long afterward.
Having heard about this,
Now I hasten to Sanuki Province.

Michiyuki, *au*

My decision made,
My heart travels toward the west, with the setting moon,[5]
My heart travels toward the west, with the setting moon,

---

[1] Matsuyama: The place where the Retired Emperor Sutoku was exiled and died, in Ayaka County, Kagawa Prefecture, Shikoku. This should not be confused with the Matsuyama in the neighboring Iyo Province (Ehime Prefecture); it was a village set back about a mile from the coast about halfway between Takamatsu and Marugame in today's Kagawa Prefecture. Mt. Shiramine rises up behind the village, and Emperor Sutoku's grave is located at its foot.

[2] Saga, also Saga Moor: In the northwestern part of Kyoto, a scenic place rich in poetic associations. Saigyō (1118–90; *né* Satō no Norikiyo): A monk and one of the most celebrated poets of his time. He renounced life at the age of twenty-three and lived in seclusion, traveling throughout the country. The *Sanka-shū* (Poems by a Mountain Dweller) and the *Senjū-shō,* a collection of poetic episodes, both written by Saigyō, portray him as a roaming poet-monk. While he was a layman, he had been a samurai in the service of the Retired Emperor Toba, Sutoku's father.

Kaze no yukue o shirube nite
Kaze no yukue o shirube nite
Matsuyama ni izaya isogan.[1]

Kaze no yukue o shirube nite
Matsuyama ni izaya isogan.

Kore wa Sagano no oku ni sumai suru Saigyō Hōshi nite sōrō.[2]

Sate mo Shinnin, Honnin mi-kurai no arasoi atte[3]

Shinnin na [= wa] Sanuki no Kuni Matsuyama to mōsu tokoro nite[4]
Hodonaku hōgyo narase-tamaitaru yoshi uketamawari oyobite sōrō hodo ni

Tadaima Sanuki no Kuni e to isogi sōrō.
Omoitatsu
Kokoro mo nishi e yuku tsuki no[5]
Kokoro mo nishi e yuku tsuki no

---

[3] The Emperor (Hon'in): Hon'in (pronounced Honnin in the text) actually means the Senior or First Retired Emperor. This title is used when there are two or more retired emperors. However, Hon'in is used in this Noh to designate the Emperor Go-Shirakawa, Sutoku's younger brother. The Newly Retired Emperor (Shin'in [Shinnin in the text]) is Sutoku, so called to distinguish him from the Senior Retired Emperor Toba, his father.

[4] Sanuki Province: The present Kagawa Prefecture in Shikoku.

[5] *nishi e yuku* (go to the west) is the verb for both *kokoro* (heart) and *tsuki* (moon); the nuance is that "the heart, too, travels westward, as does the moon," but we have chosen to use the image of the moon setting in the west, followed by the heart. This seems to "follow" logically after the imagery in the opening *shidai*. Also, the west was tradtionally the direction in which the Paradise of the Buddha Amida (Skt. Amitābha) was located. This was the Paradise that medieval people hoped to enter after death.

Nightly lying on pillows all unfamiliar,
Without knowing their number, along the white-cloud—
Hovering highways[6] I have traveled on, until
The Province of Sanuki I have reached at last,
The Province of Sanuki I have reached at last.

Tsuki-zerifu, *spoken*
After the speech, the Waki *sits at the* waki-za.

Having traveled quickly,
I have arrived in the Province of Sanuki.
Let me wait for someone
And ask him the whereabouts of the Newly Retired Emperor's burial place in Matsuyama

ISSEI *An old man, the* Shite, *enters and stands at the* jō-za. *He has a walking stick in hand.*

Issei, *awazu*

SHITE

The roadside grass
Is heavy with dew along the oft-trodden path.
The thought of mountain wind,
Makes the heart tremble so![7]

Mondō, *spoken*
The Waki *rises and turns to the* Shite.

WAKI

Excuse me, you venerable one there,
Are you someone who lives in this neighborhood?

SHITE

Yes, I live in this neighborhood.
You, holy man, whence do you hail and whither do you travel?

WAKI

I am the monk Saigyō, who lives in a remote corner of Saga Moor in the Capital.
The Newly Retired Emperor, who was exiled to this Sanuki Province,
Passed away soon afterward. Having heard of this,
In order to pray for his afterlife,
I have come to this place.
Please tell me the whereabouts of his burial place in Matsuyama.

---

[6] *isa ya* ***shira***— (well, **unknown**) → ***shira****-kumo* (**white** cloud) → ***kakaru*** (hanging, related to "cloud") → ***kakaru*** *tabi-ji* (such a traveling road).

[7] In lines 23–24: *Michishiba* (roadside grass) and *tsuyu* (dew) are *engo* (associated words). Lines 25–26 are given in an ancient text as *Yama kaze sasou kokoro kana*. Together with the

Iku yona-yona no kari-makura
Sono kazu isa ya shirakumo no[6]

Kakaru tabiji o sugu shikite
Sanuki no Kuni ni tsukinikeri
Sanuki no Kuni ni tsukinikeri.
Isogi sōrō hodo ni
Sanuki no Kuni ni tsukite sōrō.
Hito o ai-machi
Shinnin no go-byōsho Matsuyama o tazunebaya to omoi sōrō.

Michishiba no
Tsuyu fumi-wakuru kayoi-ji no[7]
Arashi o sasou
Kokoro kana.

Ikani korenaru jō-dono
On-mi wa kono atari no hito nite sōrō ka.

Sanzōrō kore wa kono atari no mono nite sōrō.
Osō wa izuku yori izukata e on-tōri sōrō zo.

Kore wa Miyako Sagano no oku ni sumai suru Saigyō Hōshi nite sōrō ga

Shinnin kono Sanuki no Kuni e nagasare-tamai

Hodonaku hōgyo narase-tamaitaru yoshi uketamawarite sōrō hodo ni
On-[n]ato o tomurai mōsan tame
Kore made mairite sōrō.
Matsuyama no go-byōsho o oshiete tamawari sōrae.

---

preceding lines, this would mean that the wind from the mountains invites the dew from the roadside grass away, causing it to evaporate, and that the heart would be as fearful and as fragile as the dew.

SHITE

Oh, then you are Reverend Saigyō, whose name is known all over the country.
The large mountain you see there,
That is the high mountain named White Peak.[8]
The one you see a little nearer,
That is none other than the Newly Retired Emperor's burial place, Matsuyama.
I will show you the way; so saying,

Kakaru

He conducts the holy man along.

Age-uta, *au*

CHORUS

With a traveler met as a total stranger,
With a traveler met as a total stranger,
Already steeped in friendly feelings, colorful[9]
Words cordial they exchange as they go,
Rare indeed is what lies in the depths of their hearts.
Following steep mountain paths ne'er trodden before,[10]
Over the rocks and roots they go, 'neath the gaping cliffs
On foot-paths o'ergrown with moss they walk on and on,
Even where the howling wind's sound is chilling cold,

The two stand, facing the tsukurimono.

And at Matsuyama they finally have arrived,
And at Matsuyama they finally have arrived.

Mondō, *spoken*

SHITE

This is the Newly Retired Emperor's burial place, Matsuyama—
A most pitiful sight, indeed!

The two kneel.

WAKI

So this is the grave of the Newly Retired Emperor!
In the past, he lived in a palace of jewels and gold,

---

[8] Because Saigyō is quite renowned for his travels, the *Shite* begins by pointing out one of the area's most famous sites, Mt. Shiramine ("White Peak"; a mere hill at 337 meters), which was known in legend as a place where many *tengu* lived and also as the home of the Great Tengu Sagami-bō.

[9] In *nare-some* (to become familiar), *nare* means "familiar, friendly" and *some* means "to begin" as well as "to dye," and is thus an *engo* of *iroiro no* (colorful [= various]).

[10] *Mada fumi mo minu yamamichi* (not yet trod mountain path): Cf. the following poem by Ko-Shikibu no Naishi, a court lady (1005–26) in the *Kin'yō-shū* (555*): Ōe-yama / Ikuno no michi no / Tōkereba /* ***Mada fumi mo minu*** */ Ama no Hashidate.* In the poem, Mt. Ōe and Ikuno are places in Tango Province. *Iku* in the place name Ikuno means "to go," so that the first three lines of the poem mean: "Mt. Ōe Mountain—to go there the way is far." In these lines, Mt. Ōe and Ikuno are used simply to introduce the phrase, *michi no / Tōkereba* (the

Sate wa tenga ni kakure-naki Saigyō Shōnin nite mashimasu ka ya.

Are ni mietaru taisan na [= wa]
Shiramine to mōsu kōzan nari.[8]
Sukoshi konata ni mie sōrō koso
Shinnin no go-byōsho Matsuyama nite sōrae.

On-michi-shirube mōsan to
O-sō o izanai tatematsuri

Yukue mo shiranu tabibito ni
Yukue mo shiranu tabibito ni
Haya naresomete iroiro no[9]
Nasake aru koto-no-ha no
Kokoro no uchi zo arigataki.
Mada fumi mo minu yamamichi no[10]
Iwane o tsutai tani no to no

Koke no shitamichi tadorikite
Kaze no oto sae susamajiki
Matsuyama ni hayaku tsukinikeri
Matsuyama ni hayaku tsukinikeri.

Kore koso Shinnin no go-byōsho Matsuyama nite sōrae.

Nanbō asamashiki on-(n)arisama nite sōrō zo.

Sate wa kore naru ga Shinnin no misasaki nite mashimasu ka ya.
Mukashi wa gyokurō kinden no on-sumai

---

way / Being remote), so that the poem really means nothing more than: "The way being remote, I have not yet trod nor seen Ama no Hashidate (the Floating Bridge of Heaven)." Ama no Hashidate was—and still is—one of the three most popular scenic spots in all of Japan. The background of the poem is this: Ko-Shikibu's mother, the great poet Izumi Shikibu, was in Tango Province, where her husband was the governor. When a poetry contest was going to be held at court, some thought that Ko-Shikibu would be helped by her mother. So one of her rivals asked her if she had heard from her mother, to which she answered with the above poem. Literally, the poem means that she has not yet trodden the famous Bridge of Heaven, but *Mada fumi mo minu* (not yet trodden) also means, "[I have] not yet seen a letter," with *fumi* meaning both "to tread" and "letter," indicating that she had not heard form her mother. She was praised for such a witty and impromptu riposte.

Waited on by grand ministers and high-ranking courtiers in great number,
Kakaru — Now in this remote countryside, buried under the moss he lies,
Within a graveyard, no trace of him ling'ring.
I cannot hold my tears.
Oh, my heart aches so!
Spoken — At this pitiful sight
Moved to tears, I recite thus:
Kakaru — "Even though, my Lord, in the days gone, jewel-bright were your palace floors;
After all has come to this,
What can be the use of it?"[11]

Spoken — SHITE
"Oh, that is a most impressive poem!
It touches even a humble man's heart,"
Kakaru — He says, deeply moved by Saigyō's poem.

WAKI
Indeed, at this place away from the Capital,

Age-uta, *au* — CHORUS
This man here—though a humble rustic, one can see—
This man here—though a humble rustic, one can see
The nobleness of his heart under the waves of age,[12]
Even in his rising or moving,
One perceives an air of elegant gracefulness.
Ko-uta — Greeting spring time, though flowers are in bloom,
There is no one to see them in the mountain's depths,
Even the voice of a bush warbler, singing
At a place like this, only moves one
To a feeling of deep pathos on this spring eve.

Spoken — WAKI
I say, venerable man,
When His Majesty was alive,
Who came to cheer him up?

SHITE
When His Majesty was alive,
He would think of the time when he lived in the Capital,
And throw himself into rage.

---

[11] This is the thematic poem written by Saigyō when he visited the grave of Retired Emperor Sutoku (*see* the Introduction). It also appears in the *Hōgen Monogatari, Sanka-shū,* and *Senjū-shō* in the same form.

Hyakkan keishō ni itsukare-tamaishi on-mi no

Kakaru denja no koke no shita

Hito mo kayowanu go-byōsho no uchi
Namida mo sara ni todomarazu
Ara, on-(n)itawashiya sōrō.
Kaku asamashiki on-(n)arisama
Namida-nagara ni kaku bakari
Yoshi ya Kimi, mukashi no tama no yuka totemo

Kakaran nochi wa
Nani ni ka wa sen.[11]

Ara, omoshiro no go-eika ya.
Iyashiki mi ni mo omoi-yarite
Saigyō o kanji-tatematsureba

Geni ya tokoro mo ama-sagaru

Hina-bito naredo kaku bakari
Hina-bito naredo kaku bakari
Kokoro shiraruru oinami no[12]
Tachimō sugata made
Samo miyabitaru keshiki kana.
Haru o ete saku hana o
Miru hito mo naki tani no to ni
Naku uguisu no koe made mo
Tokoro kara aware o
Moyōsu haru no iube kana.

Ikani jō-dono,
Kimi go-zonmei no ori-ori wa
Ika naru mono ka mairi mi-kokoro o nagusame mōshite sōrō zo.

Sansōrō Kimi go-zonmei no ori-ori wa
Miyako no koto o oboshimeshi-idashi
On-gekirin no shikiri nareba

---

[12] Line 72: *Ama-sagaru* (away from the Capital) is a pillow word (*makura-kotoba*) for *hina-bito* (humble rustic) in lines 73–74. Lines 75–76: *oi-**nami*** (age-old-**waves**) → ***tachi**-mō* (**to rise** and move about).

This attracted demonic beings to him,
The *tengu* who follow Sagami-bō of White Peak.
Except for them, no one came to wait on him.
Kakaru — This old man, too,
Used to come here to sweep the ground beneath the trees
And to console his mind.
Recites — "Though the beach plover's footprints in the Capital leave behind traces,
I shall at Matsuyama remain, crying bitterly."[13]

Au

CHORUS

Now let me take leave of you, farewell, saying thus,
As he rises to go, the waves of old age return.[14]
To a venerable and solitary tree—
The instant he was seen to draw near,
Like a shadow, his form has faded out of sight.

NAKAIRI *Accompanied by* raijo *music, the* Shite *makes an interim exit into the* tsukurimono.

AI-KYŌGEN *The music changes to* kyōgen raijo. *The* Ai-kyōgen, *a minor* tengu, *enters, tells about the Retired Emperor, and the monk Saigyō and the poem he composed before the grave mound. Then he announces that all the* tengu *should accompany Sagami-bō, their leader, and attend the party to be held in honor of Saigyō.*

AI

I who appear here now am a tree-leaf long-nosed demon in service to the Great Goblin Sagami-bō on Mt. Shiramine in the land of Sanuki. Now, the 75th emperor, Sutoku, was the first son of Emperor Toba. But he was forced to abdicate the throne in favor of Prince Konoe, and Sutoku was given the position of Newly Retired Emperor. When Emperor Konoe died, the next in line was Retired Emperor Sutoku's firstborn son, Prince Shigehito, but through the machinations of Cloistered Empress Bifukumon'in,[15] Retired Emperor Toba's fourth son was placed on the throne under the name Go-Shirakawa. This

---

[13] Lines 95–96: A poem by Sutoku (*see* the Introduction).

[14] Lines 98–99: *tachi-kaeru oi no nami* (rise and return the age-old waves, in which "rise" is an *engo* of "waves") → ***Oki*** **(to rise** [related to "waves"], **offing)** → ***Okina*** **(old man)** → **Okina-sabi (oldman-like, venerable)** → ***sabishiki*** (**lone**some) → ***sabishiki*** *ko no moto* (beneath a **lonely** tree). *Tachi-kaeru* (to rise and return) is an *engo* of *nami* (waves), and is reminiscent of the imagery in lines 75–76 (*see* Note 12).

Maen chikazuki tatematsuri
Ano Shiramine no Sagami-bō ni shitagō tengu-domo
Mairu yori hoka wa yo no sandai wa naku sōrō.
Kayō ni mōsu rōjin mo
Tsunezune mairi kokage o kiyome
On-kokoro o nagusame mōshishi nari.
Hamachidori ato wa Miyako e kayoedomo

Mi wa Matsuyama ni ne o nomi zo naku.[13]

Itoma mōshite saraba tote
Mata tachi-kaeru oi no nami[14]
Okina sabishiki ko no moto ni
Tachi-yoru to mieshi ga
Kage no gotoku ni usenikeri.

(*The original Japanese text of the Ai-kyōgen is omitted here.*[15–29])

---

[15] Bifukumon'in: The daughter (Tokuko; 1117–60) of the Middle Counselor and later Prime Minister Fujiwara no Nagazane, she was taken as a concubine by Toba after he became a Retired Emperor. After the birth of Konoe (Toba's eighth son) she was named *nyōgo,* or Imperial Concubine; and after Konoe's accession, she was made Empress.

turn of affairs brought discord between Sutoku and Go-Shirakawa. Sutoku staged a revolt against his brother and war broke out. Among his allies, Sutoku had, from the ruling class, the Uji Great Minister of the Left,[16] and, from the warrior class, the Rokujō Lieutenant of Imperial Police Tameyoshi[17] and his son. These he made his generals. The allies of Emperor Go-Shirakawa were, from the ruling class, the Chancellor and Minister of the Interior Tadamichi,[18] and, from the warrior class, Yoshitomo[19] of the Minamoto clan and Kiyomori[20] of the Taira clan. The battle began on the 11th day of the 7th month of the 2nd year of the Hōgen Era during the Hour of the Tiger. The battle was brought to a close during the Hour of the Dragon,[21] with defeat for Sutoku. And on the 10th day of the 8th month of the same year, Sutoku was banished to

---

[16] *Uji no Aku Safu* (The strong Governor of the Left) = *Uji no Sadaijin* (the Uji Great Minister of the Left): Fujiwara no Yorinaga (1120–56). As the second son of Tadazane [1078–1162], the former Chancellor and Prime Minister (*Dajō-daijin*), he was the younger brother of the current Prime Minister, Tadamichi (*see* Note 18), and the chief official of the Great Council of State.

[17] *Rokujō Hōgan Tameyoshi:* Minamoto no Tameyoshi (1096–1156), the senior member of his clan at the time and heir to his grandfather Yoshiie, one of the most renowned heroes of the age. He was called Rokujō because his residence was at the intersection of that street and Horikawa. This was the famed *Kawara no In* (Riverside Mansion) of the great statesman and poet Minamoto no Tōru (*see* the play *Tōru; see also* Note 29 below). Tameyoshi was the son of Yoshitomo, who fought on Go-Shirakawa's side. The son mentioned is Tametomo (1139–70), who fought with his father in the Hōgen rebellion and was banished to the island of Ōshima (Izu), from which legend states that he escaped to the Ryūkyūs (Okinawa), becoming the ancestor of the Ryūkyūan royal family.

[18] *Kanpaku Naidaijin Tadamichi:* Chancellor and Minister of the Interior Fujiwara no Tadamichi (1097–1164), the eldest son of Tadazane and elder brother of Yorinaga. He succeeded his father as Chancellor in 1121, became Regent (*sesshō*) at the accession of Sutoku (1123), and Prime Minister (*Dajō-daijin*) in 1129. Retired Emperor Toba recalled the father and made Tadamichi give up the chancellorship to him, but he resumed it in 1140 when his father retired from public life.

[19] Minamoto no Yoshitomo (1123–60) was the son of Tameyoshi. He was the only member of the Minamoto clan who sided with Taira no Kiyomori (*see* Note 20), with whom he beseiged and took the palace of Shirakawa, which had been defended by his father and brother, Tametomo. He pleaded in vain for his father's life, but Kiyomori had him executed. After peace had been established, Yoshitomo was slighted over and over by Kiyomori, who took more and more power. Eventually, Yoshitomo rebelled (the Heiji Uprising; (January 19–February 5, 1160)), and set fire to the palace of Retired Emperor Go-Shirakawa (*see* Note 28 below), whom he had earlier defended. Defeated in battle, he escaped, but he was murdered by one of his own men. His wife, Tokiwa Gozen, fled with her three children—including Yoritomo and Yoshitsune (*see* the introduction to *Kurama Tengu*). Arrested by Kiyomori, she

the island of Naojima[22] where he was placed in a residence that was surrounded on all four sides by sturdy walls with only a single gate. Except for servants who brought him his meals three times a day, no one at all came to visit him. Truly, while it is a well-known axiom that nothing or no one can withstand the changes of fortune in this world, after thirty-eight years of holding court in the capital in jeweled towers and golden palaces, with one hundred courtiers under his sway, protected by his Imperial guards, and reciting poems to the moon above his Southern Pavilion,[23] faced with such sudden sadness, tears never ceased to flow from Sutoku's eyes. His sole activity from that time forward was the copying of the five Great Vehicle sutras[24] for the salvation of his soul in the afterlife. Upon completion, around the spring of the first year of the Heiji

---

became his concubine, but he made the mistake of sparing her children—who were later to bring about the fall of the Heike.

[20] *Heike no Kiyomori:* Taira no Kiyomori (1118–81) was ostensibly the son of Taira no Tadamori, but legend has it that he was actually the son of Retired Emperor Shirakawa. If this is true, it means that he fought against his own half-brother, Sutoku. After the Hōgen rebellion, his power grew by leaps and knew no bounds. He was involved in the deposing and enthroning of several emperors, finally imprisoning Go-Shirakawa, exiling the Chancellor and the Prime Minister, and forcing Emperor Takakura (Go-Shirakawa's son) to abdicate in favor of his own grandson Antoku, then two years old. The first to rebel were Prince Mochihito (another son of Go-Shirakawa) and Minamoto no Yorimasa (see *Yorimasa* in *Warrior Ghost Plays*). Although defeated, the whole Minamoto clan and other dissatisfied parties rose up. Even though Kiyomori died before the struggle was over, he and his entire clan were destroyed. The saga can be read in *The Tale of the Heike.*

[21] The Hour of the Tiger in the previous line was actually a two-hour period between 3 and 5 AM; the Hour of the Dragon was a scant four hours later, from 7 to 9 AM.

[22] Naojima: A small island in the Inland Sea off the coast of Sanuki (Kagawa Prefecture), roughly north-northwest of Takamatsu.

[23] *Nanrō no tsuki ni usobuki* ("reciting poems to the moon of/o'er the Southern Pavilion"): This alludes to a line in a T'ang poem by Li Po (701–62), which refers to the biography of Yü Liang in the *Chin-shu* (The Book of the Chin Dynasty), telling how in ancient times, a certain man of Chin used to call together his friends to have "moon-viewing parties" at his "Southern Pavilion" in order to write poems on the autumn full moon.

[24] *Gobu no Daijō-kyō o asobashi* (he amused himself with the five Mahāyāna ["Great Vehicle"] sutras): These are the five great sutras of the Mahāyāna tradition, closely associated with the Tendai sect. They are: the *Kegon-kyō* (Avataṁsaka [Garland] Sutra), *Daihōdō Daishū-kyō* (Mahā-sannipāta [Great Collection] Sutra), *Daibon Hannya-kyō* (Mahā-prajñā-pāramitā [Great Wisdom and Perfection] Sutra), *Myōhō Renge-kyō* (also called *Hoke-kyō;* Saddharma-puṇḍarīka [Lotus of the Wonderful Law] Sutra), and *Daihatsu-nehan-gyō* (Mahāparinirvāṇa [Great Extinction] Sutra). Sutoku "amused" himself by copying them and later casting them into the sea.

Era,[25] Sutoku requested that his sutra scrolls be placed on Mt. Yawata, near the Imperial Palace, in the temple Ninnaji, but his request was refused by the Abbot and the scrolls were returned to him.[26] Sutoku was so angered by the return of the scrolls he had copied as penitence for the evil he had committed that, unable to bear the flames of his rage, he made up his mind to take revenge by allying himself with the forces of evil. What a frightfully angry man he then became! To accomplish his purpose, he took the form of a long-nosed goblin, letting his nails grow and neglecting to comb his hair, and donning persimmon-colored priest's robes and the long hempen stole[27] of the warrior priest. At the end of his Great Vehicle sutra scrolls, he inscribed an oath in his own blood. Then he cast his scrolls into the depths of the sea. In sympathy with the rage of Sutoku, the Great Goblin Sagami-bō decided to aid him in accomplishing his purpose by approaching the emperor. And due to this and many other disasters brought about by the living spirit of Sutoku of Sanuki, in the first year of the Heiji Era, on the ninth day of the eleventh month, in response to the urgings of Lord Nobuyori,[28] Yoshitomo staged a revolt against the em-

---

[25] *Heiji gannen* (the first year of the Heiji Era): 1159, the same year in which Minamoto no Yoshitomo and Fujiwara no Nobuyori (*see* Note 28) led a revolt against Taira no Kiyomori in which they were defeated and killed. Because of the date, it is known as the Heiji uprising.

[26] *Yawata-yama:* Mt. Yawata (also spelled Yahata). Another name for Otoko-yama, a small hill 20 km south of Kyoto (which is "near the Imperial Palace" when compared with Naojima). It was thus called because of the famous Iwashimizu Hachiman shrine on its summit. (Yawata is a different reading of the characters for Hachiman, who was the tutelary deity of the Minamoto clan, and the apotheosis of the great military commander, Emperor Ōjin [201–310]). Ninnaji: The headquarters of the Shingon sect within the Imperial capital, it was a temple headed by a Prince of the Blood. At this time, the Abbot was none other than Kakushō, the fifth prince of Emperor Toba and thus the younger brother of both Sutoku and Go-Shirakawa.

[27] *Suzukake chōken* (long hempen robe): The *suzukake* was a linen or hempen outer robe worn by *yamabushi,* and, if this account reflects the beliefs of the times, by *tengu* (see also *Adachigahara,* Note 1).

[28] *Nobuyori-kyō:* Fujiwara no Nobuyori (1133–59), a descendant of Michitaka (953–99; known as the Nijō Chancellor). At first favored by Retired Emperor Go-Shirakawa, when repeatedly passed over for favors he joined with Yoshitomo against the emperor and the Taira. They burned the palace of Go-Shirakawa and captured the two emperors (Go-Shirakawa and his son Nijō). Nobuyori proclaimed himself Prime Minister, but was beseiged by Kiyomori's eldest son, Shigemori (1138–79). He was captured and beheaded.

peror. But as no one can escape the winds of transience, Sutoku expired in a place called Shido in the second year of the Chōkan Era, on the sixth day of the eighth month, at the age of forty-six, and they turned him into smoke at Shiramine.[29] When the springs and autumns of fifty years had already come and gone with no one visiting Sutoku's tomb to offer prayers for the repose of his soul, the monk Saigyō traveled from the capital all the way to the Imperial tomb at Matsuyama. The soul of Retired Emperor Sutoku appeared to Saigyō in the form of an aged man and guided him to Sutoku's tomb. When he arrived, Saigyō recited a poem that goes, "Even though, my Lord, / In days gone by, jewel-bright / Were your palace floors, / After all has come to this, / What can be the use of it?" Upon hearing this, the spirit was so overjoyed that the old man disappeared like passing mist, and Sutoku soon will reappear in his own form to perform a Bugaku dance to last the whole night long to entertain and comfort Saigyō. Then Sagami-bō and all his long-nosed demon host will come to participate in the proceedings as well. So, I say to one and all: Prepare your hearts for that! Prepare your hearts for that!

---

[29] Shido: A place with a bay of the same name known for its pearl divers; it is the venue of the fifth-group Noh *Ama,* in which Fujiwara no Fusasaki (681–737; Minister of State and founder of the regent line, or northern branch, of the Fujiwara clan) is fathered there of an *ama* (pearl diver) by Fujiwara no Fuhito (659–720; Grand Minister of State). For more information, see the synopsis of the play in the Introduction of this volume, p. 13).

Shiramine nite kemuri to nashi tatematsuri ([they] turned [him] into smoke at Shiramine): That is, they cremated his remains, so that he became as smoke rising over Shiramine. Compare this to the famous poem by Ki no Tsurayuki (883–946) in the *Kokin-shū* (473), written when the poet visited the site of Minamoto no Tōru's Riverside Mansion: *Kimi masade / Kemuri taenishi / Shiogama no / Ura-samishiku mo / Mie-wataru kana* (Without you, my Lord, / The smoke no longer rises / From the old salt kilns / At sad Shiogama Bay— / Seen as des'late and forlorn). In the poem: ***shiogama*** (salt kilns) → ***Shiogama** no **Ura*** (Shiogama's Bay) → ***ura**-samishiku* (**desolate** and forlorn); *see also* the synopsis of *Tōru* in the Introduction of this volume (pp. 10–11).

—ACT 2—

DEHA *After the* deha *music, the* Chorus *sings, followed by the* Shite, *who sings from within the grave, which is represented on the stage by the* tsukurimono.

Deha, *sings, awazu*	CHORUS
	"The five elements are primarily all non-existent. For what reason should one care for one's own self? The spirit that guards the body flies in the moonlit night."[30]
Sings from within the tsukurimono, *awazu*	NOCHI-SHITE
	How now, Saigyō,
Speaks	You have come a long way as far as here. Which is most touching, indeed. Also, the poem you have recited Has moved my heart so very deeply
Kakaru	That I am going to reveal myself to you.
	CHORUS
The cloth covering the grave is removed.	Hardly has he spoken these words than the grave begins to rumble and shake And the Imperial form has appeared,
Ō-nori	Truly the Imperial form so graceful and noble, Truly the Imperial form so graceful and noble, With features exquisite as sweet-smelling flowers,
The Shite *comes out of* the grave.	Here too, like the cloud-bound sky of the Capital City,[31] The moon casts her light on the sparkling dancing sleeves. (*Off rhythm*)

HAYA-MAI *by the* Shite, *after which he continues to dance.*

	CHORUS
Noru	Time passes fast with nocturnal dancing and music, Time passes fast with nocturnal dancing and music.

---

[30] Lines 102–4: The first three lines of a quatrain expressing Buddhist philosophy, the source of which is not identified (*see* Nogami, 5:362n). The fourth line goes: "The troubled soul deprived of its body moans in the autumn wind." *Go-un* (the five *skandhas* [aggregates] = assembly of five constituents): in the Buddhist view, all of existence is made up of five constituents, namely, matter, sensation, cognition, will, and consciousness, which are all considered to be empty and illusory.

[31] *Koko mo* ***kumoi*** (Here, too, a well of clouds) → ***kumoi*** *no* ***Miyako*** (the "cloud-ranked" [=

Goun moto yori mina kore kū
Nani ni yotte heizei kono mi o aisen.
Ku o mamoru iukon na [=wa] yagetsu ni tobu[30]

Ika ni Saigyō

Kore made haru-baru kudaru kokorozashi koso
Kaesu-gaesu mo ureshikere.
Mata tadaima no eika no kotoba
Kokoro ni somite omoshirosa ni
Ide-ide sugata o arawasan to

Ii mo aeneba gobyō shikiri ni meidō shite

Gyokutai araware-owashimasu.

Makoto ni taenaru gyokutai no
Makoto ni taenaru gyokutai no
Hana no kaobase taoyaka ni
Koko mo kumoi no miyako no sora no[31]
Tsuki mo terisou mai no sode

Kakute yaiu mo toki sugite
Kakute yaiu mo toki sugite

"of high status"] Capital, often translated as the "cloud-bound Capital," a place in which only those with rank as high as the clouds live. Thus, the term is often written "cloud-dwelling." In the current Kongō text, it appears as "cloud-well," but Nogami, also drawing upon Kongō texts, gives it as "cloud-dwelling") → ***Miyako*** *no sora* ***no tsuki*** (the Capital's sky's moon), which brings to mind ***tsuki no Miyako*** (moonlit Capital). See *Kuzu*, Note 1, for another juxtaposed occurrence of *kumoi* and *tsuki no Miyako*.

Waving and turning the sleeves of his royal robe,
He seemed to enjoy dancing. However,
Again the bygone day's sad experience in the Capital
Reviving in his memory,
The royal figure in fierce anger
Strikes those in his presence with terrifying awe.
(*Off rhythm*)

Noru

But what is that! Look at that? From Shiramine,
But look at that! What is that? From Shiramine's
Summit the wind comes blowing down violently,
Thunder and lightning in quick succession fill the entire sky,
The rain begins to fall down from clouds near and far[32]
The figures of *tengu* are seen to make their appearance.
(*Off rhythm*)

The Shite *sits in the* tsukurimono.
HAYA-FUE *The* Nochi-tsure, *Sagami-bō, the great* tengu, *and after him, the Second* Tsure, *a minor* tengu, *enter and stand on the* hashi-gakari.

Sings, awazu

NOCHI-TSURE

Let me tell who I am.
On Shiramine for many years I have lived;
One named Sagami-bō is no other than myself.

Spoken

It so happens that the Newly Retired Emperor
Passed away here at Matsuyama.
We regularly come to this place
To comfort His Majesty.

Kakaru

So, with all these *tengu* following me,

Noru

CHORUS

With our wings spread side by side, in a great number,
With our wings spread side by side, in a great number,
We have come flying here to Matsuyama
To give worship in the Imperial presence.
All those rebellious subjects
We're going to beat and kick to death, to the last person,

[32] *Ame* ***ochi*** (rain **falls**) → ***ochi**-kochi* (**far** and near).

Gyoi no tamoto o hirugaeshi
Mai-asobi-tamaishi ga
Mata inishie no Miyako no uki koto o
Oboshimeshi-idashi
Gekirin no on-sugata
Atari o haratte osoroshi ya.

Are, are, miyo ya Shiramine no
Are, are miyo ya Shiramine no
Yamakaze araku fuki-ochite
Kaminari inazuma shikiri ni michi-michite

Ame ochi-kochi no kumo ma yori[32]

Tengu no sugata wa arawaretari.

Somosomo kore wa
Shiramine ni sunde toshi o furu
Sagami-bō to wa waga koto nari.
Sat emo Shinnin omowazu mo
Kono Matsuyama ni hōgyo naru
Tsunezune sandai mōshi-tsutsu
On-kokoro o nagusame mōsan to
Sho-tengu o hiki-tsurete

Tsubasa o narabe kazu-kazu ni

Tsubasa o narabe kazu-kazu ni

Kono Matsuyama ni tobi-kitari
Gyokutai o haishi tatematsuri
Gekishin no tomogara o
Kotogotoku tori-hishigi kekoroshi

And set to right the humiliation of Mt. Kuai-chi.[33]
Let the royal heart be comforted, we pray you!
(Off rhythm)

MAI-BATARAKI *by the* Nochi-tsure Sagami-bō *and the other* tengu.

SHITE

Ō-nori.

Having listened to these words, His Majesty is deeply pleased,

CHORUS

Having listened to these words, His Majesty is deeply pleased,
Expressing his appreciation in many gracious words.

The Shite *stands.*

As for the *tengu,* all of them
Bow low, their heads touching the ground, and worship His Majesty.
Let us take leave, says the leader, and by many *tengu*
Accompanied, into the sky he is seen to fly up,
Where the dawning light shimmers on Shiramine,[34]

The Tsure *exits. The* Shite *stamps the* tome-byōshi *at* jō-za.

Where the dawning light shimmers on Shiramine, o'er the tree tops,
They fly about until they vanish out of sight.

---

[33] Mt. Kuai-chi (also Huichi): A Chinese mountain near Tsui-li, where Kou Chien (5th century BC), King of Yüeh, was defeated by Fu-ch'ai, King of Wu. Later Kou Chien defeated and killed Fu-ch'ai. The proverb, "to wash away the shame of Kuai-chi" originates from this story. In the Noh text, the word "shame" is omitted. Cf. *Kurama Tengu,* line 229, Note 52.

[34] *Akeyuku sora mo* ***shira***— (the dawning sky also white) → ***Shira****mine* (White Peak).

Kaikei o susugase mōsu-beshi[33]
Eiryo o nagusami owashimase.

Sono toki Kimi mo yorokobi owashimashi,

Sono toki Kimi mo yorokobi owashimashi

Gyo-kan no mi-kotoba kazu-kazu nareba
Tengu mo ono-ono
Kōbe o chi ni tsuke haishi tatematsuri

Kore made nari tote sho-tengu o
Hiki-tsure kokū ni agaru to mieshi ga
Akeyuku sora mo Shiramine no[34]
Akeyuku sora mo Shiramine no kozue ni

Mata tobikakette usenikeri.

鞍馬天狗

KURAMA TENGU

和上臈も。さも花やかなる御有様にて
姿も心も荒天狗を。師匠や坊主と御賞還ハ。や坊主と御賞還ハ。

My noble lord, a blooming youth in an attire of flowery splendor,
This goblin, rude and fierce in appearance and in mind,
You venerate so, calling him teacher and master.

Introduction

Kurama Tengu is one of the five *tengu-mono* (goblin pieces) among the *gobanme-mono* (fifth-group Noh) plays. In this type of play, as a rule, the *tengu* usually approach men to injure or work mischief on them. All *tengu* plays are in two acts. In Act 1, the *tengu* appear as *yamabushi* (mountain-ascetic priests), except in *Dairoku-ten,* in which the *mae-shite* is a goddess who appears as a village woman. In Act 2, the *tengu* appear in their true splendor, and it is here that they do their best to trick men, but are defeated by a deity or the power of prayer.

Kurama Tengu is the only goblin play in which the *tengu* is a benevolent power: he protects youth Ushiwaka-maru, the young Minamoto no Yoshitsune (1159–89; *see below* for more details on his life), and instructs him in swordsmanship and military strategy, so that he might defeat the tyrannical rule of the Taira clan under Taira no Kiyomori (1118–81). Thus, from Ushiwaka's point of view, the Great *Tengu* of Kurama is equivalent to a guardian deity; however, from the Taira standpoint, he is just another malevolent deity bent on destroying men. Indeed, in the *Genpei Jōsuiki,* it is stated that both *tengu* and angry ghosts (*ashura*) consciously worked toward bringing about the fall of the house of Taira (*see* de Visser, p. 54).

The *Tengu*

Before launching into a discussion of Yoshitsune and the play, let us look as what a *tengu* is in Japanese folklore. A *tengu*, usually translated as "goblin," is a long-nosed, fierce-looking creature who can fly and who wields great magical power. Indeed, in *Dai-e,* a *tengu* even assumes the form of the Buddha himself. In medieval literature, the *tengu*, who were reputed to be unequalled masters of the martial arts, were often portrayed as enemies of Buddhism. In popular tales, the *tengu* often kidnap young children (as described in the Noh play *Kagetsu*). In contrast, legends also portray the *tengu* as benevolent guardians and transmitters of supernatural skills, as in *Kurama Tengu*. They are often portrayed as, or associated with, *yamabushi* (lit: "one who lies down [= sleeps] in the mountains"; for more on *yamabushi, see* Note 33 to the play); this may be because *tengu* are also seen as manifestations of *yama no kami,* or guardian deities of certain mountains.

De Visser, especially in the section on the *Tengu Meigikō* (p. 82) of Teinin (1704–86), gives the following list of the great *tengu* of Japan (and the mountain or area with which they are associated): Sōjō-bō (Mt. Kurama); Tarō-bō (Mt. Atago); Jirō-bō (Mt. Hira); Sanjaku-bō (Mt. Akiba); Rihō-bō (Kōmyō); Buzen-bō (Mt. Hiko); Hōki-bō (Mt. Daisen); Myōgi-bō (Kozuke); Sankijin (Itsukushima); Zenki-bō (Mt. Ōmine); Kōken-bō (Mt. Kazuraki); Tsukuba Hōin (Mt. Tsukuba); Tarō-bō (Mt. Fuji); Naigubu (Mt. Takao); Sagami-bō (Mt. Shiramine = Hakufū); Jirō-bō (Mt. Izuna; also associated with the fox deity); Ajari (Higo); etc. Other mountains often encountered in *tengu* legends include Mts. Hiei and Kōya (the two headquarters of Japan's esoteric Buddhist sects, which vied for supremacy throughout the Heian era [794–1185]; and those mentioned in the *Konjaku Monogatari, Shaseki-shū,* and *Ōkagami*), Mt. Akagi (Sugino-bō), Takayama (*Konjaku Monogatari*), and Mt. Kinpu (Zenki-bō). Note that the -bō part of their names is normally used in the names of Buddhist monks.

It is interesting to note that although the word *tengu* itself is written with the Chinese characters for "Celestial Hound," the word was originally used in ancient Chinese literature to mean a malevolent star, such as a flaming meteor or comet. In the *Records of the Historian* of Ssu-ma Ch'ien (Ch. 27, 1.31), it says: "It has the shape of a large moving star" that falls to earth, "resemb[ling] a dog," and with "flames flaming up to heaven." But T'ang-dynasty poet Tu Tzu-mei (dates unknown) describes such *t'ien-kou* in his "Poem on Celestial Dogs" as creatures able to fly above the clouds, living on high mountains, having great magical powers, and being the size of gibbons (*wan-k'ang*) and nearly equal to the gods (*see* de Visser, pp. 30, 32). Already, they are much more like Japanese *tengu.*

Yet even in ancient Japan, the word *tengu* was used for astronomical phenomena. The *Nihongi* [Chronicles of Japan] says that in the ninth year of the reign of Emperor Jomei (637), "a great star flew from east to west, and there was a noise like that of thunder. . . . Of this, the Buddhist priest Min said: 'It is not the shooting star, but the Celestial Dog, the sound of whose barking is like thunder' " (*Nihongi* 231–32). Aston (2:168n5) states that the Celestial Dog was considered to be a group of seven stars called Amatsu Kitsune (Heavenly Foxes) near the constellation Cancer (perhaps the constellation Pyxis [Compass]). However, by the time of the *Utsubo Monogatari,* which predates and is quoted in both the *Makura-zōshi* (ca.

1000) and the *Genji Monogatari* (ca. 1004?), *tengu* were considered mountain demons who deluded men.

At about the time that the *tengu* legends became most prominent, certain adepts of the esoteric Shingon (Mt. Kōya) and Tendai (Mt. Hiei) schools of Japanese Buddhism followed the rules of Shugendō, established by the semi-legendary ascetic En no Ozuno (634–early 8th cent.), and retired to mountain recesses to practice austerities and develop their occult powers. Known as *yamabushi* ("those who sleep in the mountains"), they also trained in the martial arts to strengthen their bodies and their minds. Folklore soon attributed to them such magical powers as the ability to fly, and these beliefs may be the origin of the legends of the *tengu*. They often made pilgrimages to mountains associated with *tengu*, traveling through the mountain wilderness on special paths between certain temples at which they assembled in such places as Mt. Ōmine (in Yoshino, south of Nara), Mt. Kinpu (north of Kōfu), and the Kumano shrines (in southeastern Kii, south of Nara).

The Play and Its Sources

The setting of the play is Mt. Kurama in the northern district of Kyoto. After the defeat and death of his father, Ushiwaka and two elder brothers were captured by the Heike with their mother, Lady Tokiwa. Their lives were spared on condition that Tokiwa become a mistress of the Heike leader, Taira no Kiyomori. Ushiwaka was sent to Kurama Temple to become a monk when grown up. The Noh develops as follows:

Act 1

1) A *yamabushi,* who is actually a goblin in disguise, enters and introduces himself to the audience as a priest living in Archbishop's Valley on Mt. Kurama. He has heard about a flower-viewing party to be held in the Western Valley this day, so he has come to see the flowers as an outsider.

2) The *Kyōgen,* a temple servant of the Western Valley, enters with a letter of invitation, and meets the flower-viewing party from the Eastern Valley. Some priests and several temple boys enter, and among them is the young Ushiwaka (who goes by the Buddhist name of Shanaō). The priest reads the letter, and they all go to sit under the trees to view the flowers.

3) The temple servant performs a dance to amuse the young temple boys. Then he sees the *yamabushi*, and is about to drive him away. The priest stops him, and tells the party it is best to leave the place and come back the next day. So they all exit, except for Ushiwaka.

4) The *yamabushi* sings, referring to the behavior of these people, which is against the spirit of the spring season, when strangers and acquaintances should be enjoying flowers together, and against the true spirit of Buddhism as well. Ushiwaka invites the *yamabushi* to approach the trees and

look at the flowers. The *yamabushi* is deeply touched. A song is sung to hint at the awakening of warm feelings in their hearts.

5) The chorus sings about the fate of Ushiwaka, comparing him to the moon behind the trees, as well as to a mountain cherry, blooming alone after the season.

6) When dusk falls, guided by the flowers, the *yamabushi* takes Ushiwaka to all the places in and near Kyoto famed for their cherry blossoms.

7) Asked his identity by Ushiwaka, the *yamabushi* tells him that he is the Great Goblin of the mountain, and that Ushiwaka should learn military arts so that he may destroy the Heike. Saying that he will come to meet Ushiwaka the next day, he disappears, flying over the clouds.

Ai-kyōgen
A few *Ai-kyōgen* enter as small tree-leaf goblins. They are to fight with Ushiwaka, to help him practice military arts. However, they are scared, and exit without meeting the boy.

Act 2.

1) Ushiwaka enters with a halberd in hand, and sings, describing his appearance as a handsome and brave youth, which would inspire awe even in demons and fiends.

2) The Great Goblin, the *Nochi-shite,* enters in his own form in the magnificent attire of a *tengu*, and, after telling who he is, mentions the names of famous goblins from various provinces, who attend on him, making the mountains and trees shake as they approach. (They do not appear on stage.)

3) Ushiwaka tells the Goblin that he refrained from wounding the small goblins even slightly, lest he should be scolded by his teacher. The Goblin is moved by the boy who thinks so dearly of his teacher, and in a *katari,* he tells Ushiwaka how Chang Liang (Jpn. Chōryō; d. 168 BC) learned the secrets of military tactics from the great master Huang Shih Kung, having moved that master by his reverent attitude toward him.

4) The Goblin encourages the boy, an offspring of a renowned Genji general, and promises that he will help and protect him so that he may finally conquer the Heike. The Goblin bids farewell to Ushiwaka, and flies up to the tree tops and disappears.

According to the *Heiji Monogatari* and the *Gikeiki* (Chronicle of Yoshitsune), Ushiwaka stayed at Kurama Temple until he was fourteen years old. Then he left the temple and went to Hiraizumi in the northernmost province of Mutsu (in the present-day Iwate Prefecture), where he stayed under the protection of Fujiwara no Hidehira (1096–1187) until the outbreak of the war between the Heike and the Genji. The Goblin's prediction came true. In this war, the young Genji leader Yoshitsune, the one-time Ushiwaka, helped to destroy the Heike and thereby clear the past shame of his family.

As for Ushiwaka's learning military arts from a goblin, one of the old printed versions of the *Heiji Monogatari* briefly mentions how the boy practiced the art with a goblin at night. Apart from these basic facts, *Kurama Tengu* is largely fiction. There are many popular stories and *jōruri* songs of the time that tell all sorts of fantastic stories about Ushiwaka as a young boy and a handsome youth, making him one of the most popular historical figures in Japan. Some scholars attribute the source of such stories to a contemporary *jōruri* song, no longer extant. It is considered that *Kurama Tengu* may have also been based more or less upon that source.

Kurama Tengu is a play of great dramatic appeal, but what is the secret of its appeal? First of all, its *Shite* is a goblin. The goblin, usually portrayed as a conceited, inhuman monster, is here presented as a being with a human heart who laments the coldness of people toward a stranger, is moved by the tenderness of a young boy, and takes cares of him like a father. This humanity in a non-human being, this tenderness in a hard-hearted monster, is one of the secrets of the play's great dramatic appeal.

No less dramatic is the *Kokata,* the young Ushiwaka. His personal background itself is so deeply dramatic as to be sung or narrated about in numerous songs and tales, as has already been mentioned. His popularity as a dramatic subject can be attested to by the number of Noh plays about him. He appears in ten plays currently performed, as a *shite,* as a *tsure*, or as a *kokata* playing either a child's or an adult's part. (They are: *Ataka, Eboshi-ori, Funa-Benkei, Hashi-Benkei, Kumasaka, Kurama Tengu, Settai, Shōzon, Tadanobu,* and *Yashima.*) Only one other character appears in such a large number of Noh plays—Ono no Komachi, yet even she appears only in five Noh in the current repertoire.

In *Kurama Tengu*, Ushiwaka is presented as a charming young boy who captivates the heart of a goblin, and as a brave youth who practices military arts in order to achieve his ambition. Thus, there is a combination of two characters of great and antagonistic dramatic appeal—a wild, rough *yamabushi* priest, who later appears as a powerful supernatural goblin, and an elegant and youthful temple page, each devoted to the other.

In addition to these two characters, the songs in *Kurama Tengu* are of a great lyrical beauty that intensifies the dramatic effects. For example, the scenes of the rendezvous of the Goblin and Ushiwaka are accompanied by songs quoted from classical sources that describe the beautiful mountain landscape with cherry blossoms in full bloom.

Near the top of Mt. Kurama, about 1.6 km from the temple's main hall, is the vale called Sōjōgadani (Archbishop's Valley), where the goblin is said to have taught Yoshitsune, and from which one can easily descend the other side of the mountain to the Kibune River and Kibune Shrine. It is

Kibune Shrine to which the *Gikeiki* tells us that Ushiwaka went every night; and it is the same shrine that figures prominently in the play known as *Kanawa* (The Iron Crown; in *Troubled Souls*), which is based upon an episode in the *Tale of the Heike.* Transformed into a demon so that she might kill the faithless man and his lover, in the Noh, a jealous woman is subdued by the power of the legendary yin–yang master (*onmyōji*) Abe no Seimei (fl. post-1005).

In the *Gikeiki,* the following account is given of Yoshitsune's nightly escapades:

> Ushiwaka completely forgot all traces of his studies, and thought only of rebellion day and night. "If I'm going to lead a revolt, I must master unparalled fighting techinques," he thought. . . .
>
> In the depths of Mt. Kurama there was a dale called Sōjōgadani, where someone had long ago built a shrine to the god of Kibune, who performed great miracles, and where learned holy men had practiced devotions. It had been a place of wonders—the sound of bells, and the beating of the Shinto priests' *kagura* drums, could always be heard. . . . But the miraculous powers of the buddhas had weakened the powers of the gods. The abandoned buildings were now the abode of goblins, and after the sun had set in the west, weird specters shrieked, frightening away all those who might have come in order to seclude themselves in retreat.
>
> After Ushiwaka heard about the place, he pretended to work at his studies as usual during the daytime, but at night, . . . he began going regularly to Kibune Shrine alone, wearing armor called Shikitae (a gift from the abbot) and a sword with gold fittings. "Hail, O Great and All-Merciful deity, O Great Bodhisattva Hachiman," he would pray with joined palms. "Preserve the Genji! If you grant my wish, I shall build you a magnificent shrine with twenty-five hundred acres of fields." Having made this his vow, he would turn and face the southwest, and would pretend that the surrounding bushes and shrubs were the Taira family members. Then he would slash away with all his might at one of two great trees, which he dubbed Kiyomori. . . . And then at dawn he would return to his quarters and lie down under the covers without anyone ever knowing about it.
>
> —Gikeiki, *"Ushiwaka's Visits to Kibune," 44–45*

And in the *Heiji Monogatari*, the following passage can be found:

> The youngest brother, Ushiwaka, became a student of Ācārya Gakujitsu of Kurama Temple's Zenrinbō (Hall of the Zen Forest), himself

a disciple of Ācārya Rennin of the Tōkōbō (Hall of the Eastern Light), and came to be called Shanaō. When he was about 11, he remembered what his mother had told him, and saw the genealogies of various houses, and thus learned that he was truly the scion of Emperor Seiwa in the tenth generation and of Rokuson-ō [Tsunemoto] in the eighth generation; the successor of Tada no Mitsunaka (Manjū); the descendant of the Iyo Lay Priest, Yoriyoshi; the progeny of Hachiman Tarō Yoshiie; the grandson of the Rokujō Magistrate, Tameyoshi; and the youngest son of the former Chief of the Imperial Stables of the Left, Yoshitomo. It was terrible, the more he thought of fulfilling his father's true ideal and overthrowing the Taira clan. In the day, he studied all day long, but at night he was taught martial arts all night long. In Sōjōgadani, it is said that he studied military techniques with a *tengu* every night, among them, "quick feet" and "flying stance"—things that cannot be thought of as any human techniques.

—Heiji Monogatari, *An Old Printed Version; "Ushiwaka's Flight to Oshu,"* 462

Kurama Tengu is classified as a fifth-group (or ending) Noh by all five schools. Kunio Komparu places it among the *hataraki* pieces of the fifth group, and Haruo Nishino places it in his *Tengu-mono* (goblin pieces) subcategory of the fifth group, but we have classified it as the only *Tengu-mono* of the fifth group with a *mai-bataraki.*

Scene: Sōjōgatani ("Archbishop's Valley"), near the top of Mt. Kurama, north of Kyoto, above and behind the buildings of Kurama Temple.

Time: Spring (the third lunar month), in the late Heian period (approx. 1172).

Characters and Costumes:

Mae-shite A *yamabushi* priest (the Great Goblin in disguise), wearing a *chōkin* headpiece, a *suzukake* stole over a *mizugoromo* robe, an *atsuita kitsuke,* a white *ōkuchi* divided skirt, and a small sword, carrying prayer beads.

Kyōgen A servant from the Western Valley, wearing a *noriki-zukin* headdress, a *mizugoromo* robe, and a striped *noshime kitsuke,* carrying a letter.

Mae-kokata Ushiwaka-maru (as Shanaō), wearing a *nuihaku kitsuke* and *chigo-bakama* (acolyte divided skirt).

Mae-kokata Taira children (4 or 5), dressed like Ushiwaka-maru.

Mae-waki A priest of the Eastern Valley, wearing *sumi-boshi* head gear, a *mizugoromo* robe, a plaid *atsuita,* and a white *ōkuchi* divided skirt, carrying prayer beads.

Mae-waki-tsure Lesser priests in attendance, dressed like the *Waki.*

Nochi-kokata Ushiwaka-maru, wearing a white *hachimaki* headband, a white *mizugoromo* robe, an *atsuita kitsuke,* and a white *ōkuchi* divided skirt, carrying a *naginata* halberd.

Nochi-shite The Great Goblin of Mt. Kurama, in a typical *tengu* costume, wearing an *ō-beshimi* mask, a colored *hachimaki* headband, an *aka-gashira* long red wig, a great *tokin* headpiece, an *atsuita kitsuke* under a lined *kariginu,* and a *hangire* divided skirt, carrying a large feather fan.

Ai-Kyōgen *Konoha tengu* ("Tree-leaf Goblins"; usually 2).

Dance action: *Mai-bataraki*

Author: Attributed to Miyamasu (The origins of this late Muromachi-period actor-playwright, to whom *Eboshi-ori* [in *Troubled Souls*] is also attributed, remain obscure.)

Kurama Tengu

鞍馬天狗

—ACT 1—

NANORI *The* Shite, *a* yamabushi, *enters and stands at the* jō-za.

Nanori, *Spoken*

SHITE

This person lives
At Archbishop's Valley in the inner heights of Mt. Kurama,[1] a *yamabushi* priest.
Now, at this temple,
A flower-viewing party is going to be held. Having heard about this,
I have a mind to betake myself there and as an outsider to see the tree tops in bloom.

The Shite *withdraws to the* kōken-za *and sits down. The* Kyōgen, *a temple servant, enters with a letter and stands at the* jō-za. *During his speech, several* Kokata *enter, among them, Shanaō, in last place, followed by the* Waki, *the head priest, and two or three* Waki-tsure, *attendant priests. They stand on the* hashi-gakari.

Spoken

KYŌGEN

I am one
Who serves in the Western Valley at Kurama Temple.
Now, surrounding this same temple, there are a Western Valley and an Eastern Valley,[2]
And each valley alternately serves as host for the annual flower-viewing party.
This year it is the turn of the Western Valley to be host
But as the people from the Eastern Valley have not yet arrived,

---

[1] Mt. Kurama is directly north of Kyoto's Imperial palace. Halfway up the mountain is a large Buddhist temple, Kurama-dera, founded in 770, when, according to the legend, a monk named Gantei had a dream that he should allow himself to be guided to a sacred site while sitting on on the saddle of a white horse. He followed the instructions given in the dream and his horse brought him to the foot of Mt. Kurama. Climbing the mountain, he was attacked by a fierce demoness, but he was then rescued by the Buddhist deity, Bishamon-ten. In gratitude, Gantei built a small thatched temple at the site of his rescue and dedicated it to the guardian deity known in Japan as Tamon-ten or Bishamon-ten (Skt. Vaiśravaṇa). Bishamon-ten was regarded as a powerful protector who would defend the capital from all evil coming from the north. However, the mountain is more famous for the legendary Kurama Tengu, a human-like creature who was highly proficient in martial disciplines. Archbishop's Valley (pronounced "Sōjōgatani" in the Kanze school, the actual place is today pronounced "Sōjōgadani") is a large dale on the mountainside that lies 1.6 km northwest of the temple's main hall. The

Kayō ni sōrō mono wa
Kurama no yama[1] no oku Sōjōgatani ni sumai suru
  yaku-sō nite sōrō.
Sate mo tōzan ni oite1
Hanami no yoshi uketamawari oyobi sōrō aida

Tachi-koe yoso nagara kozue wo mo nagamebaya to zonji sōrō.

Kayō ni sōrō mono wa.
Kurama no Nishitani no tera ni tsukae-mōsu nōriki nite sōrō.
Satemo tōzan ni oite Nishitani, Higashitani tote goza sōrō.[2]

Mainen ban ni atarite hanami no kai no goza sōrō.

Tōnen wa Nishitani no ban nite sōrō.

Higashitani no menmen imada oide naku sōrō aida

Gikeiki (pp. 44–45) states that it "had been a place of miracles, . . . but the glory of the buddhas and the power of the gods had become weakened. . . . The abandoned buildings had become the abode of goblins."

Note that *tōzan* in the next line, which would normally be translated "this mountain," is given as "this temple," since major temples are referred to as "mountains," and their names are written with the suffix *–san* / *–zan*.

[2] Sōjōgatani fell off in a Western Valley and an Eastern Valley on opposite sides of the mountain, the Western Valley leading down to Kibune River and Kibune Shrine, the setting of the revengeful-fiend play *Kanawa* (in *Troubled Souls*). As mentioned in the next line, the priests living in the two valleys apparently took turns holding flower-viewing parties. This year, it is the turn of the Western Valley to host the event. In the following speech, sometimes the following phrase is included, as indicated by Sanari (2:949): *Toko ni tōnen wa ichidan to migoto nite sōrō* (Truly, this year, the cherries are blooming in unusual splendor).

I have received orders to deliver this letter to them;
I must set out on my way quickly.
I wonder what the people of the Eastern Valley could be up to,
For by all rights they should be here already.

The Kyōgen *looks toward the* hashi-gakari *and sees Ushiwaka-maru, accompanied by five or six young boys, as well as the Priest of the Eastern Valley* (Waki) *and his attendant priests.*

Mondō

KYŌGEN

Well, and here they come.

The Kyogen *approaches the group and sits on the floor, bowing toward them as he speaks.*

KYŌGEN

I wish to speak to you.
I have come bearing a letter from the Western Valley.

WAKI

What's that? You say you have a letter from the Western Valley?
Well, then, I will look at it.

KYŌGEN

That I do, indeed, and here it is.
Please read it at once.

The Waki *reads the letter.*

WAKI

Well, well. "The cherry blossoms in the Western Valley are at their best now.
Why is it that we do not have the pleasure of your visit?
Please permit us to send you a word. An old poem goes:

Kakaru

'Should you miss them now, you would surely regret it—flowers at their best,

Spoken

There's not a bud yet to bloom, nor a single petal falling!' "[3]

---

[3] Lines 26–27: Sanari and others state that the source of the poem is unknown, but that it is attributed to "Lord Sadayori," or Fujiwara no Sadayori (995–1045). Nishino (1998: p. 87, n10) notes that the *Yōkyoku Shūyōshō* also attributes the poem to Sadayori, but it does not appear in either version of the *Sadayori-shū* (in KT 3-1 and *Zoku Gunsho Ruiju,* 430). Although all commentators remark that the source poem remains undiscovered, compare it with this poem by Nijō no Tametō (1341–81), which appears in the *Dairin gushō* (KT 6-1): ***Kyō mizu wa** / **Kainakaramashi** / **Chiri mo sezu** / **Saki mo nokosanu** / **Yama-zakura** kana* (Should you miss them now, / You would surely lament it— / Neither do they fall, / Nor 's there a bud left to bloom. / The wild mountain cherry—ah!). Though different poems, they are obviously very

Kono fumi o mochite maire to no on-koto nite sōrō.
Mazu isoide mairabaya to zonji sōrō.
Makoto ni Higashitani no menmen wa nani o shite oraruru ka.

Mohaya on-ide arisō na mono ja.

Iya kore e on-ide nite sōrō.

Ikani mōshi sōrō.
Nishitani yori no on-tsukai nite mairite sōrō.

Nani to Nishitani yori no fumi to sōrō ya.

Sate wa myōzuru nite sōrō.

Nakanaka no koto, sunawachi kore ni on-fumi no sōrō.
Goran sōrae.

Naninani Nishitani no hana ima o sakari to miete sōrō ni

Nado on-otozure ni mo azukarazaru.
Ippitsu keijō seshime sōrō. Koga ni iwaku:

Kyō mizu wa kuyashikaramashi hana-zakari

Saki mo nokorazu, chiri mo hajimezu.[3]

---

closely related, as can be seen by looking at the bold sections, which are identical in both poems. It cannot be due to coincidence that *yama-zakura* in Tametō's poem is echoed by the *yama-zato* in the poem based on Yorimasa's that follows almost immediately.

As Ze-ami's nephew and successor, On-ami (1398–1467) is recorded as having performed the play in the year Kanshō 6 (1465; *see* Sanari 2:947), it is possible that Tametō's poem is actually the foundation poem (*honka*) for the *waka* in the play. In any event, if the poem in the play is really by Sadayori, then it is obvious that Tametō's later poem is very closely based upon it.

Kakaru

What an interesting poem!
Even if we get no tidings,
We should be waiting under the trees.

Age-uta, *au*

CHORUS

When cherry trees bloom,
We will send you a message, said men on the mountain,
We will send you a message, said men on the mountain,
Here comes their messenger. Put the saddle on the horse—[4]
Saddle-horse Mountain's pale cherries[5] are in full bloom;
Being guided by the branches plucked to guide the way,
Never lost in the mountain depths, under the trees,
Let us sit together and view the flowers.

They enter the stage and sit down at the waki-za *and before the* daishō.

Spoken

WAKI

Is there a servant here?

KYŌGEN

At your service, Your Reverence.

WAKI

Since there are some young boys with us,
I request that you sing and dance something for them.

KYŌGEN

As you say, Your Reverence.

KOMAI *by the* Kyōgen, *who sings while he dances.*

---

[4] Lines 31–34: These lines are based on a poem by Minamoto no Yorimasa (1106–80) written on the topic of "cherry blossoms" that appears in the *Yorimasa-shū* (KT 3-1: 63): ***Hana sakaba** / **Tsugeyo to iishi** / **Yama**-mori **no** / Kuru oto sunari / Ko**ma ni kura** oke* (When cherry trees bloom, / Let us send you a message, / Said the men on the mountain— / Their approach can now be heard; / Put the saddle on the horse.)

In the play, the author has replaced *koma* (a more poetic term for horse) with the more prosaic *uma*. There is also wordplay: *uma ni **kura*** (saddle on the horse) → ***kura**ki **Kura**ma* (dark Kurama, where the brightness of the cherry blossoms contrasts nicely with the dark image of the mountain); in another sense, *uma no **kura*** is a *jo-kotoba* (*see* Glossary) that "introduces" Mt. **Kura**ma (here, the association is one of sound).

[5] "Pale cherries" (*uzu-zakura*): Originally, *uzu* was a kind of decoration used on a Chinese-style (= highly ornate) saddle (cf. Nishino 1998: p. 87, n11); *uzu-zakura* is a special type of

Geni omoshiroki uta no kokoro.
Tatoi otozure naku tote mo
Kokage nite koso matsu beki ni

Hana sakaba
Tsugen to iishi, yamazato no,
Tsugen to iishi, yamazato no,
Tsukai wa kitari, uma no kura.[4]

Kurama no yama no uzu-zakura[5]

Ta-ori shiori o shirube nite
Oku mo mayowaji saki tsuzuku.
Kokage ni nami-ite izaiza hana o nagamen.

Ikani nōriki.

On-mae ni sōrō.

Shōnin o tomonaite aru aida
Nani nite mo ikkyoku kanade sōrae.

Kashikomatte sōrō.

---

cherry, for which Mt. Kurama is famous, and whose blossoms are of a pale (*usui*) pink hue. Compare this poem written by Sadayori (*Sadayori-shū,* no. 45, in KT 3): "***Usu-zakura to iu*** *o hito no mote* ***kitari*** *kereba*": *Kore ya kono /* ***Oto*** *ni kikitsuru /* ***Usu-zakura*** */* ***Kurama no yama*** *ni /* ***Sak****eru naru beshi* ("On when people come especially [to view] the pale cherry blossoms": Indeed, yes, indeed, / These pale pink cherry blossoms / Can hear the jingling sound of / Uzu on saddles, on Mt. / Kurama, making them bloom).

Note that I have made bold words in the poem that also appear in the text around this area. Sadayori's poem seems to be a link that ties many of these images together. Indeed, I have highlighted *oto* (above), since it is only Sadayori's poem that serves as the 'link' between Yorimasa's poem and the actual Noh text.

Note that this pun works because in ancient orthography *uzu* and *usu* were written with exactly the same *kana*—i.e., no marks were used to indicate the voicing of consonants.

Of charming toys, there is an abundance:
Pâpier-maché faces and painted boy dolls,
Pretty peasant knots, and knots of bamboo grass,
Yamashina knotted cords, and whirling pinwheels,
Nesting inside a calabash, a tiny titmouse,
Pair of migrating birds snuggled in a walnut,
Pretty tiger-brindled puppy dog,
Self-righting Daruma doll, whirling rattle drum,
A colorful ball—and a small bow that dances!

During the komai, *the* Shite *enters and proceeds to near the* metsuke-bashira *and sits down cross-legged with a resounding thump. The* Kyōgen *sees him.*

KYŌGEN

Huh? There is a *yamabushi,* whose face I've never seen before.
Those from other temples are never allowed to attend the ceremonies of our temple.
I will inform His Reverence of this matter.
To the Waki — Excuse me, Your Reverence, I have a matter to convey to you.
There is an unfamiliar *yamabushi* over there.
He is a most outrageous fellow.
Let us chase him away from here.

WAKI

Wait! Indeed, this party
Is attended by the children of two eminent families, the Genji and the Heike.
An outsider like him has no place here.
However, to tell him so would be an act of discrimination. Therefore,
It would be best that they see the flowers tomorrow.
For today, I beg you all to leave this place.

KYŌGEN

No, no, as it is the honorable law here,
Let us chase him away from here.

WAKI

No, it is enough for all of us to leave this place.

KYŌGEN

As you say, Your Reverence.

Itaikeshitaru mono ari.
Hariko no kao ya nuri chigo
Shishi shiya musubi ni sasa musubi
Yamashina musubi ni kaza-guruma.
Hyōtan ni yadoru yamagara
Kurumi ni fukeru tomo-garasu
Tora madara no e no koro
Okiyagari ko-boshi furi-tsuzumi
Temari ya odorimasu ko-yumi.

Yaa. Kore ni minarenu kyaku-sō no sōrō.

Sōjite tōzan ni oite tazan no yakara sankai kinsei nite sōrō aida

Kono yoshi mōshi-hikitate mōsō.
Ikani mōshi sōrō.

Are ni kyaku-sō no watari sōrō.
Kore wa chikagoro rōzeki naru mono nite sōrō.
Ottachōzuru nite sōrō.

Shibaraku. Sasugani ni kono on-zashiki to mōsu ni
Gen-Pei ryōka no tōgyō-tachi onoono goza sōrō ni

Kayō no gaijin wa shikaru bekarazu sōrō.
Shikaredomo, mata kayō ni mōseba hito o erami mōsu ni nite sōrō aida

Hana o ba myōnichi koso goran sōrō bekere.
Mazu, mazu kono tokoro o ba on-tachi arōzuru nite sōrō.

Iya, iya, sore wa gojō nite sōraedomo
Ano kyaku-sō o ottachōzuru nite sōrō.

Iya, tada on-tachi arōzuru nite sōrō.

Kashikomatte sōrō.

They all exit, leaving behind only Shanaō and the Shite.
Shanaō sits at the waki-za.

KYŌGEN

What is to be made of this?
He insists that I should refrain from doing a thing
 to which he should have no objection.
And allowing an unfamiliar *yamabushi* to desecrate this
 place makes me increasingly angry.
If it were up to me, I would give him a good hard punch!

(*The* Kyōgen *raises his fist and mimes striking the* Shite.)

Exits. Oh, how angry, how angry I am!

Sashi, *awazu*

SHITE

If, from far away, one sees a house with a cherry tree
 in bloom, he would go right in,
With no discrimination between the high and low born,
 or friends and strangers—[6]
This is the way of people in springtime, I thought.
Away from the way of worldly life is Kurama Temple,
Dedicated to Vaiśravaṇa,[7] a buddha of great mercy.
Yet these are people estranged from mercy.

Kakaru

KOKATA

Indeed, beneath the cherry blossoms, guests of half a day;
Beneath the moon, acquaintances of a single night—[8]

---

[6] Lines 75–76: Based upon a Chinese couplet by T'ang poet Po Chü-i (772–846) that appears in the *Wakan Rōei–shū* [Japanese and Chinese Poems to Sing] (115), compiled by Fujiwara no Kintō (966–1041): *Yao chien jen chia hua pien ju / Pu lun kuei chien yu ch'in shu* [***Haruka ni jinka o mite hana areba sunawachi iru / Kisen to shinso to o ronzezu***] (If, from afar, one sees a house with flowers [blooming], he would just go right in, / With no discrimination between high and low born, or friends and strangers). Note that in the original Chinese, *kuei chien* usually means "close or distant relatives," whereas the phrase was adopted in Japanese to mean "high born and lowly born"; also, *hua* in classical Chinese means simply "flowers," with a strong emphasis upon plum blossoms, whereas *hana* to the Heian courtier meant "cherry blossoms" unless otherwise modified.

Note also that the *Wakan Rōei–shū* contains three types of poems: 1) Chinese poems by Chinese authors (*shih*), 2) Chinese poems by Japanese authors (*kanshi*), and 3) Japanese poems (*waka*). When quoting Chinese poems, both the Chinese and Japanese readings are given, as above.

[7] Tamon-ten: This is another name for Bishamon-ten (Skt. Vaiśravaṇa), one of the Four Heavenly Guardians, who protects the northern quarter. Note that Kurama Temple is directly north of Kyoto's Imperial Palace. In Japan, he is also considered one of the Seven Deities of Good Fortune.

Kore wa ikana koto.
Kurushūnai koto o muyō ni sei to ōseraruru.

Kono go-zashiki o samasasuru mo kyaku-sō-dono to omoeba hara ga tatsu.

Soregashi ga mama ni naru, naraba kore o hitotsu itadakasetai na.

Hara tatsu ya, hara tatsu ya!

Haruka ni jinka o mite hana areba sunawachi iru.

Ronzezu kisen to shinso to o wakimaenu o koso.[6]

Haru no narai to kiku mono o
Ukiyo ni tōki Kurama-dera
Ho(n)zon wa daihi Tamon-ten.[7]
Jihi ni moretaru hitobito kana.

Geni ya hana no moto no hanjitsu no kaku
Tsuki no mae no ichiya no tomo[8]

---

[8] Lines 81–82: Based upon a section in Chapter 3 ("The Lesser Captain's Return to the Capital") of the *Heike Monogatari* (NKBT 29, p. 224): ***Hana no moto no hanjitsu no kaku, tsuki no mae no ichiya no tomo,*** *ryojin ga hito murasame no tsugiyuku ni ichiju no kage ni tachi-yorite, wakaruru nagori mo oshiki zo kashi* (We suffer the pain of parting even when we leave behind **guests with whom we have spent half a day beneath the cherry blossoms, or acquaintances of a single night beneath** [= gazing at] **the moon,** or a traveler with whom we have sheltered under the same tree during a passing shower). The lines in the *Heike* are themselves thought to be quoted from Part 5 of the *Jikkunshō,* a mid–thirteenth-century collection of tales illustrating moral principles and presented in ten parts: ***Hana no moto*** *to ni haru bakari o chigiri,* ***tsuki no mae ni ichiya*** *o kagiru* ***tomo*** *made mo* (Vows true only in spring beneath the cherry blossoms, a friend only for a single night beneath the moon). Teiji Ichiko (NKBT 29, p. 54) says that the reference to lodging under the same tree, which is said to derive from a no longer extant version of the *Chūin-gyō* (Skt. Antarabhāva-sūtra), and which is very common in the Noh, derives from the *Seppō Myōgen Ron: Arui wa hito-mura ni tokoro ori, ichiju no moto ni yadori, ichiga no nagare o kumu, . . . mina zensei no ketsuen nari* (Whether we live in the same village, take shelter under the same tree, [or] draw water from the same stream, . . . these are all due to karma from a previous life).

Even such encounters are bound with friendship.

Spoken Oh, I am sorry for you. Come nearer and look at the flowers.

SHITE

Ah, you have taken me by surprise! Where e'en a pining[9] cricket's
Voice[10] is stilled, this deep-mountain[11] cherry
You obey and give kind words. I appreciate it deeply. On this mountain—

Kakaru

KOKATA

I live, a wisp of white cloud
Floating all alone, by nobody known.[12]

Spoken

SHITE

Would there were someone to be my companion; e'en Takasago's

KOKATA

Pine, waiting for age-old

SHITE

Friends—a flock of ravens[13]

Age-uta, *au*

CHORUS

Laughs at and mocks me, sowing the seed of scandal,[14]
Causing word-leaves to grow, thick and wild in love-grass
Of ancient root.[15] Do not shut out the old priest, plum-tree by the hedge,[16]

---

[9] *Matsu* (pine) and *matsu* (to wait) are *jo-kotoba* for *oto / ne* (sound, and by extension here, voice), as in *matsu ga ne* (the sound of [wind in] the pines); there is also an implied pun on "waiting for a friend" (*see* Note 10).

[10] Lines 85–86: *Matsumushi no / ne* recalls lines from the *Kokin-shū*—from the Japanese Preface by Ki no Tsurayuki (ca. 872–945): ***Matsumushi no ne ni*** *tomo o shinobi* ([one] turns one's thoughts to a friend at [hearing] the cry of the pining [= pine] cricket); and from poem 202 (anonymous): *Aki no no ni / Hito* ***matsu mushi no*** */ Koe sunari . . .* (On the autumn moors, / Someone waits; the pine cricket's / Crying can be heard . . .). In the poem, *hito* ***matsu*** (waiting for someone; someone who waits) → ***matsu****mushi no koe* (pine cricket's cry; pining cricket's cry).

[11] *Ne ni tatenu* ***mi*** (body that gives off no sound) → ***mi-yama*** (deep mountains) → ***yama-****zakura* (wild cherry trees/blossoms).

[12] Lines 88–89: *Tare ka* ***shira****nu* (who I am is unknown) → ***Shira****kumo* (white clouds). *Shirakumo no tachi-*: *Shirakumo* is a *makura-kotoba* ("pillow word") for *tatsu* (rise, float up). Also, the *Renju Gappeki-shū* (RGS), a late fifteenth-century manual for word association in poetry and *renga* (linked verse) by Nijō no Kanera (1402–81), contains the following entry (26): "If 'cloud,' then 'rise.' " Nishino (1998: p. 88, n23) maintains that although the *Kokata* (Ushiwaka) chants these lines, in terms of context and content, they belong to the *Shite*.

[13] Lines 89–92: These lines are directly taken from a poem by Fujiwara no Okikaze (fl. ca. 900) in the *Kokin-shū* (909): ***Tare o ka mo / Shiru hito ni sen / Takasago no / Matsu mo***

Sore sae yoshi wa aru mono o
Ara, itawashi ya! Chikō yotte hana goran sōrae.

Omoi-yorazu ya! Matsumushi[9] no

Ne[10] ni dani tatenu mi-yama-zakura[11] o
On-tomurai no arigatasa yo, kono yama ni

Ari tomo tare ka shirakumo no
Tachi-majiwaraneba shiru hito nashi.[12]

Tare o ka mo shiru hito ni sen Takasago no

Matsu mo mukashi no

Tomo-garasu no[13]

On-mono-warai no tane maku ya.[14]
Koto no ha shigeki koi-gusa no

Oi[15] o na hedate so kakio no (m)ume[16]

---

mukashi mo / Tomo *naranaku ni* (Would there were someone / To be my companion; / E'en Takasago's / Pine, waiting for age-old friends / Is not my friend from of old). Note that in lines 91–92: *Mukashi no* ***tomo*** (age-old friends) → ***tomo****-garasu* (flock of ravens).

[14] Lines 92–93: *Tomo-garasu* (= *karasu*) is an *engo* (associated word) with "laugh" as well as with "seed." According to Sanari (2:953), *Tomo-garasu no on-monowarai no tane maku ya* (The mockery and laughter of a flock of ravens sows the seeds of scandal!) was a popular saying. RGS (396): "If 'raven' ('flock of ravens'), then 'laughter.' " Note also that the *Renga Tsukiai* (RT), a companion to the *Renju Gappeki-shū,* has this entry (115): "With 'raven,' 'pine,' " which highlights the juxtaposition of the pine with a flock of ravens.

[15] Lines 93–94: *Koi-gusa no /* ***Oi*** (growth of love-grass; love-grass of ancient [root]) → ***Oi*** *o na hedate so* (Do not shut out the old [priest]). "Love-grass" is an ancient term that was used even in the *Man'yō-shū.* The conceit is that one's love is like grasses (weeds) that grow wild and cannot be completely plucked out of one's heart. Our favorite poem on the subject is by Princess Hirokawa (fl. late 6th cent.) in the *Man'yō-shū* (4:694): ***Koi-gusa*** *o / chikara-guruma ni / nana-guruma / tsumite kōraku / Waga kokoro kara* (The grass of my love— / Many large and strong wagons, / Seven large wagons, / It would fill if it were plucked / Out of the depths of my heart). This poem is quoted in a variant form in the fourth-group Noh play *Hyakuman.*

[16] RGS (300): "If 'plum,' then 'hedge (*kakine*).' " Lines 93–97 contain several words related to plants and their growth: *tane* (seed), *maku* (to sow), *ha* (leaf), *shigeki* (thick growth), *gusa* [= *kusa*] (grass), *oi* (growth), *kaki* (hedge; also, homonymous with 'persimmon'), *ume*

That a flowery kindness be revealed in full bloom.
Flowers have their appointment for three months in springtime;[17]
After an intimacy of only one night,
What will it be like afterword? All of a sudden
My heart soars skyward, thick growth of oak leaves—[18]
Instead of intimacy,
Only yearning increases,[19] oh, how grievous!

Mondō

SHITE

Please excuse me, but there is something I would like to ask you.
While all the other boys have left,
Why do you alone remain here?

KOKATA

Well, those boys are all members of the Heike clan,
And among them, the sons of Kiyomori,[20] lord of Aki Province. As it is
They are made much of by the entire Temple, and are the favorites of other cloisters, flourishing like cherry blossoms in season.[21]

Kakaru

Although I belong to the same temple,
I suffer humiliation in every way,
By the moon and flowers forsaken.

(plum), and *hana* (flower = cherry blossoms), and line 100 contains *nara* (oak). Concerning hedge (*kakiho*) → shut out, cf. RGS (178): "If 'hedge,' then 'separate/shut out.' "

[17] Line 97: Most commentators note that this line is quoted from an unknown source. NKBZ and NKBT both point out that *sanshun* means three months [in spring], while Itō says it means *haru sangatsu,* or "March, in spring." We have opted for the former, agreeing with Nishino that it means "the three months of spring" (*Yōkyoku Hyakuban,* p. 89, n27). Nishino adds that the phrase can be found in the *Ken'en* (Garden of Sayings).

[18] *Kokoro no sora ni* ***naru*** (my heart soars skyward) → ***nara****shiba no* (thick growth of oak leaves). *Narashiba* is a *jo-kotoba* for *nareru* (become intimate) in the next line (*see also* Note 19).

[19] Lines 100–102: Based on this poem by Kakinomoto no Hitomaro (d. 708–15) in the *Shin Kokin-shū* (11:1050): *Mi-kari suru / Kariba no Ono no /* ***Narashiba no / Nareba masarade / Koi*** *zo* ***masa****reru* (On the hunting ground, / The field for th' Imperial hunt, / Stand the leafy oaks; / Instead of intimacy, / Only yearning increases). An earlier, variant text of the poem appears in the *Man'yō-shū* (12: 3048) as an anonymous work.

[20] Taira no Kiyomori (1118–81), appointed governor of Aki Province in 1146, and traditionally said to have been a son of Emperor Shirakawa (1053–1129), was virtual dictator of the court and the government from the end of the Heiji Uprising (1160; *see* note 19 to *Matsuyama Tengu*) until his death. His sons included Shigemori, Munemori, Tomomori, and Shigehira, the last three of which feature in the Noh plays *Yuya, Funa-Benkei,* and *Senju,* respectively.

[21] *Ichiji no shōkan tazan no oboe:* This phrase means that the children of the Heike nobility

Sate koso hana no nasake nare.
Hana ni sanshun no yaku ari.[17]

Hito ni hitoyo o nare-somete
Nochi ikanaran uchitsuke ni
Kokoro sora ni narashiba no[18]

Nare wa masarade
Koi no masaran,[19] kuyashisa yo.

Ikani mōshi sōrō.

Tadaima no chigo-tachi wa minamina on-kaeri sōrō ni
Nani tote go-ichinin kore ni ha goza sōrō zo.

Sanzōrō tadaima no chigo-tachi wa Heike no ichimon.
Naka ni mo Aki no Kami, Kiyomori,[20] ga kodomo taru ni yori

Ichiji no shōkan tazan no oboe toki no hana tari.[21]

Mizukara mo dōzan ni ha sōraedomo
Yorozu menboku mo naki koto-domo nite
Tsuki ni mo hana ni mo suterarete sōrō.

---

were greatly respected and appreciated by Kurama Temple and thus by other temples, too.

Toki no hana tari: In the context of this play, the phrase means "like cherry blossoms in season." Note that Ze-ami often used the phrase *toki no hana* in his aesthetic treatises to indicate a wonderful, brilliant style of acting or stage presence that did not last—it was not true talent, but either the blush of youth or something fortuitous that evoked the right mood for the performance. It it used to refer to "the quickly fading beauty of the moment," like the beauty of youth, that fades with the passing of time.

Although Japanese commentators do not mention it, this phrase seems to be taken from Ze-ami's own writings. Note that in the *Fūshi Kaden* (ZZ, 56), Ze-ami wrote: *Tatoeba, haru no hana no koro sugite, natsukusa no hana o* ***shōkan*** *senzuru jibun* (*ji* = *toki*) *ni, haru no hana no fūtai bakari o etaran shite ga, natsukusa no hana wa nakute, sugishi haru no hana o mata mochite idetaran wa,* ***toki no hana*** *ni au beshi ya* (For example, when the season of spring flowers has passed and it is time to admire the grasses of summer, an actor who can only perform in the style of spring flowers will be unable to perform in the style of summer grasses; this portrayal of spring flowers after their time has passed should not take place, since the flowers should match the season). Note that "spring flowers" above means by convention "cherry blossoms," which matches the imagery in the play. Indeed, both the line in the play and the line from Ze-ami seem to be "in season." The end of the passage from Ze-ami means that no performance can be beautiful unless it is timely—which for him meant unless it matches the season in which it takes place.

SHITE

Spoken Oh, how distressing!
But in spite of all, your lordship[22] is
The third son Tokiwa[23] bore to your father.
Taking the character *sha* of Bishamon,
You were named Shanaō.[24]

Kakaru Oh, how distressing! Now that I know who you are—
Here at Kurama,[25] the moon is dark behind the trees,[26]

Sage-uta, *au*

CHORUS

By nobody seen, the cherry tree blooming in a
mountain hamlet,
After the flowers in other places have gone,
It should bloom,[27] if it blooms at all.
Ah, your distressing state moves one to deep pity.

Age-uta, *au* Pine wind[28] blows mournfully where flowers have fallen,
Pine wind blows mournfully where flowers have fallen,

---

[22] *Wajōrō: Wa* is a contraction of *waga* (my), and *jōrō* is a term used in addressing one whose rank is higher than one's own; thus, although we could have opted for "My Lord," we have rendered the phrase here as "your lordship." Haga and Sasaki (1:639n) point out that *jōrō* was originally a term used for senior Buddhist monks, and was later applied to higher ranking ladies (and also men) of the court. Much later in the Edo period, it came to be used for higher ranking courtesans of the pleasure quarters.

[23] Tokiwa Gozen, at first a lady-in-waiting to Emperor Konoe's widow, Fujiwara no Tashi (1140–1201), she later became a concubine of Minamoto no Yoshitomo (1123–60), to whom she bore three sons, the youngest of whom was Yoshitsune (1159–89?), who was thus half-brother of Yoritomo (1147–99) and Noriyori (1156–93) by a different mother. Yoshitomo had in all eight sons.

[24] Although the play derives the name Shanaō from the *sha* of Bishamon, the guardian deity of Kurama Temple, Itō (2:33) points out that the *Gikeiki* and other sources say that the name was formed of the *shana* of Birushana (Skt. Vairocana; also Dai-Nichi Nyorai, the principal Buddha of the Shingon sect), and, indeed, they are written with the same characters. This may well be, but the Iwanami (NKBT) version (p. 47) of the *Gikeiki* simply states: *On na o ba kaerarete Shana to zo mō[shi]keru* (He changed his name and was called Shana), without offering any derivation. The passage does go on, however, to add: *hibi ni Tamon ni nyūdō shite, muhan no koto o zo inorarekeru* (daily he entered the hall of Bishamon and prayed for the success of his revolt), which would seem to indicate that his name was indeed derived from the *sha* of Bishamon.

[25] *Tokoro no* ***kurai*** (here it is dark) → **Kura**ma.

[26] "The moon is dark behind the trees": From the sound of the word **Kura**ma comes the association with being dark (***kurai***), as seen in Note 25, which leads to the idea of *kokage no tsuki* (the moon [dark] in the shade of the trees) or *kogakure no tsuki* (the moon hidden by the trees), which itself leads on to the idea in the next line of the moon being unseen by anyone (*see* Note 27).

[27] Lines 119–21: Based upon a poem by Lady Ise (fl. early tenth century) in the *Kokin-shū* (1:68): ***Miru hito mo*** / ***Naki yamazato*** *mo* / ***Sakura-bana*** / ***Hoka no chirinan*** / ***Nochi*** *zo* ***saka****mashi* (By nobody seen, / The cherry tree blooming / In a mountain hamlet— / After other flow'rs had fall'n, / That it might not bloom till then!). Note that *hoka* is highlighted,

Ara, itawashi ya sōrō.
Sasu ga ni wajōrō[22] wa,
Tokiwa-bara[23] ni wa san-nan.
Bishamon no sha no ji o katadori
On-na o mo Shanaō to tsuke-mōsu.[24]
Ara, itawashi ya, on-mi o shireba
Tokoro mo Kurama[25] no kokage no tsuki[26]

Miru hito mo naki yamazato no sakura-bana

Yoso no chirinan nochi ni koso
Sakaba,[27] saku beki ni,
Ara, itawashi no on-koto ya!
Shōran[28] hana no ato toite
Shōran hana no ato toite

---

even though a different word, *yoso,* is used in the play: this is because the meaning is the same.

[28] According to Itō (2:33), *shōran* (pine wind) is a word used in *kanshi* (poetry in Chinese by Japanese authors) that was taken over as a phrase for use in pure Japanese *waka* poetry as *matsu no arashi* (pines in a storm / storm in the pines). These lines are derived from a poem by the Priest Jakuren (1139?–1202) in the *Shin Kokin-shū* (2:155): *Chirinikeri / Aware urami no / Tare nareba /* ***Hana no ato tou*** */ Haru no yamakaze* (The flow'rs have fallen. / Ah, whose jealously could have / Caused them to scatter? / The [stormy] mountain winds of spring / That visit still the "flowery grave"). Note that the characters for *yamakaze,* or "mountain winds," when written together as a single character, form the word *arashi,* or "storm."

Compare these phrases from other Noh plays—*Hanagatami:* ***Matsu no arashi*** *mo / Itsu shika ni /* ***Hana no ato tote*** */ Natsukashiki* . . . (The storm in the pines, too, / When indeed did it come, / Leaving this flowery grave? / Oh, how sad the memory . . .) [Itō 3:105]; *Tomonaga:* ***Hana no ato tou matsu****kaze ya /* ***Yuki*** *ni mo urami naruran* (The wind in the pines visits the flowery grave, / Becoming jealous even of the snow) [Itō, 2:414; Shimazaki, 2-1:176–77]; *Taisanpukun:* ***Matsu*** *no kaze /* ***Yuki*** *ni nari-yuku* ***hana*** *naraba /* ***Ato tou*** *tote mo yoshi mo nashi* (In the pine wind, / Like piling snow, flowers fall. / Then a visit [by the pine wind] after they are gone [or: mourning for what has passed away]— / What good can it be?) [Shimazaki, idem]; or *Futari Shizuka:* ***Yama****-zakura /* ***Yuki*** *ni fuki-nasu* ***hana no matsu****kaze / Shizuka ga* ***ato*** *o* ***toi****-tamae* (From the mountain cherries, / Like snow, flowers are blown by the pine wind / Quietly, for Shizuka's repose please pray.) [Shimazaki, 3-3: 60–61].

It should also be noted that in his *Go-on* (Five Tones), Ze-ami wrote: ***Hana no ato tou matsu****kaze wa /* ***Yuki*** *ni ya shizuka naruran* (The wind in the pines visits the "flowery grave" / And even the snow becomes quiet and calm). Ze-ami quotes this phrase from the play *Shizuka* by his dead father (Kan-ami), but it no longer remains in the current repertoire. Omote and Katō (p. 209) note that the phrase does not appear in the current versions of *Yoshino Shizuka* and *Futari Shizuka;* yet the resemblance to the closing lines of *Futari Shizuka* (given above) cannot be ignored. It is interesting to note also that Shizuka Gozen, the heroine of these plays, was later to become the lover of Yoshitsune; thus, in a play about Yoshitsune himself, these lines could meaningfully be adapted from lines in those plays or from Ze-ami's own quotation of them.

Falling down as flakes of snow, or as rain,[29]
The sad cries of a monkey echo in the clouds,
Breaking the heart of the one who hears them—[30]
The des'late landscape of a broken heart,
Where twilight is still lingering in the flowering tree tops,
The temple bell is heard tolling; night is slow to come.
Further along it is dark, on Mt. Kurama's mountain path,[31]
With cherry blossoms as our guide,

The Shite *lifts the* Kokata.

Let us go this way. Come with me, I pray.

Sage-uta, *au*

The Shite *goes about the stage with the* Kokata.

During these past days I accompanied you,
Showing you one renowned place after another.[32]
Sometimes we saw at
Atago and Takao the earliest flowers,
At Hira and Yokawa, those slow to blossom.
Yoshino and Hatsuse,[33] celebrated places—

---

[29] The word *yuki* (snow) at the head of this line in Japanese suggests that the author was familiar with at least the similar lines in *Tomonaga, Futari Shizuka,* or the *Go-on.*

Compare this couplet from a Ch'ü-era *fu*-style poem by Sung Yü (fl. third cent. BC) included in the *Wen Hsüan* (a Chinese classic covering a millennium of writing from the Chou dynasty on; see *Monzen,* 2:440–41): *Tan wei chao yun, mu wei hsing yü* [*Akatsuki ni asagumo to narite, yūgure ni tori-**yuku ame to naru***] (At dawn, I become the morning clouds; at evening, I become the passing shower). Note that the playwright has changed "clouds" to "snow" (*yuki*), perhaps to reflect the lines mentioned above in Note 28.

These words were uttered by a Celestial Maiden who appeared near the summit of Mt. Wu in eastern Szechwan to Hsiang, the King of Ch'ü. These lines, or poems based upon them, also appear in the Noh plays *Tōru* (in this volume), *Suma Genji, Funabashi* (*see* Shimazaki, *Restless Spirits,* p. 210), and *Uneme,* as well as in the "Aoi" chapter of *Genji* (cf. Tō no Chūjō's poem [Genji, 2:101]: ***Ame to nari*** */ Shigururu sora no / Ukikumo o / Izure no kata to / Wakite nagamen* [Has she become rain? / In these stormy, rain-filled skies, / Filled with brooding clouds, / In which direction, I wonder, / Should I look, then, to find her?]). The phrase is often quoted in stories, poetry, and Noh to describe not only the weather, but also the departed soul wandering midway between this world and the next as a cloud or as rain.

The tale of the Ch'ü king is also referred to in a line from a poem entitled *Kung-tzu hsing* (Song of a Young Lord) by Liu T'ing-chih (fl. ninth cent.) in the *T'ang Shih Hsüan* (see also *Kanshi Taikan* 1:662): *Wei yün wei yü, Ch'ü Hsiang wang* (As clouds she became [at dawn], as **rain she became** [at night], King Hsiang of Ch'ü).

Compare also this line from a *shih*-style poem by Middle T'ang poet Liu Yü-hsi (722–842), written upon the death of his wife: *Wei yü, wei yün, ching pu ch'ih* [***Ame to nari*** *kumo to ya narinikemu ima wa shirazu*] (Has she become rain? Or has she become clouds? Now I do not know), which is itself thought to be based upon either the *Wen Hsüan* original or the Liu T'ing-chih poem. Note that the entire line (see *Genji* 2:101; *see also* 314) is quoted by Tō no Chūjō a few lines before his poem.

Although this note may seem long, the educated viewers of the playwright's time would

Yuki to furi, ame to naru.[29]
Aien kumo ni sakende wa
Harawata o tatsu to ka ya,[30]
Kokoro sugo no keshiki ya.
Yūbe o nokosu hana no atari
Kane wa kikoete yo zo osoki.

Oku wa Kurama no yamamichi no[31]

Hana zo shirube naru.
Konata e irase tamae ya.

Satemo kono hodo o-tomo shite
Mise mōshitsuru na-dokoro no.[32]
Aru toki wa
Atago, Takao no hatsu-zakura,
Hira ya Yokawa no Oso-zakura,
Yoshino, Hatsuse[33] no na-dokoro o

---

have been expected to know all these references, and thus all the feelings and moods of the originals, and *Genji,* would overlap with their experience of the play itself.

[30] Lines 126–27: The previous line being based upon a Chinese poem led to these lines being based upon two different poems that appear adjacent to each other in the *Wakan Rōei–shū.* The first (No. 454) is by late T'ang poet Hsieh Kuan: *Pa hsia ch'iu shen / Wu ye chih ai yüan yüeh* [*Hakō ni aki fukashi / Goya no* ***aien*** *tsuki* ***ni sakebu***] (Autumn deepens in the gorges of Pa, / At dawn [lit. at the fifth watch of the night], the mournful monkeys howl at the moon); the playwright has moved away from "snow" and "rain" to "clouds" and "moon." The second (No. 455) is by Po Chü-i: *Chiang ts'ung Pa hsia ch'ü ch'eng tzu / Yüan kuo Wu-yang shih tuan ch'ang* [*E wa Hakō yori hajimete ji o nasu / Saru wa Buyō o sugi hajimete* ***harawata o tatsu***] (The Yangtze at first flows in the form of [the character for] Pa near the [three] gorges [of Pa]; / Beyond Wu-yang [a place south of Mt. Wu], the [doleful cries of] monkeys first break the hearts [of those who hear them]). Obviously, the association between line 125 and lines 126–27 are the references to Mt. Wu and mournful sounds.

[31] *Oku wa* ***kurai*** (In the depths it is dark / Further along [the path] it is dark) → ***Kurama no yama*** (Mt. Kurama) → ***yama****-michi* (mountain path).

[32] *Kono hodo o-tomo shite / Mise mōshitsuru na-dokoro* (During these past days I accompanied you, / Showing you one renowned place after another): These lines indicate the passage of time (how much is not indicated), during which the *tengu* has accompanied the young Yoshitsune to see the various spots around the Imperial capital famous for their cherry blossoms (*see also* Note 33).

[33] All of these places—Atago and Takao (in present-day Kyoto prefecture), Hira and Yokawa (Shiga), and Yoshino and Hatsuse (Nara)—in addition to being renowned for their beautiful cherry blossoms, are also centers of Shugendō, the ascetic Buddhist sect of the *yamabushi.* They are also famous for their association with *tengu.* Thus, it was to these places known for unsurpassed martial arts that the Great Goblin took Yoshitsune, in order to further his training as a military leader.

We have visited all, there is none left unseen.

Rongi, *au*

KOKATA

"As I think of it,
I can't help wondering who in the world you are,
You who do so much to amuse and cheer me up.
May I ask who you are? Tell me your name, I pray."

SHITE

"I will not hide my name from you any longer.
I am one who has lived on this mountain for many years,
The Great Goblin is none other than I.[34]

CHORUS

You should learn all the secrets of military arts so that
You may defeat and finally destroy the Heike clan.[35]
If such be what you set your heart on,
Tomorrow I will come here again and will meet you.
Fare thee well." With these words the *yamabushi* goes,
Knitting through the ravines of Archbishop's Valley,
Treading on the clouds he went flying away;
Treading on the mounting[36] clouds, he went flying away.

The Shite *kneels to the* Kokata.

INTERIM EXIT (NAKA-IRI) *Accompanied by raijo music, the* Shite *makes an interim exit. The* Kokata *exits after him.*

AI-KYŌGEN *Accompanied by raijo music, two* Ai-kyōgen, *an* omo *and an* ado, *small "Tree-Leaf" goblins, enter, to help Shanaō practice military arts.*

OMO

I who appear before you here am a Tree-Leaf Goblin who lives in Archbishop's Valley in the recesses of Mt. Kurama. (*Looks at* Ado:) And for what have you come out here?

ADO

I am not sure just what for, for I came out here just because you did.

---

[34] According to de Visser (p. 82), the Great Tengu of Mt. Kurama was named Sōjō-bō. Presumably, the valley on Mt. Kurama was named after the Buddhist cleric who had once lived there (*Gikeiki*, 44–45), and the *tengu* took his name from that of the valley.

[35] For more detail on the passing down of secret military arts, *see* Note 47 below. Note that the Hōshō, Konparu, and Kita (*shimo-gakari*) schools substitute three lines for lines 148–

Mi-nokosu kata mo araba koso.

Saru nite mo,
Ikanaru hito ni mashimaseba
Ware o nagusame tamōran.
On-na o nanori owashimase.

Ima wa nani o ka tsutsumu beki.
Ware kono yama ni toshi hetaru

Dai-tengu wa ware nari.[34]

Kimi hyōhō no daiji o tsutaete
Heike o horoboshi tamō beki nari.[35]
Samo oboshimesareba
Myōnichi sankai mōsu beshi.

Saraba to iite kyaku-sō wa
Dai-Sōjōgatani o wakete
Kumo o funde tonde yuku tatsu[36]
Kumo o funde tonde yuku.

(*The original Japanese text of the* Ai-kyōgen *is omitted here.*)

49: ***Kimi*** *Minamoto no tōryō nite, /* ***heihō*** *o uke-tatematsuri, /* ***Heike o*** *utase mōsan tame . . .* (As you are a leader of the Minamoto clan, / You should receive instruction on military strategy / in order that you might strike down the Heike clan).

[36] Lines 154–55: *kumo → tatsu.* RGS (26): "If 'clouds,' then 'rising/mounting.' "

OMO

If that is the case, I will narrate to you the reason I am here. Listen well.

ADO

With all my heart.

OMO

To begin with, on this mountain, those from the Western Valley and those from the Eastern Valley always meet each year to hold a flower-viewing party. This year it is the turn of the Western Valley to act as host. So the Eastern Valley priest came here with his acolytes and young wards to attend the party.

But the Great Goblin became so jealous that he decided to come and have a look, so he disguised himself as a *yamabushi.* But he was discovered by a servant, who insisted that they chase him out on the strength of the law that forbids the participation of outsiders from other temples, but the head priest said that there is a special dispensation for *yamabushi* at this temple, and that the flowers could be viewed just as well tomorrow. So he took his entourage and went right back home, leaving the son of Yoshitomo, Master Shanaō, behind, all by himself, and with a heavy heart.

When the Great Goblin saw what had happened, he questioned Master Shanaō about the reason for the dispersal of the priest and his entourage. Master Shanaō responded that the young wards were all scions of the Heike nobles, some of them even being sons of Kiyomori; they are made much of by the entire temple, and are also the favorites of other cloisters. Then, Master Shanaō added that though he himself is of this temple, he was very embarrassed about the position in which the Great Goblin had been placed, abandoned by both the moon and the flowers, and that he felt great pity for him.

When the Great Goblin heard this, he was deeply moved and said to Master Shanaō: "You are a chief of the Genji Clan, and when you said once in the past that you wanted to go flower viewing, I took you to see the blossoms on mounts Yoshino, Hatsuse, Atago, and Takao. Then you earnestly requested that I convey to you the great secrets of military strategy so that you could use them to overthrow the Heike Clan. Well, as you are both talented and clever, the secrets of the hidden hairpin, the hidden leaf, and the sign of the mist, I have already completed conveying to you."[37]

And now, today, here we are, you and I, two Tree-Leaf goblins who have come here as well for the purpose of crossing swords with Master Shanaō.

What do you think?

ADO

I think that I am ready and willing to cross swords.

OMO

As Master Shanaō has received all the great secret teachings, it will not be easy to cross swords with him.

ADO

Well, I am certainly ready to cross swords with him.

OMO

In that case, let us now cross swords as a warming up exercise

They spar.

ADO

Yatto-na, yatto-na.

OMO

Ei, yatto-na, yatto-na. Do you know your strength now, do you know your strength?

ADO

Forgive me, oh, forgive me. I will not cross swords any more. I'm going home, I'm going home.

The Ado exits. The Omo *follows him as far as the* metsuke-bashira.

OMO

Wait, oh, wait. What is this? He has already disappeared.

It will be most difficult for me to cross swords with Master Shanaō all alone. I will call to Master Shanaō to come out here, to show him that I have indeed come here at least, and then I will go home.

Faces the Curtain. I say, Master Shanaō, Master Shanaō, I say! (Exits.)

---

[37] These are three techniques of the art of the ninja: *kōgai-gakushi* ("hidden hairpin"), the concealing of nail-shaped projectiles (shuriken) or small *kozuka*-type daggers in the hair or clothing; *konoha-gakure* ("hidden in the leaves of trees"), literally, hiding in the leafy shade, included such techniques as leaping up into leafy branches to hide oneself, tossing a handful of leaves in the wind to conceal one's movements, etc.; and *kiri no in* ("the sign of the mist"), the use of small chemical smoke-bombs to create smokescreens to enable one to "disappear."

It is interesting to note that as Ze-ami was himself the grandson of the sister of Kusunoki no Masashige (1294–1336), defender of the Southern Court and sworn enemy of the Northern Court and its Ashikaga shogunate, he probably had training in the techniques of the Iga ninja. Indeed, many believe that his firstborn son, Motomasa, was murdered shortly after visiting Iga in 1430—indicating close connections between Ze-ami's family and the Southern Court, as well as with Iga-style ninjutsu, even a century after Masashige's death. It is also interesting to draw parallels between the Noh-style movement and that of the ninja.

—ACT 2—

ISSEI *The* Kokata *enters, accompanied by* Issei *music, and stands at the* jō-za.

Sashi, *awazu*

KOKATA

Shanaō is attired in
A pale-cherry-blossom–colored single underrobe,[38]
A transparent silk robe with woven patterns,[39]
The sleeve-strings tied and hung across the back,
And light armor sewn with white thread,[40] a halberd with a white grip held in hand,

CHORUS

Issei, *awazu*

Before him, even the demons in Heaven or fiendish gods
Will scatter away like wind-blown mountain cherry blossoms.[41]

The Kokata *goes to the* waki-za.

Flower-bright is the boy's attire.

Ō-BESHI *Accompanied by* ō-beshi *music, the* Nochi-Shite, *the Great Goblin, enters and stands by the first pine.*

Sings, awazu

NOCHI-SHITE

Here I am, I am here, at last,
In the mountain recess of Kurama, in Archbishop's Valley
For many years I have lived,
The Great Goblin am I.

Chū-nori

CHORUS

Now about the goblins in attendance,

---

[38] *Usu hana-zakura* (lit: pale cherry-blossom) is the name given to a style of wearing many robes in layers such that the outermost robe is white and the innermost, crimson. However, since the text very clearly states that Yoshitsune wore a single robe (*hitoe*), the term here is interpreted as the color of the robe, which is assumed to be very pale pink, the color of pale cherry blossoms. This term creates a lovely echo of the *uzu-zakura* mentioned at the beginning of Act 1 (*see* Note 5).

[39] *Kenmon-sha:* a thin, semi-transparent, gauze-like silk with floral patterns woven into the fabric. The name of the robe, *hitatare* (< *tareru*, to drip) is an *engo* with *tsuyu* (sleeve-strings / dew).

[40] *Shiraito no haramaki:* This *haramaki* ("that which is wrapped around the abdomen") was part of a warrior's formal armor, and it is here described as being sewn together with white string. *Ito* (string/thread) is an *engo* with *hitatare* (outer robe), *tsuyu* (sleeve-strings), *musunde*

Sate mo Shanaō ga idetachi ni wa
Hada ni wa usu hana-zakura no hitoe ni[38]
Kenmonsha no hitatare no[39]
Tsuyu o musunde kata ni kake
Shiraito no haramaki,[40] shirae no naginata.

Tatoeba tenma kijin nari tomo

Sa koso arashi no yama-zakura.[41]

Hanayaka narikeru ide-tachi kana.

Somosomo kore wa
Kurama no oku Sōjōgatani ni

Toshi hete sumeru
Dai-Tengu nari

Mazu on-tomo no tengu wa

(tied), and *kake* (hung). The *shira* of ***shira**ito* is repeated in ***shira**e* (white grip). Note that in the Genpei (Minamoto–Taira) conflict, white is the color of the Genji (Minamoto), while red is the color of the Heike (Taira).

[41] *Sakoso* ***araji*** (they are not that [strong]) → ***arashi*** *no* ***yama*** (mountain of wind/storm = Arashiyama) → ***yama**-zakura* (mountain [= wild] cherries). The last half of line 162 thus means "the wind-blown wild cherry blossoms on Arashiyama." *Araji* is a conventional *jo-kotoba* for Arashiyama, a mountain northwest of Kyoto famed not only for its autumn foliage, but also for the beauty of its cherry blossoms. Note that this pun works because in ancient orthography *araji* and *arashi* were written with exactly the same *kana*—no marks were used to indicate the voicing of consonants.

Pray tell me who they are. From Tsukushi,[42]

SHITE

Mt. Hiko's Buzen-bō.

CHORUS

From Four Provinces?[43]

SHITE

Hakufū's Sagami-bō,
Daisen's Hōki-bō;

CHORUS

Izuna's Saburō, Fuji's Tarō,
Ōmine's Zenki and his Followers,
Kazuraki, Takama—
No need to tell any further names away from the Capital.[44]

SHITE

Hira,

CHORUS

Yokawa,

SHITE

Nyoi-ga-dake,

CHORUS

The Shite *enters the stage and dances to the song.*

On Takao's peak lives the highly conceited one,[45]
To men working mischief, over Mt. Atago,[46]
Floating in a stretch of mist or changed into a cloud.

SHITE

The moon is darkened, while all over Archbishop[47]

CHORUS

Valley, they make the mountain tops shake violently,

Noru

The tree-withering wind, the roaring waterfall—

---

[42] From here, lines 169–81, there follows a list of the *tengu* and their mountain abodes (*see also* the Introduction to this play). Note that Zenki (l. 175) was under the control of the founder of Shugendō, En no Gyōja (*see also* the discussion of him in the introduction to the play).

[43] Lines 171–72: Four Provinces = the island of Shikoku; Hakufū = Mt. Shiramine.

[44] Lines 176–77: Based on an anonymous poem in the *Shin Kokin-shū* (990): ***Yoso** ni nomi / Mite ya yaminan / **Kazuraki** ya / **Takama** no yama no / **Mine** no **shira**kumo* (Just from far away, / Could I only gaze at you, / As I view the white clouds o'er / Katsuraki's peak / and the mount of Takama?). A slightly variant version of the same poem appears in the *Wakan Rōei-shū* (409). The playwright obviously had this poem in mind when writing lines 172–77, as they contain the words *shira* (Hakufū = Shiramine), *mine* (Ōmine), and *yoso* (further off / away from) of the poem.

[45] *Gaman **taka**shi* (highly conceited) → ***Taka**o no mine* (Takao's peak).

Taretare zo? Tsukushi ni wa[42]

Hiko-san no Buzen-bō.

Shishū ni wa[43]

Hakufū no Sagami-bō;
Daisen no Hōki-bō.

Izuna no Saburō, Fuji Tarō.
Ōmine no Zenki ga ichitō.
Kazuraki, Takama—
Yoso made mo arumaji.[44]

Hira,

Yokawa,

Nyoi-ga-dake,

Gaman Takao[45] no mine ni sunde
Hito no tame ni wa Atago-yama[46]
Kasumi to tanabiki kumo to natte.

Tsuki wa Kurama no Sōjōga[47]

Tani ni michi michi mine o ugokashi
Arashi kogarashi taki no oto—

---

[46] *Hito no tame ni* ***ada*** (on men [working] mischief / [taking] revenge for someone's sake) → ***Ata****go-yama* (Mt. Atago). Since the character for *ada* can also be read *ogori-takaburi* (highly conceited), *gaman takashi* is a *jo-kotoba* for *ada.* Note that the phrase as it occurs in the current printed text (of the Kanze school) could also be read *hito no tame ni ai* (for the sake of men, love), suggesting that Sōjō-bō decided to help Yoshitsune overturn the Taira tyranny because of his love for mankind. Note also that this pun works because in ancient orthography *ada* and *ata* were written with exactly the same *kana*—no marks were used to indicate the voicing of consonants. Note that Mt. Atago is the scene of a fourth-group Noh titled *Shikimi Tengu,* which is no longer performed (*see* Goff 1991: 146–49 for a translation).

[47] Lines 246–47: *Tsuki wa* ***kurai*** (the moon is darkened) → ***Kura****ma no Sōjōga- / Tani* (in Kurama's Archbishop's Valley). One could merge the two images to make the sentence read: "In the pale moonlight, it is dark in Kurama's Archbishop's Valley."

All this commotion is the work of the goblins.

The Shite stands at the jō-za.
Spoken

SHITE

How now, Master Shanaō!
I have sent you some small goblins;
How did you show the fruit of your hard training?

KOKATA

Well, some small goblins come just now, so
I thought I would wound them slightly, to show the fruit of my hard training. However,
I was afraid I might be scolded by my teacher, so I thought better of it.

SHITE

Kakaru
Spoken

Oh, it is sweet of you to say so!
Since you think so dearly of your teacher,
I will tell you a story.

KATARI *The* Shite *sits on a stool at center stage.*

Katari, *Spoken*

SHITE

Now, there was a man named Chang Liang, a retainer of the first Emperor of the Former Han dynasty.[48]
This is how he learned the secrets of military tactics from Huang Shih Kung.

One day the two men met on horseback, when, one did not know how it happened,
The other man dropped his left shoe.
"I say, Chang Liang, pick up that shoe and put it on my foot," he said.
Chang Liang thought him very rude. However, he picked up the shoe and put it on his foot.

---

[48] What follows (lines 196–210) is based upon the account in the *Records of the Historian* (pp. 238–52), written around 100 BC. Chang Liang (Jpn. Chōryō; (d. 168 BC), marquis of Liu, had failed in an attempt to assassinate the First Emperor of Ch'in. One day he met an old Taoist sage whose name has come down to us as Huang Shih Kung (Old Man "Yellow Rock"), since he promised that Chang would meet him again as a yellow rock at the foot of Mt. Kucheng). Just as the *San Kuo Chih* (*Romance of the Three Kingdoms*) relates how Liu Pei had to visit the young military strategist Chuko Liang (also known as K'ung-ming), three times before being received, Huang Shih Kung tested Chang as described in the play; most versions of the legend tell of three tests, but the play portrays only two. The sage eventually taught Chang the secrets of military tactics and gave him a copy of *The Patriarch Lu Shang's Art of War*.

Tengu-daoshi wa obitatashi ya.

Ikani Shanaō.
Tadaima shō-tengu o mairasete sōrō ni
Keiko no kiwa o ba nanbō on-mise sōrō zo.

Sanzōrō tadaima shō-tengu-domo kitari sōrō hodo ni
Usude o mo kiritsuke, keiko no kiwa o mise mōshitaku wa sōraitsuredomo

Shishō ni ya shikarare mōsan to omoi-totomarite sōrō.

Ara, ito hoshi no hito ya.
Sayō ni shishō o daiji ni oboshimesu ni tsuite
Saru monogatari no sōrō katatte kikase mōshi sōrō beshi.

Satemo Kan no Kōso no shinka Chōryō to iu mono[48]

Kō Sekikō ni kono ichi daiji o sōden su.

Aru toki bashō nite yuki-aitari shi ni nani to ka shitariken.

Hidari no kutsu o otoshi.
Ikani Chōryō, ano kutsu totte hakase yo to iu.

Yasukarazu wa omoishikadomo kutsu o totte hakasu.

Chang Liang later threw his lot in with Liu Pang (r. 206–194 BC), who founded the Former Han dynasty (206 BC–AD 25). Ssu-ma Ch'ien states (p. 252): "It was surely the will of Heaven that Chang Liang was so often able to save the first emperor of Han when he was in trouble." Indeed, it could be said that Chang Liang was instrumental in enabling Liu Pang to establish the Han dynasty and set the stage for the later defeat of Ch'ü, whose armies were led by Hsiang Yü, who is memorialized in the Peking Opera *Pa-wang Pieh-chi* (known in the West as "Farewell, My Concubine") and the visional fifth-group Noh play *Kō-u,* in which the ghosts of the general and his lady tell of his defeat and death. Chang Liang is himself the subject of a realistic fifth-group Noh play, *Chōryō,* which describes the tests that both Huang and a dragon (a manifestation of the Bodhisattva Avalokiteśvara [Jpn. Kannon]) put him through.

After this, Chang Liang met him once more on horseback. This time,
He dropped both his left and right shoes.
"I say, Chang Liang, pick up those shoes and put them on my feet," he said.

Kakaru

Again he thought him very rude,

Spoken

However, he thought,
"Well, if I am to learn any secrets from this man—"
So he picked up the shoes the man had dropped.

Chū-nori

CHORUS

The Shite *mimes the action.*

Chang Liang holds the shoes in his hands, and
Chang Liang holds the shoes in his hands, and
Approaching Shih Kung on his horse,
Puts them on his feet. Whereupon his heart melted, and he taught Chang Liang the secrets of military tactics.

SHITE

In the same way as this man, you, my noble lord,

CHORUS

In the same way as this man, you, my noble lord,
A blooming youth in an attire of flowery splendor,
This goblin, rude and fierce in appearance and in mind,
You venerate so, calling him teacher and master,
Because you wish to learn all the secrets of military arts,
In order that you might overthrow the proud Heike Clan.
Oh, laudable indeed is your ambition!

Noru

As for the names famed for their military achievements,

MAI-BATARAKI by the *Shite*. After the dance, the *Shite* stands at the jō-za.

The Shite *dances to the song.*

CHORUS

As for the names famed for their military achievements,
Among the four families Gen-Pei-Tō-Kitsu,[49] especially

---

[49] Since the steady increase in the number of Imperial princes was draining the financial resources of the Court, many were caused to give up their Imperial status, granted family names (since even today the Imperial family has no family name), and made the heads of new families of high-ranking nobility. In line 223 three of the four families mentioned are descended from Imperial princes (sons of emperors), and they are: the Minamoto (**Gen**), from Prince Sadazumi, son of Emperor Seiwa (851–81); the Taira (Hei/-**pei**), from Prince Katsura-

Mata sono nochi izen no gotoku bashō nite yuki-aitari shi ni, kondo wa

Hidari, migi no kutsu o otoshi.
Yaa, ikani Chōryō, ano kutsu totte hakase yo to iu.

Nao yasukarazu.
Omoishikadomo.
Yoshi, yoshi kono ichi daiji o sōden suru ue wa to omoi
Ochitaru kutsu ottotte

Chōryō kutsu o sasagetsutsu,
Chōryō kutsu o sasagetsutsu,
(M)uma no ue naru Sekikō ni
Haksekeru ni zo. Kokoro toke heihō no ōgi o tsutaekeru.

Sono gotoku ni wajōrō mo,

Sono gotoku ni wajōrō mo,
Samo hanayaka naru on-(n)arisama nite
Sugata mo kokoro mo ara-tengu o

Shishō ya bōzu to go-shōkan wa
Ikani mo daiji o nokosazu tsutaete
Heike o utan to oboshimesu ka ya,

Yasashi no kokorozashi ya na.
Somosomo buryaku no homare no michi,

---

bara, son of Emperor Kanmu (736–805); and the Tachibana (**Kitsu**), from Prince Naniwa, son of Shōtoku Taishi (572–621), and thus grandson of Emperor Yōmei (540–87). The fourth family is the Fujiwara (**Tō**), which claimed descent from the deity Ame-no-koyane no Mikoto, a retainer of the sun goddess, Amaterasu Ōmikami, the progenetrix of the Imperial Family; it was this close descent from the gods that the Fujiwara used in order maintain their proximity to, and actual control over, the Imperial house for so long.

The Minamoto Family has its source[50]
In Emperor Seiwa, being his royal descendants.
Having roughly considered the trend of the times, I would say,
You should drive the conceited Heike to the Western Seas;
Having mastered the art of flying freely on the clouds afloat over smoking blue waves,[51]
You will destroy the enemy and clear the shame of the past.[52]
I will help you to achieve this purpose.
It is now time we should part.
Fare thee well." Having spoken this, he is about to leave.
Ushiwaka, who is loath to part, clings to the goblin's sleeves.
Indeed, it is hard to part.
Even at battles fought on the remote Western and Shikoku Seas.
Shadow-like, never leaving you,
I will assist you, fighting side by side with your men-at-arms.

---

[50] Lines 287–88: *Kano ie no* ***mina****moto* (that house's source = the source of the Minamoto house) → ***mina****kami wa* ***kiyo****shi* (the upper water [= the surface of the water] is pure) → ***Sei****wa Tennō no kōin* (directly descended from Emperor Seiwa). Note that the *kiyo* of *kiyoshi* and the *sei* of *Seiwa* are written with the same character.

The first man to receive the name Minamoto was the seventh son of Emperor Saga (785–842). The four principal Minamoto families were those descended from the emperors Saga, Seiwa, Uda (867–931), and Murakami (926–67). Yoshitsune was a member of the Seiwa Genji clan.

[51] *Enpa* = waves like smoke; distant waves so wild their spray forms a smoke-like mist over the surface of the waters; *sōha* = blue waves = the wide sea. These phrases appear in various works. In the "Initiate's Chapter" (The Imperial Lady Becomes a Nun) of the *Heike Monogatari* (Ichiko, 507) is this phrase: ***Sōha*** *michi* ***tō****shi, omoi o saikai senri no kumo ni yose* (Her thoughts lingered on the clouds a thousand leagues distant o'er the western sea, far away on the paths of the boundless blue waves). Note that *tō*, which means "distant, far away," is also pronounced *en* (i.e., it is homonymous with *en* [smoke]), and that *enpa* (misty, or smoky, waves) in the text used by Itō (cf. p. 37) was originally written as distant waves. In the RGS (No. 26), this entry is found: "If 'clouds,' then 'floating,' . . . 'waves.' " ***Kumo*** (clouds) is underlined as it is an *engo* of *en* (smoke). The lines are themselves based on a Chinese couplet by Tachibana no Naomoto in the *Wakan Rōei–shū* (646): ***Sōha*** *michi* ***tō****shi, kumo senri / Hakubu yama fukashi, tori hito koe* (The distant lanes of the blue waves, clouds for a thousand

Kano ie no minakami wa[50]
Seiwa Tennō no kōin to shite.
Ara-ara jitestu o kangae kitaru ni,

Ogoreru Heike o saikai ni okkudashi.

Enpa-sōha[51] no fu-un ni higyō no jizai o ukete

Kataki o tairage, kaikei o susugan.[52]

On-mi to mamoru beshi.
Kore made nari ya
O-itoma mōshite tachi-kaereba
Ushiwaka tamoto ni sugari tamaeba

Geni nagori ari.
Saikai, shikai no kasen to iu tomo

Kage-mi o hanarezu
Yumi-ya no chikara o soe mamoru beshi.

---

leagues, / The white mist of the deep mountains, the bird's solitary cry). As Nishino (2000: 93n14) also points out, these lines from a popular *enkyoku* (Hayakawa, 1912: *Enkyoku-shū* 4: *Umibe* [Seashore; p. 571]) bear comparison: ***Sōha*** *michi* ***tō****shi, kumo no nami, kemuri no nami o shinogite* (The roads [along] the blue sea are far away, and, enduring waves of clouds and waves of smoke [= mist], . . .).

[52] "Clear the shame of the past": *Records of the Historian* (pp. 47–59) relates the tale of Kou Chien, king of Yüeh, who was defeated and humiliated at Mt. Kuai-chi (sometimes transliterated Hui-chi; it took place in 496 BC) by Fu-ch'ai, king of Wu. Kou Chien went into seclusion on Mt. Kuai-chi, and ten years later defeated Wu, clearing the disgrace of the past (= the shame of Kuai-chi). This episode is also told in Sun Tzu's *Art of War,* and is also narrated in great detail in the "War Between Wu and Yüeh" chapter of Book Five of the *Soga Monogatari* (225–40), which ends with the words: *Etsu-ō wa,* ***Kaikei*** *no haji* ***o susug****i, un no hiraki, yo ni sakau nari. Ima no Tokimune wa, haji o susugu to iedomo, ichimei o ushinau nari. Tatoe ni mo naru bekarazu to zo mōshikeru* (It was said: The King of Yüeh avenged the disgrace of Kuai-chi, improved his fortune, and prospered in the world. [Soga no Gorō] Tokimune will take revenge and **clear** his **shame**, but will lose his life. How different, indeed, are their fates!"). One cannot help but hear the playwright saying, "just as Yoshitsune will avenge his father's death, clear the shame of the past, and overthrow the Heike rule, but will lose his life and die."

Believe and trust in me, quoth he, and the evening shadows darken,
Believe and trust in me, quoth he, and as night grows dark, to Kurama's[53]
Tree tops up he flew and then disappeared from sight.

---

[53] Lines 238–39: *Tanome to* ***iu*** ("Trust in me," quoth he) → ***yū**kage* ***kura**ki* (the evening shadows darken / as night grows dark) → ***Kura**ma no kozue* (Kurama's tree tops).

These lines, discussing trust as the night grows dark, are reminiscent of two poems by Izumi Shikibu. The first, one of her most famous poems (and one thought by many to have been her death-poem), appears in the *Shūi-shū* (1342): ***Kuraki*** *yori /* ***kuraki*** *michi ni zo / iri bekinu / haruka ni terase / yama no ha no tsuki* (Out of the darkness, now upon a darker path I have to set out. Though so distant, shine on me, moon above the mountain ridge!). With its imagery of the dark path, it alludes to the parable of the Magic City within the Lotus Sutra. The other appears in the *Shin Kokin-shū* (408): *Tanometaru / hito wa nakeredo / aki no yo wa / tsuki mite ne-beki / kokochi koso senu* (Even though there is no one I am waiting for, on this autumn night, I just gaze upon the moon, without any thought of sleep.).

They also call to mind lines that appear in another play about Yoshitsune, *Funa-Benkei,* that time, sung by Lady Shizuka, after performing a *chū-no-mai:*

SHITE: *Tada tanome. Shimeji-ga-hara no sashimo-gusa*
(Have but faith in me, you, who are like moxa-weeds on Shimeji Moor,
CHORUS: *Ware yo no naka ni. Aran kagiri wa.*
(While within this faithless world, I continue still to dwell.)

These lines comprise an anonymous poem in the *Shin Kokin-shū* (1917, where it begins *Nao . . .*) that is attributed to the Bodhisattva Kannon enshrined in Kyoto's Kiyomizu Temple. It is recorded that it was addressed to a grieving woman who had lost all hope and wanted to take her own life.

Tanome ya tanome to yūkage kuraki,
Tanome ya tanome to yūkage Kurama no[53]
Kozue ni kakette usenikeri.

昭君

SHŌKUN

これハ胡國の夷乃大将軍。呼韓邪單于が。幽霊なり

Of the Great General of the alien land of the Huns,
Hu Han-yeh Shan-yü, / This is the ghost.

Introduction

The heroine of the Noh *Shōkun,* whose full Chinese name is Wang Chao-chün (Ō Shōkun in Japanese; the characters mean "Royal Radiant Lady"), was one of numerous women in the harem of Emperor Yüan-ti (reigned 48–33 BC) of the Former Han Dynasty of China. At that time the northern border of China was menaced by the invasions of the barbarian Huns (Hsiung-nu). When the Khan of All the Huns, Hu Han-yeh *Shan-yü* (Ko Kan'ya Zennu in Japanese, r. 58–31 BC),[1] came to China asking for assistance in subduing rebellious uprisings in his land, the Han Emperor, who hoped for a peaceful relationship with the northern neighbor, offered him one of his consorts, and selected Chao-chün from among numerous women.[2] The story of Chao-chün as the heroine of a tragic episode in Chinese history is told in Japanese story books such as the *Konjaku Monogatari,* the *Soga Monogatari,* and the *Kara Monogatari.* The various versions of the story are more or less alike. The following is an outline of the story as told in Book 10 of the *Konjaku Monogatari:*

> Long ago during the reign of the Han Emperor Yüan-ti, daughters of ministers and noblemen celebrated for beauty were summoned to wait on the Emperor. Their number amounted to four or five hundred, so that many of them had no chance of ever meeting the sovereign. When the Hun ruler came to China to pay tribute, Yüan-ti thought of making the unwelcome visitor go home by giving him one of his many consorts, the one who was the least attractive. However, he could not make the selection of the women, many of whom he had never seen. Therefore, he had artists

[1] Hu Han-yeh appears to be not his name but his title as one of the two rival Hsiung-nu khans ruling at the time. Although the name is sometimes given as Hu Han-hsieh, we have used this reading, as it is closer to the Japanese reading of Ko Kan-ya. Also, *shan-yü* is the Chinese term used to signify sovereign, or khan.

[2] During his visit to the Han capital in 33 BC, he was presented with five women from the Imperial harem, one of whom was Wang Chao-chün.

draw the portraits of them so that he could make the selection from these portraits. The women, who did not want to go to the land of barbarians, bribed the painters, so that they would make the portraits more attractive than they actually were. Among the women there was one named Wang Chao-chün, who was the most beautiful of all. Trusting in her own beauty, she did not bribe her painter, so he portrayed Chao-chün as an ugly woman. Thus it was decided that she should be offered to the barbarian emperor.

Yüan-ti summoned Chao-chün and took a look at her. To his great surprise he found her as beautiful as a radiant jewel, compared with whom other women were "as dirty as mud." The Emperor was sorry to give her to a barbarian. However, the Hun Khan already knew that Chao-chün was selected to be his wife, and demanded her of Yüan-ti, who had no choice but to give her up.

Seized with deep grief, Chao-chün lamented her fate, but in vain. The Emperor, too, missed her greatly. His heart ached to see willow branches waving in the spring wind, or autumn leaves falling in thick piles in the garden.

The Hun Khan, very pleased to have Chao-chün, had taken her home on horseback, with his men playing music on the *biwa,* a type of lute. When they arrived home, the Hun Emperor made her the Empress and proved himself a devoted husband. In spite of this, Chao-chün's mind found no solace. It is said that people at that time criticized her, saying that her misfortune was all because she was too confident of her beauty and did not bribe the artist. (After her marriage with Hu Han-yeh, Chao-chün gave birth to two sons. After her husband's death, she is said to have married her own stepson and borne two girls.)[3]

The source of inspiration for the Noh *Shōkun* is the story told in the above-mentioned books. The Noh is of the type of *gobanme-mono* (fifth-group Noh) classified as *oni-mono* (Demonic-spirit Noh). *Oni* here means: 1) a deity from hell; 2) a human spirit or ghost with an infernal atmosphere about it. According to Ze-ami, the *shite*-ghost of a *shūshin-mono* (attachment piece) is a sort of *oni,* to be distinguished from the warrior-ghost in *shura* (battle)-Noh (cf. Omote pp. 24–25). In *Shōkun,* the *oni* in the second sense appears as the ghost of Chao-chün's husband, the Emperor Hu Han-yeh (Ko Kan'ya), who looks frightening, like a demon. A

---

3 "[Chao-chün] became a favorite of [the Hu Han-yeh *shan-yü*] and gave birth to two sons. Only one of these seems to have survived, I-t'u-chih-ya-shih. When the Hu Han-yeh *shan-yü* died in 33 BC, Wang Chao-chün, with Chinese Imperial permission, followed the custom of the Hsiung-nu and became a wife of the new *shan-yü.* In her new marriage she had two daughters." (Twitchett, 236)

large part of the Noh is fiction, with fictitious characters, including Chao-chün's parents, who lament the separation from their daughter. Like all other *oni-mono, Shōkun* is made up of two acts. In the first act, the scene is the home of Chao-chün's old parents, who in deep grief constantly take care of the willow tree, Chao-chün's keepsake, sweeping the leaves fallen under the tree. The father remembers an old belief that one can see the image of a person by putting a keepsake of this person before a mirror and reflecting its image in it. So he puts a mirror in front of the willow tree. In the second act, the ghost of Chao-chün appears to make her image appear in the mirror. She is followed by Hu Han-yeh's ghost, who is shocked by his own dreadful appearance in the mirror and goes away, leaving Chao-chün, whose image appears alone in the mirror that reflects truth.

The Noh develops as follows:

—*Act 1*

1) Accompanied by *nanori-bue,* the *Waki,* a villager, enters, and in a soliloquy says that he is going to visit his neighbors, Pai-t'ao ("White Peach") and his wife, Wang-mu ("Royal Mother"), whose daughter, Wang Chao-chün, an imperial consort, has gone to the Land of the Huns to be married to the barbarian emperor.

2) Accompanied by music, the *Shite,* Pai-t'ao, and the *Tsure,* his wife Wang-mu, enter and sing about their daughter, Chao-chün, and about the willow tree that she planted as a souvenir. They sweep the willow leaves fallen on the ground, singing about their sorrow as they work.

3) The *Waki,* the neighbor, speaks to the couple, expressing his sympathy and asks them how Chao-chün came to be sent to the alien land. The father's story of Chao-chün told to the neighbor—with details concerning the selection of the ladies by their portraits, and the bribing of the painters by the women—is rendered in *kuri, sashi,* and *kuse.*

4) Pai-t'ao recalls old stories telling how one can see the image of a person dear to him by looking at the reflection of this person's keepsake in a mirror. He relates this in an exchange with his wife. Then he puts a mirror at downstage center, and, sitting before it, he weeps.

5) The *Shite* makes an interim exit. The *Ai-kyōgen,* a villager, accompanies him half way, talking kindly to him, and then returns and in a soliloquy relates the story of Wang Chao-chün, and in an announcement asks people to be kind to her parents.

—*Act 2*

6) Accompanied by *issei* music, the *Kokata,* Chao-chün's ghost, enters and says in *sashi* that she is so sorry to see her parents grieving for her sake that she has come to reveal her visional form to them.

7) The *Nochi-shite,* the ghost of Hu Han-yeh, the Khan of the Huns, en-

ters running, accompanied by *haya-fue* music. He sees that Chao-chün's mother is terrified by his demonic appearance. He approaches the mirror and sees his image reflected in it. The Chorus sings:

> "How very terrible appears that countenance!
> I am so ashamed. With these words he goes away." (lines 214–15)

However, instead of making an exit, the *Shite* continues to act during the next and final sections, making dancing gestures to a song that compares a mind clear as the crescent moon to a mirror that reflects truth.

Among the six Noh grouped as *oni-mono,* both *Shōkun* and *Funa-Benkei* are different from the rest in that, while their second act is visional, their first act is realistic. Moreover, in these plays, the *Shite* in the second act is a different character from that in the first. The same is true with *Ukai,* which is visional in both the first and second acts. Of the three Noh with such a characteristic, the transition from the first to the second scene is made in *Funa-Benkei* and *Ukai* without any problem, but not so in *Shōkun.* Toward the end of the first act, Chao-chün's father places a mirror at center stage, hoping to see his daughter's image reflected in it. Then he exits. In the second act, when Chao-chün's ghost appears to reveal her image in the mirror, the father is not there to see it.

We have other examples of a similar situation. In the first act of *Fujito,* an aged woman, the *Shite,* comes to accuse a warrior, who has killed her son, a fisherman, after he obtained strategic information from him. This scene is realistic. In the second act, the *Nochi-shite,* the ghost of the fisherman, appears where a memorial service is being held for him by the warrior. A similar situation takes place in *Tenko.* In this play, the *Mae-shite* is an aged father who laments the death of his son, who was put to death for disobeying an Imperial order. In the second act, at the Emperor's order, a service is held for the deceased boy, whose ghost, the *Nochi-shite,* appears and dances in joy. The first act of *Tomonaga* takes place at the burial place of the young warrior Taira no Tomonaga, whose death is mourned by his benefactress, the *Mae-shite.* In the second scene, Tomonaga's ghost appears at the service being held for him. In these three Noh, the first act describes the sorrow of the bereaved; the second act, the gratitude of the dead for the service held for him. In them, the two scenes are more or less independent of each other, so that the switch from realistic to visional, or the difference in the identity of the *shite* from the first to the second act, presents no problem. (*Tomonaga* and *Tenko* are included in *Battle Noh* [vol. 2:1] and *Restless Spirits* [vol. 4:1] in the Noh Series.)

On the other hand, in *Shōkun,* although the same scene is continued from the first to the second act, there is an abrupt break in the flow of the dramatic narration. At the beginning of the second act, the ghost of Chao-chün, as *Kokata,* or *Tsure,* enters and sings a few lines, then she just remains sitting. There is no exchange with her mother, who has remained on stage after the exit of the father. Then the Emperor of the Huns, the *Nochi-shite,* enters, and sings only one sentence, telling who he is. This is very unusual for the first song of a *Nochi-shite.* At this point, the mother, who has spoken not a word to her daughter, expresses her terror at the dreadful appearance of the second apparition. The apparition in reply says that it is the ghost of Hu Han-yeh, who has come to see Chao-chün's parents, only to be told by the mother that there is no use in her meeting one who looks so dreadful. From this point on, it is a short one-man performance of the *Nochi-shite.* The *Nochi-shite* sees himself reflected in the mirror, while the Chorus sings that, ashamed of his dreadful form, the barbarian Emperor goes away. This is the end of the drama. Actually, he remains on the stage as the player of the epilogue, dancing to the final song, which is about how the cloudless-clear mind of a man is a mirror that reflects truth. The play ends without any hint of why Hu Han-yeh appears as a demonic being. Although he is a barbarian, the play presents him as a man with a human heart, who comes to see his bride's parents, but who then disappears, ashamed of his appearance. Such structural irrelevance has been attributed to revisions made to the original version written in an earlier period.

Recently attempts at revisions have been made, some making the ghost of Chao-chün the *Nochi-shite.* In the version performed by Kanze actor Makio Umewaka (now Manzaburō III, son of the great Manzaburō Umewaka II and great-grandson of the legendary Minoru Umewaka), the *Shite* and *Nochi-shite* roles are played by two different actors, and Pai-t'ao remains on the stage. Also, the ghost of Chao-chün is played not by a *kokata* but an adult actor, performing as a *Tsure.* Although this makes for a large number of characters upon the stage, it is not unprecedented (cf. *Eboshi-ori, Ataka,* or the *oni-zoroe* variation of *Momiji-gari*), and seems to flow more smoothly when performed, in comparison with the conventional form of the play.

Side by side with the structural flaws pointed out above, in *Shōkun* we also find passages of great lyrical appeal. In Chinese and Japanese classic literature, many poems are found that describe the beauty and tragedy of Chao-chün. The Noh abounds in quotations from, and allusions to, these celebrated poems. These, as well as the willow and mirror as the thematic symbols, play important roles in achieving the dramatic effect. From the ancient Chinese tradition of offering a wreath of willow to a friend leaving for a remote land, the tree became a symbol of separation, and the expression, "to break a willow branch" has come to mean "to part with a friend." We find this expression woven into an *age-uta* (*see* the text, line 43, and the note). Also, willow branches swaying gently in the spring wind are compared to the graceful form of a woman, and its green leaves to her eyebrows. *Shōkun* has examples of this imagery. As for the mirror, since prehistoric times it has been held as a revered object in Japan. Even today mirrors are used at shrines as symbols of deities. They were rare, precious objects, and there were many people who had never seen one.

Thus, a mirror came to be looked at as something with supernatural power and associated with mysterious stories. *Matsuyama Kagami,* a miracle Noh in the fifth group, is about a girl who pines for her dead mother and looks at her own image in the mirror, her mother's keepsake, believing her own reflection to be her mother's, until the mother's ghost actually appears in the mirror. (There is also a Kyogen comedy on the mirror theme—*Kagami Otoko* [The Man and the Mirror], in which a country man brings back from the Capital a mirror for his wife, but when she sees her image reflected, she explodes, thinking he has brought back another woman!) There are countless poems about the image of a dear one reflected in a mirror. Examples include one by Lord Genji, composed when he was leaving for Suma in self-exile:

Mi wa kakute	Although I myself
Sasuraenu tomo	Shall go adrift from you,
Kimi ga atari	From my beloved's side
Saranu ***kagami*** *no*	Never shall this mirror leave,
Kage wa hanareji.	Nor my shade reflected there.

and by Lady Murasaki in answer:

Wakarete mo	Though separated,
Kage dani tomaru	Should your image stay behind,
Mono naraba	As I wish it would,
Kagami *o mite mo*	Then looking at the mirror,
Nagusametemashi.	My heart would find some comfort.

In addition to the willow and mirror, there is a third symbolic image that is closely associated with the first two, and it is the peach blossom. There are poems that compare Chao-chün's eyebrows to willow leaves, and her face to a peach blossom. In the Noh, Chao-chün's father's name is Pai-t'ao (Hakudō, or Hakutō), which means "white peach.' Her mother's name, Wang-mu (Ōbo), is the same as the goddess known in Chinese mythology as the Western Sovereign Mother (Hsi Wang-mu [Seiōbo]), the eponymous protagonist of a third-group Noh. In this deity's garden there grows a peach tree that bears fruit every three thousand years—fruit that renders one immortal. Indeed, it is these peaches that gave Sun Wu-k'ung, the "magic monkey," eternal life. (*See* the translation of *Seiōbo* in *God Noh,* vol. 1 of

The Noh Series.) Chao-chün's father tells about a man who saw the image of his deceased sweetheart, an immortal, by placing a peach branch in front of a mirror. This man's name is T'ao-yeh (Tōyō), meaning "peach leaf." In China and Japan, the peach is associated with magic power, longevity, and a land of magic. The peach blossom is closely associated with the mirror in lines 157–60, where a well-known poem about the water as a mirror for the blossoms is quoted:

Toshi o hete	For many years past,
Hana no kagami to	Like a mirror for blossoms
Naru mizu wa	Became the water;
Chiri-kakaru o ya	When flower dust falls on it,
Kumoru to iuran.	We may say, it is cloudy.
	—Lady Ise, *Kokin-shū* (44)

The author of *Shōkun* is not identified. Scholars consider that it is an old work by one who belonged to the Konparu school.

Scene Chao-chün's father, Pai-t'ao's home in the village of Hsiang-ho, in Hupei Province, China.

Season March by the lunar calendar

Characters and costumes

Waki Pai-t'ao's neighbor, who wears an *atsuita kitsuke,* a white *ōkuchi* divided skirt, and a *sobatsugi.*

Mae-shite Chao-chün's father, Pai-t'ao, wearing an *akobu-jō* or *Sankō-jō* mask and a plain *noshime* or plaid *atsuita kitsuke* under a *mizugoromo* robe, carrying a broom.

Tsure Chao-chün's mother, Wang-mu, wearing an *uba* mask, a wig band in subdued colors over a white wig, a *surihaku kitsuke* under a *karaori* in subdued colors, and a *yori-mizugoromo* robe.

Kokata (Nochi-tsure) Chao-chün's ghost, wearing a *tsure* mask (if *nochi-tsure*), a colorful wig band over a black wig, a crown, a *surihaku kitsuke* under a white or colored *ōkuchi* divided skirt, and a colorful *karaori* worn in the *tsubo-ori* style.

Nochi-shite The ghost of Chao-chün's husband, the Khan, Hu Han-yeh, wearing a *ko-beshimi* mask, a Chinese crown, an *atsuita kitsuke* with bold patterns in horizontal stripes under a *hangire* divided skirt, and a *happi* or lined *kariginu* robe.

Ai-kyōgen A villager.

Author: Unknown.

Shōkun

昭君

—*Act 1*—

NANORI-BUE *The* Waki, *a villager, enters and stands at the* nanori-za.

Nanori, *spoken*

WAKI

I am an inhabitant of the village of Hsiang-ho in China.[1]
In this village live a man and his wife, named Pai-t'ao
and Wang-mu.[2]
They have a daughter
Who is named Chao-chün.
By imperial decree, she went to wait on His Majesty, who
loved her deeply.[3]
However, certain circumstances led to her being sent
to the Land of the Huns,[4]
To the profound grief of her parents.
Since they are my neighbors,
I am going to call on them and see how they are faring.

The Waki *sits at the* waki-za.

ISSEI *The* Shite *enters, preceded by the* Tsure. *They are both carrying brooms. The* Shite *stands by the third pine; the* Tsure, *by the first pine; and they are facing each other.*

Issei, *awazu*

SHITE & TSURE

Flowers fall so that [5]
Under the shade of the tree,
Unknown to heaven above,
We find that it is snowing!

ASHIRAI *The two enter the stage. The* Shite *stands at the* jō-za; *the* Tsure, *before the two drummers.*

---

[1] The place, said by legend to have been in Hopei (Hebei) province, is not identified. Read as Kōho in Japanese we tried to find the correct Mandarin reading. Today, the Hsiang-ch'i Ho (river) pours into the Yangtze Ho at a place called Hsiang-ch'i. About 45 km away, there is a place known as Chao-chün Village, which claims to be her birthplace. If that is true, then perhaps the place name given is that of the river, abbreviated to Hsiang Ho (although, strictly speaking, that would be Kōka in Japanese). It is interesting to note that Mt. Wu of the "clouds and rain" poem (*see* Note 29 to *Kurama Tengu*) is rather close by.

[2] The names are fictitious. The father's name is written in the Kanze text as "White Peach," which is a symbol of longevity, which is what he hopes for his daughter. And peaches of immortality are also grown in the garden of Hsi Wang-mu (Sovereign Mother of the West),

Kore wa Morokoshi Kōho[1] no sato ni sumai suru mono nite sōrō
Sate mo kono tokoro ni Hakudō Ōbo[2] to mōsu fūfu no sōrō

Ichinin no sokujo o motsu
Sono na o Shōkun to nazuku.

Mikado ni mesarete go-chōai kagirinakarishi tokoro ni[3]

Saru shisai ate Kokoku e utsusarete sōrō[4]
Fūfu no hito no nageki tada yo no tsune narazu.
Kinjo no koto nite sōrō hodo ni
Tachi-koe tomurawaba ya to omoi sōrō

Chiri kakaru[5]
Hana no kokage ni tachi-yoreba
Sora ni shirarenu
Yuki zo furu.

---

which reflects the mother's name, Wang-mu. Thus, the names are filled with the stuff of legends.

[3] Actually, the Emperor had never seen Chao-chün until she was presented to him just as she was leaving for the Land of the Huns. This is how the mistake was made that sent her off, hitherto sight unseen, as the bride of a barbarian ruler.

[4] The Japanese term is Ko, but the Chinese is Hsiung-nu. Rather than Tatar or Mongol, we have opted for the cognate Hun.

[5] From a poem by Ki no Tsurayuki (ca. 872–945) in the *Shūi-shū* (64*): Sakura chiru / Ko no shita-kaze wa / Samukarade /* ***Sora ni shirarenu / Yuki zo fur****ikeru* (Where cherry blossoms / Fall in the shade of the tree, / Though the wind 's not cold, / Unknown to heaven above, / We see that snow has fallen.)

Sashi, *awazu*

SHITE
We are villagers of Hsiang-ho in China.
SHITE & TSURE
Pai-t'ao and Wang-mu are our names,
We are man and wife.
TSURE
Although, as you see, we are humble people,
We have a daughter celebrated for her beauty.
SHITE & TSURE
She is named Chao-chün.
Her beauty surpasses others'.
As it is, she was called to the Imperial City,
Her name was changed to Ming-fei,[6]
And there she waited on the Emperor.
SHITE
In spite of this good fortune,
The karma from her former lives
Must still have been binding her—
SHITE & TSURE
She was selected from all the others
And was sent to the Land of the Huns,
Ten thousand miles distant from the Han Emperor's
Palace,[7]
Making a journey under an alien sky.

The two weep.

The very thought fills our hearts with grief.
SHITE
However, the courtiers who accompanied her,
To break the tedium of the long journey,
Would play on their flutes and stringed instruments
as they went.
SHITE and TSURE
The practice of playing the lute on horseback[8]
Began at that time, according to what people say.

---

[6] Lady Ming = Ming-fei (Jpn. Mei-hi = Radiant Concubine) or Ming-chün (Mei-kun). This line is based on the following fact: During the time of Emperor Wên, the first emperor of Western Chin (211–65), because the emperor's given name was Ssu-ma Chao, people called the beauty Ming-chün ("Bright Lady") instead of Chao-chün ("Radiant Lady"), out of deference to the emperor. Sanari (3: 1581) notes that an ancient text called the *Ku-ching Hsueh-hsien* (Jpn. *Kokon Gakusen*) states: *Wang Ming-chün, pen-mei Chao-chün, i ch'u Wên-ti hui, ku Chin-jen wei chi Ming-chün* [*Ō Mei-kun wa, honmyō Shōkun nari, Bun-tei no imina ni fururu o motte, yue ni Shin-bito kore o Mei-kun to iu*] (Wang Ming-chün's real name was Chao-chün; but it was the same as Emperor Wên's true name, for which reason, people in Chin times called her Ming-chün).

Kore wa Morokoshi Kōho no sato ni sumai suru

Hakudō Ōbo to mōsu
Fūfu no mono nite sōrō nari.

Kahodo ni iyashiki mi naredomo
Bimei o arawasu musume ari.

Shōkun to kare o nazukete tsutsu
Yōgan hito ni suguretari.
Sareba Teito ni mesarete nochi
Mei-hi to sono na o aratamete[6]
Tenshi ni mamie owashimasu.

Kahodo imijiki mi naredomo
Na o mo zenze no shukuen
Hanare yarazaru yue yaran

Shonin no naka ni erawarete
Kokoku no tami ni utsusare
Kankyū banri no hoka ni shite[7]

Minarenu kata no tabi no so
Omoi-yaru koso kanashikere.

Saredomo gubu no kannin-domo
Ryokō no michi no nagusame ni
Kenk(u)an no kazu o sōshi-tsutsu

Bashō ni biwa o hiku koto mo[8]
Kono toki yori to kiku mono o.

---

[7] From a Chinese poem by Ōe no Asatsuna in the *Wakan Rōei-shū* (701): *Hu-chiao yi-sheng shuang hou meng / Han-kung wan-li yüeh ch'ien ch'ang* [*Kokaku hitokoe shimo no nochi no yume / Kankyū banri tsuki no mae no mono-omoi*] (By a single note from a Hun ram's horn, after the frost [fell] the dream was broken; / Ten thousand miles from the Han Emperor's palace, beneath the moon sad thoughts break my heart).

[8] Although in literature there are references to the lute (Ch. *p'i-p'a;* Jpn. *biwa*) being played to amuse Chao-chün, it was not the first time that they played the instrument on horseback. The theme of Chao-chün playing the lute on horseback has long been a favorite subject of Chinese painting.

Sage-uta, *au* — The image of Chao-chün in her portrait. . . .[9]
The Shite *weeps.* — Now they recognize that it did tell truth.
Age-uta, *au* — The pair of painted eyebrows of Chao-chün,
The pair of painted eyebrows of Chao-chün[10]
Were the color of young green leaves newly sprouted,
Now in late spring, spinning the thread of weeping willows[11]
When the mind gets lost in a tangle of confusion,
Together with the rising wind, let us go and[12]
Sweep the dust fallen in the shade of the tree,
Sweep the dust fallen in the shade of the tree.

Kakeai, *kakaru*

SHITE

Now together let us sweep and clean the garden,
Says the aged father, with his broom ready to work.

TSURE

Indeed, my thought turns to the spring of the past long gone,[13]
An aged woman, looking frail as a spider's
Thread, and barely able to endure the pain, and yet,
With a sash tucking up both sleeves, on which wind-blown tears like bright gems[14]
Fall, heavy grief I bear for the sake of the child.[15]

SHITE

As an ordinary man of humble status,

---

[9] Lines 37–38: From the second couplet of the quatrain entitled "Wang Chao-chün" in Chapter 14 of the *Collected Poems of Po Chü-i,* which also appears in the *Wakan Rōei-shū* (697): *Chou-k'u hsin ch'in ch'iao-ts'ui chin / Ju-chin ch'ueh szu hua-t'u chung [Shūko shin kimu-shite shōsui-shi tsukinureba / Ima wa kaette gato no uchi ni nitari*] (Because of grief and suffering she was worn out, / So that now she looks like her portrait).

[10] Lines 39–41: From the first couplet of a quatrain entitled "The Willow" in Chapter 17 the *Collected Poems of Po Chü-i,* which also appears in the *Wakan Rōei-shū* (104): *Wu-nü-miao hua heng szu fen / Chao-chün-ts'un liu ts'ui yü mei* [*Bu-jo-byō no hana wa fun yori mo ku-renai ni nitari, / Shōkun-son no yanagi wa mayu yori mo ao nari*] (The flowers at the shrine of the Goddess of [Mt.] Wu are redder than rouge; / The willow in the village of Chao-chün is of deeper green than her eyebrows).

[11] Lines 42–43: *Haru ya **kuru*** (Is spring **growing old**?) → ***kururan ito*** (will be **spinning thread**) → ***ito**-yanagi* ("**thread**" willow = **weeping** willow), with *kuru* meaning: 1) "to grow late / old," with an allusion to Chao-chün; and 2) "to spin," leading to *ito* (thread) and *ito-yanagi* (weeping willow). *Midaruru* (tangle, confusion) is an *engo* of *ito* (thread). In *ori goto ni* (every time when . . .), *ori* in the sense of "bending /breaking" is related to the willow from

Gato ni utsuseru omokage mo[9]
Ima koso omoi-shiraretare.
Kano Shōkun no mayuzumi wa
Kano Shōkun no mayuzumi wa[10]
Midori no iro ni nioi shimo

Haru ya kururan ito-yanagi no[11]

Omoi-midaruru ori goto ni
Kaze morotomo ni tachi-yorite[12]
Kokage no chiri o harawan,
Kokage no chiri o harawan.

Iza iza niwa o kiyomen to
Ōji wa hawaki o tazusaetari.

Geni ya kokoro mo mukashi no haru[13]

Oi no sugata mo sasagani no
Ito-kurushi to wa omoedomo
Kaze musubu namida no sode no tama-dasuki[14]

Kakaru omoi mo ko yue nari.[15]

Tada yo no tsune no shizu no o to

---

the custom of breaking willow branches to make a wreath to give to a friend as a farewell token; in the sense of "weave" or "fold," it is an *engo* of "tangle" and "spin" and "thread."

[12] In *tachi-yorite* (approaching), *tachi* in the sense of "to rise" is an *engo* of *kaze* (wind), and in the sense of "cut," is an *engo* of "thread," as is *-yori* (*yoru:* twist) as well.

[13] Lines 49–50: *Kokoro mo mukashi no haru:* The meaning of this phrase is that the time when the heart was young is now in the distant past. Compare these lines to this poem by (Takatsukasa) Fujiwara no Mototada (1247–1313) from the *Shin Gosen-shū* (83): *Aware ni **mo** / **Mukashi no haru** no / **O**mokage o / Mi sae **oi**ki no / Hana ni miru kana* (Even in sorrow / The youth of past springs leaves a / Trace that can be seen; / The body is like an old / Tree whose flow'rs can still be seen); *Oi no chikara mo **sasa*** (the aged one's strength **small**) → ***sasa**gani* (small crab, a pillow-word for *kumo* meaning "spider") → ***ito*** (**thread**) → ***ito** kurushi* (**very** painful).

[14] The verb *musubu* is used in two ways: 1) in the sense of "blowing something together into something," meaning, "the wind blows the tears on the sleeves into jewels"; 2) in the sense of "to tie," meaning "to tie two sleeves with a sash in order to tuck them up."

[15] ***Kakaru*** (to **fall**) also means "such" and leads to ***kakaru*** *omoi* (**such** grief).

People will look upon me, oh, how very shameful!

TSURE

The sun is about to set behind the mountain,[16]

Spoken SHITE

The curfew tolls, announcing a windy evening;

Kakaru TSURE

Although I feel the coldness on my wind-blown sleeves,

SHITE

Since we do this for our own child,

TSURE

I do not feel the chill.

Shidai, *au* SHITE & TSURE

In the shade of the tree where fallen leaves lie thick,[17]
Stormy winds, too, will come scattering the dust.

CHORUS

awazu In the shade of the tree where fallen leaves lie thick,
In the shade of the tree where fallen leaves lie thick,
(au) Stormy winds, too, will come scattering the dust.
Age-uta, *au* Indeed, in this life where we live, sorrowful things,
Indeed in this life where we live, sorrowful things
Trouble ever the hearts of us dust-like beings—[18]
Not to be brushed away is the dew on our sleeves,
The drops of tears we let fall increase in number.
Blown by the wind the
Autumn leaves fall and float on the water. Let them
Stay on our sleeves even for a short while.
Sage-uta, *au* Where our tears fall dew-like, with the moon's image,
Where our tears fall dew-like, with the moon's image
We had a glimpse of our loved one for an instant,
The two sit down. Only on the bamboo grass, gem-white hail is falling
The Shite *listens.* With a sound that is scarcely audible.

---

[16] Lines 56–57: *yama no ha ni **iri*** (behind the mountain range to **set**) → ***iri**ai no **kane*** (**curfew bell**) → ***kane**te shirasuru* (**in advance** to tell).

[17] Lines 61–65: This *shidai* deviates from the standard form, as shown below.

Line	Standard form	*Shōkun*
1	by character(s), in rhythm	by characters, in rhythm
2	by character(s), in rhythm	by characters, in rhythm
3	by character(s), in rhythm	by Chorus, free rhythm
4	by Chorus, in rhythm	by Chorus, free rhythm
5	by Chorus, in rhythm	by Chorus, in rhythm (?)

Hito moya miruran hazukashi ya.

Hi wa yama no ha ni iriai no[16]

Kanete shirasuru yū arashi

Sode samushi to wa omoedomo

Kono tame nareba

Samukarazu.

Ochiba no tsumoru kokage ni ya[17]
Arashi mo chiri to narinuran.

Ochiba no tsumoru kokage ni ya
Ochiba no tsumoru kokage ni ya
Arashi mo chiri tonarinuran.
Geni yo no naka ni uki koto no
Geni yo no naka ni uki koto no
Kokoro ni kakaru chiri nomi wa[18]
Harai mo aenu sode no tsuyu
Namida no kazu ya tsumoruran.
Kaze ni chiri
Mizu ni wa ukamu ochiba o mo
Shibashi sode ni yadosan.
Namida no tsuyu no tsuki no kage
Namida no tsuyu no tsuki no kage
Sore ka to mireba samo arade
Ozasa no ue no tama-arare
Oto mo sadaka ni kikoezu.

---

[18] Lines 68–70: *Chiri* (dust) in the above lines recurs in line 68: *chiri no mi* (dust-like beings), a common expression, comparing man to dust. (Cf. the Roman Catholic admonition on Ash Wednesday: Gen. 3:19—*Quia pulvis es et in pulverem reverteri* ["For thou art dust and unto dust thou shalt return."]) In *kokoro ni kakaru* (hanging on the mind, to worry), *kakaru* mean "such" and "to fall" and is related to *chiri* (dust [which was thought to "fall"]); *harai* (to brush off [said both of the dust and of the dew]) and *tsumoru* (to increase, to pile up) are also *engo* of *chiri. Mi* in the sense of "the body part of a robe" is an *engo* of *sode* (sleeve) in the next line.

Spoken

SHITE

I am so tired
That I think I will rest.

The Waki *stands.*

WAKI

Speaks.

Excuse me, is Pai-t'ao at home?

SHITE

Who is it?

WAKI

It is I.

SHITE

Please come in.

The Waki *sits.*

WAKI

Mondō, *spoken*

I have come to express
My deep sympathy about Chao-chün. It is so painful to imagine your grief.

SHITE

I thank you for your kind visit.

WAKI

By the way, there is something I would like to ask you.
You sweep the ground under this willow tree, never leaving the place.
I would like to know why.

SHITE

When Chao-chün was sent to the Land of the Huns,
She planted this willow.
"If I should die in the Land of the Huns,
This willow would also die," she said.

Kakaru

And, look! The branches on one side are already dead.

WAKI

Indeed, no wonder that you grieve so much.
But for what reason was Chao-chün sent to the Land of the Huns?

Kuri, *awazu*

SHITE

The time when Chao-chün was sent to the Land of the Huns. . . .
As we recall the long gone past,

CHORUS

It was at the time when peace was brought to the land
For the first time.

Amari ni kurushū sōrō hodo ni
Yasumaba ya to omoi sōrō

Ika ni kono ya no uchi ni Hakudō no watari sōrō ka.

Tare nite on-(n)iri sōrō zo.

Iya soregashi ga mairite sōrō

Konata e on-(n)ide sōrae.

Ika ni mōshi sōrō
Sate mo Shōkun no on-koto go-shinjū sasshi mōshite sōrō

On-tomurai arigatō.

Mata mōsu beki koto no sōrō.
Kono yanagi no ko no moto o tachi-sarazu shite kiyome tamō

Nani to mōshitaru on-koto nite sōrō zo.

Shōkun Kokoku e utsusareshi toki
Kono yanagi o ue-oki
Ware Kokoku nite munashiku naraba
Kono yanagi mo karyōzuru to mōshitsuruga
Goran sōrae haya kata-e no karete sōrō.

Geni geni on-nageki mottomo nite sōrō.
Sate sate Shōkun (n)a nani shi ni Kokoku e wa utsusare-tamai sōrō zo.

Satemo Shōkun Kokoku ni utsusareshi

Sono inishie o tazunuru ni

Tenga o osameshi

Hajimenari.

SHITE
At that time, the military power of the Huns was so
strong that
There was no prospect of their quick surrender.
CHORUS
So it was proposed that peace should be made,
And to prove the sincerity of the treaty
Our Majesty made a promise to send a lady of
beauty to that land.
Whereupon
Kuse, *au* An imperial order was issued, which said:
"There are three thousand women in our favor,[19]
We do not know how to select one out of them.
Let the figures of these court ladies
Of enchanting beauty and graceful nobleness,
Like the Screens of the Sages and Saints,[20]
Be painted in portraits true to life, so that
If we find an inferior one among them,
All we have to do is select that woman
And bestow her on the King of the Land of Huns,
And thus let peace reign in all lands under the sun."
When the Imperial order was announced,
Ladies of the royal court in great number
Were deeply disturbed, not knowing what to do.
They negotiated with the painters,
All sending them bribes, and tried to win them over,
Until they made promises in the ladies' favor.
SHITE
Because of this, their figures portrayed by the artists,
CHORUS
One and all of them, were beautiful beyond words.
Their hair was like willows gently waving in the wind,
Their faces, like peach blossoms laden with dew
That seemed to deepen the flowery color ever more.
Among these ladies Chao-chün was
A woman of great beauty whom none could equal,
and

---

[19] "Three thousand women in our favor": Cf. the opening of the *Chang-hen ge* (Jpn *Chō-gon ka;* The Song of Everlasting Sorrow; lines 19–20) by Po Chü-i in his lyric on the love between T'ang emperor Hsüan-tsung (r. 713–56) and his "Precious Consort," Yang K'uei-fei: *Han-kung chia-li san-ch'ien jen / San-ch'ien ch'ung-ai tsai yi shen* [***Kankyū** no keiri **sanzen-nin** / Sanzen **no chōai** isshin ni ari*] (In the **Han** Majesty's harem were **beauties three thousand**

Shikareba Kokoku no ikusakō-oshite

Shitagō koto goshi-gatashi.

Sareba tagai ni wa bokushite
Sono shirushi hito tsunakaran (n)ya tote
Bijin no ichinin tsukawasu beki on-(n)yakusoku no arishi ni

Somo Kan-(n)ō no senji ni wa
Sanzen-nin no chōai[19]
Izure o wakuru kata mo nashi.
Moromoro no kyūjo no
Kōshoku kōi no sugata o
Kenshō no shōji ni[20]
Nise-e ni kore o arawashi
Naka ni otoreru sama araba
Sunawachi kare o eramite
Ko-ō no tame ni tsukawashi
Tenga no un-(n)o shizumen to
Ringen narase tamaeba
Kazukazu no kyūjo tachi
Kore o ika ni to kanashimi
Ekakeru hito o katarai
Mina mainai o okuri-tsutsu
On-(n)yakusoku no arishi yue

Sareba utsuseru sono sugata

Izure o miru mo tae ni shite
Ryū hakkaze ni taoyaka ni
Tōgan tsuyu o fukunde
Iro nao fukaki sugata nari.
Naka nimo Shōkun (n)a
Narabu kata naki bijin nite

[in number]; / but the **Imperial favor** to be bestowed on three thousand was poured on only one).

[20] Screens of Sages and Saints: Sliding screens with the portraits of thirty-two ancient Chinese sages and saints. Far from being in some ancient Chinese palace, they are actually in the Shishin-den Hall of the Japanese Imperial Palace in Kyoto.

Thus she was the Emperor's great favorite.
This must have made her feel confident of herself,
She remained calm and unperturbed.
However, her image rendered in a portrait
Impressed all as so plain and unattractive that
Although the Emperor loved her
Very deeply, the thought must have occurred to him that
For a man of virtue no selfish
Thoughts existed.[21] As he reflected in this way,

A mirror is placed at jō-za.

He found no other way but to have Chao-chün
Sent away to the remote barbarian land.

Spoken

SHITE

Long ago there was a man named T'ao-yeh,[22]
Who was deeply in love with a fairy.
After her death,
When he put peach blossoms before a mirror,
He would see her image reflected there.
This willow, too, is the very image of Chao-chün.

The Shite *and* Tsure *both stand.*

Come here, let us see the reflection of the tree in the mirror, and thus see her image.

Kakaru

TSURE

But that was the image of a fairy,
Not comparable to our daughter.

Spoken

SHITE

No, no, it is not only that. In a mirror
We see the reflection of those who are dear to us.

Kakaru

TSURE

What was it that reflected a dream-like figure?

Spoken

SHITE

A mirror spotless clear that Hsien-yang possessed.[23]

---

[21] This is thought to have been a popular saying such as, "The Imperial word is like sweat," meaning that what the emperor said is not to be retracted, or "A virtuous man speaks no joke."

[22] The sources of these passages are unknown. The name T'ao-yeh (Tōyō) means "Peach Leaf." The peach has been considered to have magic power to drive away evils. In Japan, people used to put peach leaves in the bath to heal prickly heat.

[23] *Shin'yō ga mochishi masu-kagami:* Sanari (3: 1587n) says that he cannot decipher Shin'yō (*shin'yau*). Yokomichi and Omote (1: 171, n27) say that it is an unidentified person's name, but we wonder if it could it be Hsien-yang, the capital of the Yellow Emperor of Ch'in? They also say that the Hōshō, Kita, and Konparu texts they consulted give the word as *shinnyō*. It is very tempting to think that the word might have been the Buddhist term *shinnyo* (Skt. *tathatā*), which means, "thusness, the ultimate reality, as-it-is-ness, the Truth." The term *shinnyo* appears in many Noh texts, including *Arashiyama, Dai-e, Funabashi, Makiginu, Yamanba,* and *Yumi Yawata,* among others. It is often used in connection with the moon, as in

Mikado no oboetarishi nari.
Sore o tanomeru yue yaran
Tada uchi-tokete arishi ni
Gato ni utsuseru omokage no
Amari iyashiku mieshikaba
Sakoso wa chōai
Hanahadashishi to mōsedomo
Kunshi ni watakushi no
Kotoba nashi[21] to ya oboshiken
Chikara nakushite Shōkun (n)o
Kokoku ni okuri-tsukawasaru.

Mukashi Tōyō to iishi hito[22]
Senjo to chigiri asakarazarishi ni
Senjo munashiku narite nochi
Momo no hana o kagami ni utsuseba
Sunawachi senjo no sugata miekeru to nari.
Kono yanagi mo sanagara Shōkun no sugata
Iza sase-tamae kagami ni utsushite kage o min.

Sore wa senjo no sugata nari
Ikade kore ni wa tatō beki.

Iya sore nomi narazu kagami ni wa
Koishiki hito no utsurunari.

Yume no sugata o utsushishi wa

Shinnyō ga mochishi masu-kagami[23]

"the moon of Truth," as can be seen in these two examples:

Arashiyama (*age-uta* leading to *nakairi*): ***Shinnyo*** *no tsuki no sumeru yo ni / Gojoku no nigori ari tote mo* (The pollution of the Five Defilements exists / Even in the world in which the Moon of Truth shines).

Yamanba (*sashi* leading to *kuse*): *Mae ni wa kaisui jō-jō to shite / Tsuki* ***shinnyo*** *no hikari o kakage* (In front, the waters of the seas flow abundantly, / And the moon displays the light of Truth).

Given the common usage of the phrase, we cannot rule out the possibility that this line was once intended to mean something like: *Shinnyo ga utsushi masu-kagami* (The clear, spotless mirror that reflected Truth)—reminiscent of the Mirror of the Forest Guardian in the Noh *Nomori,* and the mirror of the King of Hell (*see* Note 29 below). For the ancient Chinese, the mirror was itself a source of light that could illuminate the eternal darkness of the tomb; it also was thought of as a symbol of enlightenment.

Kakaru — TSURE

Who saw a reflection of his native land in a mirror?

Spoken — SHITE

It was a traveler whose name was T'u-chüeh.[24]

Kakaru — TSURE

It is an ancient story. For many years past,[25]

SHITE

The water has been a mirror for the flowers.

Au — CHORUS

The Tsure *sits before the* Chorus. *The* Shite *puts the mirror at down-stage center, and then sits at center stage and weeps.*

When flowers fall as dust, it will become clouded.
Increasing grief, in the clear and spotless mirror,[26]
Hoping in vain to see her image reflected,
Together they gaze into the mirror, weeping,
Together they gaze into the mirror, weeping.

Spoken — WAKI

I say, is anyone there?

AI

Coming from the kyōgen-za.

At your service, Sir.

WAKI

Take the old man into the house.

AI

With all my heart. (*To the* Shite:) Farewell, now please go inside.

NAKAIRI and AI-KYŌGEN *The* Shite *exits. The* Ai-kyōgen *accompanies him half way, taking him to the* hashi-gakari. *Then he returns to the main stage and tells the story of Chao-chün and her aged parents, after which he performs a dance in her memory.*

---

[24] *Toketsu to iishi ryojin nari:* Sanari (ibid.) says that he cannot decipher "Toketsu." Yokomichi and Omote (ibid.), who read it as "Togetsu," say it is an unidentified person's name. However, they also suggest that the line might be read *Tokketsu to iishi ryojin nari* = It was a captive prisoner of a tribe called T'u-chüeh (= a Turkish tribe that ruled a vast empire from the 6th to the 8th centuries in central Asia and Mongolia; it was a name taken by a branch of the Hsiung-nu [Huns] defeated by the Tatars in the fifth century; thus, they were the first "Turks," later defeated and absorbed by the Uighurs). Although anachronistic (since Chao-chün lived in the first century BC), it is not unusual for such a discrepancy to occur in a Noh text. Thus, their idea is not that far fetched, as the Chinese reading is indeed T'u-chüeh.

[25] Lines 157–59. From a poem by Lady Ise in the *Kokin-shū* (44): *Toshi o hete / Hana no kagami to / Naru mizu wa / Chirikakaru o ya / Kumoru to iuran.* For the explanation of this poem, *see* the end of the introduction to *Shōkun.*

[26] *Omoi wa . . . **masu*** (grief increases) → ***masu**-kagami* (**clear** mirror).

Furusato o kagami ni utsushishi wa

Toketto iishi ryojin nari.[24]

Sore wa mukashi ni toshi o hete[25]

Hana no kagami to naru mizu wa

Chiri kakaru hana ya kumoruran
Omoi wa itodo masu-kagami[26]
Moshi mo sugata o miru ya to
Kagami ni mukatte naki-itari
Kagami ni mukatte naki-itari

Ika ni tare ka aru.

On-mae ni sōrō

Rōjin (n)o uchi e tomonai sōrae.

Kashikomatte sōrō Saraba on-tachi sōrae.

(*The original Japanese text of the* Ai-Kyōgen *text is omitted below.*)

The Ai-kyogen, a court official, enters the stage to Ranjo *music.*

AI

I who am here before you now am an official who worked in the service of Wang Chao-chün. I it was who was ordered to deliver her to the land of the Huns.

Well, now, as there were more than 3,000 women in the Han court, the Emperor ordered that portraits of them all be painted, so that he could gaze upon them day in and day out. But everyone was afraid that theirs would be the most ugly portrait. For that reason, all the woman of the court, each and every one, pleaded with the painter, bribing him to paint them beautifully. Therefore, the painter applied all the skills of his brush, giving them faces like moonlit flowers, making them all beautiful beyond words, so that it was quite impossible to distinguish one from another. And among the court ladies, there was one called Chao-chün. Priding herself on being the most beautiful of all the 3,000, it never occurred to her to bribe the painter to get special favors concerning her portrayal. So, since she offered the painter neither gift nor bribe, the portrait he painted had not the slightest resemblance to her.

Now, for some years previous to this, General Hu Han-yeh, Khan of all the Huns, had been laying siege incessantly upon the Han Capital. Their army could not be stopped, and one year the Khan made a proposal of peace on the condition that the Emperor make him a gift of one of the women from his court. Thus, in the interest of bringing an end to all hostilities, the Emperor agreed to the Khan's request.

So, in order to decide which court lady would be chosen, he took all the portraits and examined them, and, when he perceived that Chao-chün's portrayal was inferior to the others, he decided to send her to the land of the Huns.

Then, in order to take her leave of the Emperor, Chao-chün was granted an audience before him for the very first time. And when the Emperor saw her face glowing with radiance, he was amazed to see that she was truly a great beauty whom none could equal. Though he fervently desired to rescind his decision, the word of an emperor, like perspiration once excreted, can never be retracted, so, with great reluctance, he dispatched her to the land of the Huns. Then, the court painter, Mao Yen-shou, who had unjustly depicted

Chao-chün in such an unflattering manner, was punished for his crime, and the Emperor had him beheaded in broad daylight.

As for Chao-chün, as she set out from the Capital, there was nothing that could console her. Therefore, sitting in her carriage, she played the lute to comfort herself as much as she was able, but even so its four strings called forth copious tears. She thus wept pitiful tears until they reached the land of the Huns. She spent her days and nights longing for the Capital she so loved—but it was naught but a fleeting memory. In the end, her heart was filled with such great sorrow that she finally passed away, and was interred within the ground without ceremony. But after a time, purification rites were held over her grave, after which her parents received the grievous news of her demise, at which they sorrowed greatly.

But recently I heard that just before Chao-chün had departed for the land of the Huns, she planted a willow with her very own hands, saying, "If I should die in the land of the Huns, this willow shall also wither and die."

Now, one day, her parents noticed that one branch of the willow had begun to lose its color, and they raised their voices in fear and lamentation, sitting at the foot of the willow each day until the sun left the sky.

And this reminds me of another thing that I have heard. They say that while all of the grass in the land of the Huns is dried and devoid of color, and that there is not a single blade of green grass or green leaf on any tree, the grass around the grave mound of Chao-chün grows with such a vivid viridian hue that it has come to be called the "Green Mound."

Thus, as I am convinced that Chao-chün's spirit has caused the grass on her grave in the land of the Huns to take on the lush green of the Capital, as well as the willow in the Capital to display the withered colorlessness of the land of the Huns, I have decided to go and offer my condolences to her parents, and then to gaze upon that willow tree. (*He performs a circuit of the stage during the above, so that he has arrived by the time he recites the next line.*)

Sung I shall perform a special dance in her honor.
And now, as a memorial performance, I shall do a single dance.

Sings while dancing. Does a 3-part Dance.

And not long after, the enchanting sound of the biwa,
Now I do remember well Chao-chün,
Now I do remember well Chao-chün's
Figure like a willow tree waving in spring winds,
Its swaying branches yielding to the ruler of the Huns,
The pledge that together bound them was not shallow,
Green the thread that thus linked them,
And their teardrops fell like precious beads of jade,
Like the music and this dance, all must fade away.

Exits.

—ACT 2—

ISSEI *The* Kokata (Nochi-tsure), *Chao-chün's ghost, enters and stands by the first pine.*

Sashi, *awazu*

KOKATA (NOCHI-TSURE)

Of one who was sent to the Land of the Huns,
Wang Chao-chün, this is the ghost.
My parents, lamenting our separation,
Under a willow tree now in spring,
Weep so bitterly. How piteous!
In haste I will make my form appear in the mirror,
So that my father and mother may see my image.

Issei, *awazu* / *The* Shite *enters the stage.*

On this vernal night,[27]
When the moon casts her light through mist,
I appear and,

CHORUS

Though hazy and indistinct,
Reveal my shadow.

The Tsure *sits on a stool before the flutist.*

HAYA-FUE *The* Nochi-shite, *the ghost of Hu Han-yeh, enters running and squats before the mirror.*

Kakaru

TSURE

How terrible! I see an image like a demon
That makes my hair stand on end.
Who can it be
That reveals his shadow reflected in the mirror?

---

[27] Lines 175–76: From a poem by Ōe no Chisato in *Shin Kokin-shū* (55): *Teri mo sezu / Kumori mo hatenu / **Haru no yo no** / **Oborozukiyo ni** / Shiku mono zo naki* (Not in full bright-

Kore wa Kokoku ni utsusareshi
Ō Shōkun no yūkon nari.
Sate mo chichi hawa wakare o kanashimi
Haru no yanagi no kono moto ni
Naki kanashimi-tamō itawashisa yo.
Isogi kagami ni kage o utsushi
Chichi hawa ni sugata o mie mōsan.
Haru no yo no[27]
Oborozukiyo ni arawarete

Kumori nagara mo
Kage mien.

Osoroshi ya oni to ya iwan omokage no
Mi no ke mo yodatsu bakari nari.
Ika naru hito nite mashimaseba
Kagami ni wa utsuri-tamōran.

---

ness, / Nor totally veiled in cloud / **On a vernal night, / The moon casts her light through mist**— / There is none to surpass this!)

NOCHI-SHITE

Of the Great General of the alien Land of the Huns,
Hu Han-yeh *Shan-yü,*[28]
This is the ghost.

TSURE

Those who live in the alien Land of the Huns are human beings.
The figure I see now is not of a man.
What I have never seen but have heard about,[29]
A demon of Hell, can this be? How terrible!

SHITE

I, Hu Han-yeh (*spoken*) *Shan-yü,* too, am no longer of this life.
Like Chao-chün, her parents
To see, I have come.

TSURE

Kakaru

There is no meeting
With one so terrible to look at.

Spoken

SHITE

But why are you so terrified?

Kakaru

TSURE

You are unaware of your own appearance.
Go and look at the mirror.

SHITE

Let me (*spoken*) look at myself reflected in the mirror

Kakaru

And see if I really appear so dreadful.

Spoken. The Shite *rises and looks in the mirror.* Kakaru

So I approach the mirror and look hard—
It is no wonder that you are terrified.

Noru. *The* taiko *joins in.*

CHORUS

The head is crowned with entangled brambles of hair,
The head is crowned with entangled brambles of hair,

SHITE

That separates itself from the roots and rises,

CHORUS

Not to be tied up with twisted paper string, so

SHITE

With a piece of wild creeping ivy it is bound.

---

[28] *See* the introduction.

Kore wa Kokoku no ebisu no Taishō Ko Kan(n)ya Zennu ga[28]

Yūrei nari.

Kokoku no ebisu wa ningen nari.

Ima miru sugata wa hito narazu.
Me ni wa minedomo oto ni kiku[29]
Meido no oni ka osoroshi ya.

Ko Kan(n)ya Zennu mo munashiku naru

Onajiku Shōkun ga chichi hawa ni
Taimen no tame ni kitaritari.

Yoshi nakarikeru taimen kana.
Sugata o miru mo osoroshi ya.

Somo osoru beki iware wa ika ni.

Kokoro ni shiranu waga sugata
Kagami ni yorite mi-tamae to yo.

Ide ide kagami ni kage o utsusan.
Makoto ni kyo-otoki sugata ka to
Kagami ni tachi-yori yoku yoku mireba
Osore-tamō mo ara dōri ya.

Odoro o itadaku kami suji wa
Odoro o itadaku kami suji wa

Nushi o hanarete sora ni tachi

Moto yuisara ni tamaraneba

Sane kazura nite musubi sage

---

[29] *Me ni mienu oni* (the demon that is invisible to the eye) is a common phrase.

CHORUS

From the ears, chains are hanging in place of rings,
so that

SHITE

It seems that I appear to you

CHORUS

As a demon. I am so ashamed!
Approaching close to the mirror
And standing and sitting down
I look and see a demon there, not a human.
Is that myself, or is it not? Even to myself
How very terrible appears that countenance!
I am so ashamed. With these words he goes away.

Hira-nori. The Shite *dances to the song.*

Indeed the painted eyebrows of Chao-chün,
Indeed the painted eyebrows of Chao-chün
Are like unto the color of the willow's leaves.
The clear mirror that reflects the sins of people[30]
Will never allow this to remain unrevealed.
On the days when the flowery image is cloud-bound,
The absent mind, trouble-laden, drifts up skyward, where,
Its light faintly visible, shines the crescent moon—[31]
Cloudless-clear is the mind, to be looked upon as
A mirror that reveals truth in its reflection,
A mirror that reveals truth in its reflection.

The Shite *stamps the* tome-byōshi.

---

[30] "The clear mirror that reflects . . ." means the mirror hanging in the office of the King of Hell, in which one sees reflected all the sins committed by a person during his lifetime.

Sane kazura nite musubi sage
Mimi ni wa kusari o sagetareba

Kijin to mitamō

Sugata mo hazukashi
Kagami ni yori-soi
Tattemo itemo
Oni to wa miredomo hito to wa miezu.
Sono mi ka aranu ka ware naraba
Osoroshikarikeru kaotsuki kana.
Menboku nashi tote tachi-kaeru.
Tada Shōkun no mayuzumi wa,
Tada Shōkun no mayuzumi wa,
Yanagi no iro ni kotonarazu
Tsumi o arawasu jōhari wa[30]
Sore mo kakure wa yomo araji.
Hana ka to miete kumoru hi wa
Uwa no sora naru mono-omoi
Kage mo honoka ni mikazuki no[31]
Kumoranu hito no kokoro koso
Makoto o utsusu kagami nare,
Makoto o utsusu kagami nare.

---

[31] *honoka ni **mi*** (faintly **seen**) —> ***mi**kazuki* (**third**-day moon = crescent moon). *Mikazuki* is an introductory word (*jo-kotoba*) for *kumoranu* (not clouded).

熊坂

KUMASAKA

熊坂も長刀かまへ。たがひにかゝるを待ちけるが。

Kumasaka, too, holds his halberd level; they
Each mutually wait for the other's attack . . .

Introduction

The Noh *Kumasaka* presents a story about Kumasaka no Chōhan, a legendary highwayman who broke into an inn and was killed by the youth Ushiwaka-maru (later known as Minamoto no Yoshitsune, a great hero; *see* the introduction to *Kurama Tengu*). In the Noh, a traveling monk is accosted by a stranger, a monk like himself, and is asked to say a prayer for someone whose grave is in the shade of a tall pine tree they can see off in the distance. The stranger takes the traveler to his hermitage, where a great number of arms, such as halberds and iron staffs, are placed against a wall of the altar room. To the wonder-stricken traveler the stranger says that the area is infested with thieves and highwaymen who attack people night and day. On such occasions, the monk fights with them and drives them away, so that he is looked up to by the people in the neighborhood as someone they can rely on. Then, as if in excuse of his prowess, which might seem unfit for a monk, he tells how the buddhas themselves use force to save people. The story ended, he seems to retire into his bedroom. However, in the morning the traveler finds himself lying on the grass in a field. In the second act, the ghost of Kumasaka appears to the traveling monk and tells how he attacked the goldmonger Sanjō no Kichiji Nobutaka, and was killed by the young Ushiwaka-maru.

Similar stories about the burglars who attacked the goldmonger Kichiji and were killed by Ushiwaka-maru (also Ushiwaka) are told briefly in such military stories as the *Heiji Monogatari* and *Gikeiki* ("The Chronicle of Yoshitsune"). However, the name Kumasaka no Chōhan is not found among the names of burglars mentioned in them. The Noh *Eboshi-ori* (The Hat-maker), a sword-fighting piece among the fourth-group plays, tells the same story realistically. While in *Kumasaka,* the *Shite* is the ghost of the highwayman, who shadow-fights with young Ushiwaka, in *Eboshi-ori* the living Kumasaka appears with his followers and actually fights with Ushiwaka and is killed by him. There is a genre of popular dance and music play named *Kōwaka-mai,* which also has a piece named *Eboshi-ori.* The highwayman's name in this play is Kumasaka no Chōhan (Chōhan of Kumasaka). Probably this and the two Noh in question are the only cases in which the name Kumasaka no Chōhan is mentioned. It is considered that he is largely a legendary character, and possibly not the one who attacked the goldmonger, although one version of the *ai-kyōgen* of *Kumasaka* (that given in this translation) tells the *Waki* monk how Kumasaka became a thief. (For further details, *see* the Introduction to and translation of *Eboshi-ori* in *Troubled Souls from Japanese Noh Plays of the Fourth Group,* CEA series No. 95.)

Kumasaka is a fifth-group Noh in the subgroup known as *tōjō-mono* (warring-ghost pieces), a group of visional Noh, in which the ghost of a warrior tells the *Waki,* typically a Buddhist monk, the story of the battle he fought. (For *tōjō-mono, see* the Introduction to the Fifth-Group Noh.) Exceptionally, the *Shite* of *Kumasaka* is not a warrior, but a highwayman. Still, leading a large number of thieves, he made a night attack at an inn, fought, and was killed. Thus, the story is typical of a *tōjō-mono,* and the play is structured according to the standard pattern of a visional Noh. The play is unique in that its *Mae-shite* appears in the form of a monk without a mask. Since the *Waki* is also a monk, we see on the stage two characters, protagonist and antagonist, attired exactly alike, except for the colors of their under collars—that of the *Shite* being light blue, and that of the *Waki,* dark blue. The effect is very unusual. This happens only in *Kumasaka.* Unlike a majority of fifth-group Noh, *Kumasaka* has neither a *mai* nor a *mai-bataraki.* Instead, the long final scene is a one-man performance by Kumasaka's ghost, who describes his fighting with Ushiwaka through a dance accompanied by the Chorus.

One of the structural characteristics peculiar to some visional Noh is found at the beginning of this scene, in which the night attack is described in an exchange between the *Shite* and the *Waki,* with the *Waki* singing as if he were one of the participants or an eye-witnesses (lines 150–66). Such a structural peculiarity, rare in Western theatre, points to the narrative elements in Noh. Similar examples are found, among others, in *No-no-Miya* in the third-group and *Ukai* (The Cormorant Fisher) among the fifth-group Noh. The penultimate section, in which Kumasaka throws away his halberd and tries to grapple with Ushiwaka, is sung in the heavy and impressive *ō-nori* rhythm, accompanied by all four instruments, including the *taiko* (the stick drum). In the final section, in which the rhythm changes to the quiet *hira-nori* (ordinary rhythm) without *taiko,* the ghost tells how, mortally wounded, he faded away like dew or frost on the moss on the roots of the pine tree, the site of his grave. Although the play thus ends pathetically, on the whole it is written in a language fit for a character like Kumasaka, an uncultured villain. We even come across a comical expression unusual in

Noh, such as: "Indeed, we can steal only while we are alive. There is no way left for us but to retreat," sung by the Chorus for Kumasaka when he sees his men slain one after another by Ushiwaka. There are similar lines in *Eboshi-ori* also. What adds to this humorous effect is the mask worn by the *Nochi-shite,* such as *chōrei-beshimi* or *kuro-beshimi,* large-sized grotesque masks with huge round golden eyes, a nose with huge nostrils, and an oversized mouth that is tightly shut as if compressed in a long line. A mask with such an exaggerated expression is more comic than awe-inspiring. These masks are worn exclusively by the *Nochi-shite* of this Noh and *Eboshi-ori.* In spite of all such features, the rogue is not entirely a stranger to pious aspiration. He appears as a monk in the first act, and in his talk with the traveling monk, he compares his prowess to the buddhas' swords of mercy. Some philosophical remarks he makes on man's ignorance of truth seem to be his self-reflection on his own fault. These lines and the pathetic finale combined achieve a dramatic effect one could associate with *Dr. Jekyll and Mr. Hyde.*

Scene Akasaka in Mino Province, present-day Gifu Prefecture.
Season September by the lunar calendar.
Characters and costumes
Waki A traveling monk, in a monk's costume consisting of *sumi-bōshi* head gear and a plain *atsuita kitsuke* under a *mizugoromo* robe, carrying prayer beads.
Mae-shite The ghost of Kumasaka no Chōhan in the form of a monk, in a costume similar to the *Waki's,* with prayer beads in hand. He does not wear a mask.
Nochi-shite The ghost of Kumasaka no Chōhan, wearing a *kuro-beshimi, chōrei-beshimi,* or *Kumasaka* mask, his head covered in a headdress named *Chōhan-zukin* (used exclusively in this Noh and in *Eboshi-ori*), a *dan-atsuita kitsuke* in subdued colors, with or without a *happi* robe over it, and a *hangire* divided skirt.
Ai-kyōgen A villager.
Author Not identified.

Kumasaka

熊坂

—Act 1—

SHIDAI *The* Waki, *a traveling monk, enters and stands at the* nanori-za, *facing the pine tree painted on the back panel.*

Shidai, *au*

WAKI

A sad being who renounces life and himself,
A sad being who renounces life and himself,
Whither and till when is he to drift about thus?

Jidori, *awazu*

CHORUS

The Waki *turns around and faces front.*

A sad being who renounces life and himself,
Whither and till when is he to drift about thus?

WAKI

Nanori, *spoken*

I am a monk from the Capital City.
I have not yet visited the eastern provinces,
So I have decided to make a pilgrimage to the East.

Michiyuki, *au*

The mountain is crossed[1]
And this must be the Ōmi Road, with the lake
And this must be the Ōmi Road, with the lake
And Foamy Ford's woods in view, stretching far across,
The Long Bridge of Seta is quickly left behind,
Noji and Shinowara lie still in night's veil,[2]
Rising at morn as I tread the dew-laden path,
A place they call Greenfield Moor, in spite of the name,[3]
Already touched by autumn colors, Scarlet Slope
Hamlet lies in the declining light of the sun,
The hamlet lies in the declining light of the sun.

YOBI-KAKE *The* Waki *goes toward the* waki-za. *The* Shite, *in the guise of a monk, enters, calling to the* Waki, *who stops.*

---

[1] Lines 9–13: The mountain: Mt. Ōsaka, in the present Shiga Prefecture, was the site of Ōsaka Barrier, the first barrier on the road from Kyoto to Lake Biwa and the East. It appears in classical poetry as a place where people come and go, exchanging farewells. It was also the site of the play *Semimaru,* which appears in *Troubled Souls.* One of Prince Semimaru's own poems on the barrier is: *Kore ya kono / yuku mo kaeru mo / wakarete mo / shiru mo shiranu mo / Ōsaka no seki* (So indeed this is / Where men going and coming / Are separated / And, acquainted or not, meet— / Ōsaka [*Troubled Souls,* pp. 43, 66 (ll. 90–19)]; it appears in both the *Gosen-shū* and the *Hyakunin Isshu*). Indeed, in the Japanese preface to the *Kokin-shū,* Ki no Tsurayuki (ca. 872–945) mentions Ōsaka Barrier as an *uta-makura* for meeting and parting. Ōmi is the ancient name of Shiga Prefecture, the area surrounding Lake Biwa. *Mizu-umi*

Ushi to wa iite sutsuru mi no
Ushi to wa iite sutsuru mi no
Yukue itsu to ka sadamuran.

Ushi to wa iite sutsuru mi no
Yukue itsu to ka sadamuran.

Kore wa Miyako-gata yori idetaru sō nite sōrō.
Ware imada Tōgoku o mizu sōrō hodo ni
Tadaima omoitachi Tōgoku shugyō to kokorozashi sōrō.

Yama koete[1]
Ōmi-ji nare ya mizu-umi no
Ōmi-ji nare ya mizu-umi no
Awazu no Mori mo mie-wataru

Seta no Nagayashi uchi-sugite
Noji Shinowara ni yo o komete[2]
Asa tatsu michi no tsuyu fukaki
Na koso Aono-ga-hara nagara[3]

Irozuku iro ka Akasaka no
Sato mo kure-yuku hikage kana
Sato mo kure-yuku hikage kana.

---

no ***awa*** (lake's foam) → ***Awazu*** (a place name; literally, **Foamy** Ford). *Mie-**wataru*** (visible **far across**) → ***wataru*** (to cross) → *Seta no Nagahashi* (Seta Long Bridge), which spans the Seta River where it flows from the southern end of the lake. It is also interesting to note that the name of the barrier, which is written as "Meeting Barrier," is closely followed by Awazu, which is homonymous with "not meeting."

[2] Noji, Shinowara: Places near Lake Biwa. ***Shino**wara* → ***Shino*** (a type of bamboo with thin stems, that grows low like grass) → ***yo*** (joint in the stem of bamboo, grass) → ***yo** o komete* (all **night**).

[3] Lines 16–17: Aono-ga-hara (Greenfield Moor), Akasaka (Scarlet Slope): places in Mino Province, in the present Gifu Prefecture.

Yobi-kake
Spoken

SHITE
You, you holy man there, I have something to ask you.

Mondō, *spoken*

WAKI
Are you calling me? What is it that you want to ask me?

SHITE
Today is the date of death of a certain person. Please pray for the repose of his soul.

WAKI
That is what a monk is glad to do.
Tell me, for whom am I to pray?

The Shite *stops by the first pine.*

SHITE
Even if his name is not told, . . .
Over there you see a solitary pine tree,
And a little way down, a patch of grassland.
That is the old burial ground of the man.
I say this because it is a place untrodden by men.

WAKI
What a story!
To pray for somebody without knowing the name, I wonder if that is right.

The Shite *enters the stage and stands at* jō-za.

SHITE
There is nothing wrong about that.
"All in Buddha's Universe are equally blessed."[4]

Kakaru

WAKI
"Freed from life and death. . . ."

SHITE
To free him,

Age-uta, *au*

CHORUS
If your prayer should be bestowed on his person,
If your prayer should be bestowed on his person,
Even though his name remains unrevealed to you,
The person who rejoices,
Should be the one for whose repose you pray, thank Buddha!
Since prayer saves even grasses and trees, all on earth,[5]

---

[4] Lines 33–34: Lines chanted in prayer. *Shōji* (life and death) in *Shuri* ***shōji*** (freed from life and death) is at the same time the first word of the imperative phrase, ***Shōji*** *o hanare yo* (From life and death be freed!).

Nō, nō, arenaru on-sō ni mōsu-beki koto no sōrō.

Konata no koto nite sōrō ka, nanigoto nite sōrō zo.

Kyō wa saru mono no meinichi nite sōrō, tomuraite tamawari sōrae.

Sore koso shukke no nozomi nare,
Sarinagara tare to kokorozashite ekō mōsu-beki.

Tatoi sono na wa mōsazutomo
Are ni mietaru hitoki no matsu no
Sukoshi konata no kayawara koso
Tadaima mōsu kofun nare.
Ōbuku naraneba mōsunari.

Ara nani tomo naya
Tare to na o shirade ekō wa ikanaran.

Yoshi sore totemo kurushikarazu.
Hōkai shujō byōdō riyaku[4]

Shurri shōji o

Hanare yo tono

On-tomurai o mi ni ukeba
On-tomurai o mi ni ukeba
Tatoi sono na wa nanorazu tomo
Uke-yorokobaba
Sore koso nushi yo arigata ya.

Ekō wa sō-moku koku-do made[5]

---

[5] *Sōmoku kokudo* (grasses and trees, all on earth): The beginning of a phrase that ends *shikkai jōbutsu* (one and all attain Buddhahood), a common saying said to originate in the *Chūin-gyō* (Antarabhāva Sutra).

Letting none left unabsolved, though you may not
know
The name of the person for whom you are praying,
It should be a prayer none the less—
It would never be that he remains unredeemed.

Spoken SHITE

Will you come this way?
My hermitage is over there. I pray you to pass
the night there.

WAKI

Then let me accompany you.

The Shite *sits center stage; the* Waki, *at the* waki-za.

Spoken WAKI

Excuse me,
I thought that I would say a prayer in the altar
room. However,
On the altar you have no icons, painted or
carved in wood.
Against one wall you have put a long halberd,
And in place of a crosier, an iron staff,
And all sorts of weapons you have in a thick row.
What does this mean?

SHITE

Well, I am only a novice.
As you see, around here,
There are Tarui, Ōhaka, Scarlet Slope
And many other hamlets. However,
The paths leading to them
Lie across Greenfield Moor grown with tall grass,
And through Ōhaka and Koyasu Woods' dense growth,
So that, even during the day, when it rains,
Highwaymen and burglars
Knock down travelers' baggage. Even the
town-bound
Maid-servants and hired women
Have their clothes stripped off and wail aloud.
On such an occasion, this monk
Arms himself with that halberd,
"Leave it to this monk,"
He calls out. Sure enough,
Calamities have been thus fended off for the nonce.
On such an occasion, people around the place

Morasaji nareba wakite sono

Aruji ni to kokoro-ate naku tomo
Sate koso ekō nare
Ukamadewa ikaga aru-beki.

Sarabe konata e on-(n)iri sōrae,
Gusō ga anjitsu no sōrō ni ichiya o akashite on-tōri sōrae.

Saraba kō mairōzuru nite sōrō.

Ikani mōshi sōrō,
Jibutsudō ni mairi tsutome o hajimyōzuru to zonji sōrō tokoro ni

Anchi-shitamō-beki ezō mokuzō no katachi mo naku

Ippeki ni wa ō-naginata
Shujō ni arazaru kane no bō
Sono hoka hyōgu wo hisshito tate-okare sōrō wa
Nani to mōshitaru on-koto nite sōrō zo.

Sanzōrō kono sō wa imada shohosshin no mono nite sōrō ga
Goran sōrō gotoku kono atari wa
Tarui, Ōhaka, Akasaka tote
Sono sato-zato wa ōkeredomo
Aida, aida no michi-sugara
Aono-ga-hara no kusa takaku
Ōhaka, Koyasu no mori shigekereba
Hiru to mo iwazu ame no uchi ni wa
Sanzoku yotō no nusubito-ra
Taka ni o otoshi sato-gayoi no

Gejo ya hashita no mono made mo
Uchi-hagitorare naki-sakebu.
Sayō no toki wa kono sō mo
Rei no naginata hissage-tsutsu
Koko oba gusō ni makaseyo to
Yobawari-kakureba geni wa mata
Ichido wa samo naki toki mo ari,
Sayō no toki wa kono tokoro no

Look up at this monk as one to be counted on, and
They all rejoice. "So what I have done was right,"
I would think, and that was the only thought I had.
How astounding for a monk to have such a thought!
Kuse, *au* An achievement untestifiable,

CHORUS

Unfit for a monk, this feat of violence,
Surely you must think this a foolish story.
However, even among Buddhas,[6]
Amitābha has his powerful sword, Rāgarāja
Has an arrow notched on his strategic bow;
Vaiśravaṇa with his halberd held level
Beats devils, making them surrender,
And thus clearing the land of all calamities.

SHITE

As it is, attachment, and pity, its offspring,[7]

CHORUS

Should surpass Devadatta's five deadly sins;
Murder committed for a good cause
Exceeds the Bodhisattvas' Six Ways to Nirvana,
I hear.
We look at this, and listen to that,
We judge other people but not our own future.[8]
'T is none but the mind that gets lost or is enlightened.
Therefore they say thus: "Be the teacher of your mind.[9]
Do not look up to your mind as your teacher."
We find this word among our ancient sayings.

---

[6] Lines 81–86: "Amitābha has his powerful sword": Cf. this saying from the *Panchou-tsan* of the Chinese Pure Land master Shan-tao (613–81): *Li-chien chi Mi-t'o hao, i-sheng ch'uang-nien chiang* [*Riken sunawachi Mida no gō, issei shōnen zai mina nozoku*] (The powerful sword is none other than the calling of Amitābha's name; one call of [his] name absolves all sins). Rāgarāja, or Rāga Vidyārāja (Aizen Myō-ō): A Buddhist deity, an emanation of Mahā-Vairocana (Great Sun Buddha). The icon of this deity is shown with either two or three pairs of hands, and in the six-handed form typically holds a vajra thunderbolt and a bell, a bow and an arrow, and a stick and a lotus. He (sometimes she) is the embodiment of love and respect. Vaiśravaṇa (Tamon-ten; also, Bishamon-ten): One of the four Buddhist deities who guard the four quarters of the Buddhist Universe, his area being the north. He is represented as an armored warrior god, holding a sacred tower in one hand, and a halberd in the other. He is the deity enshrined in Kurama Temple (*see* the introduction to *Kurama Tengu*).

[7] Lines 87–90: These four lines contains two pairs of comparisons: 1) attachment, and mercy (pity) born of attachment, are better than Devadatta's five deadly sins; 2) murder for a good cause is better than the Bodhisattvas' Six Ways to Nirvana. Devadatta, Śākyamuni Buddha's cousin, committed the five deadly sins of killing one's father, killing one's mother, killing an

Tayori ni mo naru mono zokashi to
Yorokobi-aeba shikaru-beshi to
Omou bakari no kokoro nari.
Nanbō asamashiki yo-o-sute-bito no shozon zōrō zo.
Shishō naki tegara

Niawanu sō no udedate
Sakoso okashi to obosuran
Sarinagara hotoke mo[6]
Mida no riken (n)ya Aizen na (= wa)
Hōben no yumi ni ya o hage
Tamon na (= wa) hoko o yoko-taete
Akuma o gōbuku shi
Sainan (n)o harai-tamaeri.

Sareba aijaku jihishin na (= wa)[7]

Datta ga gogyaku ni sugure
Hōben no sesshō wa
Bosatsu no rokudo ni masareri toka.

Kore o mi kare o kiki
Ta o zehi shiranu mi no yukue [8]
Mayou mo satoru mo kokoro zo ya.
Sareba kokoro no shi to wa nari [9]
Kokoro o shi to sezare to
Furuki kotoba ni shiraretari.

---

arhat (a high-ranking disciple of Buddha), disturbing a community of monks (*samgha*), and causing the Buddha's body to bleed. Later he repented and attained nirvana. Because of the concise wording, the first comparison is interpreted differently by different commentators. We interpret it as follows: Attachment, as well as mercy, which is caused by attachment, are sins, but they are better than the five deadly sins committed by Devadatta.

The Bodhisattvas' Six Ways to Nirvana (Jpn. *rokudō*, or *ropparamitsu;* Skt. *ṣaṭ-pāramita;* literally, the Six Perfections): Six virtues a bodhisattva should cultivate to attain Nirvana: *dāna* (donation), *śīla* (observance of the commandments), *kṣānti* (forbearance), *vīrya* (persevering efforts to do good and abstain from evil deeds), *dhyāna* (meditation), and *prajñā* (attaining wisdom).

[8] *Ta o **ze-hi shi*** (others **to justify or deny** = to judge others as right or wrong) → ***zehi shi**ranu mi no yukue* (**right or wrong** un**known**, un**known** is one's future).

[9] The quotation is from *Mahā-parinibbana-suttanta* (Jpn. *Nehan-gyō*). According to Sanari (2:938), the Chinese text is: *Yüan tso shih hsin, fu shih yü hsin* [*Gan ni, kokoro no shi to wa nari, kokoro o shi to sezare*] (You must desire to be the teacher of your mind; you must not make your mind your teacher).

But the story-telling such as this,
If spun at length, will last till the break of day.
Pray, go to bed and be rested, you holy man.
I, too, will have some sleep. Good night.
  Having spoke thus,
The Shite *rises.* He was seen to retire into the bed-room, then
His figure faded out, the hermitage, too, was gone,
Leaving but the grassy field. It was in the pine shade
That the traveler has passed the night. Oh, how strange!
That the traveler has passed the night. Oh, how strange!

NAKAIRI *The* Shite *makes an interim exit.*

AI-KYŌGEN *The* Ai-kyōgen, *a villager, enters. Asked by the* Waki, *he tells him about Kumasaka no Chōhan, how he stole people's goods all his life, till he was defeated and was killed by the boy Ushiwaka-maru. The villager thinks that the one who appeared to the traveler must be Kumasaka's ghost, and exhorts the monk to pray for the departed soul. The villager exits.*

AI

I am a resident of the post-town known as Scarlet Slope. As I am feeling somewhat lonely today, I have decided to go out to Greenfield Moor to enjoy myself. (*Separately:*) Oh, this monk I see here is unfamiliar to this area. (*To the monk:*) You, there, you holy monk. Where might it be that you hail from?

WAKI

I am a monk from the Capital City. Are you someone who resides in this vicinity?

AI

It is as you say, Sir. I do indeed reside in this vicinity.

WAKI

That is good to know. Now, please come closer, as there is something I would ask you.

AI

With all my heart. Now, just what might it be that you seek to know?

WAKI

Although it will probably seem most strange, this is what I want to know. As this place from of old abounds with all sorts of evil doers, could you please tell me all you know about them?

Kayou no monogatari
Mōsaba yo mo akenamashi,
Oyasumi are ya o-sō-tachi
Ware mo madoroman saraba to

Menzō ni iru yo to mie-tsuruga
Katachi mo usete anjitsu mo
Kusamura to narite matsukage ni
Yo o akashitaru fushigi sa yo
Yo o akashitaru fushigi sa yo.

(*The Japanese original of the* Ai-kyōgen *text is omitted.*)

AI

You ask me about something of which I have heard not a thing. There is no one like that around this place. But as there was once a man in these parts called Kumasaka no Chōhan, who committed much evil against the people, for which he lost his life, I will relate to you everything I know concerning him.

WAKI

Please do so immediately.

AI

Katari (*chanted in a narrative style*)

To begin with, the one known as Kumasaka no Chōhan was born in the land of Kaga.[10] Now, his first act of robbery was when he stole his own uncle's horse and took it to another village, where he sold it.

That is all I know about that particular incident, but upon that occasion, Chōhan was convinced that there is nothing more amusing than robbery. What this means is that he made up his mind to possess nothing at all of his own, but to rob others of their possessions to his heart's content to provide for his wife and children and live a life of ease. And this is what he meant by declaring that nothing was more amusing than robbery. And it is said that he came to be called Kumasaka no Chōhan, known to one and all as the most skillful robber in the land.

He traveled throughout the land to gather all the robbers in the nation together under him, and led them here and there, where they committed countless acts of evil, taking the lives of many people and indulging in banditry and piracy as well. And it was at this very place that he received the final punishment of Heaven.

To be more specific, long ago, in the capital, there lived a famed gold merchant named Sanjō no Kichiji Nobutaka. Each and every year he would transport a huge amount of his treasures to Oshū.[11] Now, the band of robbers kept spies posted in all parts of the country and in every village to keep each other informed of matters that needed to be dealt with, and the transport of treasure to

[10] Kaga Province was situated on the Japan Sea side of Honshu, and comprises the southern part of the present-day Ishikawa Prefecture.

[11] Oshū was Chinese name for Mutsu Province, in the northeastern part of Japan, which comprises the present-day Fukushima, Yamagata, Miyagi, Iwate, and Aomori prefectures.

Oshū by Kichiji was brought to their attention as one such matter. So robbers from all the areas where they resided, including Kumasaka, gathered on Greenfield Moor, forming a band that was some seventy strong, who swore to join forces to rob Kichiji of his treasures. They determined to act as soon as they heard of his departure from the capital.

But as fate would have it, the son of Yoshitomo named Ushiwaka was at that time in training at Kurama Temple in the secrets of military strategy.[12] For some reason or other, this Ushiwaka asked Kichiji to allow him to join the treasure caravan on the journey to Oshū. The band of robbers, having not the least inkling of this development, decided to attack that very same night. But Ushiwaka came out fully armed, wielding his swords here and there until he had slashed to death nearly all the bandits and inflicted wounds both light and heavy on all those who remained.

Those who escaped with their lives ran hither and thither in search of shelter, creating a most pitiful sight, indeed. Only Chōhan, being the most stout-hearted of them all, pressed on into the fray. But Ushiwaka, being who he was, calmly crossed swords with Chōhan and dealt him a fatal blow with the greatest of ease.

Spoken

As I mentioned earlier, I know very little of the details of the actual end of Kumasaka, what I have thus far related to you being everything I know of the matter. Now, tell me, just what is the specific matter you wish to learn about?

WAKI

That is a most compelling story, indeed. Although there is no reason for what I am about to ask, a short while ago, a solitary monk appeared before me. Saying that since today is the anniversary of a certain person's death, he asked me to read the sutras and perform a Buddhist service for the repose of that person's soul. But when I asked him who that person might be, he told me in great detail about the various evil doers in these parts. And when he retired into the bed-chamber, his figure seemed to fade

[12]*See* the Introduction to *Kurama Tengu* in this volume.

away, and his hermitage, too, was gone, leaving but the grassy field. Was it not a most strange happening, indeed?!

AI

As you say, Sir, it was indeed a most strange occurrence. Well, now, I would venture to say that due to the great nobility and virtue of your heart, the ghost of Kumasaka has appeared to you at this very spot, for I am convinced that you have done deeds great enough to provide you with powers sufficiently deep to call such a spirit forth. The reason he comes forth is that there is no one else who will pray for his salvation. So I advise you, if you will, to remain here for a time and offer prayers for the repose of his soul.

WAKI

What a strange thing this is, indeed. I have determined that I will stay here awhile, recite the blessed sutras, and pray for the repose of that person's soul with all my heart.

AI

If there is anything more that you require, do not hesitate to call upon me.

WAKI

I will certainly call upon you.

AI

With all my heart. (*Exits.*)

—ACT 2—

The Waki *sits at the* waki-za, *and begins to chant.*

Machi-utai, *au*

WAKI

I lie for the night,[13]

---

[13] Lines 106–17: From the following poem by Kakinomoto no Hitomaro (d. 708–15) in the *Man'yō-shū* (1994; where it is listed as Anonymous) and *Shin Kokin-shū* (1374): *Natsuno yuku / Oshika no tsuno no / Tsuka no ma mo / Imo ga kokoro o / Wasurete omoe ya* (ending *Wasurezu omoe / Imo ga kokoro o* in the *Shin Kokin-shū*); (In the summer field roams / The deer, with its antlers still / Short, e'en for a while— / My beloved one's tenderness / Never, never to forget). In the second and third phrase of the poem there are alliterations of *tsu* and *no* sounds. In line 106, *fusu* (to lie down) is an *engo* (associated word) of *shika* (deer). *Tsuka no ma* (short distance / short while) modifies both antlers and sleeping time. The first three phrases serve to introduce *tsuka no ma* (a short while). This *machi-utai* (waiting song) is similar to those used in in *Nishikigi, Ominameshi,* and *Motomezuka,* attachment pieces in the

Hitoyo fusu[13]

---

fourth group. For your reference, the *machi-utai* from *Ominameshi,* which quotes the same poem, is:

Machi-uta, *au* WAKI

I lie for the night,
Short as summer deer antlers, by the grass-grown graves,
Short as summer deer antlers, by the grass-grown graves;
For the soul that appeared from behind the grass,
I offer prayers, chanting aloud the holy words.

Awazu I pray to Buddha, may the deceased soul be delivered from
Life and death, and swiftly attain nirvana!

Not for a while as short as summer deer antlers
Not for a while as short as summer deer antlers
Falling into slumber, while the autumn wind blows
On the bed of grass beneath the pine, where all night
I chant aloud prayers for the departed soul,
I chant aloud prayers for the departed soul.

DEHA *The* Nochi-shite, *the ghost of Kumasaka no Chōhan, enters, carrying a halberd on his shoulder, and proceeds to the first pine, where he stands the halberd upright upon the floor.*

Sashi, *awazu*

NOCHI-SHITE

In the southeast the wind rises; in the northwest the clouds are not quiet.[14]

Issei, *awazu*

The evening is dark,
The night wind is blowing hard in the mountain shade,

CHORUS

Making tree tops and branches
Rustle aloud.

SHITE

The moon will not be out before the break of day.

Noru

CHORUS

Though the moon comes out, the sky will be bound in mist.

The Shite *goes toward the curtain, re-enters the main stage, stands at* jō-za, *and faces the* Waki.

Break in! Go at it! I shout to those ahead and in the rear,
To right and left paying attention, looking out sharply.
Thus I took away people's treasures, an atrocious deed!
This earthly attachment still binds me fast. Pray, look at me.
How abhorrent! (*Ends off rhythm*)

Spoken

WAKI

I see that you are Kumasaka no Chōhan.
Please tell me how it all happened.

Sings, awazu

SHITE

Well, there was a man named Sanjō no Kichiji Nobutaka,[15]

---

[14] Line 112. Cf. the following lines in *Chōbuku Soga, Kureha,* and *Shiga,* sung in homage of a peaceful time: *Tōnan kumo osamarite / Seihoku ni kaze shizuka nari* (In the southeast, the clouds have cleared; in the northwest, the wind is quiet). The origin of these lines is unknown.

Oshika no tsuno no tsuka no ma mo
Oshika no tsuno no tsuka no ma mo
Neraren mono ka akikaze no
Matsu no shitabushi yo mo sugara
Koe butsuji oya nashinuran,
Koe butsuji oya nashinuran.

Tōnan ni kaze tatte seihoku ni kumo shizuka narazu,[14]

Yūyami no
Yokaze hageshiki yamakage ni

Kozue ko no ma ya
Sawaguran.

Ariake-goro ka itsu shika ni

Tsuki wa idete mo oboroyo naru-beshi,

Kiri-ire seme yo to zengo o gejishi

Yunde ya mete ni kokoro o kubatte

Hito no takara o nbaishi akugyaku

Shaba no shiushin kore goran ze yo,

Asamashi ya

Kumasaka no Chōhan nite mashimasu ka,
Sono toki no arisama on-monogatari sōrae.

Sate mo Sanjō no Kichiji Nobutaka tote[15]

---

[15] Sanjō (Third Street): Of the main streets running from east to west in Kyoto, the third one from the north.

The Shite *sits on a stool at center stage.*

A merchant who dealt in gold.
Every year he collected quite a few bagfuls of treasures,
Which he loaded on horses and took to the north.

Spoken

"Ah, let me take that!" I thought,
"But who is there to join me?"

Kakaru

WAKI

Of many who came from different provinces,[16]
Who were there specially?

SHITE

Kakujō from Kawachi Province,[17]

Spoken

And Surihari Tarō and his brother
Were matchless as assailants from the front.

Kakaru

WAKI

And those from the Capital, . . .
Who among many were the prominent ones?

Spoken

SHITE

Emon of Third Street and the Little Monkey of Mibu.[18]

Kakaru

WAKI

For skill in torch fighting, or fighting with a sword,

Spoken

SHITE

Surely there was none who surpassed these.

Kakaru

WAKI

As for those from the northern countries, from the province of Echizen came. . . .[19]

SHITE

Matsuwaka of Asō and Kurō of Mikuni, (*Ends in speech*)

Kakaru

WAKI

As for Kaga Province, from Kumasaka came[20]

Spoken

SHITE

This Chōhan first of all,
As well as strong-armed rogues,
Seventy of them, who came to assist.

Kakaru

WAKI

Along the roads Kichiji was traveling—
In fields, on mountains, and at post-towns,
Men were stationed to spy on him.

---

[16] Lines 132–66: In this exchange between the two characters, the *Waki* sings as if he had actually witnessed the scene.

[17] Kawachi: A province in the southeastern part of the present Osaka Prefecture.

Kogane o akinō akindo atte
Mainen suda no takara o atsumete

Taka ni o tsukutte Oku e kudaru.
Appare kore o torabaya to
Yoriki no ninju wa tare-tare zo.

Sate kuni-guni yori atsumarishi[16]
Naka ni torite mo taga arishi zo.

Kawachi no Kakujō[17]
Surihari Tarō kyōdai wa
Omote-uchi ni wa narabi nashi.

Sate mata Miyako no sono uchi ni
Ōki naka ni mo taga arishi zo.

Sanjō no Emon Mibu no Kozaru[18]

Hitomoshi no jōzu wakegiri ni wa

Kore-ra ni ue wa yomo kosaji.

Sate Hokkoku ni wa Echizen no[19]

Asō no Matsuwaka Mikuni no Kurō

Kaga no Kuni ni wa Kumasaka no[20]

Kono Chōhan no hajime to shite
Kukkyō no tegara no shiremono-ra
Shichi-jiu nin na (=wa) yoriki shite

Kichiji ga tōru michi sugara
No ni mo yama ni mo shuku tomari ni
Metsuke o tsukete kore o misu.

---

[18] Sanjō (Third Street): *See* note 15. Mibu: An area in the central part of Kyoto.
[19] Echizen: The present-day Fukui Prefecture.
[20] Kaga Province: *See* Note 10.

Spoken

SHITE

Now he arrived here at the post-town of Scarlet Slope,
A strategic place for attack,
With many roads running in four directions to aid our retreat.
While still early in the evening, we saw him waited on by courtesans
And passing time in all sorts of entertainments.

Kakaru

WAKI

Late at night Kichiji and his brother
Went to bed and fell soundly asleep.

SHITE

A sixteen- or seventeen-year-old small man was there (*Ends in speech*)
With eyes which were by no means those of a common man.
If a door were slightly left open, or some thing
Should make the faintest sound, that would alert him.

Kakaru

WAKI

And thus he sat up all night without lying down,

Spoken

SHITE

So it was that Master Ushiwaka never dreamed.

Kakaru

WAKI

For the thieves, good luck had run out.

SHITE

Now is the time!

WAKI

Be quick!

SHITE

Break in!

In chū-nori. *The* Shite *dances to the song.*

CHORUS

Scarcely had they finished shouting thus than,
Scarcely had they finished shouting thus than,
Vying with one another, burning fiery brands
They threw in quick succession and rushed inside
With such violent force that even a demon god
Would have found it hard to turn his face toward them.
However, Master Ushiwaka,
Without betraying the slightest air of fear,
Draws his small sword and brandishing it, fights with them.

Kono Akasaka no shuku ni tsuku.

Koko koso kukkyō no tokoro nare,
Nokiba mo shihō ni michi ōshi.

Mireba yoi yori iukun sue

Suhaku no asobi toki o utsusu.

Yo mo fuke-yukeba Kichiji kyōdai
Zengo mo shirazu fushi-tarishi ni

Jiuroku-shichi no ko-otoko no

Me no uchi hito ni sugure-taruga

Shōji no sukima mono-ai no
Soyo tomo suru o kokoro ni kakete

Sukoshi mo fusade arikeru o

Ushiwaka-dono to wa yume ni mo shirazu

Un no tsukinuru nusubito-ra

Kigen na (= wa) yoki zo

Haya

Ire to

Iu koso hodo mo hisashikere
Iu koso hodo mo hisashikere
Mina waresaki ni to taimatsu o
Nage-komi nagekoji midare-iru
Ikioi wa yōyaku-jin mo
Omote o muku-beki yō zo naki.
Shikaredomo Ushiwaka-go
Sukoshi osoruru keshiki naku
Kodachi o nuite watari-ai

A lion jumping up, a rushing tiger,[21]
A bird flying about, exhausting all the tricks,
He attacks and fights so that, unable to resist,
Thirteen burglars, who come foremost to the attack,
Struck down one after another, lie dead side by side.
The rest of them are wounded and drop their swords,
Some have their armor stripped off, and make a
  narrow escape,
Deeming it fortunate that their lives have been saved
  for them.
Kumasaka says to himself thus:
"This fellow who has dealt with these men in this
  way,
Killing them away, he must be a demon god.
He cannot possibly be a human being.
Indeed, one can steal only while one is alive.[22]
There is no way left for us but to retreat."
Supporting himself with his halberd,
Crestfallen and humiliated he retreats.

SHITE

Kumasaka, however, thought thus,

CHORUS

Kumasaka, however, thought thus,
Why so much ado about that youngster?

Even if he kills like that, there should be a limit.
If Kumasaka should fight, exhausting all his arts,
Whatever demon in heaven or fiendish god he may
  be,[23]
Catching him in the air, I'll break him into pieces,
The departed souls of those who were slain,
Let me console them thus and lead them to repose.
So, turning back now in mid-stride,
Grasping his old halberd closely at his side,
With a folding panel door guarding his back,
He stands awhile spying upon the small young man.
Master Ushiwaka, seeing the man,

---

[21] Lines 177–78. "A lion jumping up, . . . / A bird flying about": Conventional similies describing quick-action fighting.

Shishi funjin koran (n)iu[21]
Hichō no kakeri no te o kudaki
Seme-tatakaeba koraezu
Omote ni susumu jiusan nin
Onaji makura ni kiri-fuserare
Sono hoka te oi tachi o sute
Gusoku o nbaware hōhō nigete

Inochi bakari o nogaru mo ari.

Kumasaka iuyō
Kono mono-domo o te no shita ni

Utsu wa ikasama oni-kami ka
Ningen nite wa yo mo araji,
Nusumi mo inochi no arite koso[22]
Ara shiyō ya hikan tote
Naginata tsue ni tsuki
Ushiro-metaku mo hiki-keruga

Kumasaka omou yō

Kumasaka omou yō
Monomonoshi sono kaja ga

Kiru to iu tomo sazo aruran
Kumasaka hijitto furū naraba
Ikanaru tenma kijin naritomo[23]

Chiu ni tsukande mijin ni nashi
Utaretaru mono-domo no
Ide kyōyō ni hōzen tote
Michi yori totte kaeshi
Rei no naginata hiki-sobame
Ori-tsumado o kodate ni totte
Kano ko-otoko o neraikeri.
Ushiwaka-go wa goranjite

---

[22] "One can steal only while one is alive": The same speech is made by Kumasaka in a similar scene in *Eboshi-ori,* a sword-fighting piece in the fourth group (in *Troubled Souls*).

[23] The same line is used to describe a similar scene in *Eboshi-ori.*

Draws out his sword and holds it closely to his side,
And, with some distance in between, he waits for
him.
Kumasaka, too, holds his halberd level; they
Each mutually wait for the other's attack, but then
In irritation Kumasaka, stamping his left foot,
As if he were piercing through an iron wall, thrusts
his halberd,
Which the young man with his sword deflects to
the left.[24]
Kumasaka, running after him, thrusts out his halberd,
On which the boy alights jumping, so turning up
the blade;
As the man draws backward, the boy jumps off
to the right.
Again swinging his halberd, Kumasaka slashes,
But it is stopped in mid-air and is struck aside.
As Kumasaka slashes again, the boy jumps up
And becomes invisible, his form fading out of sight.
This way and that, as Kumasaka goes looking for
the boy,
All of a sudden, unexpectedly from behind,

The Shite *jumps and squats.*

The youth strikes him through the opening of his armor.
"Ah, what a story! By the youngster there
That I should be slashed in this way! How exasper-
ating!"
Quoth he, but Heaven so decrees that
His fortune runs out. Oh, how very regrettable!

Ō-nori

"If I fight with weapons, I shall never beat that
youth." (*Ends off rhythm*)

Ō-nori

The Shite *gives the halberd to the* kōken.

"If I fight with weapons, I shall never beat that
youth,
Let me catch him with my hands," saying thus, he
drops his halberd and
Spreading out his arms wide apart,
Here to the end of a long corridor and there a dead-end,
Chasing and pursuing the boy, he tries to take him,
and yet,

---

[24] Lines 213–20. In *Eboshi-ori* and *Hashi-Benkei*, there are similar descriptions of Ushiwaka's supernatural agility in fighting action, which he acquired while he learned military

Tachi nuki sobame mono-ai o
Sukoshi hedatete machitamou.

Kumasaka mo naginata kamae
Tagai ni kakaru o machikeru ga
Iratte Kumasaka sasoku o fumi
Teppeki mo tōreto tsuku naginata o

Hasshi to utte yunde ni koseba[21]

Okkake sukasazu komu naginata ni
Hirari to noreba hamuki ni nashi

Shisatte hikeba mete e kosu o

Ottori-naoshite chō to kireba
Chiu ni te musubu o hodoku te ni
Kaette haraeba tobi-agatte
Sono mama miezu katachi mo usete
Koko ya kashiko to tazunuru tokoro ni

Omoi mo yoranu ushiro yori
Gusoku no sukima o chō to kireba
Kowa ikani ano kaja ni
Kiraruru koto no haratachi sa yoto

Iedomo tenmei no
Un no kiwame zo munen naru.
Uchimono-waza nite kanou maji,

Uchimono-waza nite kanou maji,

Tedori ni sen tote naginata nage-sute

Ōde o hirogete
Koko no menrō kashiko no tsumari ni
Okkake ottsume toran to sure domo

---

arts from the goblin of Mt. Kurama. For more details, see also *Kurama Tengu,* translated in this book.

Like a mayfly, lightning, or the moon in the water,
Though visible to the eye, he cannot be caught with hands.

SHITE

Again and again heavy wounds are inflicted on me,

CHORUS

Again and again heavy wounds are inflicted on me,
The Shite *squats.* The fighting spirit and bodily strength weaken,
And weaken until (*Ends off rhythm*)

Hira-nori

SHITE

Near the roots of this pine tree,

CHORUS

Like the dew or frost on the moss,
The Shite *rises.* I faded out, a story told of days gone by.[25]
The Shite *prays to the* Waki. Please offer prayers to save my after-life, he says,
While cocks crow, announcing the break of day,[26]
The night's dusk whitens, the day dawns at Scarlet Slope,[27]
The Shite *stamps the* tome-byōshi *at* jō-za. And in the pine shade the form has faded,
And in the pine shade the form has faded out of sight.

---

[25] Lines 242–43: *monogatari* ***su*** (story to tell) → ***Sue*** *no yo* (later- or after-life). Although this rhetorical subtlety is virtually untranslatable, we have opted to translate *Kieshi mukashi no monogatari su*— as "I faded out, a story told of days gone by." This seems to get across the nuance of the original.

Kagerō, inazuma mizu no tsuki kaya
Sugata wa mire domo te ni torarezu.

Shidai, shidai ni omode wa oinu

Shidai, shidai ni omode wa oinu
Takeki kokoro chikara mo yowari
Yowari-yukite

Kono matsu-ga-ne no

Koke no tsuyu, shimo to
Kieshi mukashi no monogatari[25]
Sue no yo tasuke tabi-tamae to
Iutsuke mo tsuge-wataru[26]
Yo mo shira-shira to Akasaka no[27]

Matsukage ni kakurekeri
Matsukage ni koso wa kakurekeri.

---

[26] *Iu* in the sense of "to say" is related to the preceding line, and, in the sense of "evening," leads to ***iu**tsuke no tori* (**evening**-announcing bird = a cock).

[27] *Yo mo shira-shira to **ak**—* (night whitening it **dawns**) → ***Ak**asaka* (Scarlet Slope). The image is of a shift from the "white" of the lightening night to the scarlet of sunrise.

車僧

KURUMA-ZŌ

シテ：　苔を振り上げ、車を打つ
ワキ：　おう車を打たば、行くべきか。

SHITE: *And lifting the stick, he strikes the carriage.*
WAKI: *Ah, if you strike the carriage, will it go?*

Introduction

Kuruma-zō (The Carriage Priest, or the Priest on Wheels) is one of the five *tengu-mono* (goblin pieces) whose *Shite* is a *tengu* (goblin). (For more on *tengu,* see the explanation on the goblin pieces in the Introduction to Fifth-Group Noh as well as the Introduction to *Kurama Tengu.*) With the exception of *Kurama Tengu,* the *Shite* goblin makes an attempt to obstruct Buddhism, and is punished by a *tsure* deity or defeated by a *waki* priest. In *Zegai* and *Kuruma-zō,* a *tengu* approaches a priest and tries to seduce him. What is unique about *Kuruma-zō* is its *Waki.* While the *Waki* characters in the other *tengu-mono* are more or less stereotyped, *comme-il-faut* characters, the *Waki* in the title role of *Kuruma-zō* is of almost equal importance to the *Shite.* While the *Shite* is a typical *tengu,* the *Waki* priest, nicknamed *Kuruma-zō* (Carriage Priest) because he goes about in a carriage and preaches while sitting in it, is a fascinating character who accepts the goblin's challenge to oral combat, made in the debate-like style of questions and answers practiced by Zen monks. Also he beats the goblin in the contest of their magic powers.

The following is an outline of *Kuruma-zō:*

—Act 1

1) The *Waki,* the Carriage Priest, enters. (He is supposed to be in his carriage.)

He sings an introductory song, *shidai,* and a travel song, *michiyuki,* at the end of which he arrives at the foot of Nishiyama (Western Hills) in the northwestern part of Kyoto. He goes to sit in the *tsukurimono* representing a carriage, in order to look at the landscape. (The *jidori* in this Noh, quite exceptionally, is in rhythm. This happens only in this Noh and *Settai,* a human-interest play in the fourth group.)

2) The *Shite,* a *tengu* named Tarō-bō, enters in the form of a *yamabushi* priest, and calls to the priest and asks him a question in the form of a *waka:*

Ukiyo oba	In this wretched life,
Nani to ka meguru	How do you go driving round,
Kuruma-zō	O Carriage Priest?
Mada wa no uchi ni	Within the rut of the wheel,
Ari to koso mire.	I see you still remaining.

In the poem, "the rut of the wheel" is the circle of Birth and Death within which men go round and round in eternal transmigration, unable to get out of it and attain Buddhahood. The priest in answer recites:

Ukiyo oba	In this wretched life,
Meguranu mono o	I do not go driving round,
Kuruma-zō	This Carriage Priest,
Nori mo uru-beki	How could I drive the carriage?—
Waga araba koso.	Neither I nor wheel exist.

The first three lines of the priest's poem are basically a repetition of the goblin's poem with only a change in person, and the second line which in the first poem is in the form of a question is changed into a negative answer. The last couplet is a characteristic Zen-style answer, which looks at both what is and what is not as one. *Nori* (to ride/drive) also means Buddha's Law, and to be able "to ride or drive" also means "to obtain the Law, to become enlightened." In the last line, *Waga* means "I" as well as "wheel, ring." Questions and answers go on, with the wheel as axis, ending with a reference to the Three Vehicles of the Book of Parables in the Lotus Sutra.[1] The goblin realizes that the priest is able to drive his carriage out of the burning house, and returns to his abode on Mt. Atago.

3. *Nakairi* (interim exit) and *ai-kyōgen:* The *Shite* makes an interim exit, accompanied by *tengu raijo* music. Then the music changes to *kyōgen ranjo* and the *Ai-kyōgen,* a petty goblin, enters. (As a rule, the interim exit of a *tengu* is accompanied by *tengu raijo,* and then a minor deity or petty goblin enters accompanied by *kyōgen ranjo.*) In a soliloquy, he tells what has happened between the goblin Tarō-bō and the priest on wheels, then approaching the priest, tickles him, trying in vain to make him laugh. (Although the translation includes the *ai-kyōgen,* for comparison, an alternative *ai-kyōgen* is also given at the end of this introduction.)

[1] In the Lotus Sutra (Saddharmā-puṇḍarīka-sūtra), a father coaxes his children out of their house, which is on fire, by offering them three carriages drawn by goats, deer, and oxen. In this parable, the father is the Buddha, and the children trapped in the burning house are sentient beings. The Burning House represents the world burning with the fires of old age, sickness, and death. The teachings of the Buddha are like the father getting the boys to leave their pleasures for the greater pleasure of attaining buddhahood.

—*Act 2*

4) The *Nochi-shite* Tarō-bō enters in the gorgeous costume of a great *tengu,* accompanied by *ō-beshi* music, which is played at the entrance of a *tengu.* He calls to the priest and tries to convert him to demon worship, challenging him to a contest of their magic powers.

5) The priest, indifferent to what the goblin says, looks at the landscape in fascination. The goblin lures the priest, saying, "If it is a beautiful season, why not turn the carriage about in the snow and play in Saga Moor?" When the priest answers, "Play if you would, like gossamer thread, but never can you pull my mind," the goblin strikes the carriage. Then the following remarks by the *Waki* and the *Shite* lead to an allusion to the *Ten Oxherding Pictures* (lines 95–100):

WAKI Ah, if you strike the carriage, will it go?
If you strike the ox, it will go.
SHITE Indeed, the carriage has no mind.
And there is no ox to strike.
WAKI You fool! Don't you know the Way of Man and Ox?
Why don't you strike the ox that is visible?
SHITE The ox that is visible! What do you mean?
And how about Man and Ox?

The *Ten Oxherding Pictures* illustrate the Buddhist concept of the mind, comparing it to the relationship between a man and an ox through ten illustrations that originated in China and were widely used in Japan in the teaching of Zen. The following are descriptions of the ox-herding pictures painted by the Sung-dynasty Zen master Kuo-an Shih-yuan (J. Kakuan Shien; fl. ca. 1150): 1) *Seeking the Ox:* A boy stands in a field, not knowing where to go. On the ground we see the footprints of an ox, his mind. 2) *Seeing the Tracks:* The boy finds the footprints and runs in pursuit. 3) *Seeing the Ox:* The boy sees the ox, though only the hind part as it runs away. 4) *Catching the Ox:* The boy tethers the ox, which continues to run, dragging the boy. 5) *Taming the Ox:* The ox is tamed and is obediently led by the boy. 6) *Riding the Ox Home:* The ox is freed from the tether, and goes, following the notes of the flute the boy plays while sitting on the ox's back. 7) *Ox Forgotten, Self Alone:* The ox is safely in the cowshed. The youth, forgetting about the ox, calmly watches the moon. 8) *Both Ox and Self Gone:* With both the self and the ox gone, nothing remains, and this is illustrated by a circle with nothing inside, indicating the state of fulfillment: "Being is non-being, and non-being is being." The illustrations of the progress of the boy's mind end here. The two remaining pictures are about what stands above. 9) *Returning to the Source:* Taking all things as they are. Flowers are red and willow trees are green. 10) *Entering the Market with Bliss-bestowing Hands:* One who has attained perfection should teach people even in the market.)

The priest, when asked by the goblin if he can make the carriage go, strikes it. The carriage then turns into a flying vehicle and smoothly proceeds along the Way of the Law. The goblin worships the priest in awe and disappears.

Kuruma-zō is a short play of a simple structure. Unlike other goblin plays, it has no special action such as *mai-bataraki* (dancing action) or *uchiai-bataraki* (fighting action). Its language style is straightforward, concise, without poetic embellishment. The effect is like a black-ink drawing by a Zen priest. This is what is expected of a play whose main feature is the Zen-style *mondō*—a question-and-answer debate—between the *Shite* and the *Waki.* We can imagine that the play appealed to the audience of the time when poems with *bon mots* were much prized. There are anecdotes about critical situations saved by *bon mots* functioning like a *deus ex machina.* Also, stories about preachers who entertained audiences with poems containing *bon mots* are found in the story books of the Muromachi period (1333–1573). The *Waki* of the Noh *Kuruma-zō* can be considered one such preacher.[2]

This Noh, whose main feature is Zen-style questions and answers, naturally has a deep Buddhist coloring, with *Kuruma* (Carriage/Vehicle) as the key word. In Japanese, the word means both "vehicle" and "wheel." In the sense of "vehicle" or "carriage," *kuruma* is associated with the Vehicle of the Law that takes men to Buddha's realm. This leads to the reference to the parable of Three Vehicles told in the Lotus Sutra (lines 35, 43–44), and the ox-carriage of this story leads to the *Ten Oxherding Pictures,* the eighth drawing of which, an empty orb, stands for the Zen concept of being, as well as the circle within which men go round and round in eternal transmigration (cf. lines 23–27). The two wheels of a carriage are made a symbol of the law of dualism (lines 70–76):

CHORUS Good and evil are like two wheels of a carriage.
SHITE There is the Law of Buddha, and of men.
CHORUS Blind attachment,
Side by side with Enlightenment.

[2] Cf. Gensei Tokue, "A Study of *Kuruma-zō,*" *Kanze* (Nov. 1984).

SHITE	There are Buddhas and there are men.
CHORUS	There is Priest on Wheels,
SHITE	And Tarō-bō, the ascetic.

The drama attains the climax as the Law's Wheels go flying over mountains and rivers, defying the goblin's attempt at hindrance. Coming at the end of a play written in simple, laconic language, this fantastic finale makes the audience feel as if suddenly thrust into the land of a fairy tale. No less impressive is the effective use of a poem. After his entrance, the *Nochi-shite* goblin recites an old poem:

Atago-yama	On Mt. Atago
Shikimi-ga-Hara ni	And over Aniseed Field
Yuki tsumori	Snow having fallen,
Hana tsumu hito no	Of those who gather flowers
Ato dani mo nashi.	Not even a trace is seen.[3]

This, one of the few poems quoted in the play, effectively portrays the bleakness of the background. And at the same time, it conjures up an image that is the opposite of bleakness, the fascinating image of a crimson flower in the snow.

Very little is known about the identity of the Kuruma-zō in the Noh, except that he is probably one of those street artists in the form of a Zen priest, who entertained the audience reciting poems containing *bon mots* as he preached from his carriage. Tokue and Sanari (*Yōkyoku Taikan,* 2: 964) both mention a legendary seven-hundred-year-old priest, who preached in Kyoto in a broken carriage, and was nicknamed Kuruma-zō (sources: *Shinzan Gyōjō-ki; Wa-Kan Sansai Zu-e, Yamashiro Kaijōji*). It is likely that the Noh is based on the story of this priest, as well as on the priests who preached from their carriages and were called *kuruma-zō.* As to what the priest's carriage is like, the Noh tells us nothing, except that it moves without being pulled by a man or an ox. The stage prop of the vehicle placed at the *waki-za* looks more like a large chair than a carriage, with oversized wheels on either side, in which the priest sits throughout the performance after his arrival speech. The author of *Kuruma-zō* is unknown. The play is in the repertory of all five Noh schools.

---

[3] *See* Note 12 to the translation.

Scene	Saga Moor, Yamashiro (in the northwestern part of Kyoto)
Season	Winter (December in the lunar calendar)

*Characters and costumes**

Waki	The Carriage Priest, wearing a headdress in the dignified *shamon* style, a plaid *atsuita kitsuke* under a *mizugoromo* robe, a priest's stole, and a white *ōguchi* divided skirt, carrying prayer beads in one hand.
Mae-shite	The goblin Tarō-bō in the form of a *yamabushi* priest, wearing a *tokin* headgear, a patterned *atsuita kitsuke* in subdued colors (or a bold plaid *atsuita kitsuke*) under a *mizugoromo* robe, and a white or colored *ōguchi* divided skirt, with a *yamabushi* stole (*suzukake*), and carrying a short sword and holding prayer beads in one hand.
Nochi-shite	The goblin Tarō-bō in the costume of a great *tengu,* wearing an *ō-beshimi* mask, a wig of long red hair, a red and gold brocade headband, a great *tokin* headgear, a colorful *atsuita kitsuke* with patterns in bold horizontal bars under a *happi* and *kariginu* robe, and a *hangire* divided skirt, carrying a large feather fan in one hand, and with a striking stick inserted in his sash at the back.
Ai-kyōgen	A petty goblin nicknamed Mizogoe Tengu (Gutter-Jumping Goblin).

Author	Unknown.

* *For technical terms in Japanese concerning costumes, see the Glossary.*

Translation of the alternative *ai-kyōgen* (from Sanari, 2: 968–69), between lines 59 and 60:

> *When the* Shite *has made his interim exit accompanied by* tengu raijo *music, the music changes to* kyōgen ranjo, *and the* Ai-Kyōgen, a *Mizogoe Tengu (Gutter-Jumping Goblin) enters, and soliloquizes, standing at the* nanori-za (= jō-za).

GUTTER-JUMPING GOBLIN (spoken): I who am here am called Gutter-Jumping Goblin, and I live around Mt. Atago. The reason I am named the Gutter-Jumping Goblin is this: Once, when I was going from northern Kyoto to southern Kyoto, I jumped over a wide gutter with success. I proudly told my feat to others. Tarō-bō thought that I was a conceited petty goblin and started calling me Gutter-Jumping Goblin.

Now, there is one named Priest on Wheels, a holy priest, who thinks that he is the holiest of all. Tarō-bō thought him too conceited. So, assuming the form of a *yamabushi,* he went to Saga Moor and called to him, "I say, Priest on Wheels!" The Priest on Wheels answered nonchalantly, "What is it?" Tarō-bō asked him, "In this floating life, how do you go driving round, you Priest on Wheels? Within the rut of wheels I see you still remaining." The Priest on Wheels said in answer, "In this floating life, I do not go driving round, This Priest on Wheels. How could I drive the carriage?— Neither I nor wheel exist." But who is it that says thus? This is what is called "whose wheel," a Zen word, an interesting thing, methinks. There is this poem: One asks, "Whose is it?" / And one answers, "Whose is it? / Whose wheel is that wheel?" / That may be a rabbit's ears / Or the cry of a hawk.[4] This is the most esoteric Zen jargon of all, indeed!

After this, there were such questions and answers exchanged as: "In an empty cavern cool wind blows." "Only my name gossiped about rises like Mt. Takao's high peak." So you live on the black peak of Atago Mountain, I guess." "How about your carriage?" "One escaping from a house on fire." "Though it goes round?" "It does not go round." "Though one pulls it," "No one pulls."—and so on, until Tarō-bō was so hard driven that, saying he would return to Mt. Atago, but that he would return again for more questions and answers, he went home. He has told me, a petty goblin nicknamed Gutter-Jumping Goblin, to go to harass the Priest on Wheels. So I have come out. While I have been talking, already I have come to Saga Moor.

Where is the Priest on Wheels? Oh, there he is. How nonchalant he looks! No wonder Tarō-bō hates him. Let me talk to him. (*To the* Waki:) I say, Priest on Wheels! Priest on Wheels! (*Separately:*) What a story! He is as cool as a deer bitten by a mosquito on his antler. If he should speak to me, and if I should make a wrong answer, that would never do. Generally speaking, there is nothing more unbearable for a man than to be tickled. So if I can make him laugh by tickling, then I will drive him into the demonic realm. So I tickle, tickle, tickle! (*He makes the gesture of tickling.*) Is this not funny, Priest on Wheels? The Priest on Wheels' nose is so large! In front of his nose, a mouse with her young on her back goes this way and that, this way and that. Is this not funny, Priest on Wheels? What a story! It is very hard to drive him into the demonic realm. I will call out Tarō-bō and go home. (*Facing the curtain:*) Yo, ho! Tarō-bō, Tarō-bō! (*He exits.*)

---

[4] Surely this "Zen poem" was created especially for this *Ai-kyōgen.* The text gives it as: *Taso to iu / Taso to tōru / Taso no wa wa / Usagi no mimi ka / Tobi no shaku,* but as "*tobi no shaku*" means "the measure of a hawk," we have opted for "cry" as being more appropriate in this case. It should also be noted that a popular 4-character expression goes *Enmoku, toji,* or "A hawk's eyes, a rabbit's ears," meaning that one can see as well as though he had hawk's eyes and hear as well as if he had rabbit's ears.

Kuruma-zō

車僧

—Act 1—

A tsukurimono *representing a carriage is placed at the* waki-za.

SHIDAI *The* Waki, the *Kuruma-zō, enters and stands at the* jō-za, *facing the pine painted on the back panel.*

Shidai, *au*	WAKI Well into the life beyond, the Priest on Wheels may drive,[1] Well into the life beyond, the Priest on Wheels may drive, Embedded in eternal sleep for how long?[2]
Jidori, *au* *The* Waki *faces front.*	CHORUS Well into the life beyond, the Priest on Wheels may drive, Embedded in eternal sleep for how long?
Age-uta (michiyuki), *au*	WAKI Cloudy and snow-filled Is the sky over Dark Mountain peak, with the snow,[3] Is the sky over Dark Mountain peak, with the snow Powdering over Saga Moor and Storm Mountain, The sound of the waterfall reverberates through The thick layers of cloud; on the Ōi River A raft for the night's bed, with a floating pillow,[4] Spreading a single sleeve that, also, is snow-white;[5]
At the end of the song, the Waki *steps into the carriage.*	The Sky hangs low, the sun soon makes its course westward, And beneath the Western Mountain I have soon arrived And beneath the Western Mountain I have soon arrived
Tsuki-zerifu, *spoken*	Let me halt the carriage here

---

[1] In *nochi no yo kakete* (to the next life reaching), *kakete* (reaching out) also means "to drive" and is an *engo* (associated word) of *kuruma* (carriage). *Kakete* ***kuru*** (driving **come** = **come** driving, running) → ***kuruma*** (carriage).

[2] In *toko-ne* (eternal sleep), *toko* also means "bed" and "floor," and is an *engo* of *nemuri* (sleep) and carriage. Exceptionally, the *jidori* of this *shidai* is in rhythm.

[3] *Sora wa* ***ogura*** (sky is gloomy, darkling) → ***Ogura*** *no mine* (Dark Mountain peak). Ogura, Saga, Arashiyama (Storm Mountain), Ōi River, and Nishiyama (Western Hills) are all the

Nochi no yo kakete Kuruma-zō[1]

Nochi no yo kakete Kuruma-zō

Tokone no nemuri itsumade.[2]

Nochi no yo kakete Kuruma-zō

Tokone no nemuri itsumade.

Furi-kumoru
Sora wa Ogura no mine no yuki,[3]
Sora wa Ogura no mine no yuki,
Chiruya Sagano no Arashi-yama,
Taki no hibiki mo koe soete
Kasanaru kumo no Ōi-gawa
Ikada no toko no uki-makura [4]
Katashiku sode mo shirotae no[5]
Sora mo hodonaku meguru hi no

Nishiyamamoto ni tsukinikeri,

Nishiyamamoto ni tsukinikeri.

Shibaraku kono tokoro ni kuruma o tate

---

names of the places around the Saga district in the northwestern part of Kyoto. *Chiru* (scatter) and *arashi* (storm) are *engo. Kasanaru kumo no* ***ōi*** (layers of cloud in great quantity) → ***Ōi-****gawa* (**Ōi** River).

[4] In *uki-makura* (floating pillow), *uki* means both "floating" and "sad."

[5] Lines 13–15: *Katashiku sode* (singly spread sleeve): Means "to sleep alone." Lovers used to spread their sleeves and sleep upon them. *Shiro-tae* (literally, "white cotton") modifies the sleeve, and the following word, *sora* (the sky); *meguru hi* (moving sun) → Western Hills.

The Waki *sits down.* — And look at the landscape.

YOBIKAKE *The* Shite, *Goblin Tarō-bō in the form of a* yamabushi *priest, enters, calling to the* Waki.

Yobikake, *spoken*

SHITE

I say, Priest on Wheels!

WAKI

What is it?

SHITE

In this floating life—[6]

WAKI

In this floating life?

SHITE

Sings, awazu — In this floating life, how do you go driving round, you Priest on Wheels?[7]

Halting at jō-za — Within the rut of the wheels
I see you still remaining.

WAKI

In this floating life, I do not go driving round, This Priest on Wheels.

Spoken — How could I drive the vehicle—Neither I nor wheel exist.

SHITE

"How could I drive the vehicle—Neither I nor wheel exist."! Who says so?

Sings, awazu

WAKI

In an empty cavern cool wind blows.

Spoken

SHITE

Only my name gossiped about rises like Mt. Takao's high peak.[8]

WAKI

So you live on the black peak of Atago Mountain, I guess.

---

[6] Lines 21–42: These lines are in the style of *mondo*, questions and answers practiced by Zen priests, in which answers are made in a most fantastic way. For example, to the *Shite's* question, "Who says so?" the *Waki* answers, "In an empty cavern cool wind blows," meaning that all is emptiness.

[7] Lines 23–25, and 26–27, are in the form of *waka*, thirty-one syllable poems divided into five phrases.

[8] Lines 30–31: From a poem by Hachijō no Ōigimi (fl. early Heian period) in the *Shūi-shū*

Yo mo no keshiki o nagamyōzurunite sōrō.

Ika ni Kuruma-zō,

Nanigoto zo.

Ukiyo oba[6]

Ukiyo oba

Ukiyo oba nani to ka meguru Kuruma-zō[7]

Mada wa no uchi ni
Ari to koso mire.

Ukiyo oba nani to ka meguru Kuruma-zō[7]

Nori mo uru-beki waga araba koso.

Nori mo uru-beki waga araba koso to iu wa ta so.

Kūdō kaze suzushi.

Waga na nomi Takao no yama ni ii-tatsuru[8]

Hito wa Atago no mine ni sumu na.

---

(562): *Naki* ***na nomi / Takao no Yama*** *to /* ***Ii-tatsuru / Hito wa Atago no / Mine ni*** *ya aruran* (**Only** vain **rumor** / To **Takao Mountain's height** / **You make to rise high**. / **The black peak of Mt. Atago,** / That must be your dwelling place.) The poem was sent to a man whom, the poetess thought, was responsible for false gossip about her. In the name of the mountain, *Taka* means "high." *Ata* in Mt. Atago can mean "wicked," although, perversely enough, it is written with the character that means "love." Mts. Takao and Atago are in the northwestern part of Kyoto. Mt. Atago was a legendary dwelling place of *tengu* goblins.

SHITE
And your dwelling place, where is it?
WAKI
Not at one same place.
SHITE
How about your carriage?
WAKI
One escaping from a house on fire.[9]
SHITE
Though it goes round,
WAKI
It does not go round.
SHITE
Though one pushes it,
WAKI
It cannot be pushed.
SHITE
Though one pulls it,
WAKI
No pulling—

Sings, awazu
SHITE
The carriage of the priest.

Chū-nori
CHORUS
Out of the Triple World, unpeaceful as a house on fire[10]
Escaped to safety, the Three Vehicles on wheels;
you, Priest,
Though going round, straight was the Way.
Ah, he did make it go! He did make it go!

Age-uta, *hira-nori*
Men see and hear this,
Shocked out of wits, heads empty as sky, cloud and
water,[11]
Shocked out of wits, heads empty as sky, cloud and
water

---

[9] Lines 35, 43–44: See note 1 to the Introduction to this play. From the Lotus Sutra (Saddharmā-puṇḍarīka-sūtra), Book Three, "Parables." In this book Buddha is compared to a father who coaxes his children out of a burning house by offering them three carriages, drawn either by oxen, deer, or sheep (or goats). When they exit, he actually gives them something better, jewel-encrusted carriages drawn by pure white bullocks. The three lesser vehicles are seen as inferior forms of Buddhism, while the bullock carriage is the ultimate One Vehicle that leads to buddhahood.

[10] From "Parables," as explained in Note 9. *San-gai* (Triple World): In addition to the

Sate osō no sumika wa.

Issho fujiu.

Kuruma wa ika ni.

Kataku no shussha.[9]

Meguredo

Megurazu

Osedo

Osarezu

Hikumo

Hikarenu

Kuruma-zō no

Sangai Muan yunyo kataku oba[10]
Idetaru Mitsu no Kuruma-zō kana.

Meguru mo sugunaru michi narikeri
Ō nori-etari nori-etari.
Mikiku hito
Kokoro soranaru kumomizu no[11]

Kokoro soranaru kumomizu no

---

worlds of past, present, and future, according to Buddhist concepts, the world of men is divided into three parts: 1) the world of greediness; 2) the world of pretty colors, where those who could leave the world of greediness live; 3) the uncolored world, which transcends the colored world; another system divides the three realms of the world of transmigration thus: 1) the realm of desire; 2) the realm of form; and 3) the realm of non-form. The verb "to escape" in line 43 is related to both the Three Vehicles and the Priest on Wheels.

[11] In *Kokoro sora* (mind [is] empty), *sora* (empty; sky) leads to *kumo mizu* (clouds and water) and to *fuka* (deep).

Deep above, heaven soars up to heart-chilling height,
Stormy winds's voices roar all over Atago Mountain,
Until peak after peak resounds loud with echoes.
Although there is no path for a carriage,
My dwelling place is on Atago Mountain.
To the hermitage of Tarō-bō
Let me invite you, do come and see me, Priest on
 Wheels,
He called aloud, and on evening mountain
Cloud sinister he disappeared into the sky,
Borne on the cloud he disappeared into the sky.

NAKAIRI *Accompanied by* raijo *music, the* Shite *makes an interim exit.*

AI-KYŌGEN *After the* Shite *has made his interim exit, the music changes to* kyōgen ranjo, *and the* Ai-kyōgen, *a petty goblin, enters and, standing at the* nanori-za, *narrates what has happened between the* Kuruma-*zō and Taro-bō.*

AI

I who appear here now am a Mizugoe Tengu, a gutter-jumping, long-nosed goblin in service to the great long-nosed goblin Tarō-bō of Mount Atago. The matter for which I have come here at this time is of no great import. I am simply here to visit a noble resident of this place who is called Kuruma-zō. He was once a man of high position, but he was thrown into such a state of sorrow by the loss of his wife that he took the tonsure and became a monk. Now, I have heard nothing of the details for his reason for taking the name Kuruma-zō, but it is known that he has a great fondness for riding in a cart, and the strange thing about it is that it is not drawn by oxen or man, rather all he has to do is get inside and touch it with his holy horsehair fly-swatter and it takes flight, making it possible for him to fly through the air over mountains, peaks, rivers, and seas to wherever he might desire to travel. This wondrous personage possesses a heart that is filled with unlimited conceit. Thus, my master Tarō-bō, unsettled by Kuruma-zō's great pride, is determined to bring him down from the way of the Buddhist Law to make him walk in the Way of Demons. He gathered all his long-nosed demon relatives and discussed what could be done to accomplish this purpose, and it was decided that, first of all, Tarō-bō should

Fukadatsu sora mo susamashiku
Arashi mo koe-goe ni Atago-yama
Mine doyomu made hibiki-aite
Kuruma-ji wa nakeredomo
Waga sumu kata wa Atago-yama
Tarō-bō ga anjitsu ni
Onniri areya Kuruma-zō to

Yobawarite iuyama no
Kurokumo ni norite agarikeri
Kurokumo ni norite agarikeri.

(*The Japanese original of the* Ai-Kyogen *has been omitted here.)*

have a confrontation with Kuruma-zō. Hearing that Kuruma-zō was to fly about Saga Moor today, Tarō-bō took this advantageous opportunity to come here and confront the Priest on Wheels by means of the Poetry Enlightenment Method, calling out to him, saying, "In this floating life, / How do you go driving round, / You Priest on Wheels? / Within the rut of the wheels / I see you still remaining." One of my sort might think at first thought that this referred to the wheels of the cart, but it is, in fact, nothing of the kind. There is an ancient code known as the Laws of Zen that consists of 1,700 articles, including the original Honor Wheel, "Whose Wheel," and the Wheel of Ten Thousand Oaks. So what Tarō-bō meant by his reference to the Wheel was that Kuruma-zō still exists in the realm of the first of those Wheels. But Kuruma-zō, being a man of great pride and not easily put down, responded with: "In this floating life, / I do not go driving round, / This Priest on Wheels. / How could I drive the carriage— / Neither I nor wheel exist." This is also not a reference to the wheels of his cart, but rather, an answer that takes the cart wheels as a metaphor for demonstrating that he is not confined to the realm of the first wheel of the ancient code of laws. Kuruma-zō went on to explain that it is impossible to gain access to the Three Worlds in the context of the Past, the Present, and the Future, and that "it is only when one casts one's gaze beyond those Three Worlds, keeping detached from either joy or regret, emptiness or silence, and keeping one's heart free of pride, that one finds that there is no longer any wheel upon which one is obliged to ride." Hearing this, Tarō-bō realized that he was dealing with a man of overwhelming power, so, with the greatest regret for failing to accomplish his determined purpose of dragging Kuruma-zō down to his own Way, he reluctantly set out for home. But I, petty long-nosed demon that I am, have made up my mind to go and confront this Kuruma-zō who utters such foolish words and see what I can do to make him laugh, for if I can elicit even the tiniest chuckle from him, it will serve to detract his heart and draw him down to the Way of Demons.

First, I must hurry on my way to find him and have a look at him for myself. I wonder just where he might be? (*He makes a circuit of the stage.*) Oh, there he is crouching down over there. I will speak to him. (*He approaches the* Waki.) I say, I say, Priest on Wheels, Priest on Wheels! What is this? He appears to be deaf. But if he were deaf, he would likely not have been able to carry out the discussion he had with Tarō-bō earlier. I will do what I can to make him laugh. (*He cavorts about in front of the* Waki, *singing and dancing to orchestral accompaniment.*) Kuruma-zō, Priest on Wheels, Kuruma-zō, Priest on Wheels, I will make you laugh. Kuruma-zō, Priest on Wheels, laugh, I say, Kuruma-zō! Right in front of your nose, Priest on Wheels, with a baby rat on my back, I stumble that way, I stumble this way. Stumble, leap, and stumble. Laugh, oh, Kuruma-zō, laugh, Priest on Wheels! (*All of this has no effect on the priest.*)

There is not even as much of a reaction as when a bee stings a deer's horns! What shall I do? It is said that there is nothing that elicits laughter from a human being so surely as to tickle his flesh, so now I will tickle him and make him laugh. (*Singing and dancing to orchestral accompaniment as before.*) Kuruma-zō, I will make you laugh. I will now tickle the Priest of Wheels. Tickle, tickle, tickle, tickle. I tickle here, I tickle there. Laugh, oh, Kuruma-zō, laugh, you Priest on Wheels! I tickle here and there as well. (*He touches Kuruma-zō with his left hand, which Kuruma-zō strikes with his fan.*) Ow, ouch! Ow, ouch! Well, I must say, what a frightful person! What a frightful person! I have tried all sorts of things just now, but I failed to elicit even the tiniest grin from him. And on top of that he struck me with his horsehair flyswatter. This is most likely another manifestation of the Laws of Zen. And it appears that those Laws of Zen are most painful! There is not much the likes of me can do against them. I think that I must quickly inform Tarō-bō of what has taken place.

I say, all you petty long-nosed demons, listen to me well. I have performed a vast variety of tricks in the presence of this priest here, but he has not shown the least tendency to laugh, so I am now of the opinion that the occult powers of this Priest on Wheels are of such great strength that even the power of one thousand oxen would not be capable of overpowering him. So I order to you to go quickly and tell Tarō-bō that he should come out here again himself, preparing himself by taking all possible prudent precautions. Prepare your hearts and do this, I say, prepare your hearts and act with alacrity.

Ō-BESHI *The* Nochi-shite, *Tarō-bō, the goblin, enters and stands by the first pine.*

Sashi, *awazu*

SHITE

On Mt. Atago and over Aniseed Field, snow having fallen,[12]
Of those who gather flowers, not even a trace is seen.

Spoken

Indeed on the snow-covered mountain there is no path.

The Shite *looks at the* Waki.

But how about the ruts of your wheels, Priest on Wheels?[13]
"Nobody can equal me in holiness"—
Is there not a trace of such conceit in your mind?
If there is, then freed from attachment and desires,
Can you pull or move on, Priest on Wheels?

Issei, *awazu*

The Way of Demons as well,[14]

The Shite *enters the main stage.*

Let it be your concern, Priest on Wheels.

CHORUS

Good and evil are like two wheels of a carriage.

SHITE

There is the Law of Buddha, and of men.

CHORUS

Blind attachment
Side by side with Enlightenment.

SHITE

Noru

There are Buddhas and there are men.

CHORUS

Awazu

There is the Priest on Wheels,

SHITE

And Tarō-bō, the ascetic.[15]

Noru

CHORUS

If you say prayer, then I will pray.
As for the miraculous power,

The Shite goes near the Waki *and squats. Ends off rhythm.*

I shall not stand beneath you,
I shall not stand beneath you.
Come, Priest on Wheels,
Let's compare our powers.

---

[12] Lines 60–61: From a poem by Sone no Yoshitada (ca. 923–ca. 1003) in the *Fuboku-shō* (9951): ***Atago-yama/ Shikimi-ga-Hara ni / Yuki tsumori / Hana tsumu hito no / Ato dani** zo **naki*** (**On Mt. Atago / And over Aniseed Field, / Snow having fallen, / Of those who gather flowers, / Not even a trace is seen**.)

Atago-yama Shikimi-ga-Hara ni yuki tsumori[12]

Hana tsumu hito no ato dani mo nashi.
Geni setchiu ni sanro nashi.
Sate sharin na (= wa) ika ni Kuruma-zō.[13]

Ware hodo tattoki mono araji to
Manjin no shinro ato nakaran (n)ya.
Shikaraba mujakuhō yokushin ni
Hikuka utsuru ka Kuruma-zō
Madou ni mo[14]
Kokoro o yose yo Kuruma-zō.

Zennaku futatsu wa ryōwa no gotoshi.

Buppō areba sehō ari

Bonnō areba
Bodai ari

Hotoke areba shujō mo ari

Kuruma-zō areba

Tarō-bō no gyōja mo ari[15]

Inoraba inoru-beshi
Gyōseba gyōtoku mo
Otorumaji to yo
Otorumaji to yo
Iza Kuruma-zō
Gyō-kurabe sen.

---

[13] The question about the ruts of wheels is related to the "trace of conceit" in line 64.

[14] The goblin reveals his intention of tempting the priest.

[15] Tarō-bō, the ascetic: "Ascetic" refers to a *yamabushi* priest. A *tengu* usually appears in the form of a *yamabushi.*

Spoken

WAKI

No matter how you try to disturb me,
Neither do I heed nor contend with you.
From the first I am no more or less than what I am.[16]

Sings, awazu

Oh, what a beautiful season!

Spoken

SHITE

Indeed, if it is a beautiful season,
Why not turn the carriage about in the snow
And play in the Moor of Saga?

The Shite *goes toward the* shite-bashira.

WAKI

Play if you would, like gossamer thread,[17]
But never can you pull my mind.

SHITE

Do you say I can't? That can never be, I say,
And lifting the stick, he strikes the carriage.

Strikes the carriage.

WAKI

Ah, if you strike the carriage, will it go?
If you strike the ox, it will go.[18]

SHITE

Indeed, the carriage has no mind.
And there is no ox to strike.

WAKI

You fool! Don't you know the Way of Man and Ox?
Why don't you strike the ox that is visible?

SHITE

The ox that is visible! What do you mean? And
what about Man and Ox?

WAKI

No matter how you strike, they will not go.

SHITE

If you strike, will they go?

WAKI

Without doubt.
Now see how I strike the white bull in the alley,[19]
saying thus,

---

[16] The phrase *fuzō fugen* comes from the Heart Sutra (Prajñā Pāramita Hṛdaya Sūtra): *Ze shōhō kūsō: fushō, fumetsu; fuku, fujō; fuzō, fugen* (All things by their very nature partake of emptiness: they neither arise nor perish; they are neither defiled nor pure; they neither increase nor decrease). It would have easily been recognized by the audience.

[17] *Ito-yū,* the Japanese word for gossamer, is written in two Chinese characters, *ito* (thread) and *yū* (to play, idly moving). *Hiku* (to pull) in the next line is an *engo* of *ito* (thread).

Ika ni nanji samataguru tomo
Sore ni wa yoraji arasowaji
Ware wa moto yori fuzō fugen[16]
Ara omoshiro no jisetsu ya na.

Geni omoshiroki jisetsu naraba
Setchiu ni kuruma o megurashi
Sagano no hara nite iza asoban.

Asobaba asobe itoiu no[17]
Waga kokoro oba hikareme ya.

Nadoka wa hikade aru-beki to
Shimoto o furi-age kuruma o utsu.

Ō kuruma o utaba yuku-beki ka
Ushi o utaba yuku-beshi ya.[18]

Geni, geni kuruma wa kokoro nashi
Sate ushi o utanmo araba koso.

Oroka ya nanji nin-giu no michi
Mietaru ushi oba nado utanu.

Mietaru ushi to wa sate ika ni somo nin-giu wa

Utsu tomo yukaji

Sate osō no utaba yuku-beki ka.

Naka-naka no koto
Ide-ide saraba roji no byakugo o utte misen to[19]

---

[18] Lines 95–100: An allusion to the *Ten Oxherding Pictures. See* the introduction to the play for more details.

[19] The "white bull" is mentioned in the same parable explained in Note 9: "There was a large white bullock, fat, young and strong, with a beautifully shaped body, tethered to a treasure carriage. . . . This was given to the children."

Sings, awazu

Lifting the *hossu,* I strike the air.[20]

Au

CHORUS

Oh, look at that, what a strange sight! The carriage—
Oh, look at that, what a strange sight! The carriage
Begins to move and turn about, and what till now
To all appearance seemed a vehicle on frail wheels,
Although there is no ox, and no man to drive it,
With little effort it begins to move on,
Turning into a flying carriage.

Rongi, *au*

The little carriage goes
Along the path through the field in the mountain shade,
Preaching the Way of Holy Law as it drives on,
To the great benefit of people high and low.

The Shite *dances to the end.*

SHITE

This is the place known
As "Weary-life's Saga." Well-named indeed![21]
On the snow-covered ancient path leave deep traces[22]
The ruts of the wheels. Along the steep mountain way
In heavy snow the carriage would never go.

CHORUS

E'en if this should be a path on Snowy Mountains[23]
Riding the Way of Holy Law's carriage, smoothly—

SHITE

Will it go on, or will it not, while in this field

CHORUS

Grass-grown, the little carriage, with rain joining in,

SHITE

The Shite *beats the carriage, then stops.*

I strike, but it will not go.

---

[20] *hossu:* A scepter-like object that a priest holds in hand at ceremonies. It has a long tuft of white hair (obtained from a horse's tail) tied at one end. It is this object that the *Ai-kyōgen* calls a "fly-swatter."

[21] The name of the "Saga" district can also mean "nature, way," so that this out-of-the-way, lonesome place came to be referred to in numerous poetic allusions as *asukiyo no Saga* (weary life's way).

[22] *Yuki no* ***furu*** (snow falls) → ***furu****-michi* (old pathway). *Ato* (traces) is related to *Yuki no furu-michi* (snow-covered ancient path) and *kuruma no wadachi* (the ruts of wheels). The line is from a poem by Ariwara no Yukihira (818–93) in the *Gosen-shū* (1075), made on the occa-

Hossu wo agete kokū o uteba[20]

Fushigi ya na kono kuruma no
Fushigi ya na kono kuruma no
Yurugi megurite ima made wa
Ashi-yowa–guruma to mietsuru ga
Ushi mo naku hito mo hikanu ni
Yasu-yasu to yari-kakete
Tobu kuruma to zo naritarikeru.
O-guruma no
Yama no kageno no michi sugara

Nori no michi nobe yugyō shite
Kisen no riyaku nasu to ka ya.

Tokoro kara
Koko wa ukiyo no Saga nare ya[21]
Yuki no furu michi ato fukaki[22]
Kuruma no wadachi wa ashi-biki no

Ōyuki ni wa yo mo yukaji.

Geni sessen no michi nari to[23]
Nori no kuruma-ji tairaka ni

Yuku ka yukanu ka kono hara no

Kusa no o-guruma ame soete

Utedomo yukazu

---

sion of Emperor Kōkō's visit to Serikawa in Saga: ***Saga*** *no yama / Mi-**yuki** taenishi / Seri-kawa ya /Chiyo **no furumichi** / **Ato** wa arikeri* (To **Saga** Mountain / Though royal visits have ceased, / By Serikawa,/ On the **Old** Chiyo **Path** / **The traces** have still remained.) Serikawa is a river in Saga; *mi-yuki* (imperial visit) can also mean "deep snow" and is thus an *engo* of *ato* (trace). Cf. *Kogō,* line 120, in *Troubled Souls.*

[23] *Sessen* (Snowy Mountains): An ancient name of the Himālaya Mountains, where Śākyamuni served two holy hermits as their disciple, cutting firewood and drawing water from a stream.

CHORUS
When I try to stop it, it moves,
SHITE
This carriage being
CHORUS
Endowed with the Wheel's great power,[24]
Saga, Ogura, Ōi, and Arashi
Mountains and Rivers it crosses flying past,
Though I try to bewitch him, he is not to be disturbed.
Indeed, a man one encounters rarely is this Priest
on Wheels!

The Shite *worships the* Waki *and stamps the* tome-byōshi *at* jō-za.

Oh, how reverend! How aweful! With these words,
Having dissolved his demonic spell, the great
goblin chief
Joins his hands in worship and disappears from sight.

---

[24] "The Wheel's great power": The original Japanese is *Nori no chikara* (Law's power), in which *nori* (law, dharma) also means "to ride," which was made "Wheel [of the Law]" in this translation because of the strong association with *hōrin* (Wheel of Dharma = Wheel of the [Buddha's] Law).

Tomureba susumu

Kono kuruma no

Nori no chikara tote[24]
Saga, Ogura, Ōi, Arashi no
Sanka o tobi-kakette
Genwaku suredomo sawagaba koso
Makoto ni kidoku no Kuruma-zō kana

Ara tattoya osoroshiya to
Mashō o yawarage dai-tengu

Gasshō shite koso usenikere.

鵺

NUE

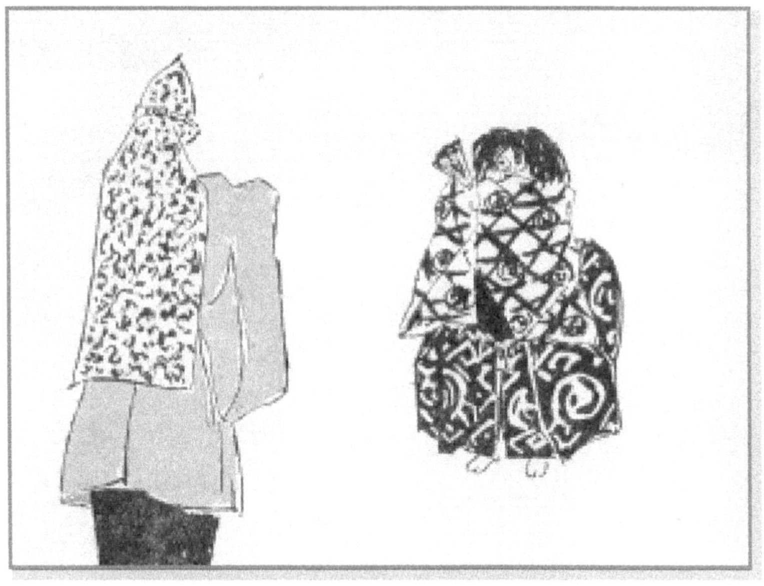

真如の月乃夜汐に浮かみつゝ
これまで来れり。ありがたや。

Over the truthful moon's / Nocturnal tidal water drifting,
To this place I have come. / Ah, thanks be to the Buddha!

Introduction

A *nue* (pronounced in two syllables, NÚ-eh) is a legendary monster, which had the face of a monkey, the body of a badger, and the limbs of a tiger, with a snake for a tail—rather reminiscent of a chimera. It is called *nue* because its voice resembled that of a bird by that name, a kind of large-sized wood thrush.[1] According to the *Heike Monogatari,* this monster came flying nightly on a bank of black clouds over the Imperial Palace and tortured the Emperor, until it was shot down by Minamoto no Yorimasa, a Genji general. In the Noh, the ghost of the monster appears to a traveling monk with a wish to attain nirvana by his prayer. The killing of the monster by Yorimasa is told at length twice in the Noh, first in the *kuri–sashi–kuse* in the first act, and then toward the end of the second act, faithfully following the lines in the *Heike Monogatari,* vol. 4, the "Nue" chapter. The following is a translation of the tale as told in the *Heike,* based on the Kakuichi version.

> IN THE EMPEROR KONOE's reign, in the Ninpei era (1151–54), it so happened that the Emperor was nightly seized with terror and lost consciousness.[2] At the Imperial order, high priests celebrated for the power of their prayers offered masses on a grand scale, but they all proved ineffective. The Emperor would suffer at the hour of the Ox,[3] when, from the direction of the forest of East Sanjō (Third Street) Palace wood, a bank of black clouds would appear and spread over the Imperial Palace, and the Emperor would be seized with terror. So a conference was held at court. . . . "We should appoint a warrior who will guard the Palace," they argued, and from among the warriors of the Genji and Heike, they

[1] The word *nue* is actually written with a single character that is itself made up of two independent characters: on the left is the character *yoru* (night); on the right, the character *tori* (bird)—so the composite new character should mean "night bird," which it does. The *nue* is another name for the bird known as *tora-tsugumi,* or White's Brown Thrush. This is the largest thrush in Japan. Its cry is an eerie high, thin whistle, alternating with an even higher, shrill whistle at a very slow pace, and it usually sings at night, which is why it gained the popular name of "nightbird."

[2] Quoted in *Nue* in Act 1, lines 112–13; act 2, line 203.

[3] The hour of the Ox was actually a two-hour period spanning 1–3 AM.

> selected Yorimasa, who at that time was only the Head of the Imperial Armory. . . . I no Hayata, his most trusted retainer, was the only one who accompanied him. Yorimasa wore a double-layered hunting robe. Fledged with the tail feathers of a copper pheasant were the couple of arrows with sharp points that he carried with a bow thickly bound with rattan. He seated himself on the South Hall (Shishinden)'s front verandah. . . . A speck of black cloud formed itself and, approaching, spread out all over the Imperial Palace. As Yorimasa, lifting his eyes, looked sharp, in the cloud he recognized a figure of some strange monstrous creature. . . . Taking an arrow and notching it, "Pray, help me, Great Bodhisattva Hachiman"[4]—thus he offered a prayer in his heart, and, stretching his bow, shot the arrow with a swish. Sure enough he felt the arrow hitting its mark. "Hurrah! I made it!" he shouted aloud in triumph. I no Hayata, swiftly approaching, caught what came falling down, and in quick succession pierced it through nine times. Then people high and low, lighting a fire, looked at it, and saw that its head was like a monkey's, its body like that of a badger, its tail was a snake, and its limbs were like those of a tiger. It cried in a voice that resembled a wood thrush (*nue*). Far, far beyond what "terrible" could express was the appearance of the creature.[5] The Emperor was pleased so much that he gave Yorimasa an imperial sword named "Lion King." The Grand Minister of the Left, Uji, received it, and, to give it to Yorimasa, he stepped half down the flight of stairs in front of the Imperial seat, . . . when up in the clouds a cuckoo passed by, calling two or three times. At this, His Lordship the Grand Minister of the Left recited, "The lowly cuckoo / His name in the cloud-bound sky / Far above has uplifted"; thus he declaimed to Yorimasa, who, bending down his right knee to the ground, recited thus: "What time the full-drawn bow moon / Went shooting down and was gone," and, the sword bestowed upon him, he withdrew from the Imperial presence. . . . It is said that the monster was put into a dugout boat and cast away.[6]

Upon comparison, we will see that the above section in the *Heike Monogatari* is transplanted almost word-for-word into the Noh to the amount of some sixty lines, divided into two parts, the *kuri–sashi–kuse* in the first act, and a section toward the end of the second act. There are several factors that made such a lengthy literal transplanting from prose into poetic passage possible. The first Noh section in question, the *kuri–sashi–kuse,* narrates Yorimasa's shooting of the monster. Of these three parts, the *kuri* and *sashi* are in free rhythm, not restricted by the rules about the number of syllables per line and are in a sort of recitative style of singing. A prose sentence easily rends itself to *kuri* and *sashi* singing. As for the *kuse,* it is the thematic song of a Noh, which is narrative. As it is, although it is in regular

[4] The deity known as Hachiman was actually the apotheosis of the warrior emperor Ōjin (AD 201–310). He was the patron of warriors and the tutelary deity of the Minamoto clan. (Cf. *Matsuyama Tengu,* Note 26.)

[5] Quoted in the *Nue,* Act 1, lines 112–57.

[6] Quoted in *Nue,* Act 2, lines 211–25.

rhythm, its construction involving word and music is different from other types of rhythmical songs, such as a *michiyuki* (travel song), *age-uta,* or *rongi.* In the latter group of songs, basically each line is made up of twelve syllables divided into two sections of seven and five, which are respectively distributed over two divisions of an eight-beat bar into five and three beats. The effect is melodious tending to monotony if continued without variation. A *kuse* is composed of lines of irregular numbers of syllables, and these lines are not distributed on the one-line-to-eight-beats system, with the end of a line falling on the eighth syllable. (The reader will easily understand this irregularity by counting the number of syllables in each line of the *kuse* in the English and Japanese texts in the translation of the Noh, and comparing the results with the *michiyuki,* or the *rongi,* which comes immediately after the *kuse.*) These lines of different lengths are distributed over eight beats regardless of the beginning and end of each line, many lines not beginning with the first beats, and not ending with the last but continuing to the first beat of the next eight-beat measure. This musical characteristic facilitates setting prose lines to music. In addition, the musical tone of a *kuse* is also different from other rhythmical songs, the effect of which is pedestrian rather than floating or flying, an effect appropriate for a narrative type of song such as a *kuse.*

•	1	•	2	•	3	•	4	•	5	•	6	•	7	•	8
. . . wore		a	dou –	ble		lay	– ered	hun	–	ting	robe	//			
. . . *fu*	–	*ta*	– *e*	*no*	·	*ka* –	*ri* –	*gi*	–	*nu*	*ni*	//			
Fledged		with	the	tail		fea	– thers	of		a	cop –	per	phea	–sant	were –
Ya	–	*ma*	– *do* –	*ri*		*no*	*o*	*ni*		*te*	*wa*	*i*	*da*	*ri*	*ke*–
–	–	–	.	The		cou	– ple	sharp	–	point	– ed		ar	– rows	That
ru	–	–	.	*To*	–	*ga*	– *ri*	*ya*		*fu*	– *ta*	*su*	– *ji*	/ *shi*	– *ge*
he		car	– ried	with		a	bow	thick	–	ly	bound	with	rat	– tan	
dō		*no*	*yu* –	*mi*		*ni*	*to* – *ri*			*so*	– *e* –	*te*	–	–	

In this example, the first line consists of a measure of only 6 beats (known as *ichiji*); the next three lines have the full 8 beats, but the second line has more than the usual twelve syllables (E: 13; J: 14); the third line has only eight; and the last line has twelve, but they begin within the eight-beat measure allotted to the previous line.

The same explanation largely applies to the second transplantation toward the end of the second act. This section continues the narration in the *Heike Monogatari,* from where it was stopped short in the first act, telling about Yorimasa receiving the Imperial sword in reward, and composing the cuckoo poem. On the whole, this section is in *chū-nori* rhythm, which has more than eight syllables to a line, often as many as two syllables to one beat. On the other hand, some syllables are often stretched out over many beats, as if in an attempt at adjustment. This results in quickness of tempo, rhythmical variety, and a feeling of excitement, elements that make the chanting more narrative than song-like. It is a style that facilitates the adoption of a prose work in the same way as a *kuse.* The element that facilitates a literal adoption is found also in the original story itself. The Kakuichi version of the *Heike Monogatari,* which is the script used by the chanters of the story, is written in a style fit to be sung or recited. In connection with the literal adoption of the original work, Ze-ami says in his remarks on how to write a *shura-Noh:* "If the hero is a celebrated Genji or Heike general from the *Heike Monogatari,* it is of special importance that you write . . . just as it is written in that story."[7]

We have dwelt at length on the subject of literal adoption as well as on the musical and linguistic structure of certain types of Noh songs, in the belief that such information is essential to a full appreciation of such Noh.

The action of *Nue* takes place as follows:

Act 1

1) The scene of the Noh is Ashiya, also Ashinoya (literally, "Reed Cottage"), a village on the seacoast in the present Hyōgo Prefecture. In the first act, after the entrance of the *Waki* and his usual initial songs and speech, there is an exchange between him and the *Ai-kyōgen,* a local person. The monk asks for a night's lodging, but is refused because of a law that forbids the lodging of strangers. The villager tells the monk to stay at a nearby chapel, warning that it is haunted by something that emits light. The monk says that he can protect himself with the Buddhist Law's power.

2) When the two have withdrawn to their seats, the *Shite,* the *Nue,* enters accompanied by *issei* music. It is wearing a ghostly mask and a wig of long black hair hanging low down its back, and carrying a pole in hand. It is supposed to be floating on the sea in something like a dugout log, steered with the pole. In the brief initial songs, it compares itself to the blind turtle of a Buddhist sutra, drifting in the ocean, hoping to come upon a piece of floating wood, which will take it to the Other Shore.[8] To the monk who wonders at the strange apparition, the boatman tells says it is the ghost of the *Nue* who lost its life, shot by Yorimasa's arrow. After the story about the killing of the *Nue* is told in *the kuri–sashi–kuse,* as translated above, the first act ends with a *rongi,* which describes the *Nue* boarding the dugout log and drifting away over the sea, leaving terrible cries behind. The *ai-kyōgen* tells the tale again in great detail.

Act 2

3) As the monk is reciting the sutra and praying for the soul of the *Nue,*

---

[7] Quoted from Ze-ami's *Sandō,* as given in Omote, p. 138. The original text is: *Keryō, Gen-Pei no meishō no jintai no honzetsu naraba, koto ni koto ni Heike no monogatari no kore . . . o hakarau beshi.*

he sees a monstrous figure appear before him and they chant the sutra in unison. The rest of the second act is the presentation of the second half of the *Heike* story, accompanied by the *Shite's* dancing action. The play ends with the *Nue's* address to the moon over the mountain ridge, to cast her light down where it is drifting jellyfish-like on the ocean waves.

In the *Heike Monogatari,* the story of the *Nue* is one of the additional episodes told after the main story, which is Yorimasa's revolt. The hero of the episode is Yorimasa, not the *Nue,* who is merely a monstrous beast, as we see in the above passage adopted into the Noh. However, in the Noh, apart from the sections transplanted from the *Heike,* the monster is treated as a being with human feelings and reason, as the following lines indicate:

> "I wanted to become a monstrous enemy of Buddhism / And molest the Buddhist and Imperial Laws." (Lines 195–96)
>
> "Indeed, to think of it, rather than Yorimasa's arrow, / It was the Imperial punishment that struck me down. / It is only now that this truth comes home to me." (Lines 209–11)
>
> ". . . the sword bestowed upon him, / He withdrew from the Imperial presence. / Yorimasa thus uplifted his name, / While my infamous name ran adrift, in a dugout log / They stuck me, . . ." (Lines 226–30)

The above lines tell the motive for the *Nue's* harassing the Emperor, his self-accusation, and his jealousy and frustration, and all this turns the *Nue* from a mere monstrous animal into a being with a human heart.

Between the *Nue* as a human-like being and Yorimasa who killed it we find certain parallels. Yorimasa, who fought as an Imperialist in the two rebellions of the Hōgen and Heiji eras, felt that he was not fairly rewarded. Twice he presented to the court a poem alluding to his slow promotion and was given a higher rank on both occasions. In spite of this, he plotted a revolt at the age of seventy-six, attempting to enthrone a royal prince, and killed himself when the revolt failed. Thus, like the *Nue,* he was a malcontent, jealous of the promotion of his rivals; he harassed the Imperial court; and he perished when his attempt failed. Yorimasa and the *Nue,* like Beowulf and Grendel, like St. Michael and the Dragon, can be seen as two opposite forces, like yang and yin, the Apollonian and the Dionysian.[9] Yorimasa was also a celebrated poet, as we see in the cuckoo passage in the *Heike Monogatari.* When he was about to fall on his sword, he composed a poem in which he compared himself to a piece of fossil wood, a tree that, having fallen into a bog, or that had fallen and become buried in the earth,

---

[8] *See* Note 8 to the play.

[9] Cf. Elizabeth Oyler, "The *Nue* and Other Monsters in *Heike Monogatari,*" HJAS 68:2 (Dec. 2008), p. 27.

never blossoms but rots away, becoming like a fossil: "I, a fossil wood, / From coming into blossom / Forever estranged, / And this is the final fruit, / Ah, the bitterness of it!"[10] Like Yorimasa, the *Nue* compares itself to fossil wood. It appears to a traveling monk, singing: "In darkness confined, like fossil wood, / And yet not resting buried forever— / The lost soul, whereto does it still attach itself?"[11] While most of the above parallels are coincidences, by making the *Nue* compare itself to fossil wood the playwright has elevated the drama from a mere monster tale to the metaphysical level. One thing that supports such a reflection is yet another parallelism found between *Nue* and a modern European short story. In "Der Jäger Gracchus" (The Hunter Gracchus) by Franz Kafka, a hunter named Gracchus, when shooting a chamois, fell down a cliff and died. (He was shooting, not shot like the *Nue;* but like the *Nue* he fell from a height and died.) They put him in a coffin and put the coffin into a bark, which was to take him to *das Jenseits* (the Other Shore). But something went amiss, and the bark has been drifting ever since for countless years, just like the dugout bark into which they put the *Nue's* body.[12] The approach of Gracchus' bark to a village is announced by an oversized dove, and *nue* is the name of a type of oversized thrush, whose voice the monster's voice resembles. In the Noh, a traveling monk hears the terrible cries of the *Nue* as it disappears at the end of the first act. In the Kafka tale, the Burgomaster comes to meet Gracchus, and the dead hunter tells him his story. When the Burgomaster asks him if he is going to stay at his village, the dead hunter replies that he does not know, for his rudderless bark is driven by the wind that blows from the Land of the Dead. Minor details aside, the two works are very alike in their both being stories of the dead eternally drifting on the earthly water without any hope of ever attaining the Other Shore.

The Noh presents the *Nue* as a being with two different faces: a monstrous beast as told in the *Heike Monogatari,* and as a being with a human heart. While the sections that present the *Nue* as a monstrous beast are faithful adoptions of the *Heike* in a straightforward narrative style, the sections not based on the original story are written in a style of great linguistic subtlety, quoting and alluding to well-known classic poems. The scene is a place celebrated for its associations with poetry—Nada on the seacoast of

---

[10] See *Yorimasa,* in *The Noh* series, Vol. 2, Book 2: *Warrior Ghost Plays* (*see* especially the Introduction to *Yorimasa* [p. 102], and lines 239–42).

[11] Quoted from *Nue,* lines 53–55.

[12] In terms of the eternal wandering of the boat, we cannot help but notice the parallel with the legend of *Der Fliegender Holländer,* or the Flying Dutchman.

[13] There is a passage in the *rongi* of *Matsukaze* that alludes to this poem by Ariwara no Narihira (825–80), which appears in both the *Ise Monogatari* (Episode 87) and the *Shin*

Ashiya (or Ashinoya). The name is frequently used in the Noh to heighten poetic effects. The *Waki's* travel song (*michiyuki*) ends with his arrival at Ashiya. The *Shite* in his initial *mondō* with the *Waki* refers to himself as "salt maker of Nada at Ashinoya." The phrase is a part of one of the well-known poems in the *Ise Monogatari*. The poem is recited alternately by the *Shite* and the *Waki* during a *mondō* (lines 85–87). The play ends with a song describing the *Shite* finally drifting to a floating bar on the coast of Ashinoya.[12]

We have already referred to Yorimasa's last poem, in which he compares himself to fossil wood, and the *Nue's* comparing itself to fossil wood. A third and the most beautiful poetic reference is found in the final song. The monster describes itself as one rotting in the dugout boat, shut out from the light of sun and moon, drifting from darkness unto darkness. He addresses the moon on the mountain ridge, pleading it to shed its light afar. Woven into this passage is the following poem by Izumi Shikibu: *Kuraki yori / Kuraki michi ni zo / Irinu beki / Haruka ni terase / Yama no ha no tsuki* (Out of the darkness / On an even darker path / I must now set out. / Shine on me though far away, / Moon above the mountain ridge; lines 235–39). The last word of the poem, *tsuki* (moon) comes at the head of line 239 as the first word of the next phrase, *Tsuki to tomo ni* (Moon together = together with the moon), in the final couplet*: Tsuki to tomo ni kaigetsu mo irinikeri / Kaigetsu to tomo ni irinikeri* (. . . O Moon! With her, the moon floating on the sea waves also has sunk, / And with the moon floating on the sea waves it has sunk). In the last couplet there are three moons: the moon on the mountain ridge, the moon floating on the sea, and the sea moon, which can be the moon's reflection, or a jellyfish, a word written in two Chinese characters, *kai* (sea) and *getsu* = *tsuki* (moon), here alluding to what drifts about jellyfish-like on the sea. All these moons disappear, leaving only darkness behind.

Nue, unlike most of the Noh of the group to which it belongs, is a visional Noh with structural characteristics peculiar to this type of Noh. It resembles a *shura*-Noh in that its *Shite* tells a story of defeat to a monk and begs him to pray for his soul. It comes even closer to another type of visional Noh,

---

Kokin-shū (1590): *Ashinoya no / Nada no shioyaki / Itoma naki / Tsuge no o-gushi mo / Sasade kinikeri* (At Ashinoya, / Nada's salt-maker woman / Has no time, so that / Even a small boxwood comb / She's never worn in her hair). It is sung by the *Shite* in solo, which is a highlight of the play (see *Matsukaze,* lines 100–102, and the notes to those lines on pp. 170–71, in *The Noh* series, Vol. 3: *Woman Noh,* Book 2. According to Ze-ami, this *rongi* was taken from an old and no-longer extant version of the play *Tōei.*)

the attachment piece, whose *Shite* cannot attain nirvana because of his earthly attachment. The songs in this type of Noh are full of poetic allusions expressed with great linguistic subtlety, and the same applies to *Nue.* However, in one point *Nue* differs from usual visional Noh, in which the ghost or supernatural being first appears in the form of an ordinary person. In *Nue,* from the first act, the *Shite* appears in a strange form, which makes the *Waki* remark, "To all appearance you do not look like a human."

The first phrase sung by the *Mae-shite, Kanashiki kana ya* (Woe to me), is quoted in Ze-ami's *Go-on* without the author's name. A quotation in *Go-on* without the author's name is considered an indication that the work is by Ze-ami. Based on this, as well as in consideration of its style, some scholars consider that *Nue* was written by Ze-ami. Another relationship of *Nue* with Ze-ami is the use of the phrase *raku-raku rai-rai,* which describes the falling down of objects like stones. In *Nue,* the phrase describes the *Nue,* which, shot by Yorimasa, comes falling down from the clouds (line 207). The same phrase is used in Ze-ami's *Kakyō,* to describe a puppet falling down in pieces from the stage with its manipulating strings cut off (*see* the note to line 207).

Scene Village of Ashiya (Ashinoya) in Settsu Province, present-day Hyōgo Prefecture.

Season April by the lunar calendar.

*Characters and costumes:**

Waki A traveling monk, wearing a *sumi-bōshi* and a plain *noshime kitsuke* under a *mizugoromo* robe, carrying prayer beads in one hand.

Mae-shite The ghost of the *Nue,* wearing an *ayakashi* or *awa-otoko* mask, a long, black *kuro-gashira* wig, and a plain *noshime* or *atsuita kitsuke* under a *mizugoromo,* carrying a steering pole in hand.

Nochi-shite The ghost of the *Nue* in its own form, wearing a *ko-tobide* or *saru-tobide* mask, a long, red *aka-gashira* wig, a *dan-atsuita kitsuke* under a *happi* robe, and a *hangire* divided skirt, carrying a striking stick in one hand.

Ai-kyōgen A local man.

The author Attributed to Ze-ami.

* *For the technical terms in Japanese concerning costumes, see the Glossary.*

Nue

—ACT 1—

SHIDAI *The* Waki, *a traveling monk, enters and stands at the* jō-za, *facing the pine tree painted on the back panel.*

Shidai, *au*

WAKI

Fleeing from life, one goes adrift under the sky,[1]
Fleeing from life, one goes adrift under the sky,
The places he has left behind, where do they lie?[2]

Jidori, *awazu*

CHORUS

The Waki *turns and faces front.*

Fleeing from life, one goes adrift under the sky,
The places he has left behind, where do they lie?

Nanori, *spoken*

WAKI

I am a monk who travels, visiting places in various provinces.
Recently I have been to Mi-Kumano.
Now I intend to travel to the Capital.[3]

Michyuki, au

After a short while,
Returning past the Barrier on the Road of Ki,[4]
Returning past the Barrier on the Road of Ki,
I went further ahead to Izumi Province,
And when the wood of Shino had been traversed,[5]
A pine field came into view and a hamlet far,[6]
Suminoe here on the Bay of Naniwa
And to the village of Ashiya I have come,
And to the village of Ashiya I have come.

---

[1] *Yo o* ***sute*** (life to renounce) → ***sute****-bito* (renounced man = monk) → ***tabi*** (travel): one who has renounced life is a sort of traveler in that he has no permanent home → ***tabi*** *no sora* (traveling sky; going under the sky as a traveler): a phrase that implies loneliness, *Sehnsucht*, and all such sensations of a traveler.

[2] *Koshikata* (what is left behind): Means both the renounced past and the places the traveler has passed. It is only coincidental, but it is quite thought-provoking, to note that the name of the era in which this human-hearted monster appears, Ninpei, means Equal Compassion.

[3] Mi-Kumano ("The Three Kumanos"): The three great shrines in the Kumano region, in the southern part of Kii Province, present Wakayama Prefecture. *Mi* = three, also an honorific prefix. The three shrines (and the deities enshrined within them) are: Kumano Nachi Shrine (Katsumiko no Kami; Kumano Hayatama no Kami; Kumano Fusumi no Kami); Kumano Hayatama Shrine, also called Shingū [New Shrine] (Kumano Hayatama no Kami); and Kumano Nimasu Shrine, also called Hongū [Original Shrine] (Katsumiko no Kami).

[4] *Kaeri-****ki*** (return–**come**; **come** back) → ***Ki*** *no ji no seki* (**Ki** Road Barrier) on the border between Kii and Izumi provinces.

[5] *Shinoda no Mori* (Shinoda Wood): In Izumi Province, present-day Osaka Prefecture; an *uta-makura,* that is, a place well known in classical poems. The *Kokin Rokujō* (Six Quires of Ancient and Modern [Japanese Poetry]) compiled in 987 by Minamoto no Shitagō, or Prince Kaneakira, was one of several *ruidai waka-shū* (topically categorized *waka* collections) that

Yo o sutebito no tabi no sora[1]
Yo o sutebito no tabi no sora
Koshikata izuku naruran.[2]

Yo o sutebito no tabi no sora
Koshikata izuku naruran.

Kore wa shokoku ikken no sō nite sōrō.

Ware kono hodo wa Mi-Kumano ni mairite sōrō.
Mata kore yori Miyako ni noborabaya to omoi sōrō.[3]
Hodo mo naku
Kaeri Kinoji no Seki koete[4]
Kaeri Kinoji no Seki koete
Nao yuku sue wa Izumi naru
Shinoda no Mori o uchi-sugite[5]
Matsubara mieshi tōzato no[6]
Koko Sumiyoshi ya Naniwa-gata
Ashiya no Sato ni tsukinikeri
Ashiya no Sato ni tsukinikeri.

---

were heavily used by *waka* poets for reference, and it contains this poem (II, *Yama*, no. 1049): *Izumi naru / Shinoda no mori no / Kusu no ki no / Chie ni wakarete / Mono o koso omoe* (Like a spring becomes / Izumi's Shinoda Wood, / whose camphor trees have / a thousand branches of wisdom— / That keep my thoughts flowing on). As the wood is close to Kuzunoha Shrine, let us relate the tale of Kuzunoha, another non-human creature with a heart, here.

Kuzunoha was a fox who took human form and in the guise of a maiden married Abe no Yasuna, a twelfth-century nobleman who had saved the fox from hunters. Kuzunoha bore him a child, who would become the future famous yin-yang master, Abe no Seimei. Ultimately Kuzunoha was compelled by various circumstances (depending on the version of the legend) to reclaim her fox nature and return to her natural home in Shinoda Wood. So with unbearable sadness she abandoned her husband and son, after writing this famous farewell poem: *Koishiku ba / tazunekite miyo / izumi naru / shinoda no mori no / urami kuzunoha* (If you long for me, / Come then and search for me in / Shinoda Forest, / there in Izumi Province. / With regret, Kuzunoha).

[6] *Tōzato* (lit. "far hamlet") alludes to a nearby place named Tōzato Ono ("Far Hamlet of Littlefield"). This place, as well as the three places mentioned next, Suminoe, Naniwa-gata (Naniwa Bay), and Ashiya ("Reed Cottage") are all in Settsu Province, present-day Osaka Prefecture, and are all *uta-makura* well known in classical poetry.

Tsuki-zerifu, *spoken*

Having hurried,
Already I have arrived at the village of Ashiya in the province of Settsu.
As dusk has fallen,
I will seek lodging for the night.

Facing the hashi-gakari.

Is there some one of this place?

AI-KYŌGEN

Standing by the first pine.

You ask for a person of this place.
What can I do for you?

WAKI

I am a monk who is traveling, visiting various provinces.
Will you give me a night's lodging?

AI-KYŌGEN

That is a problem.
There is a strict law
That forbids us to give a night's lodging to a traveler.
So it is impossible to give you lodging.

WAKI

I understand about the law,
And yet I beg you to let me pass a night at your place.

AI-KYŌGEN

No, no, we cannot break the strict law.
You had better hurry on.

WAKI

So you will not give me shelter.

The Waki *is about to go.*

AI-KYŌGEN

Stop! I will give you shelter.
I say, I will give you shelter.

WAKI

I am very happy.

AI-KYŌGEN

Pass the night in the chapel on the headland there.

WAKI

Was the chapel built by you?

AI-KYŌGEN

No, it was not built by me.
It is a chapel built by a group of us.

WAKI

Then if I stay at that chapel,
I do not have to ask your permission.

Isogi sōrō hodo ni
Kore wa haya Tsu no Kuni, Ashiya no Sato ni tsukite sōrō.

Hi no kurete sōrō hodo ni
Yado o karabaya to omoi sōrō.
Tokoro no hito no watari sōrō ka

Tokoro no mono to o-tazune wa
Ika yō naru goyō nite sōrō zo.

Kore wa shokoku ikken no sō nite sōrō.

Ichiya no yado o on-kashi sōrae.

Sono koto nite sōrō.
Kono tokoro no taihō nite
Ōrai no mono ni yado kasu koto wa kinsei nite sōrō aida
Narimōsumajiku sōrō.

Gotaihō wa saru koto nite sōraedomo
Hira ni ichiya o akasasete tamawari sōrae.

Iya, iya taihō o yaburu koto wa narimōsazu sōrō.
Tōtō on-tōri sōrae.

Sate wa ryōken naku sōrō ka.

Ara o-yado o mairasetaku sōrō.
Nō, nō, oyado o mairashō.

Shūchaku mōshite sōrō.

Ano susaki no midō e on-tomari sōrae.

Sono midō wa kata-gata no tateraretaru midō nite sōrō ka.

Ware-ra no tatetaru midō nite wa nashi.
Yori-aite tatetaru dō nite sōrō.

Sono midō ni tomari sōraeba
Kata-gata ni karu made mo naku sōrō.

AI-KYŌGEN

I tell you, to that chapel.
Every night some thing that emits light comes.
So be careful.

WAKI

I will pass the night there, for I have the power of the Law to help me.

The Waki *sits at the* waki-za. *The* Ai-Kyōgen *sits at the* kyōgen-za.

AI-KYŌGEN

That is a very strong-willed monk, indeed!

ISSEI *The* Shite, *a monstrous boatsman, enters and stands at the* jō-za.

Sashi, *awazu*

SHITE

Woe is me! This body, a caged bird,[7]
The soul, one should deem, the blind turtle and its floating wood,[8]
In darkness confined, like fossil wood,[9]
And yet not resting buried forever,
The lost soul, whereto does it still attach itself?

Issei, *awazu*

Floating and sinking,
In tears that beat in waves, the dugout log,[10]

CHORUS

Driven by yearning unbearable
For the past

SHITE

To reminisce to the heart's full,
There is little time.[11]

---

[7] A caged bird: Cf. "like a caged bird longing for clouds" in the *Heike Monogatari,* vol. 10, "Yashima Inzen" (The Retired Emperor's Letter), originally a phrase in a letter by Taira no Kanemori (d. 990; one of the 36 Poetic Geniuses) in Chinese that appears in the mid–Heian-period collection of Chinese writings known as the *Honchō Monzui,* vol. 6.

[8] "the blind turtle and its floating wood": In the Lotus Sutra (Saddharma-puŏÿarīka-sūtra, Book 27, "The Story of King Resplendent"): "A buddha is as hard to meet as an *udumbara* flower [which blooms but once every three thousand years], or as the one-eyed tortoise meeting the hole in the floating log" (Katō et al., p. 335). This teaching points out the rareness of the chance to be led to the Way of Buddha, and compares it to a blind turtle infinite kalpas old, that floats up from the bottom of the sea only once every hundred years. If it then encounters a piece of drifting wood and is lucky enough to be able to put its head through a hole in the wood, it will be led to the shore. (This parable also appears in chapter 15 of the Samyutta Nikāya, which is the most likely source of the allusion in the Lotus Sutra.)

Sarinagara ano dō e wa
Yona yona hikari-mono ga nobori sōrō aida
Kokoroete on-tomari sōrae.

Hōriki o motte tomari sōrō beshi.

Ara sun'ei osō ni wa aru.

Kanashiki kana ya mi wa rōchō[7]
Kokoro o shireba mōki no fuboku[8]

Tada anchiu ni nmoregi no[9]
Saraba nmoremo hatezushite
Bōshin nani ni nokoruran.
Uki-shizumu
Namida no nami no utsuo-bune[10]

Kogarete taenu
Inishie o

Shinobi-hatsu–beki
Hima zo naki.[11]

---

[9] "like fossil wood": The first allusion to Yorimasa's poem, in which the poet-warrior compares himself to fossil wood.

[10] Lines 55–57: *Uki-**shizumu*** (floating and **sinking**) → ***namida** no nami* (**tears** in waves), in which *namida* is an *engo* (associated word) of *shizumu* (to sink), from an expression, "to sink in tears," (to weep bitterly) → ***utsu**o-bune* (**dug**out boat), in which *utsu* meaning "to beat" is related to *nami* (waves, which "beat" the shore). "Floating wood," "fossil wood," and "dugout boat" in lines 51, 52, and 56 effectively present the image of a vessel, and the one in it, drifting in darkness. *Utsuo-bune **kogarete*** (dugout boat driven) → ***kogarete** taenu* (yearning unbearably), with *kogarete* meaning "to be rowed" and "to yearn."

[11] There is little time: In poetic writings, a fisher is often presented as being busy at his work with no time for anything else. A well-known poem about a busy fisher is quoted later on (*see* lines 85–91; Note 16).

Kakaru

WAKI

How strange! Where the night's darkness deepens
over the sea waves,
Shadow-like comes drifting an object.
I see that, just as I have been told,
It is shaped like a boat, and yet
It seems to be only a piece of fossil wood.
The form of the man in it is not clearly visible.
What a strange thing!

Spoken

SHITE

"A strange thing"—you who say thus,
Who are you?

Kakaru

Naturally, this woeful being adrift is like some
fossil wood,
Unknown to men. Thinking thus,
Pray, stop wondering.[12]

WAKI

Well, it is only because a villager
Has told me that a most strange boatsman
Comes drifting nightly.[13]
You look exactly like what he told me of,
So I wonder at your appearance.

SHITE

Spoken

A villager, you mean, of Ashiya,
A fisher who boils the salt water of Nada,[14]
A man of his sort, why do you think him strange?

Kakaru

WAKI

If you are one of those fishers who boil the salt water
of Nada,
Instead of attending to your trade, your nightly
coming here like an idle man is very strange.[15]

Spoken

SHITE

Indeed, my looking like an idle man
Seems strange to you, and you have reason.

---

[12] Lines 71–72: In *uki mi* (sad being), *uki* means both "sad" and "floating." "Fossil wood / Unknown to men": From the following passage in Ki no Tsurayuki's Japanese Preface to the first Imperial anthology, the tenth-century *Kokin Waka-shū* (Ozawa, 54): *Iro-gonomi no ie ni umoregi no, hito shirenu koto to narite:* In the houses of amorous people, [poetry] is like fossil wood, submerged, unknown to men." Like fossil wood he describes Japanese poetry, since it had become an obscure pastime of lovers, in contrast to Chinese writing, which was given priority at that time and was used in official documents.

Fushigi ya na! Yo mo fuke-gata no uranami ni

Kasuka ni ukami-yoru mono o
Mireba kikishi ni kawarazu shite
Fune no katachi wa arinagara
Tada nmoregi no gotoku naru ni
Noru hito kage mo sadaka narazu
Ara fushigi no mono ya na.

Fushigi no mono to uketamawaru
Sonata wa ikanaru hito yaran.
Motoyori ukimi wa nmoregi no

Hito-shirenu mi to oboshimesaba
Fushin na (= wa) nasase tamaiso to yo.[12]

Iya kore wa tada kono sato-bito no
Samo fushigi naru funa-bito no
Yoru-yoru kitaru to ii-tsuru ni[13]
Mireba sukoshi mo tagawaneba
Ware mo fushin (n)o mōsunari.

Kono sato-bito to wa Ashinoya no
Nada no shio kumu ama-bito no[14]
Tagui o nani to utagaitamou.

Shio yaku ama no tagui naraba

Waza oba nasade itoma arigeni yoru-yoru kitaru wa fushin nari.[15]

Geni, geni itoma no aru koto o
Utagaitamō mo iware ari

---

[13] *Yoru-yoru* means both "night after night" and "drifting and drifting."

[14] Lines 78–79. The name of the place Ashinoya, also Ashiya, means "Reed Cottage" (of a poor fisherman). Nada, the name of the place, also means "sea channel where waves rise high." "The salt maker of Nada at Ashinoya" is a poetic phrase; *see also* lines 85–87 and Note 16.

[15] "Like an idle man": From the poem quoted in lines 85–87; *see* Note 16.

There is this old poem: “Here at Ashiya,”[16]

Kakaru — WAKI

“The salt maker of Nada, As she has no time,
Her small comb made of boxwood, She came
without wearing it.”

SHITE

I, also, have no time free from surging sad thought,[17]

WAKI

By the tide water driven,

SHITE

The boatman

Age-uta, *au* — CHORUS

Came without combing the sea on his dugout log,[18]
Came without combing the sea on his dugout log,
Dream, or real, all this? When the day has dawned,
you will
See. No seaweed they would cut here at Ashiya.
Sleep just one night, and for the fisherman
Say a prayer and enlighten his soul’s darkness.
Ah, thanks be to Buddha! You traveler,
You are one who has discarded this earthly life.
In name only am I a cast-away little boat,[19]
Hoping to board the saving ship by the Law’s power,
Hoping to board the saving ship by the Law’s power.

Spoken — WAKI

To all appearance you do not look like a human.
Who are you? Tell me your name.

---

[16] Lines 85–91. A poem in Episode 87 of the *Ise Monogatari.* The particle *wa* (= as for) in the fourth line is *mo* (even) in the original. *Sasazu* (without wearing) in the fifth line is used in different senses in lines 89—*shio ni* ***sasare*** (by the tide **pushed**)—and 91—***sasade*** *kinikeri* (without **poling** came). This last phrase is basically a repetition of the fifth line of the original poem, but the meaning is different. *See also* Note 12 to the Introduction.

[17] Lines 88–89: *itoma* ***na***— (time being none) → **na**mi Shio (waves) → *shio* (tide). In *shio ni* ***sas****are* (by the tide **pushed**), ***sas****(u)*— also means “to steer a boat” and leads to *funabito* (boatman). The occurrence of *itoma na[shi]* (no time) shortly after two occurrences of *itoma ari* and *itoma no aru* (having time = idle) in lines 82 and 83 makes it stand out even more conspicuously.

[18] Lines 91–95: ***utsu****o-bune* (dug-out boat) → ***Utsu****tsu ka yume ka* (Reality or a dream?), from a poem in the *Ise Monogatari* (Episode 69): *Kimi ya koshi / Ware ya yukiken / Omōezu / Yume ka utsutsu ka / Nete ka samete ka* (Was it you who came, / Was it I who went to you? / I remember not. / Was it a dream? Was it real? / Was I asleep or awake?). *Yume* (dream) leads to *akete koso miru* (when day breaks one sees), in which ***miru*** (to see) leads to ***miru****me* (sea

Furuki uta ni mo Ashinoya no[16]

Nada no shioyaki / Itoma nami /
Tsuge no ogushi wa / Sasazu kinikeri.

Ware mo uki ni wa itoma nami no[17]

Shio ni sasarete

Funa-bito wa

Sasade kinikeri utsuo-bune[18]
Sasade kinikeri utsuo-bune
Utsutsu ka yume ka akete koso

Mirume mo karanu Ashinoya ni
Hitoyo nete ama-bito no
Kokoro no yami o toi-tamae.
Arigataya tabi-bito wa
Yo o nogaretaru on-mi nari.
Ware wa na nomi zo sute-obune[19]
Nori no chikara o tanomu nari,
Nori no chikara o tanomu nari.

Nani to mimōsedomo sara ni ningen to wa miezu sōrō.
Ika naru mono zo na o nanori sōrae.

---

weed). *Ake* also means "to open," and in *akete miru,* there is the meaning, "one opens (something) and sees," which has nothing to do with the context here. In *Ashinoya ni / Hito-yo nete* (At Ashinoya ["Reed Cottage"] / for one night to sleep), *hito* means "one," and *yo* means both "night" and "joint of the root of the reed" is a phrase associated with "Reed Cottage." Cf. the following poem in the *Senzai-shū* (807) by a Lady-in-Waiting (fl. 1175–81) in the service of Princess Kōkamon'in (d. 1181): *Naniwa-e no / Ashi no kari-ne no / Hito-yo yue / Mi o tsukushite ya / Koi-wataru-beki.* The poem can be paraphrased as follows: "Because of just one night of casual sleep, short as a joint on the root of the reed they cut, am I to long for him to death?" In the poem, *kari-ne* means both "casual sleep" and "cut root." *Mi o tsukushi* means "to worry or endeavor to death," while *miotsukushi* is "a stake erected in the water to mark the flow of the current and depth of the sea." *Miotsukushi* is especially associated with Naniwa Bay.

[19] *sute-obune* (cast-away little boat): From *yo o nogaretaru on-mi* (life-discarded one) in line 98, leads to *nori,* which means both "to board" and the Buddhist "Law of Dharma."

SHITE
There was one who, during the reign of the Emperor Konoe,[20]
Hit by Yorimasa's arrow,
Lost his life, a creature called the *Nue.* This is his lost soul.
I will tell you in detail how it happened.
Please pray for my afterlife.

WAKI
So you are the lost soul of the *Nue.*
Tell me in detail how it happened.
I will pray for your afterlife with all my heart.

Kuri, *awazu*
The Shite *sits at center stage.*

CHORUS
It so happened that, in the Emperor Konoe's reign,
In the Ninpei era,[21]
The Emperor was nightly assaulted by fits of illness.

Sashi, *awazu*

SHITE
At the Imperial order, high priests celebrated for the power of their prayer
Offered masses on a grand scale,
But they all proved ineffective.

CHORUS
The Emperor would suffer at the hour of the Ox,[22]
When, from the direction of the East Sanjō Palace wood,[23]
A bank of black clouds would appear
And spread over the Imperial Palace, and the Emperor would be seized with terror.

SHITE
So a conference was held at court:

CHORUS
"Surely this must be the doing of some monster.
We should appoint a warrior who will guard the Palace," they argued,
And from among the warriors of the Genji and Heike

---

[20] The Emperor Konne: Konne is an alternative reading of the name, and one that lent itself to being sung in Noh chants. It is usually given as Emperor Konoe (1139–55; r. 1141–55).

[21] Ninpei era: The era of Equal Compassion, 1151–54.

[22] the hour of Ox: *See* Note 3 to the Introduction.

Kore wa Konne no In no gyō ni[20]

Yorimasa ga yasaki ni kakari
Mei o ushinaishi Nue to mōshishi mono no bōshin nite sōrō.

Sono toki no arisama kuwashiku katatte kikasemōshi sōrō beshi.
Ato o tōte tamawari sōrae.

Sate wa Nue no bōshin nite sōrō ka.
Sono toki no arisama kuwashiku katari sōrae
Ato oba nengoro ni tomurai sōrō beshi.

Sate mo Konne no In no gozai-i no toki
Ninpei no koro ni[21]
Shushō yona-yona gonō ari

Ugen no kōsō kisō ni ōsete

Daihō o shuserarekeredomo
Sono shirushi sara ni nakarikeri.

Gonō wa ushi no koku bakari nite arikeru ga[22]
Tō-Sanjō no mori no kata yori[23]

Koku-un hitomura tachi-kitatte
Goten no ue ni ōeba kanarazu obie-tamaikeri.

Sunawachi kugyō sengi atte

Sadamete henge no mono naru-beshi
Bushi ni ōsete keigo aru-beshi tote

Genpei ryōka no tsuwamono o senzerarekeru hodo ni

---

[23] East Sanjō Palace: Situated to the southeast of the Imperial Palace, in the northeastern part of Kyoto, the residence of an Empress Dowager, and then of the Fujiwara family. Sanjō: Third Street, from the north, the third main street running east and west.

They selected Yorimasa.[24]

Kuse, *au*

Yorimasa at that time
Was the Head of the Imperial Armory.[25]
Among the retainers he deemed dependable,
I no Hayata
Was the only one who accompanied him.
Yorimasa wore a double-layered hunting robe,
Fledged with the tail feathers of a copper pheasant were
The couple of arrows with sharp points
That he carried with a bow thickly bound with rattan.
He seated himself on the Palace's front verandah and,
For the time of royal suffering,
He waited, counting every minute passing by.
After a while, as had been expected,
A speck of black cloud formed itself and, approaching,
Spread out all over the Imperial Palace.

To the end of the kuse *the* Shite *mimes the action.*

As Yorimasa, lifting his eyes, looked sharp,
In the cloud he recognized a figure of some strange, monstrous creature.

SHITE

Taking an arrow and notching it,

CHORUS

"Pray, help me, Great Bodhisattva Hachiman,"[26]
Thus he offered a prayer in his heart,
And, stretching his bow, shot the arrow with a swish.
Sure enough he felt the arrow hitting its mark.
"Hurrah! I made it!" he shouted aloud in triumph.
Where the victim had fallen, I no Hayata
Swiftly approached, and in quick succession,
No less than nine times he pierced it through with his sword.
Lighting a fire they looked at it and saw that
Its head was like a monkey's, its tail was a snake,
Its fore and hind legs were like those of a tiger,
It cried in a voice that resembled a *nue*.

---

[24] [Minamoto no] Yorimasa: A Genji general (1104–80); *see* the Introduction.
[25] Head of the Imperial Armory: Yorimasa was posted to this office after the *Nue* affair.

Yorimasa o erami-idasaretari.[24]
Yorimasa sono toki wa
Hyōgo no Kami to zo mōshikeru.[25]
Tanomitaru rōdō ni wa
I no Hayata
Tada hitori meshigushitari.
Waga mi wa futae no kariginu ni
Yamadori no o nite haidarikeru

Togari-ya futasuji
Shigetō no yumi ni tori-soete

Goten no ōyuka ni shikō shite
Gonō no kokugen (n)o
Imaya, imaya to machi-itari.
Saru hodo ni an (n)o gotoku
Koku-un hitomura tachi-kitari

Goten no ue ni ōitari.
Yorimasa kitto mi-agureba
Unchiu ni ayashiki mono no sugata ari

Ya totte uchi-tsugai

Namu Hachiman Daibosatto![26]
Shinjiu ni kinen shite
Yoppiki hyō to hanatsu ya ni
Tegotae shite hata to ataru.
Etariya ō to yasakebi shite
Otsuru tokoro o I no Hayata
Tsutto yorite tsuzuke sama ni
Kokono-gatana zo saitarikeru.

Sate hi o tomoshi yoku mireba
Kashira wa saru, o wa kuchinawa,
Te-ashi wa tora no gotoku nite
Naku koe nue ni nitarikeri

---

[26] Great Bodhisattva Hachiman: The Shinto god Hachiman is identified with a Buddhist Bodhisattva; *see also* Note 4 to the Introduction.

The Shite *sits at center stage.*
Rongi, *au*

Far, far beyond what "terrible" could express was the appearance of the creature.
Indeed, this is a well-known story, telling of
Your worldly attachment. I pray, turn it into
A power to let you float up from where you're sunk.

SHITE

To let me float up,[27]
The way is none. On the seacoast a shallow green
Three-horned elm tree was growing, its leaves would tell that,
When one is sinking, one is bound to float up.

CHORUS

Indeed, being bound by karma from former lives. . . .[28]

SHITE

Of all days and months, specially on this very eve,

CHORUS

By one no longer of this life to be joined. . . .[29]

SHITE

The Shite *rises with the pole in hand.*

The bamboo pole held in hand, in the dugout boat

CHORUS

He seemed to get in, and then,

SHITE

Over nocturnal waves

CHORUS

Floating up and sinking down,
Now seen, now lost to sight, intermittently,
Again and again one hears *Nue's* shrill voice
How horrible! How very terrifying!
Indeed, how horrible! How very terrifying!

NAKAIRI *The* Shite *drops the pole by the* shite-bashira *and makes an interim exit.*

---

[27] Lines 161–64. *tayori **naki*** (way none) → ***nagi**sa* (sea**coast**) → ***asa*** (shoal; shallow, pale) → ***asa-mi**dori* (pale green) → ***mizu*** (water) → ***mi-zuno*** (three horns) → ***mizuno**-gashiwa* (**three-horned** elm) → *shizumu wa ukamu en* (sinking is bound with floating, with *en* meaning "[karmic] bondage = when one sinks, there is a chance of floating up, whereas there is no floating up for one who already floats), from the following poem by Lady Kojijū (fl. twelfth century), in the *Shoku-Kokin-shū* (1290): *Omoi-amari / **Mizuno-gashiwa ni** / Tō koto no / **Shizumu** ni **uku** wa / Namida narikeri* (Sick with love I let / The triple-horned leaves of elm / Divine my fortune— / If they sink, what comes afloat? / Woe is me! It is my tears). There was an ancient custom of telling fortunes by throwing a *mizuno-gashiwa* leaf into water. If it floated up, it meant good fortune; if it sank, it was an omen of bad luck. It should be noted

Osoroshi nandomo oroka naru katachi narikeri.

Geni kakurenaki yogatari no
Sono ichinen (n)o hiru-gaeshi
Ukamu chikara to nari-tamae.

Ukamu-beki[27]
Tayori nagisa no asa-midori
Mizu no kashiwa ni arabakoso

Shizumi wa ukamu en narame

Geni ya tashō no en zo tote[28]

Toki mo koso are koyoi shimo

Nakiyo no hito ni aitake no[29]

Sao tori-naoshi utsuo-bune

Noru to mieshi ga Yoru no nami ni

Ukinu shizuminu
Mietsu kakure tae-dae no
Ikue ni kikuwa nue no koe
Osoroshi ya susamashi ya,
Ara osoroshi ya susamashi ya!

(*Below, the original Japanese text of the* Ai-Kyōgen *has been omitted.*)

---

that Lady Kojiju was reputed to be the most beautiful, intelligent, and independent lady in the Court at the time. She had many love affairs and left many excellent poems of passion. She was once the center of an amorous battle between Emperor Go-Shirakawa, Taira no Tadanori (Heike), and Minamoto no Yorimasa (Genji).

[28] *tashō no en* (former lives' bondage or karma): From the proverbial phrase: "Bound by the karma from former lives, strangers come to take shelter under the same tree, or draw water from the same river." (*Cf.* 135n 8).

[29] *hito ni* ***ai*** (by one **joined** = to encounter) → ***ai****-take* (**joined** bamboo), in which *take* (bamboo) implies "flute," and the phrase means a way of playing on a flute → *sao* (bamboo pole of a boatman).

AI-KYŌGEN *The* Ai-kyōgen, *a local person, has come to see how the traveler is faring, and the* Waki *asks him to tell the story about the Nue. The* Ai-kyōgen *tells the story and exhorts the monk to pray for the soul of the* Nue *and withdraws.*

The Ai-Kyōgen *rises and comes to stand at the* nanori-za (= jō-za).

AI

Earlier, a wandering priest requested lodging for the night, but I explained the strict law of this place, and told him he could sleep in the chapel on the strand. I wonder whether he is still there. I think I will go take a look.

Seeing the Waki. Are you still here, Reverend Priest?

WAKI

Yes, I am still here. Are you not the man who did not give me lodging earlier?

AI

That I am, indeed. While I wanted to provide you lodging, there was no way that I could go against the strict law of this place.

WAKI

No, no, you caused me no inconvenience at all. However, there is one thing concerning which I would like to inquire, so please come closer.

AI

With all my heart. (*He crosses to center stage and sits.*)
Just what is it of which you wish to inquire?

WAKI

This is perhaps a most unexpected thing to inquire about. Long ago, during the reign of Emperor Konoe, there was a changeling beast known as the *Nue.* Concerning how it came to its end, please relate to me anything you might know about the matter.

AI

I would never have expected you to inquire of such a thing. I myself am a resident of this neighborhood, but I know very little of that matter. However, I will relate to you everything I do know, just as it was told to me.

WAKI

For that I am most grateful.

Katari

AI

Well, then, I will tell about this chimera known as the *Nue.* During the reign of Emperor Konoe, night after night, black clouds rose up from the forest of East Sanjō, filling the sky over the palace and filling the Emperor's heart with great concern. He called together all the high and noble priests and had them offer prayers, but to no avail. A great soothsayer was then summoned, and he read an oracle and announced that it was the work of some ghost or demon.

It was then decided that a warrior should be chosen to shoot the demon down. The nobles gathered to discuss who would be best, and it was determined that from among all the warriors of both the Minamoto and Taira clans, Yorimasa was the best man for the job. When called forth, Yorimasa accepted the commission. And taking along only one attendant, I no Hayata from the land of Ōmi, he went to the garden of the Imperial Palace and awaited the time of the phenomenon that troubled His Majesty.

Just as was expected, at the very same hour as always, at the beginning of the third quarter of the Hour of the Ox (about 2:30 AM), a violent wind rose suddenly from East Sanjō, accompanied by a driving rain, and a huge mass of pitch-black clouds covered the sky above the palace entirely. Yorimasa peered deep into the mass of clouds and saw a beast more fearful than words can describe. All the courtiers of the Imperial Court, both high and low—the Emperor's Chief Advisor; the Ministers of the Right and Left; fifteen Great and Middle Counselors, eight advisors, six senior officials, and a high dignitary; all the warriors of the Fifth and Sixth ranks; and all courtiers of all court ranks of all levels—and all watched with bated breath as Yorimasa calmly notched an arrow to his bow and let it fly into the very center of the clouds.

The arrow found its mark and the beast crashed to the ground in the midst of the garden. I no Hayata rushed to its side and drove his sword straight into its heart, killing it in an instant. Torches were brought forth, and everyone gathered around to get a glimpse of the beast. What they saw before their eyes possessed the head of an ape, a serpent for a tail, and the limbs and claws of a tiger. And, as its voice resembled the cry of a wood thrush, they decided that is must be the *Nue.* And for fear of incurring the wrath of its spirit, they built for it a dugout boat, into which they placed the *Nue's* body, and set it afloat in the Yodo River. It is said that the boat drifted here to Naniwa Bay, where it remained for some time, and that its spirit became so attached to this place that, to this day, it appears here night after night.

Separately.

AI

This is the extent of what I have been told about this matter, but I feel quite concerned about your reason for inquiring about it.

WAKI

Thank you for having obliged me by so courteously relating the tale. There was no particular reason behind my asking you about this matter. But just a little while ago, when I came to this chapel to spend the night, a very strange man appeared in a dugout boat.

When I expressed my doubts about his identity, he told me that he was in reality the spirit of the *Nue.* He said that he was cast into the hollow craft, which drifted to this place on the tide and stopped here, caught in tangles of seaweed and salt reeds. Because his heart is still filled with attachments to this world, he is doomed to roam this place, appearing each night as a specter. He also told me the story that you have kindly told me in detail. Then he boarded his hollow craft once more and disappeared in the waves.

AI

Oh, what a wondrous thing you speak of! As I am convinced that it was truly the spirit of the *Nue* that appeared to you, I humbly request that you offer prayers for repose of its soul before you continue on your way.

WAKI

It is a very strange and wondrous thing, indeed! And I will be happy to recite the sutras and, at this very place, to fervently offer up memorial prayers that its tormented soul may know eternal peace.

AI

If there is any other service you might require of me, please feel free to call on me again.

WAKI

I will certainly call on you if I have the need.

AI

And with all my heart I will respond. (*Exits.*)

The Waki *goes to sit at the* waki-za.

Howard Hamilton performing the *Mae-shite* role in a Kita-school performance of *Nue* on the Noh stage of Itsukushima Shrine, Miyajima, Hiroshima, around 1974. "This woeful being adrift is like some fossil wood, unknown to men." (Courtesy the late Dr. Howard B. Hamilton.)

Machi-utai, *au*

WAKI

The voice of Sacred Law and the sound of sea waves
The voice of Sacred Law and the sound of sea waves,
All preach the way of Supreme Truth opened widely.
Come and receive the Sacred Law, all night long
In this way I chant aloud the Holy Scripture,
In this way I chant aloud the Holy Scripture.

DEHA *The* Nochi-shite, *the spirit of the Nue, enters. When he comes as far as the first pine, the* Waki *joins his hands together in prayer and begins to recite the sutras.*

Sings, awazu

WAKI

"When a buddha attains nirvana and looks at the Law's Universe,
Grasses, trees, lands, one and all become buddhas."[30]

The Shite *stands at* jō-za *and joins hands in prayer.*

SHITE

Issei, *awazu*

"Sentient and insentient, all on the path to buddhahood,"[31]

WAKI

Must have trust, I say.

SHITE

Indeed, I should have trust.

Ō-nori

CHORUS

Fifty-two kinds of creatures and I are beings of kin,[32]
Toward nirvana attracted, over the truthful moon's
Nocturnal tidal water drifting,
To this place I have come. Ah, thanks be to Buddha!

The Shite *joins hands in prayer.*

Kakaru

WAKI

How strange! Here comes something before my eye.

---

[30]Lines 181–82: Although said to be found in the Chūin-gyō (Antarabhava-sūtra), these lines are not found in extant versions of this text. *Sōmoku kokudo, shikkai jōbutsu:* The origins of this saying are obscure. Although said to be quoted from the Chūin-gyō (Antarabhāva Sūtra), it does not appear in either of the surviving versions. There is, however, a similar phrase in the Mahāyāna text known as the Nehan-gyō (Mahāparinirvāṇa-sūtra): *Issai shujō shitsu yū busshō* (All living things without exception possess the Buddha-nature). But in India, the term translated as *shujō* does not include plants or inanimate beings. So the ninth-century Tendai monk, Annen (b. 841), in his *Kanjō Sōmoku Jōbutsu Shiki* (Personal Observations on the Attainment of Buddhahood by Plants and Trees; compiled 869–85) wrote this phrase for the first time. It

Minori no koe mo uranami mo

Minori no koe mo uranami mo

Mina jissō no michi hiroki

Nori o uke yo to yo to tomo ni
Kono on-kyō o dokuju suru
Kono on-kyō o dokuju suru.

Ichibutsu jōdō kanken hōkai

Sō-moku koku-do shikkai jōbutsu.[30]

Ujō hijō kaigu jōbutsudō[31]

Tanomu-beshi.

Tanomu-beshi ya!

Gojiu-ni rui mo ware dōshō no[32]
Nehan ni hikarete shinnyo no tsuki no
Yojio ni ukami-tsutsu
Kore made kitareri arigata ya.

Fushigi ya na! Mokuzen ni kitaru mono o mireba

---

appears in several Noh: *Bashō, Genzai Shichimen, Kakitsubata, Mutsura, Nue, Saigyō-zakura, Sumizome-zakura, Takasago,* and *Teika.* It should be noted that Kūkai (774–835), the founder of the Shingon sect, wrote in his *Un-ji Gi* (Meanings of the Word *Hūṁ*): *Sōmuku mata narazu, ika ni, iwanya, yushō o ya* (If plants and trees do not attain [buddhahood], how, then, indeed, shall sentient beings do so?)

[31] A variation of the words traditionally chanted at the end of the recitation of a sutra.

[32] Lines 186–88: Fifty-two kinds of creatures are those who came to Śākyamuni as he attained nirvana, mentioned in the introduction to the Nirvana Sutra (Mahaparinibbana-suttanta). *Shinnyo no tsuki no **yo*** (Truth's Moon night) → ***yo**-jio* (nocturnal tide).

Its face is like that of a monkey, its limbs are like
those of a tiger,
Exactly like what I was told is the monstrous figure.
Oh, what a terrible sight!

SHITE

I wanted to become a monstrous enemy of Buddhism
And to obstruct the Buddhist and Imperial Laws.
So I haunted around the Imperial Palace,

The Shite *dances to the song to the end.*

Flying awhile above East Sanjō woods.
At about the Hour of Ox nightly[33]
Down to the Palace roof as I flew,

Hira-nori *mixed with* chū-nori.

CHORUS

Fits of acute pain would assault the Emperor,
His whole body afflicted with torture;
Stricken with terror, he would lose consciousness.
All this was my doing, I would think, as fury mounted
in me.
Then the undreamed of happened. By Yorimasa's
Arrow I was stricken, and the monstrous soul in me
perished.

The Shite *squats on the floor.*

Like a stone I fell down and with a crash lay flat on
the ground.[34]
In an instant life fading out of me.
Indeed, to think of it, rather than Yorimasa's arrow,
It was the Imperial punishment that struck me down.
It is only now that this truth comes home to me.

The Shite *rises.*

Yorimasa's feat deeply pleased the Emperor,
And an imperial sword named "Lion King"
Was bestowed on Yorimasa at his order.
Holding the sword, the Grand Minister of Uji[35]
Was coming down, descending a flight of stairs,
When, choosing this moment, a cuckoo called,[36]
announcing itself.
The Minister at once recited:

---

[33] Line 198: See note 22.

[34] *Raku-raku rai-rai:* An onomatopoeic phrase describing the falling down of an object, in which it is broken into pieces. From the following quatrain in the *Religious Talks of Priest Getsuan* (Getsuan Sōkō, 1326–89), quoted by Ze-ami in his *Kakyō* (14. Concerning [Uniting] All the Arts through One Mind): *Shōji no kyorai suru wa, / Hōtō no kairai tari, / Issen tayuru toki, / Raku-raku rai-rai* (Birth and death, coming and going [= human life], / But a puppet on the board. / When its single string snaps, / It crashes down in pieces). This phrase is used by Ze-ami in comparing the art of Noh to a puppet worked by a string, that is, the mind of the artist (Omote, *Kakyō*, p. 100). Ze-ami follows the quotation with: *Kore wa, shōji ni rinne suru*

Omote wa saru, ashi-te wa tora.

Kikishi ni kawaranu henge no sugata
Ara osoroshi no arisama ya na.

Sate mo ware akushin gedō no henge to natte
Buppō ōbō no sawari to naran to
Ōjō chikaku henman [ni] shite
Tō-Sanjō no rintō ni shibaraku higyō shi
Ushimitsu bakari no yona-yona ni[33]
Goten no ue ni tobi-sagareba

Sunawachi gonō shikiri nite
Gyokutai o nayamashite
Obie-tamairase–tamō koto mo
Waga nasu waza yo to ikari o nashishi ni

Omoi mo yorazarishi Yorimasa ga
Yasaki ni atareba henshin usete

Raku-raku rai-rai to chi ni taorete[34]

Tachimachi ni messeshi koto
Omoeba Yorimasa ga yasaki yori wa
Kimi no tenbatto atarikeru yo to
Ima koso omoi-shiraretare
Sono toki Shushō gyokan (n)atte
Shishiō to iu gyoken (n)o
Yorimasa ni kudasarekeru o
Uji no Daijin tamawarite[35]
Kizahashi o oritamou ni
Orifushi kakkō otozurekereba[36]

Daijin toriaezu

---

ningen no arisama o tatoe nari (This is the image of the existence of man, who is born and then dies in a cycle of reincarnation). It is the use of this line that suggests that Ze-ami may have been the author of this play.

[35] The Grand Minister of Uji: Fujiwara no Yorinaga (1120–56). He was defeated and died in the Heiji Uprising, of which he was the leader (*see also* the introduction to and translation of *Kuzu* in this volume).

[36] "A cuckoo called": The cry of a cuckoo used to be described as "making a call," or "calling out its name."

SHITE

Awazu

"The lowly cuckoo /
His name in the cloud-bound sky[37] / Far above has uplifted."

Au

As the Minister declaimed thus,

CHORUS

Yorimasa, bending down his right knee to the ground,
Spread out the left sleeve of his hunting robe,
And looking up a little sideways at the moon,
"What time the full-drawn-bow moon / Went shooting down and was gone."[38]
He recited thus, and, the sword bestowed upon him,
He withdrew from the Imperial presence.
Yorimasa thus uplifted his name,
While my infamous name ran adrift, in a dugout boat[39]
They stuck me, and, like the Yodo River's water,[40]
Sometimes tarrying, sometimes drifting, the boat went as far
As Udono known for its reeds, by Reed Cottage's[41]
Seacoast the boat came to a standstill among floating bars,
And rotting away remains there the dugout boat,[42]
Shut out from sun and moon's light, from darkness down here[43]
Unto the path of darkness the way is destined.
Cast far your enlightening light from the mountain ridge,
Cast far your enlightening light from the mountain ridge,

The Shite *squats at* jō-za, *rises, and stamps the* tome-byōshi.

O Moon! With her, the moon floating on the sea waves also has sunk,
And with the moon floating on the sea waves it has sunk.

---

[37] *Kumoi* (cloud-bound sky): This common epithet connotes the Imperial Palace. The lines mean that the cuckoo has made himself known to the Imperial court, and also refers to Yorimasa, who has raised his name.

[38] In *Yumihari-zuki no iru* (literally, "bow-stretched moon's setting"), *iru* (to set, go down, sink) also means "to shoot (as a arrow)" and is thus related to *yumi* (bow). The bow-stretched moon is a crescent moon.

[39] *na o nagasu* (name to set adrift, to let one's infamous name [be] talked about); the idea of drifting leads to *utsuo-bune* (dugout boat).

[40] Lines 229–30: *Yodo-gawa no / Yodomitsu nagaretsu:* From an anonymous poem in the *Kokin-shū: Yodogawa no / Yodomu to hito wa / Miruramedo / Nagarete fukaki / Kokoro aru*

Hototogisu
Na omo kumoi[37] ni aguru kana to

Ōserarekereba

Yorimasa migi no hiza o tsuite
Hidari no sode o hiroge
Tsuki o sukoshi me ni kakete
Yumihari-zuki no iru ni makasete to[38]

Tsukamatsuri gyoken (n)o tamawari
Gozen (n)o makari-kaereba
Yorimasa wa na o agete
Ware wa na o nagasu[39] utsuo-bune ni
Oshi-irerarete Yodogawa no[40]
Yodomitsu nagaretsu yukusue no

Udono mo onaji Ashinoya no[41]
Urawa no ukisu ni nagare-tomatte

Kuchi-nagara utsuo-bune no[42]
Tsukihi mo miezu kuraki yori[43]

Kuraki michi ni zo iriniikeru
Haruka ni terase yama no ha no

Haruka ni terase yama no ha no

Tsuki to tomo ni kaigetsu mo irinikeri

Kaigetsu to tomo ni irinikeri.

---

mono o (Like Tarry-River / Tarrying—that may be how you / Think of me. And yet / A long-flowing, deep loving / Heart you should know to be there). In the poem, Yodo, the name of the river, also means "to stagnate." *Nagarete* means both "to flow" and "long continuing."

[41] Lines 231–33: *Udono mo onaji* ***ashi*** (At Udono, too, the same **reeds**) → ***Ashi****noya no* ***ura*** (**Reed** Cottage's **bay**) → ***ura****wa no* ***ukisu*** (**bay**coast's **sand bar;** *uki* also meaning "to float") → *nagare* (to flow) → *utsuo-bune* (dug-out boat).

[42] Lines 233–34: *utsuo-****bune*** *no /* ***Tsuki****hi mo miezu* (the dugout **boat,** / Shut out from the **moon** and sun's light): *fune* = *bune* (boat) is an *engo* (associated word) of *tsuki* (moon).

[43] Lines 234–38: A poem by Izumi Shikibu in the *Shūi-shu; see* the Introduction to this play.

安達原

ADACHIGAHARA

いかにあれなる客僧、止まれとこそ。

You visiting priests, there! Stop, I say!

Introduction

Adachigahara (Adachi Moor), the name of a place in the present Fukushima Prefecture in the northern part of Japan, came to be widely known through the following poem by Taira no Kanemori (?–990; Lord of Suruga Province, one of the Thirty-Six Greatest Poets) in the *Shūi-shū:*

Michinoku no	In Michinoku,
Adachi no hara no	On the moors of Adachi,
Kurozuka ni	Within the Black Mound,
Oni komoreri to	Some demons live in hiding,
Iu wa makoto ka.	They say, but can this be true?

Kanemori sent this poem to another great poet, the Lord of Michinoku Province, Minamoto no Shigeyuki, on hearing that Shigeyuki had his sisters living together in Kurozuka (literally, "Black Mound"), and he jokingly referred to the young women as demons. This episode was later included in the *Yamato Monogatari* (58), a book of tales about poems, with some enlargement, explaining that the poet proposed to marry one of the young women. When his offer was declined because the girls were too young, Kanemori composed another poem, expressing his fear that the blooming beauty of the yellow kerria roses would fade away. From this story in the *Yamato Monogatari,* Adachigahara and Kurozuka have become the legendary dwelling place of *oni* (devils or fiends), and stories and plays have been written based on the legend. The Noh *Adachigahara* is one example. *Adachigahara* is the Kanze name. The play is called *Kurozuka* in the other four schools, as well as in Kabuki.

Like the other evil-fiend plays, the dramatic story of *Adachigahara* is simple, and it is similar to the rest of the plays in the same group: a fiend attacks men but is defeated in the end. In spite of this, we notice differences among these plays in many respects. Some fiends are brought down by immortals and by prayer, and others are conquered by warriors. There is also a great variety in the types of the fiends: most of them first appear in the form of a human male, but the *Mae-shite* of *Adachigahara* appears as a humble woman, and that of *Momiji-gari* as a beautiful young lady. In some plays, the fiend appears only in the second scene, as in *Rashōmon* and *Orochi,* often without any lines to speak or sing. In some plays, men go to kill the fiend; in others, they encounter one. In three, *Ōe-yama, Momiji-gari,* and *Adachigahara,* the fiend offers hospitality to men; in *Momiji-gari* only, the demon attempts to seduce the man. In *Ōe-yama,* some warriors disguise themselves as *yamabushi* and go to a fiend's abode to kill it. The fiend nicknamed "Drunkard Boy," in the form of a blooming youth, offers *sake* to them and sings and dances for them. In the song there is an allusion to the intimate relations between priests and acolytes we come upon so often in the contemporary literature. In *Adachigahara,* the fiend attacks its guests only after they had broken their promise not to look into its bedroom. The action describing the fight between fiend and man is also different from play to play. In *Momiji-gari* and *Rashōmon,* the fiend performs a *mai-bataraki* to demonstrate its power; in *Tsuchigumo, Ōe-yama, Rashōmon,* and *Shari,* an *uchiai-bataraki* (fighting action) describes the fight between the monster and the assailant. In *Adachigahara,* an instrumental dancing action called *inori* (prayer) is performed to portray the priests trying to drive away the fiend by prayer. An *inori* is also performed in *Aoi no Ue* and *Dōjōji* (both fourth group plays), and partially in *Funa-Benkei,* where it occurs in the middle of a *mai-bataraki.* It also appears in *Hiun* in all schools except the Kanze.

In connection with the different phases of evil-fiend plays explained above, it is interesting to note that the fiends in some plays are similar to humans, while others are portrayed without any traces of humanity whatsoever. This is reflected in the masks worn by the *nochi-shite* fiends. We find the *Mae-shite* woman of *Adachigahara* to be very human. The *Nochi-shite* of this Noh wears a *hannya* mask. In spite of its angry expression, with two sharp horns, a wide-open mouth, and glaring gilt eyes, we see a trace of heart-breaking sadness hover over it, especially when the wearer hangs its head a little. Of all the fiendish Noh, a *hannya* mask is worn only in three, the other two being *Aoi no Ue* and *Dōjōji.* These Noh, classified as belonging to the fourth group, are different from the evil-fiend Noh of the fifth group in that the *Shite* in these two Noh are not real fiends, but humans who have become transformed into fiends. *Adachigahara* is the only fifth-group Noh in which a *hannya* mask is used. As a rule, the *nochi-shite* fiends, including that of *Momiji-gari,* who appears as a beautiful lady in the first act, all wear the horrifying, most un-human mask called *shikami.* This is quite reasonable when we think of the humanness of the *Mae-shite* woman in *Adachigahara.*

The Noh *Adachigahara* develops as follows:

Act 1

1) Accompanied by *shidai* music, the *Waki,* an elder *yamabushi* named Yūkei, and the *Waki-tsure,* the attendant *yamabushi,* enter, accompanied by an *Ai-kyōgen,* a servant. After a self-introduction and a travel song, they arrive at Adachi Moor in the northeastern district of Michinoku. Dusk has already fallen, and they decide to ask for a night's shelter at a cottage nearby.

2) The covering cloth is removed from the *tsukurimono* placed before the two drums, revealing a woman, the *Shite,* sitting inside a brushwood hut. In a *sashi* song, the woman sings about the autumn sadness and laments her life as a humble woman.

3) The *yamabushi* address the woman and ask for a night's shelter. The woman at first refuses their request, saying that her cottage is too mean to shelter them, but at their repeated request, she comes out of the hut and invites them in. The Chorus sings of how they are going to pass a night, with grass mats for a bed, their sleeves heavy with dew.

4) The *yamabushi* finds a spinning wheel in the room and asks the woman what it is. The woman explains that it is a tool with which a humble woman spins thread all night. At the *yamabushi's* request, the woman begins to spin thread, to show how the wheel operates. The spinning gesture is accompanied by alternating singing by the *Shite,* the *Waki,* and the Chorus, as if this is a part of the conversation between the traveler and his landlady, the latter lamenting her poor fortune, and the priest preaching that she should seek salvation by the way of Buddha. At the beginning of this section, the Chorus sings a *shidai,* based on an old poem in the *Ise Monogatari* (32): *Inishie no shizu no oda-maki kuri-kaeshi mukashi o ima ni nasu yoshi mo gana,* "As in days of old, let me spin thread, turning it, over and over; Those days of so long ago, would I'd turn them back once more!" The woman's lament and the *yamabushi's* preaching in *sashi* is followed by a *kuse,* which sings about how a human being is but a speck of dust going round and round in an eternal cycle of transmigration. The song can be interpreted as a continuation of the priest's sermon and the woman's lament.

5) The *kuse* is followed by a *rongi,* which can be considered a song the woman sings as she spins. This is one of a number of *rongi* sung as working songs that exhaustively list examples of certain objects or events. Among the plays in *The Noh* series, such *rongi* occur in *Kamo* (Vol. 1), in which the names of rivers are quoted in a song about drawing water from rivers; and in *Matsukaze* (Vol. 3, Bk. 2), in which the fisher women sing as they draw seawater, quoting names of seacoasts famous in poems. The *rongi* in *Adachigahara* sings about strings that decorated a nobleman's

court cap, a festive coach decorated with festoons, weeping cherry trees with string-like drooping branches, and so on. Then the song laments the string-long life of the poor woman, and ends with the woman making a weeping gesture, covering her face with both hands. Because of all these allusions to string-like things, this *rongi* is named *Ito no dan* (String Section).

6) The woman tells the travelers that, since the night is so cold, she is going to gather brushwood on the mountain so that she may kindle a fire for them. She leaves with a warning that they must not look into her bedroom. From a woman who so far seemed like an ordinary poor cottager, this strong admonition strikes the audience as mysterious. The priests promise that they will never look into her room.

7) *Ai-kyōgen:* The *Ai-kyōgen,* the servant, mystified by the woman's words, tells the priest that he will take a look at her room, but is forbidden to do so by the priest. He tries to sleep, but his curiosity is too strong, and more than once he attempts to approach the bedroom. Every time, the priest wakes and scolds the servant, until finally the servant gets to the bedroom unnoticed and looks inside. He finds the room full of human corpses and bones. In surprise he tells this to the priests and runs away.

Act 2

8) The *Waki* and *Waki-tsure* stand before the *tsukurimono* and sing, describing the horrible sight of the woman's room. They realize that this must be the notorious abode of the demon of Kurozuka, and they run away as fast as they can. At the end of the song, they stand at the *waki-za.*

9) Accompanied by *haya-fue* or *deha* music, the *Nochi-shite* enters, wearing the demonic *hannya* mask and carrying a bundle of brushwood on her back. On the *hashi-gakari,* the fiend calls to the priests to stop, and accuses them of looking into her room, which she was trying so hard to conceal. The *Shite* and the Chorus alternately describe the angry fiend attacking the priests amid thunder and lightning.

10) *Inori* (Prayer): The *Shite* enters the stage, chasing the Waki and *Waki-tsure,* who rub their beads at the fiend, trying to conquer it by prayer. The fight is presented by the instrumental dancing action, *inori* (prayer). The action is accompanied by all four instruments, with the three drums in rhythm. The choreographic patterns are on the whole the same from play to play, with minor differences according to the difference in the dramatic backgrounds. The action is made up of three parts. In *Adachigahara,* in the first part, the *Shite* chases the priests to a corner; in the second part, the *Shite* stands by the first pine, and brandishes her demonic wand at the priests across the *shite* pillar. In the third part, the *Shite* again chases the priests across the stage, and, standing before the *tsukurimono,* raises her wand and threatens them, with her hand on a pillar of the *tsukurimono.*

11) The fight between the fiend and the priests continues after the *inori,* the priests rubbing their beads at the fiend, and invoking the names of their tutelary deities, while the fiend chases them about the stage, until struck down by the priest's prayers, whereupon it loses all power and disappears. After the initial invocation of deities' names by the *Waki* and *Waki-tsure,* the following section, a quotation of Buddhist prayers and the invocation of the great Acalanātha (Jpn. Fudō), which is in corrupted Sanskrit, is sung by the Chorus in the special *inori-ji* (prayer rhythm).

Scene: Adachigahara, now Adachi County, in the present Fukushima Prefecture in the northern part of Japan.
Season: August by the lunar calendar, that is, early autumn.
Characters and costumes:
Waki The elder *yamabushi* Yūkei, wearing *yamabushi* costume: a *tokin* head piece, a plaid *atsuita kitsuke,* a *mizugoromo* robe over an *ōkuchi* divided skirt, a *yamabushi* stole named *suzukake,* and a small sword, carrying prayer beads in hand.
Waki-tsure Attendant *yamabushi,* attired like the *Waki,* with some difference in the colors and materials of their costumes.
Mae-shite A fiend in the form of a rustic woman, wearing a *fukai* mask and a middle-aged woman's costume: plain *noshime* or *surihaku kitsuke* under *karaori* in subdued colors.
Nochi-shite The fiend in its true form, wearing a *hannya* mask, plain *noshime* or *atsuita kitsuke,* also a red, scale-patterned *surihaku,* with an *atsuita* in subdued colors or a *nuihaku* with circle patterns on a black ground, worn like a skirt around the waist.
Ai-kyōgen The Waki's servant.
Dance-action *Inori* (Prayer)
The author Not identified.

Kogaki (Variant performances), Kanze school.
1. *Kuro-gashira* (Long-haired black wig)
Instead of the usual woman mask, the *Mae-shite* wears an *uba* (old woman) mask; the *Nochi-shite's* ordinary woman wig changes to a *kuro-gashira* ("black head"), that is, a large, bushy wig with long black hair trailing all the way down the back. The *Nochi-shite* enters accompanied by special *haya-fue* ("quick flute") music. The style of performance becomes more deliberate.

2. *Shiro-gashira* (Long-haired white wig)
The *Mae-shite* wears a *rei no onna* mask, which is worn only by a supernatural woman. The *Nochi-shite* wears a *shiro-gashira* wig with long white hair. After entering accompanied by *haya-fue* music, the *Shite* withdraws once more behind the curtain, to enter again. There are more movements than in the ordinary style, with greater emphasis on dramatic phases than in the *kuro-gashira* style. At the end, the *Shite* enters the curtain during the chanting, and the *Waki* performs the *tome-byōshi.*

3. *Nagaito no den* (Long-thread version)
The spinning movement continues longer than usual, lasting from the *shidai* song to the end of the *rongi.*

4. *Kyūshin no de* (Quick entrance)
The *Nochi-shite* enters running, accompanied by *haya-fue* music. Sometimes the *Nochi-shite* exits running. Usually this version occurs in combination with the *Kuro-gashira* or *Shiro-gashira* version.

Adachigahara

足達原

—ACT 1—

A tsukurimono *representing a brushwood hut, covered with dark cloth, is placed before the two drummers.*

SHIDAI *The* Waki, *the senior yamabushi, Yūkei, and the* Waki-tsure, *the attendant* yamabushi, *accompanied by the* Ai-kyōgen, *a servant, enter and stand at center stage, facing each other. The* Ai-kyōgen *sits at the* kyōgen-za.

Shidai, *au*

WAKI & WAKI-TSURE

Trav'ling robes we have put on, 'neath the sycamores,
Trav'ling robes with linen stoles brush the undergrowth,
Their sleeves, heavy-laden with dew, get wet and droop.[1]

Jidori, *awazu*

CHORUS

Trav'ling robes with linen stoles brush the undergrowth,
Their sleeves, heavy-laden with dew, get wet and droop.

Sashi, *awazu*

WAKI

The Waki *faces front.*

I am the senior priest of Tōkō Cloister at Nachi;[2]
Yūkei is my name.

Facing each other:

WAKI-TSURE

Hard discipline at the cost of life
Is a part of a *yamabushi's* ascetic exercises.

WAKI

The Yuya *yamabushi* pilgrimage throughout the provinces;[3]
This is the practice of all the disciples of Buddha.

WAKI & WAKI-TSURE

Now it so happens that Yūkei some time ago
Made a vow at heart
And is now on pilgrimage throughout the provinces.

---

[1] Lines 1–2. *koromo no* ***suzukake*** (robe's **stole**) → ***suzukake*** *no tsuyu* (dew on the **sycamore**). The *suzukake*, represented in costume by an alb-like stole decorated with large pompoms, was actually a light linen outer robe worn over the kimono by priests of the Shugendō sect, or *yamabushi.* Line 3. *Shioruran* would normally suggest that the sleeves of the travelers' robes were moistened by tears, but this is not the case in this play, as they are merely moistened with dew. It is interpreted as "tears" when one is departing from a lover.

[2] Lines 6–7. Nachi: One of the Three Kumano Shrines in the Province of Kii (present-day

Tabi no koromo wa suzukake no

Tabi no koromo wa suzukake no

Tsuyukeki sode ya shioruran[1]

Tabi no koromo wa suzukake no

Tsuyukeki sode ya shioruran

Kore wa Nachi no Tōkōbō no ajari[2]
Yūkei to wa waga koto nari.

Sore shashin tosō no gyōtai wa
Yamabushi shugyō no tayori nari.

Yuya no junrei kaikoku wa[3]

Mina Shakumon no narai nari

Shikaru ni Yūkei kono aida
Kokoro ni tatsuru gan (n)atte
Kaikoku angya ni omomukan to

Wakayama Prefecture), specially venerated by *yamabushi* priests. Yūkei: Not a historical personage; the text says that he is an *ajari,* or priest with the special authorization to teach. It is interesting to note that the priest Mongaku (1139–1203) practiced austerities by standing in the icy waters of Nachi Falls in midwinter for 21 days while making 300,000 recitations of the Salvation Spell of Fudō Myō-ō (*see* Note 27). Through this, he was granted special powers by Fudō, and later was instrumental in helping Minamoto no Yoritomo and the Genji rise to power.

[3] Yuya is an alternative pronunciation of the characters used for Kumano.

Michiyuki, *au*

Leaving our sacred mountain behind, we set out,
Leaving our sacred mountain behind, we set out,
Over mountains, heading for Kii Province's coast,
Past the Bay of Tide-Water Cape we sped quickly by,[4]
On Brocade Beach we wove our way, many a time
Soaked with salt, our traveling robes drooping heavily.
A long string of days having piled up, before long,[5]
A place in Michinoku, known only by name,
The bleak moors of Adachi we have reached at last,
The bleak moors of Adachi we have reached at last.

Tsukizerifu, *spoken*
Facing front:

WAKI

Having hurried,
Already we have arrived at the moors of Adachi in Michinoku.
Ah, what a nuisance! It has grown dark.
There is no hamlet about this place.
Over there I see a light of fire.
Let us go there and ask for a night's lodging.

WAKI-TSURE

Yes, let us.

The Waki *and* Waki-tsure *go to the* waki-za. *The cloth is removed from the* tsukurimono, *revealing the* Shite, *a woman, sitting inside.*

Sashi, *awazu*

SHITE

Indeed, the life of a poor and lonely one—
There is nothing in this world that is so sad.
To this woeful world weary autumn has come,[6]
And the morning wind is piercing cold. Even so,

---

[4] Lines 17–21. Kii Province: *see* Note 2. Bay of Tide-Water Cape (Shiozaki no Ura), Brocade Beach (Nishiki no Hama): Names of places on the southeastern coast of Wakayama prefecture. *Shio* (tide) → *sashi* (come in) → *sashi-sugi* (to pass by). Nishiki no Hama (Brocade Beach) → *oriori* (occasionally, in which *ori* is homonymous with "to weave"). ***oriori*** also means "breaking and breaking," and alludes to the travelers' custom of breaking roadside tree branches to mark their way = *shi**ori***, which is homonymous with "to droop" (as in Note 1), which leads to "the wet sleeves." "Traveling robes" leads to ***hi mo*** *kasanareba* (days, too, piling up), in which ***himo*** also means "string," an *engo* of "robe." *Kasanaru* (to pile up) is also an *engo* of *k(g)oromo* (robe), giving a passage filled with "clothing" words.

[5] Lines 32–33: From a poem by Minamoto no Kageakira in the *Shūi-shū* (505): ***Wabibito*** *wa* / ***Uki-yo*** *no naka ni* / *Ikerajito* / *Omōu koto sae* / *Kanawazarikeri* (**A poor, lonely one**— / Although in this **woeful world** / He doesn't want to live, / Not even a wish of his / Can e'er

Waga honzan (n)o tachi-idete
Waga honzan (n)o tachi-idete
Wake-yuku sue wa Ki no ji gata
Shiozaki no ura o sashi-sugite[4]
Nishiki no hama no
Oriori wa nao shiori yuku tabi-goromo

Hi mo kasanareba hodo mo naku[5]
Na ni nomi kikishi Michinoku no
Adachigahara ni tsukinikeri
Adachigahara ni tsukinikeri

Isogi sōrō hodo ni.
Kore wa haya Michinoku no Adachigahara ni tsukite sōrō.

Ara shōshi ya hi no kurete sōrō.
Kono atari ni wa hitozato naku sōrō.
Are ni hi no hikari no mie sōrō hodo ni
Tachi-yori yado o karabaya to zonji sōrō.

Kokoroe mōshi sōrō

Geni wabi-bito no narai hodo
Kanashiki mono wa yo mo araji
Kakaru uki-yo ni aki no kite[6]
Asake no kaze wa mi ni shimedomo

---

hope to be fulfilled). Lines 34–35: *Aki* (autumn) also means "be tired of," so that the phrase *aki no ki* (autumn has come) also means "tiredness has come," that is, "one has had enough of it." The allusion is to the following poem by Ōe no Masafusa in the *Shin Kokin-shū* (455): ***Aki kureba/ Asake no kaze*** *no / Te o samumi / Yamada no hita o / Makasete zo kiku* (When **autumn comes round / The wind in the morning** is / So cold on the hands, / I leave to it the pulling / Of the mountain field clappers.)

[6] From a poem by Priest Saijū in the *Senzai-shū* (1140): ***Madoromi****te / Sate mo yami-naba / Ikaga sen / Nezame zo aranu /* ***Inochi nari****keru* (While **one is asleep** / Suppose one ceases to be. / What would it be like?/ There would be no awakening, / **No** longer any **life left**.) *Inochi* (life) in the original poem is used in the Noh in the sense of "moments in which to take a breath, to gain respite from what one is suffering."

Not a moment of solace finds the weary mind.
Yesterday all fade away, filled with emptiness,
Only in slumber at night, one finds brief respite.[7]
How inconstant, uncertain is such a life as this!

Mondō, *spoken*

WAKI

Excuse me, is there somebody in this hut?

SHITE

Who is there?

Kakeai, *kakaru*

WAKI & WAKI-TSURE

If you are the mistress of this hut, pray listen.
We have come for the first time to Michinoku,[8]
And here on the Adachi moors are caught by night.
We know no place where we can obtain a night's lodging.
Pray, pity us
And give us a night's shelter.

SHITE

In this field far from any village,
Where the pine wind is blowing violently,
In a chamber into which the moonlight comes leaking through,
How can I let you pass the night?

WAKI

But travelers would sleep, with a bundle of grass for a pillow.[9]
A place for a brief sleep just for this one night—
Give us that accommodation, we beseech you.

SHITE

Even to myself, dreary is this cottage.

WAKI

We wish to pass the night within the brushwood door—[10]

SHITE

Though tight-locked till now, her heart opens to sympathy.

Age-uta, *au*

The Shite *comes out of the hut*

CHORUS

If that is your wish, please pass the night here, she says,

---

[7] *hajimete* ***mi*** (for the first time to see) → **Mi**chinoku

[8] *kusa-makura* (grass pillow) is a poetic term for a journey, from the practice of ancient times when travelers slept in fields and on mountains with a bundle of grass for a pillow.

[9] *shiba no to o* ***sasu*** (brushwood door to **shut / lock**) → ***sasu****ga* (**though**).

[10] Lines 61–64: *shikinamashi* (will spread) alliterates with *shiitemo* (upon repeated plead-

Mune o yasumu koto mo naku
Kinō no munashiku kurenureba
Madoromu yowa zo inochi naru[7]
Ara sadame na no shōgai ya na

Ika ni kono ya no uchi e annai mōshi sōrō

Somo ikanaru hito zo

Ika ni ya aruji kiki-tamae
Ware-ra hajimete Michinoku no[8]
Adachigahara ni yuki kurete
Yado o karu beki tayori mo nashi

Negawaku wa ware-ra o awaremite
Hitoyo no yado o kashi-tamae.

Hitozato tōki kono nobe no
Matsukaze hageshiku fuki-arete
Tsukikage tamaranu neya no uchi ni wa

Ikade ka todome mōsu beki

Yoshi ya tabi-ne no kusa-makura[9]

Koyoi bakari no kari-ne sen
Tada tada yado o kashi-tamae

Ware dani mo uki kono io ni

Tada tomaran to shiba no to o[10]

Sasuga omoeba itawashisa ni

Saraba todomari tamae tote

---

ing). *yado o* ***kari*** (lodging to obtain) → ***kari****-goromo* (hunting robe) → *katashiku sode* (single-spread sleeve). *Kari-goromo* (hunting robe) introduces *sode* (sleeve). *Kata-shiku* (without-a-partner spread): *Kata* (half, one of a pair) + *shiku* (to spread) = *katashiku* (to sleep without a mate). Here the word is used to emphasize loneliness. *Sode no tsuyu* ***fukaki*** (sleeve's dew thick) → ***fukaki kusa*** (thick grass) → ***kusa*** *no iori* (grass hut).

and sits at center. The Waki *&* Waki-tsure *sit. A* tsukurimono *of a spinning wheel is placed near the* metsuke-bashira.

And opening the humble brushwood door, she comes out.
A miscanthus mat mingled with grasses diverse
Alas, this they will spread to lie upon tonight,[11]
Upon repeated pleading, shelter is provided,
On solitary sleepers' sleeves the dew will fall thick
Within the grass cottage so narrow and shabby,
A sad night you travelers will pass on such a bed,
A sad night you travelers will pass on such a bed.

Mondō, *spoken*

WAKI

It is very kind of you to give us shelter tonight.
By the way, I see there something unfamiliar to us.
What is that thing called?

SHITE

Well, it is a "disentangling frame," or spinning wheel,
A tool humble women use as they work.

WAKI

Oh, how interesting!
If you will work at it all night, will you show us how you do it?

Kakaru

The Shite *sits before the spinning wheel.*

SHITE

Ah, how embarassing! Before the travelers'
Curious eyes to engage oneself shamelessly
In the never-ending lowly task of a humble woman!

WAKI

Tonight we are given a shelter in this house,
Thanks to the landlady's sympathy, deep at night[12]

SHITE

Moonlight comes leaking,

WAKI

In the chamber, where

Shidai, *au*

The Shite *spins thread.*

CHORUS

Pure linen thread let me spin, turning it round and round,[13]

---

[11] *Aruji no nasake* ***fukaki*** (landlady's sympathy deep) → ***fukaki*** *yo* (deep night).

[12] Lines 81–83. From a poem that Lady Shizuka, a celebrated dancer, sang, as she danced in front of Minamoto no Yoritomo, remembering her lord, Yoritomo's estranged brother Yoshitsune: *Shizu ya shizu / Shizu no oda-maki / Kurikaeshi / Mukashi o ima ni / Nasu yoshi mogana* (*Shizu*-cloth, *shizu* / With its spinning spool of yarn / Turning and turning / The past into the present— / How I long to turn things back!). *Shizu,* the name of cloth, also means "humble person," so that *shizu no oda-maki* also means "humble woman's spool of yarn."

Toboso o hiraki tachi-idezuru
Kotokusa mo majiru kaya-mushiro
Utate ya koyoi shikinamashi[11]
Shiite mo yado o kari-goromo
Katashiku sode no tsuyu fukaki
Kusa no iori no sewashi naki
Tabi-ne no toko zo mono-uki
Tabi-ne no toko zo mono-uki

Koyoi no o-yado no kaesu-gaesu mo arigatou koso sōrae
Mata arenaru mono wa mi-nare mōsanu mono nite sōrō
Kore wa nani to mōshitaru mono nite sōrō zo

Sanzōrō kore wa wakukase-wa tote
Iyashiki shizu no me no itonamu waza nite sōrō

Ara omoshiro ya
Saraba yo mo sugara itonōde on-mise sōrae

Geni hazukashi ya tabi-bito no
Miru-me mo hajizu itsu to naki
Shizu ga waza koso mono-ukere

Koyoi todomaru kono yado no
Aruji no nasake fukaki yo no[12]

Tsuki mo sashi iru

Neya no uchi ni

Maso-o no ito o kuri-kaeshi[13]

The poem is quoted from the *Gikeiki* (Chronicle of Yoshitsune) [*Kokka Taikan: Gikeiki* 9], and is based on a poem in the *Ise Monogatari* (32), in which the first line is *Inishie no* (Of the ancient times). The word *kurikaeshi* is used in three senses in the poem and the text: to spin; to repeat; to turn something back to what it was before.

[13] *umiso no* ***yoru*** (linen thread to twine) → ***yoru*** *made* (night even, even at night). *Yo* in *yoru* alliterates with *yo* (life) in the next line.

Pure linen thread let me spin, turning it round and round,
How I long to spin the past into the present!

Jidori, *awazu*

Pure linen thread let me spin, turning it round and round,
How I long to spin the past into the present!

Sings, awazu

The Shite *stops spinning.*

SHITE

A humble woman's flaxen thread she twines even at night,

CHORUS

The chore in order to make her living,
Oh, how wearisome!

SHITE

What wretchedness! Though born into the world of human beings,
I lead a life of such misery,
Torturing myself. It is sad, indeed.

Sashi, *awazu*

WAKI

Vain are the words you have spoken.
First, you should save yourself while you live in this life,
Only then you can aspire to Buddhahood.

CHORUS

Even though you live in a weary world like this,
Never free from your chore morning or evening,
If only your mind could always conform to the way of righteousness,[14]
Even though you never pray, it would never be
That you should fail to have the fruit of Buddhahood.

Kuse, *au*

We are no more than earth, water, fire, and wind[15]
Only for a little while assembling together,
Going 'round the cycle of Birth and Death,
Through the Five and Six Realms forever revolving,[16]
All this, the doing of the illusory mind.

---

[14] Lines 97–99: From an old poem attributed to Sugawara no Michizane: ***Kokoro dani / Makoto no michi ni / Kanainaba / Inorazu tote mo*** / *Kami ya mamoran* (**If only your mind / To the way of righteousness / Should always conform, / Even though you never pray,** / The gods 're sure to protect you.) Yokomichi and Omote state that the poem is attributed to Michizane (344n). It is also quoted in an *age-uta* in the play *Hanjo*. It appears in the *Nenashi-gusa, Kōhen* of Hiraga Gennai's *Furai Sanjin-shū* (145; *see also* n22), and the annotation states that the poem is recorded in Kamo no Chōmei's *Shiki Monogatari* (Tales of the Four Seasons) as having been written by the god of Kitano Shrine (= Michizane).

[15] According to Buddhist belief, all creatures are made up of five basic elements: earth, wa-

Maso-o no ito o kuri-kaeshi
Mukashi o ima ni nasabaya
Maso-o no ito o kuri-kaeshi

Mukashi o ima ni nasabaya

Shizu ga umiso no yoru made mo

Yo wataru waza koso
Mono-ukere

Asamashi ya ningai ni shō o uke-nagara

Kakaru uki-yo ni ake-kurashi
Mi o kurushimuru kanashisa yo

Hakana no hito no koto no ha ya
Mazu shōjin (n)o tasukete koso
Busshin (n)o negō tayori mo are

Kakaru uki-yo ni nagaraete
Ake-kure hima naki mi nari tomo
Kokoro dani makoto no michi ni kanainaba[14]

Inorazu tote mo tsui ni nado
Bukka no en to narazaran
Tada kore ji-sui-ka-fu no[15]
Kari ni shibaraku mo matowarite
Shōji ni rinne shi
Godō rokudō ni meguru koto[16]
Tada isshin no mayoi nari

---

ter, fire, wind (air), and metal (or ether); esoteric Buddhism adds consciousness as the sixth element.

[16] The Five Realms, or Six Realms: The lower states of existence through which beings continue their eternal transmigration, namely: *naraka-gati* (demons), *preta-gati* (hungry ghosts), *tiryagyoni-gati* (beasts), *manuṣya-gati* (humans) and *devā-gati* (deities). The six realms include *asura-gati* (warriors), where warriors' souls are condemned to eternal fighting. The term *ningai* (world of human beings) in line 89 above refers to the human realm (*manuṣya-gati*) among these six realms of existence.

As we think of human beings,
And ponder how frail our fate is, we realize
That nobody can regain youth a second time.[17]
Finally we come face to face with our old age.
As vain as a fast-vanishing dream is our life,
Why do I not renounce it? Even to myself
Vain indeed seems this mind of mine.
I blame myself bitterly, but to no avail.

Rongi, *au*
Ito no dan
(String
Section)

Tell me who it was that somewhere in the Fifth Street[18]
Came to visit the house where moonflowers were
in bloom?

SHITE

It was one wearing a hat hung with blue and white
strings
A noble person of high renown he must have been.

CHORUS

For Kamo Festival what did they decorate?

SHITE

With colored strings, they covered their coaches, we
hear.

CHORUS

When weeping-cherry's strands
In full blossom display their beautiful color,

SHITE

Drawn by the blossoms, crowds gather on a spring
eve.[19]

CHORUS

Into thread-white tufts sprouts out autumn's
pampas grass,[20]

SHITE

Waiting for the night when it will wave at the moon.

---

[17] From a Chinese poem by Ono no Takamura in the *Wakan Rōei–shū* (47): ***Hito sara ni wakai koto nashi,*** *toki subekaraku oshimu beshi / Toshi tsune ni haru narazu, sake o mun-ashiku suru koto nakare* (**Nobody is young for a second time;** cherish dearly every passing minute. Spring is not with us all year long; let us not fail to savor saké.) This poem is very much in the style of T'ang-dynasty *shih* poetry, especially that of Li Po.

[18] Lines 113–20 invoke the romantic imagery of the *Genji Monogatari,* the first four lines alluding to an episode told in the chapter *Yūgao* (The Moonflower), about Lord Genji's meeting with a woman who lived in a house where moonflowers were in bloom. However, the story in that chapter has nothing to do with a hat decorated with strings; the last two lines are related to a different scene, one that appears in the *Aoi* chapter of *Genji,* which tells about

Oyoso ningen no
Adanaru koto o anzuru ni
Hitosara ni wakaki koto nashi[17]
Tsui ni wa oi to naru mono o
Kahodo hakanaki yume no yo o
Nado ya itowazaru ware nagara
Adanaru kokoro koso
Uramite mo kainakarikere
Sate somo Gojō atari nite[18]
Yūgao no yado o tazuneshi wa

Hikage no ito no kamuri kishi

Sore wa nadakaki hito yaran

Kamo nomi are ni kazarishi wa

Itoge no kuruma to koso kike

Ito-zakura
Iro mo sakari ni saku koro wa

Kuru hito ōki haru no kure[19]

Ho ni izuru aki no ito-zusuki[20]

Tsuki ni yoru o ya machi nuran

---

people coming to see a festival procession in their coaches, which are hung with colorful strings. The "noble person" in line 116 is Genji himself.

[19] In *kuru hito ōki* (coming people many = many the people who come), *kuru* (come) also means "to spin" and is an *engo* of *ito* (thread or string) in *ito-zakura* ("thread" cherry = weeping cherry).

[20] Lines 122–23: *Ito-zusuki* is a type of pampas grass with tufts as long as *ito* (thread). In *ito-zusuki tsuki ni yoru* (pampas grass at the moon waving), *yoru* also means "to twist, twine" and is thus an *engo* of *ito*. *Tsuki ni **yoru*** (at the moon to wave) → ***yoru** o machi* (for the night to wait), with *yoru* meaning both "to wave" and "night."

CHORUS

The Shite *begins to spin.*

And here this string that a poor, humble woman yarns,

SHITE

The spinning quickens, then stops. The Shite *weeps, covering her face with both hands.*

On this life of mine so cruelly long-stretching,

CHORUS

On this life of mine so cruelly long-stretching,
I brood on all night, like Akashi Bay's beach plover,[21]
Without companion, crying aloud till morn,
Without companion, crying aloud till morn.

SHITE

Mondō, *spoken*

Priests, I have something to say to you.

WAKI

What is it?

SHITE

As it is very cold tonight,
I will go up the mountain, climbing up to cut some wood
To kindle a fire and to warm you.
Pray wait for a while.

WAKI

That is very kind of you.
If you go, we will wait for your return,
But please come home before long.

SHITE

I will be back before long.
[*The* Shite *rises to go, then stops.*]
Oh, there is one more thing.
Until I come back, do not look into this chamber!

WAKI

I understand.
We will not look in there.
Please put your mind at ease.

SHITE

Oh, how glad I am.
Be sure not to look inside, you understand?
And you priest, there, you, too, do not look inside, you understand?

WAKI-TSURE

I understand.

---

[21] Lines 127–28. *Omoi-**akashi*** (to brood till dawn) → **Akashi** no Ura (Akashi Bay). In poetry beach plovers are often associated with crying and being without companion. Compare the following poem by Saionji Kintsune in the *Shin Kokin-shū* (1331): *Tsukuzuku to / **Omoi-***

Ima hata shizu ga kuru ito no

Nagaki inochi no tsurenasa o

Nagaki inochi no tsurenasa o
Omoi Akashi no ura chidori[21]
Ne o nomi hitori naki-akasu
Ne o nomi hitori naki-akasu

Ika ni kyaku sō-tachi ni mōshi sōrō

Uketamawari sōrō

Amari ni yosamu ni sōrō hodo ni
Ue no yama ni agari ki o torite

Takibi o shite ate mōsōzuru nite sōrō
Shibaraku on-machi sōrae

On-kokorozashi arigatō koso sōrae
Saraba machi mōsōzuru nite sōrō
Yagate on-kaeri sōrae

Saraba yagate kaeri sōrō beshi.

Ya. Ika ni mōshi sōrō
Warawa ga kaeran made kono neya no uchibashi go-ranji sōrō na

Kokoroe mōshi sōrō
Mi-mōsu koto wa arumajiku sōrō
On-kokoro yasuku oboshi-mesare sōrae

Ara ureshi ya sōrō
Kamaete go-ranji sōrō na
Konata no kyaku sō mo go-ranji sōrō na

Kokoroe mōshi sōrō

---

akashi no / Ura-chidori / *Nami no makura ni /* ***Naku****naku zo kiku* (I would meditate / **Until dawn, to Akashi / Bay's crying plovers** / Listening **in bitter tears,** / Pillowed close to the sea waves.) (In the translation, the fourth and fifth lines of the original have been reversed.)

NAKAIRI *The* Shite *makes an interim exit, stopping once on the* hashi-gakari, *then walking quickly.*

AI-KYŌGEN *The* Ai-kyōgen, *the servant, enters, and while the priests are asleep, looks into the woman's bedroom, and sees countless corpses piled up inside. He tells this to the priests and runs away terrified.*

(*The original Japanese text of the* Ai-Kyōgen, *including the* Waki's *part, is omitted.*)

AI

The Ai *stands at the* jō-za.

Well, I must say, our host for this night is a most kind-hearted person, indeed. Just as we found it suddenly so dark that not only a servant like myself, but even the priest, my master, was unable to see anything at all, she offered us lodging, and, saying how cold the night had become, even went out to the mountain to gather wood to build a fire, in spite of the dark night shadows and her being a woman. What a charitable heart she has! It has been said since time long past that "Man at his best is kind-hearted; the world at its best is charitable." And this hostess of ours convinces me of its truth. Now I will go to my master and speak of this with him.

The Ai *moves to center stage and sits.*

I wish to speak with you, sir. I was just saying to myself that I have never met one with such a kind heart as this host of ours.

What I mean to say is that not only her offering us lodging, but also her going off into the depths of the mountains to collect firewood as well both seem to me to indicate a most charitable heart for a woman of this day and age. Do you not agree, sir?

WAKI

It is as you say, indeed. People with as deep a sense of charity as she possesses are truly rare. And for a woman to set out into the gloom of night, saying that she will ascend the mountain to fetch some wood with which to build a fire to keep us warm is truly most thoughtful and charitable.

AI

That is most assuredly true. But at the same time, there is one thing about all this that I find most strange. After she had left to go to the mountain, she came all the way back here only to tell you that you must not look into her bedchamber. There may well be some to whom it would be necessary to mention such matters, but do you not find it most presumptuous of her to say such a thing to such a holy priest as yourself? You see, sir, I was born with a very bad habit that has plagued me since youth. I always have a most insatiable desire to go against whatever anyone may tell me to do. Whether it be for good or bad, if someone orders me to come, that is exactly where I never want to go. And if someone is trying to hide and wishes me not to come to them, I find that that is where I must go, no matter what the cost. Thus, as our host has said that we must not look into the chamber, I find that that is exactly what I would like to do. With your permission, sir, I will just go have a look.

WAKI

No, No. As we have already given the mistress of this place our solemn word, you must not look!

AI

No, that means that it is wrong for you, sir, to look, but I made no such promise.

WAKI

No! You must not look! The darkness is deepening, and since I am going to retire for the night, you must, too. Now go to sleep!

AI

The Ai *bows.* As you say, sir. [*The* Waki *and* Waki-tsure *sleep.*]

Aside: But what is this? Oh, how I want to look! But since my master has so strongly told me not to look, I will try my best to sleep. [*He tries to sleep.*] Ah, what is wrong with me? I just cannot get to sleep! I want to see our host's chamber so very much!

The Ai *sneaks a peek at the* Waki. As my master seems to be sleeping quite soundly now, I'll just creep quietly away from his side and go have myself a look.

The Ai *stands up.* WAKI

What are you doing?

AI

The Ai *sits.* Oh, I'm only turning over in my sleep.

WAKI

Well, sleep more quietly!

AI

The Ai *bows.* As you say, sir. [*The* Waki *and* Waki-tsure *go back to sleep.*]

Aside: What is this? How sensitive to the slightest sound my master is, even in sleep! But he said that I must not look into the chamber. I tried to sleep and stayed wide awake, so I will try again to go sleep.

[*The* Ai *tries once more to go to sleep. When the* Waki *has dozed off again, he begins talking once more.*]

Ah, it's no use. The harder I try to go to sleep, the more I find that I cannot get to sleep!

[*He sneaks another peek at the* Waki.]

Well, my master certainly seems to be fast asleep this time. If that is the case, I will just creep quietly away from his side and then I will just take a quick look.

[*The* Ai *stands up and proceeds toward upstage right.*]

WAKI

Where are you going?

AI

The Ai *sits.* Uhh, I had a terrible nightmare, in which I was being led somewhere. You saved me when you called out to me. Now I will go to sleep again.

WAKI

You are certainly a noisy rascal tonight.

AI

The Ai *bows.* Forgive me, sir.

[*The* Waki *and* Waki-tsure *once more go to sleep.*]

What a predicament I am in! Over and over I lie down and try to sleep, and over and over I keep waking up! I wonder what the meaning of this can be? It is said that within the heart of man is a pillar of strength, tall and wide like the Great Buddha of Nara. So I will call upon that strength and force myself to go to sleep.

[*The* Ai *tries for a third time to go to sleep. When he notices that the* Waki *has dozed off again, he begins scheming once more. He opens his fan, and looks at the* Waki *through the ribs of the fan. He rolls over toward the* Waki, *strikes the floor, clears his throat, and makes other sounds. After testing whether the way is clear or not a few times, he goes to center stage, stands up, and starts walking on the bridgeway.*]

AI

The Ai *stands near the First Pine.* Oh, how happy, how happy I am! Finally I was able to get away!

Whenever someone tells me to look, that's when I don't want to look, but when someone tells me that I must not look, then that is when I must look. Well, well, I must hurry and take a quick look in our host's chamber.

[*The* Ai *goes over to the hut set upon the stage, opens the door, and looks in. He shuts the door suddenly and falls over backward in shocked surprise, and, falling with fright while he moves, makes his way to the First Pine.*]

AI

Oh, my! How frightful, how frightful it is! Could such a thing as this be really true?! This is indeed no ordinary matter. There are dead bodies and bones in there in such number that the piles of decaying flesh reach all the way up to the rafters. And I can see that here and there, there are many things that shine with a most unnatural light. This is most peculiar, indeed, and is a matter of great import. Therefore, I must tell my master of it quickly, lest he be killed!

[*The Ai goes to downstage right, faces the* Waki, *and gets down on his knees:*]

AI

Sir, I looked!

WAKI

Looked at what?

AI

You said I must not look, but I did look into that woman's chamber, and what I saw there was most frightening, indeed.

There were dead bodies of people, a mess of arms and legs, piled up so high that they make a mountain that reaches up all the way to the rafters. And I could see that here and there, there are many things that shine with a most unnatural light.

It is most peculiar, sir. I think it would be best, sir, to leave this place as quickly as we can.

WAKI

And just after I so carefully explained to you that we gave our word. . . . What a terrible thing you have done!

AI

The Ai *bows.*

Forgive me, sir. But I think that you should have a look for yourself.

WAKI

Well, I suppose there's no harm in it now; let us get up and cross over to the chamber in order to look within.

AI

Then please do so quickly. And while you have your look,
I will go on ahead to find lodging for us elsewhere.

WAKI

There is good sense in what you say.

AI

The Ai *stands.*

Oh, how frightful! I am going on ahead to find lodging for us elsewhere.

[*The* Ai *starts to leave via the bridgeway, and shouts the following as he leaves through the curtain:*]

Oh, how frightful! Oh, how frightful!
Help, oh, help! Help, oh, help!
Oh, how frightful! Oh, how frightful!
Help, oh, help! Help, oh, help!

—Act 2—

The Waki *and* Waki-tsure *get up; the* Waki *goes to center stage; the* Waki-tsure, *to stage right. They all face the hut and start singing the following song. When they get to the line "Their minds in confusion, and stricken with terror," they walk around the stage, the* Waki *coming to a stop at downstage center; the* Waki-tsure, *behind him.*

The Waki *and* Waki-tsure *stand before the* tsukurimono.

Kakaru

WAKI

How strange! Within our hostess's bedchamber,
Through a narrow opening looking well, I see
Pus and blood flowing everywhere in streams,[22]
Bodies bloated with stinking filth,
Flesh and fat all inflamed and rotting.
Human corpses in countless number
Are piled up as high as the rafters.
Surely this must be what we have heard rumored:
"The Black Mound upon Adachi Moor!
This is where the demon lives in hiding!

---

[22] Lines 151–53: From *Kusō* (the Nine Aspects), the nine stages of rotting of a human corpse, described in the form of Chinese poems, similar to those quoted here. Meditation on the nine aspects of death was familiar to Japanese monks; these lines were often falsely attributed to the T'ang poet Su Tung-p'o (1037–1101). Through the images these lines conjure, people hoped to drive away carnal temptations. These lines are obviously related to the description given by Śākyamuni Buddha in the Mahā-satipatthana Sutta (Great Frame of Refer-

Fushigi ya aruji no neya no uchi o
Mono no hima yori yoku mireba
Nōketsu tachimachi yūteki shi[22]
Shūe wa michite hōchaku shi
Funi kotogotoku ranne seri
Hito no shigai wa kazu shirazu
Noki to hitoshiku tsumi-okitari
Ikasama kore wa oto ni kiku
Adachigahara no Kurozuka ni
Komoreru oni no sumi ka nari

---

ence Sutra): "If a monk sees a body . . . swollen, blue, and festering, . . . [or] being devoured by various sorts of worms, . . . [or] reduced to a skeleton . . . with some flesh and blood adhering to it, . . . [or] a fleshless skeleton smeared with blood, . . . [or] reduced to bones . . . lying in a heap, . . . [or] crumbling to powder, . . . he applies this perception to his own body thus: 'Truly, this body of mine too is of the same nature; it will become like that and will not escape from it.' " (Cited in: Nyoniponika Thera, *The Heart of Buddhist Meditation,* p. 120.)

WAKI-TSURE

Oh, how terrible! We suffer this plight "in Michinoku,[23]
"In the Black Mound on Adachi Moor,
A demon lives in hiding," goes the poem.
This must be what the poet had in his mind then.

Age-uta, *au*

WAKI & WAKI-TSURE

Their minds in confusion, and stricken with terror,

The priests take quick steps toward the waki-za.

Their minds in confusion, and stricken with terror,
Not knowing which way to take, they make their escape,
Running as quickly as their legs can carry them,
Running as quickly as their legs can carry them.

HAYA-FUE (or DEHA) *The* taiko *joins the musicians. The* Nochi-Shite, *who carries a bundle of brushwood on her back, enters, walking quickly, and stops by the First Pine.*

Kakaru

NOCHI-SHITE

You priests, there! [*Spoken:*] Stop, I say!
My bedchamber which I so jealously concealed,
You exposed, stealing a look inside.
I have come to vent my rage upon you.

Sings, awazu
The Shite *drops the brushwood.*

Heart-scorching anger blazes in flames,
Billows of smoke from the Hsien-yang Palace[24]
Spew forth, scattering sparks.

CHORUS

The Shite *attacks the priests, who pray.*

Sweeping down the mountain the wind blows o'er the field,

SHITE

Thunder and lightning fill both heaven and earth,[25]

CHORUS

The sky is overcast, black as a rainy night,

---

[23] *Ukime o **mi*** (plight to witness, suffer) → **Mi**chinoku → a quotation of the thematic poem, ***Mi**chinoku no* (*see* the Introduction to this play).

[24] From a Chinese poem by Minamoto no Shitagō included in the section entitled "On Ancient Palaces" in the *Wakan Rōei-shū* (532): *Kyō Gō no horobite keikyoku ari, Kosotai no tsugu jōjōtari / Bō-Shin otoroite korō nashi,* ***Kan'yōkyū no keburi*** *henhentari* (The powerful Wu was overthrown—there are thorns and brambles; the dew of Kusu heights falls in raging streams; / The tyrannical Ch'in lost its power—there are neither tigers nor wolves; the smoke of the Hsien-yang Palace rises in blazing billows." In *The Records of the Historian,* Ssu-ma Ch'ien wrote that when the Hsien-yang (Kan'yō) Palace of Shih Huang-ti was set fire by the

Osoroshiya kakaru uki-mi o Michinoku no[23]

Adachigahara no Kurozuka ni
Oni komoreri to eijiken
Uta no kokoro mo kaku yaran to

Kokoro mo madoi kimo o keshi
Kokoro mo madoi kimo o keshi
Yuku beki kata wa shiranedomo

Ashi ni makasete nigete yuku
Ashi ni makasete nigete yuku

Ika ni arenaru kyaku sō tomare to koso
Sashi mo kakushishi neya no uchi o
Asama ni nasare mairaseshi
Urami mōshi ni kitaritari
Mune o kogasu hono-o
Kan'yō-kyū no kemuri[24]
Funpun tari

No-kaze yama-kaze fuki ochite

Narukami inazuma tenchi ni michite[25]

Sora kaki-kumoru ame no yo no

---

soldiers of Hsiang Yu of Wu, "the conflagration raged for three whole months" (p. 211), during which time it is said that black smoke filled the skies. Shih Huang-ti is also known as the Yellow Emperor, and his Hsien-yang Palace was in the Imperial capital of the Ch'in dynasty, which he founded, near Hsi-an.

[25] Lines 176–78: From the sixth episode in the *Ise Monogatari,* which tells about the hero of the tale, who eloped with an Imperial consort. It was a night of rain and thunder. Although he placed the lady in an old roadside hut, while standing guard outside, a fiend appeared who ate her "in a single gulp."

SHITE
The fiend comes to swallow the victims in one gulp,
CHORUS
The sound of its approaching footsteps,
SHITE
My iron wand lifted high to strike with mighty force,

The Shite *enters the main stage.*

CHORUS
Fill all with terror. Oh, how horrible!

INORI *During this mute dancing action, the* Waki *and* Waki-tsure *try to drive away the fiend, rubbing their rosaries in prayer, while the* Shite, *the fiend, attacks them, using a magical iron wand against them. In the first part of the* inori, *the* Shite *gets the priests into a corner; in the second part, the* Shite *brandishes the wand across the* shite *pillar; in the third part, the* Shite *again chases the priests into a corner, and with her left hand on a pillar of the* tsukurimono, *raises the wand and threatens them, and scowls at the* Waki. *The action is accompanied by all four instruments.*

After the inori, *the* Waki *and* Waki-tsure *continue to pray, rubbing their rosaries and chanting mystic mantric prayers, while the* Shite *attacks them with the wand.*

Sung, awazu
The Priests rub their rosaries at the Shite.

WAKI
In the east, Triple-Faced King of Light,[26]
WAKI-TSURE
In the south, the Demon-Quelling King of Light,
WAKI
In the west, the Dragon-Slaying King of Light,
WAKI-TSURE
In the north, the Devil-Destroying King of Light,
WAKI
And in the center, the Great Sun, The Most Holy, the great Immutable King of Light,

[26] Lines 182–86; A *dhāranī* (mystic spell) invoking the five Buddhist deities of the *Myō-ō* (*vidyā-rāja* = King of Light/Wisdom) class: Gōsanze (Trailokyavijaya [Conqueror of the Three Realms]), Gundari-yasha (Kuṇḍalī-yakŷa), Dai-itoku (Yamāntaka), Kongō-yasha (Vajra-yakŷa), and their leader, Fudō (Acala[nātha]). Like other *vidyā-rājas,* they are powerful protectors of Buddhist Law, and are presented as armed, mighty deities with an angry expression. Acala, whose name means "Immovable One," is usually portrayed with a flaming aureole burning behind his back, a sword raised high in his right hand (to cut away all obscura-

Oni hito-kuchi ni kuwan tote
Ayumi-yoru ashi-oto
Furi-aguru tecchō no ikioi

Atari o haratte osoroshi ya

Tōbō ni Gōzanze Myō-ō[26]
Nanbō ni Gundari Yasha Myō-ō
Saihō ni Dai-itoku Myō-ō
Hoppō ni Kongo Yasha Myō-ō
Chūō ni Dainichi Daishō Fudō Myō-ō

---

tions stemming from passion and ignorance), and a rope in his left (with which to bind all that might hinder). The five Kings of Light are deities of the Matrix-Store Realm (*Taizō-kai* [Garbhakośa-dhātu]), and are believed to be the manifestations of the five Buddhas of the Diamond Realm (*Kongō-kai* [Vajra-dhātu])—in the east, Ashuku (Akṣobhya); in the south, Hōshō (Ratnasambhava); in the west, Amida (Amitābha); in the north, Fukūjōju (Amoghasiddhi); and in the center, Dainichi Nyorai (Mahā-Vairocana).

WAKI and WAKI-TSURE

Oṁ huru huru candāli mātangi!
Oṁ A! Vi! Ra! Hūṁ! Khāṁ! Svāhā!
The taiko *stops.* *Hūṁ! Trat! Hāṁ! Māṁ!*[27]

Inori-ji

CHORUS

"Those who see my body[28]
Shall aspire for Nirvana;
Those who see my body
Shall aspire for Nirvana;
Those who hear my name called
Shall change from evil to good;
Those who listen to my sermons
Shall acquire great wisdom.
And those who know my mind,
Shall instantly become buddhas,
Shall instantly become buddhas," thus
Hanging hope on the Great Immutable's powerful rope,
The Waki *strikes the* Shite *with his rosary.* They continue to rub their beads, to rub their beads,
Until their prayers bring down the fiend. "Come now, stop it!"

The Shite *squats, drops her wand, and, opening a fan, holds it in her right hand. The* Waki *and* Waki-tsure *sit at the* waki-za.

SHITE

Chū-nori Until this very moment, what appeared,

CHORUS

Until this very moment, what appeared
The Shite *rises.* To be a fiendish ogress burning in anger
All of a sudden loses her power, and,
Cowering between heaven and earth,
Her dazed eyes unable to see,
Her feet failing her, she goes faltering,
Wandering this way and that upon Adachi Moor;[29]

---

[27] Sanskrit invocations and mystic syllables (*see below* for their Japanized corruptions) addressed to three Buddhist deities: line 187, to Bhaisajya-gūrū, the Medicine Buddha (Jpn. *On koro koro sendari matōgi* [*Oṁ!* (May the demon) retreat and begone! (May the demon) retreat and begone! Guard and protect us!]); line 188, an invocation of the five elements, to Mahā-Vairocana (Jpn. *On a-bi-ra-un-ken sowaka* [*Oṁ! A! Vi! Ra! Hūṁ! Khāṁ!* So be it!]); and line 189, to Acalanātha (Jpn. *Untarata kanman* [*Hūṁ! Trat! Hāṁ! Māṁ!*]). This last is an abbreviation of what is known as the Salvation Spell of Fudō: Jpn. *Nōmaku samanda bazaradan.*

On koro koro sendari matōgi
On (a)-bi-ra-un-ken sowaka
Un tarata kanman[27]

Ken ga shin ja[28]
Ho(n) bodai-shin
Ken ga shin ja
Ho(n) bodai-shin
Mon ga myō sha
Dan (n)aku shu zen
Chō ga sessha
Toku dai-chie
Chi ga shin sha
Soku shin jōbu(n)
Soku shin jōbu(n) to
Myō-ō no kebaku ni kakete
Seme-kake seme-kake
Inori fusenikeri
Sate kori yo

Ima made wa sashi mo geni

Ima made wa sashi mo geni
Ikari o nashitsuru kijo naru ga
Tachimachi no yowari hatete
Tenchi ni mi o tsuzume
Manako kuramite
Ashi-moto wa yoro-yoro to
Tadayoi meguru Adachigahara no[29]

Senda makaroshada sowataya un tarata kanman [*Namah samanta vajrānām. Caṇḍa mahā-roṣana sphotaya Hūṁ! Trat! Hāṁ! Māṁ!*] (I dedicate myself to all the Buddhas of the Vajra Realm. With your righteous anger, destroy this raging fury! *Hūṁ! Trat! Hāṁ! Māṁ!*). *On* at the head of first two lines is the well-known mantra *Oṁ*, which means "Hail!" or "All praise!"

[28] Lines 189–99: Acala's pledge to save men.

[29] *Tadayoi meguru* [*kuruma*] (wandering-this-way-and-that [wagon]) → *w**adachi*** (wheel tracks) → **Adachi**gahara.

Her abode, the Black Mound, the secret hiding place, has now been exposed.[30]

The Shite *hides her face behind her fan.*

"Oh, how disgraceful! Odious even to myself is the sight of me!"
The fiendish voice shouting thus, sounds so horrifying,[31]

The Shite *enters the* hashi-gakari, *stops & stamps.*

The fiendish voice shouting thus, so horrifying,
Mingling with the sound of the stormy night, her form has faded out of sight,

The Shite *stamps the* tome-byōshi *near the third pine.*

In the sound of the stormy night, has faded out of sight.

---

[30] Lines 211–12: ***asama*** (exposed) → ***Asama****shi* (shameful).

[31] *koe wa nao* ***susamashiki*** (the voice still **horrifying**) → ***susamashiki*** *yo-arashi* (**horrible** night storm).

Kurozuka ni kakure sumishi mo asama ni narinu[30]

Asamashi ya. Hazukashi no waga sugata to

Iu koe wa nao monosusamashiku[31]

Iu koe wa nao susamashiki
Yo arashi no oto ni tachi-magire usenikeri

Yo arashi no oto ni usenikeri

Appendix 1

Fifth-Group Noh
Currently in the Repertories of the Five Noh Schools

1. The Shimazaki Classification (1998)

Abbreviations:

The names of the Noh Schools

Ho = Hōshō; Kan = Kanze; Kg = Kongō; Ki = Kita; Kp = Konparu

Types of Noh

akki-p	*akki-mono* (evil-fiend pieces), conquered by prayer/deity
akki-w	*akki-mono* (evil-fiend pieces), conquered by warrior(s)
haya-f	*haya-mai mono* (quick-dance pieces) with female Shite
haya-m	*haya-mai–mono* (quick-dance pieces) with male Shite
igyō	*igyō-mono* (strange-apparition pieces)
igyō-d	*igyō-mono* (strange-apparition pieces) with a special dance
oni-h	*oni-mono* (demonic-apparition pieces) with once human Shite
oni-d	*oni-mono* (demonic-apparition pieces) with true demon Shite
reiken-waki	*reiken-mono* (miracle pieces) like Waki-Noh
reiken-ninjō	*reiken-mono* (miracle pieces) with human interest
tengu	*tengu-mono* (goblin pieces)
tōjō	*tōjō-mono* (warring-ghost pieces)

(The Kanze names are given below. Note that some schools use different characters.)

English Title	***Japanese Title***	***Type***	***In Repertory of***
Adachigahara (see also *Kurozuka*)	安達原	*akki-p*	only Kan
Aisome-gawa	藍染川	*reiken-ninjō*	Kan, Kp
Ama	海士	*haya-f*	all 5 schools
Chōbuku Soga	調伏曽我	*reiken-ninjō*	Ho, Kg, Ki
Chōryō	張良	*reiken-waki*	all 5 schools
Dai-e	大会	*tengu*	all 5 schools
Dairoku-Ten	第六天	*tengu*	only Kan
Danpū	檀風	*reiken-ninjō*	Ho, Kg
Funa-Benkei	船弁慶	*oni-h*	all 5 schools
Genjō	玄象	*reiken-waki*	all 5 schools
Hiun	飛雲	*akki-p*	Ho, Kan, Kg
Ikari-kazuki	碇	*tōjō*	Kan, Kg

Kappō	合浦	*igyō*	only Kan
Kasuga Ryūjin	春日龍神	*reiken-waki*	all 5 schools
Kokaji	小鍛冶	*reiken-waki*	all 5 schools
Kōtei	皇帝	*reiken-waki*	all but Kp
Kōu	項羽	*tōjō*	all 5 schools
Kurama Tengu	鞍馬天狗	*tengu*	all 5 schools
Kuruma-zō	車僧	*tengu*	all 5 schools
Kurozuka	黒塚	*akki-p*	all but Kan
(see also *Adachigahara*)			
Kusanagi	草薙	*tōjō*	only Ho
Kuzu	国栖	*reiken-waki*	all 5 schools
Matsuyama Kagami	松山鏡	*reiken-ninjō*	Kan, Kg, Ki
Matsuyama Tengu	松山天狗	*haya-m*	only Kg
Momiji-gari	紅葉狩	*akki-w*	all 5 schools
Nomori	野守	*oni-d*	all 5 schools
Nue	鵺	*igyō*	all 5 schools
Ōe-yama	大江山	*akki-w*	all 5 schools
Orochi	大蛇	*akki-w*	Ho, Kg, Ki
Raiden-A	雷電	*oni-h*	only Ho
Raiden-B	来殿	*haya-m*	Kan, Kg, Ki
Rashōmon	羅生門	*akki-w*	all but Kp
Ryōko	龍虎	*igyō*	Kan, Ki
Sesshōseki	殺生石	*igyō*	all 5 schools
Shakkyō	石橋	*igyō-m*	all 5 schools
Shari	舎利	*akki-p*	all 5 schools
Shōjō	猩々	*igyō-m*	all 5 schools
Shōki	鍾馗	*oni-h*	all but Ki
Shōkun	昭君	*oni-h*	all 5 schools
Suma Genji	須磨源氏	*haya-m*	Ho, Kan, Kg
Taema	当麻	*haya-f*	all 5 schools
Taihei Shōjō	大瓶猩々	*igyō-m*	only Kan
Taisanpukun	泰山府君	*reiken-w*	only Kg
Take no Yuki	竹雪	*reiken-ninjō*	Ho, Ki
Tanikō	谷行	*reiken-ninjō*	all but Ki
Tōru	融	*haya-m*	all 5 schools
Tsuchigumo	土蜘蛛	*akki-w*	all 5 schools
Ukai	鵜飼	*oni-d*	all 5 schools
Yamanba	山姥	*igyō-d*	all 5 schools
Zegai	善界	*tengu*	all 5 schools

2. The Classical Classification (Nogami 1943)

Note: In the following scheme, the plays are classified according to dance/action. It is given here only for comparison with the new Shimazaki classification. Those plays that are translated in this volume are given in ***bold*** type.

1. ***Hataraki- / Jun–Hataraki-mono*** (Action-Dance/Quasi–Action-Dance Pieces)
   a) SHINTAI-MONO (Deity Plays)
   Aizome-gawa, Chōbuku Soga, ***Kuzu***
   b) RYŪJIN-MONO (Dragon God Plays)
   Genzai Shichimen, Kasuga Ryūjin, Orochi
   c) KAIJIN-MONO (Non-human Spirit Plays)
   *Genzai Nue,** *Kappō, Kokaji,* ***Nue,*** *Sesshōseki*
   d) TENGU-MONO (Goblin Plays)
   Dai-e, Dairoku-ten, ***Kurama Tengu, Kuruma-zō,*** *Zegai*
   e) JUN–TENGU-MONO (Quasi–Goblin Plays)
   Chōryō, Eboshi-ori,† ***Kumasaka***
   f) KIJIN-MONO (Demonic Deity Plays)
   Danpū, Kōtei, Matsuyama Kagami, Nomori, Raiden,‡ *Shari, Shōki,* ***Shōkun,*** *Taisanpuku, Tanikō, Ukai*
   g) KICHIKU-MONO (Evil-Fiend Plays)
   Adachigahara *(Kurozuka), Hiun, Momiji-gari, Ōeyama, Rashōmon, Ryōko, Tsuchigumo*
   h) BOREI-MONO (Ghost Plays)
   Funa-Benkei, Ikari-kazuki, Kusanagi, Ko-u

   * Extant only in the Kongō School.
   † Now classified as a fourth-group play (see *Troubled Souls*)
   ‡ Nogami does not specify whether this is *Raiden-A* or *-B;* but given its placement among *Kijin-mono,* and the fact that *Raiden-B* is a *haya-mai–mono,* it can only be *Raiden-A.*

2. ***Haya-mai–mono*** (Quick-Dance Pieces)
   Ama, Genjō, ***Matsuyama Tengu,*** [*Raiden-B,*] *Suma Genji, Taema, Tōru*

3. ***Tokubestu-mai–mono*** (Special-Dance Pieces)
   Sagi, Shakkyō, Shōjō, Taihei Shōjō, Yamanba

4. ***Shugen-mono*** (Celebratory Piece)
   Taiten (Kanze only; but not considered part of the regular repertory)

Appendix 2

List of Poems
Quoted in Fifth-Group Noh

This list is abbreviated from *Poetic Allusion in Noh: A Complete List of Poems Quoted in the Current Noh Repertoire* (unpublished), compiled in Japanese by Stephen Comee, with the most generous and unstinting assistance of Chifumi Shimazaki. Although the complete list gives each quoted line in its entirety with its author and provenance, when known, and also gives the sometimes quite altered lines from the Noh, it would make this list too long to include all that information here. Therefore, we have given here only the name of the play, followed by the number of poems quoted from classical Japanese and Chinese sources. This list follows Mrs. Shimazaki's classification as given in the "Introduction to Fifth-Group Noh." It is followed by an alphabetical list for the reader's convenience.

POEMS QUOTED IN FIFTH-GROUP NOH

I. Quick-Dance Plays (6 plays)

a. *Male Plays* (4 plays)

1. **Matsuyama Tengu**—1 poem
2. **Raiden–B**—0 poems
3. **Suma Genji**—8 poems
4. **Tōru**—21 poems

b. *Female Plays* (4 plays)

1. **Ama**—10 poems
2. **Taema**—8 poems

II. Warring-Ghost Plays (4 plays)

1. **Ikari-Kazuki**—0 poems ("Funade no Narai" *kogaki*)—1 poem
2. **Kō-u**—3 poems
3. **Kumasaka**—1 poem
4. **Kusanagi**—4 poems

III. Demonic-Apparition Plays (6 plays)

a. *Demonic-Ghost Plays* (4 plays)

1. **Funa-Benkei**—5 poems
2. **Raiden–A**—4 poems
3. **Shōki**—1 poem
4. **Shōkun**—6 poems

b. *Demonic-Deity Plays* (2 plays)

1. **Nomori**—3 poems
2. **Ukai**—0 poems

IV. Goblin Plays (5 plays)

1. **Dai-e**—3 poems
2. **Dairoku-ten**—4 poems
3. **Kurama Tengu**—10 poems
4. **Kuruma-zō**—3 poems
5. **Zegai**—3 poems

V. Strange-Apparition Plays (8 plays)

a. *Dance Plays* (4 plays)

1. **Shakkyō**—6 poems
2. **Shōjō**—1 poem
3. **Taihei Shōjō**—3 poems
4. **Yamanba**—14 poems

b. *Non-Dance Plays* (4 plays)

1. **Kappō**—2 poems
2. **Nue**—6 poems
3. **Ryōko**—6 poems
4. **Sesshōseki**—2 poems

VI. Evil-Fiend Pieces (8 plays)

1. **Adachigahara** (Kurozuka)—11 poems
2. **Hiun**—4 poems
3. **Momiji-gari**—12 poems
4. **Ōe-yama**—6 poems
5. **Orochi**—4 poems
6. **Rashōmon**—6 poems
7. **Shari**—0 poems
8. **Tsuchigumo**—4 poems

VII. Miracle Plays (13 plays)

a. *God-Noh–like Plays* (7 plays)

1. **Chōryō**—2 poems
2. **Genjō**—8 poems
3. **Kasuga Ryūjin**—4 poems
4. **Kokaji**—3 poems
5. **Kōtei**—10 poems
6. **Kuzu**—4 poems
7. **Taisanpukun**—7 poems

b. *Human-Interest Plays* (6 plays)

1. **Chōbuku Soga**—0 poems
2. **Danpū**—0 poems
3. **Tanikō**—7 poems
4. **Matsuyama Kagami**—10 poems
5. **Aisome-gawa**—8 poems
6. **Take no Yuki**—14 poems

ALPHABETICAL LIST

Adachigahara (Kurozuka)—11 poems
Aisome-gawa—8 poems
Ama—10 poems
Chōbuku Soga—0 poems
Chōryō—2 poems
Dai-e—3 poems
Dairoku-ten—4 poems
Danpū—0 poems
Funa-Benkei—5 poems
Genjō—8 poems
Hiun—4 poems
Ikari-Kazuki—0 poems (“Funade no Narai” *kogaki*—1 poem)
Kappō—2 poems
Kasuga Ryūjin—4 poems
Kō-u—3 poems
Kokaji—3 poems
Kōtei—10 poems
Kumasaka—1 poem
Kurama Tengu—10 poems
Kuruma-zō—3 poems
Kusanagi—4 poems
Kuzu—4 poems
Matsuyama Kagami—10 poems
Matsuyama Tengu—1 poem
Momiji-gari—12 poems
Nomori—3 poems
Nue—6 poems
Ōe-yama—6 poems
Orochi—4 poems
Raiden–A—4 poems
Raiden–B—0 poems
Rashōmon—6 poems
Ryōko—6 poems
Sesshōseki—2 poems
Shakkyō—6 poems
Shari—0 poems
Shōjō—1 poem
Shōki—1 poem
Shōkun—6 poems
Suma Genji—8 poems

Taema—8 poems
Taihei Shōjō—3 poems
Taisanpukun—7 poems
Take no Yuki—14 poems
Tanikō—7 poems
Tōru—21 poems
Tsuchigumo—4 poems
Ukai—0 poems
Yamanba—14 poems
Zegai—3 poems

Glossary of Technical Terms

ageha A line (or two) sung by a character, sometimes by two characters in duet, that comes in the middle of a *kuse* sung by the chorus.

age-uta (high-pitched song) General term for high-pitched songs in *hira-nori. Michiyuki, rongi,* and the latter part of the *kuse,* among others, are *age-uta* type songs. See also ***sage-uta.***

ai-kyōgen, also ***ai***

1. Section of a play performed by *kyōgen-kata* (comedians) during the interval between the first and second acts. Some Noh begin with the entrance of an *ai-kyōgen* as a messenger or proclaimer, and in other Noh there are sections where *ai-kyōgen* play with other actors. These are also referred to as *ai-kyōgen.*
2. Comedian who performs an *ai-kyōgen.*

akki-mono (evil-fiend pieces) A type of fifth-group play in which an evil fiend is defeated either by a deity or the power of prayer or by warriors. An example in this volumes is *Adachigahara.*

Asakura-jo An old-man mask (named after a certain daimyo) worn by deities and ghosts of high-ranking nobles in the first act, where they appear as humble old men such as fishermen or rustics, as in *Matsu-yama Tengu* or *Tōru.*

ashirai Simple instrumental music used to accompany some action of the *shite* or the *tsure,* such as a quiet entry, moving from the *hashi-gakari* to the stage, or an onstage costume change.

atsuita ("thick board") A type of *kitsuke* (a kimono worn as an under robe) made of *atsuita-mono* ("thick-board type"), a kind of silk cloth so named because it is thick and comes folded flat around an *atsuita* (thick board), instead of around a thin board or in a roll as in the case of soft cloth. *Atsuita kitsuke* are primarily worn by male characters: one with bold patterns, by warriors in full battle attire or by demons; one with bold horizontal stripes in red and white, by young *waki*-Noh gods; a plaid one, by dignified old men and high-ranking priests. Unpatterned *atsuita* are worn by special types of humble old men and *yamabushi* priests.

au, or more properly, ***ai*** ("in regular rhythm") This word in the Noh texts indicates that the rhythm is in *hira-nori* or *chū/shura-nori* (*nori* = rhythm). Where the rhythm is in *ō-nori,* the term *noru* is used. In this series, *au,* rather than *ai,* is used because that is the term given in the Kanze-school texts; it also saves confusion, since *ai* also means *ai-kyōgen.*

awazu This word in the Noh texts indicates that the singing is "not *au,*" that is, it is sung in free rhythm.

Avalokiteśvara (Skt.) A Buddhist bodhisattva whose name means "Regarder of the Cries of the World" (Kanzeon in Japanese). The being manifested in 33 different guises, both male (Chenrezig [Tib.] and female (Kuan-yin [Ch.]), and is considered the deity of compassion.

ayakashi. A type of mask depicting a deity or ghost possessed of mysterious powers, it is used by the *mae-shite* of *Nue* or the *nochi-shite of Funa-Benkei.* It might also be used for a vindictive warrior.

beshimi, a class of masks worn by powerful deities and demons. The *ō-beshimi* ("large clenched mouth") has gold eyes and red skin that indicate terrifying power, and the clenched mouth signifies that that power is kept under close control. It is sometimes worn by the *nochi-shite* of *Kurama Tengu* and *Kumasaka,* or by the goblin of *Kuruma-zō.* The *ko-beshimi* ("small clenched mouth"), a little less fierce, has a grim countenance touched with sorrow, and it is worn by the spirits who perform an active dance called *mai-bataraki,* such as the Khan Hu Han-yeh (*nochi-shite*) in *Shōkun,* or the guardian deity in *Nomori.* The *akujō-beshimi* ("strong old man with clenched mouth"), portraying the face of a fearful old god, is sometimes used for the goblin (*nochi-shite*) of *Kurama Tengu.* The *saru-beshimi* has an ape-like visage and is used for non-human, evil creatures such as the *nochi-shite* of *Nue.* A variation painted in dark grey (black) with red outlines in the creveses is *kuro-beshimi,* a Kanze and Konparu mask used for Kumasaka roles and in special performances of *Hashi-Benke*i and *Tsuchigumo.* In addition, there is a powerful *Chōrei beshimi* (named after its creator) that is often worn by the highwayman Kumasaka in place of the *ō-beshimi.*

chōken ("long silk") A large-sleeved unlined robe made of transparently woven thick silk named *chōken,* with elegant patterns in gold or silver, worn as a dancing robe by goddesses, heavenly maidens, female spirits, and ghosts. It is also worn by elegant male characters.

chūjō A melancholy yet elegant mask worn by a high-ranking nobleman in the second act of fifth-group plays, in which he performs a *haya-mai,* such as *Genjō, Matsuyama Tengu,* and *Tōru.*

chū no mai ("medium dance") A dance in medium tempo, with the same basic choreographic pattern as *kami-mai, jo no mai,* or *otoko-mai,* as a rule accompanied by all four instruments when the dancer is a supernatural character, such as a fairy or an elfish being, and without the *taiko* if the dancer is a ghost or living person; it is performed both by male and female characters, in all categories of Noh, and frequently occurs among the fourth-group Noh. See also ***haya-mai; jo no mai.***

chū-nori ("medium rhythm") Same as *shura-nori,* the quickest of all three rhythms, with more syllables to an eight-beat line than *hira-nori* (ordinary rhythm) and *ō-nori* (large rhythm): *hira-nori* has twelve syllables to eight beats, and *ō-nori* has eight, while *chū-nori* often has sixteen (two syllables to one beat), as shown in the following example (according to the Kanze school). The quick tempo is well suited to describing quick actions and an urgent atmosphere.

•	1	•	2	•	3	•	4	•	5	•	6	•	7	•	8
			Mi -	*na*	*wa -*	*re*	*sa -*	*ki*	*ni*	*to*	–	*ta -*	*i -*	*ma -*	*tsu*
o	-	.	*Na -*	*ge -*	*ko -*	*mi*	*na -*	*ge -*	*ko-*	*mi*	*mi -*	*da -*	*re*	*i -*	*ru*
–	.	*I -*	*ki -*	*o -*	*i*	*wa*	*yo -*	*o*	*ya -*	*ku*	*ji -*	*n*	*mo*	–	–
.	*O -*	*mo -*	*te*	*o*	*mu -*	*ku -*	*be -*	*ki*	–	*yo -*	*o*	*zo*	–	*na -*	*ki* –

"Vy - ing with one a - no - ther, burn - ing fi - e - ry
brands - . They threw and threw in quick suc - ces - sion and rushed in - side
– . With such vio - lent force that e - ven a de - mon god – –
. Would have found it hard to turn his – face – to - – ward them."

Kumasaka, lines 170–74

Dainichi Nyorai (Skt. Mahā-Vairocana) The main deity, considered the Adi-Buddha, or Original Buddha, of Japan's esoteric sects, especially the Shingon sect (Mantrayāna) founded by Kūkai (*q.v.*).

daishō ("large and small") Large and small hand drums.

daishō-mae The position on the stage in front of the *daishō*—upstage center.

dan (section) There are a number of Noh plays with a song of great musical appeal, referred to by special names based on the theme of the song, such as *Koma no Dan* (The Horse Section) in *Kogō,* or *Ito no Dan* (The String Section) in *Adachigahara. Dan* are found most often among the fourth-group Noh, especially among *kyōran-mono* (mad-person Noh).

dan-noshime. See ***noshime.***

deha A type of entrance music by the three drums in *ō-nori* rhythm, with flute accompaniment in free rhythm, performed at the entrance of certain types of *nochi-shite,* such as deities, demons, spirits, heavenly maidens, and ghosts. Example: at the entrance of the *Nochi-shite* of *Kumasaka.*

demons, female In Noh, it is considered that woman are transformed into demons in three distinct stages, each having representative masks that are used in special plays: 1) *nama-nari* (beginning stage), the face of a troubled woman burning with incipient hatred (*hashihime, namanari: Kanawa*), without or with budding horns; 2) *chū-nari* (intermediate stage), the face of a woman consumed by a raging internal battle (*hannya: Aoi no Ue, Dōjōji*), with large horns; and 3) *hon-nari* (true transformation), the terrifying aspect of a completely demonic creature (*ja:* a special performance of *Dōjōji*), with great horns and fearful fangs. See also ***hannya.***

eboshi A special type of hat used for centuries in Japan, made of thick paper stiffened with black lacquer. *See* Note 1 to the Introduction to *Eboshi-ori* (*Troubled Souls*, p. 135).

engo (associated words) In poems and poetic prose, especially in *renga* (linked verse), in order to deepen and enrich the poetic effect, a word is often used with one or more *engo* (associated words) that are closely associated with it in sound or meaning. For example, *tsuyu* (dew), *musubu* (to join together / to tie), and *kusa* (grass), or *ura* (bay), *kaeru* (to return), and *nami* (waves) are used together in one poem or a passage as *engo.* Some *engo* are based on wordplay; for example, a complicated use of *engo* is often employed in a *michiyuki.* Consider this passage, from *Suma Genji: Tabi-goromo. Omoi-tachinuru asa-gasumi. . . . Yayoi no sora mo nakaba nite. Hikage nodoka ni yuku fune no. Ura-ura sugite haru-baru to. Nami no Awaji o yoso ni mite. . . . Suma no ura ni mo tsukinikeri.* (In my trav'ling robes, I've decided to set out in the morning mist. . . . Leaving in the middle of March beneath warm skies, under the gentle sunlight, our boat travels on, passing now bay after bay, traveling so far, yonder past the foamy waves, I see Awaji. . . . Till at last I have now come here to Suma Bay.) In words related to travel, we find: *tabi-goromo* (travel robes); the intensifying suffix *-tatsu,* which makes *omoi-tatsu* (to decide to do), which contains *tatsu* (to set off); *yuku fune* (traveling boat); and *haru-baru* (distant). In words related to clothing, we find: *koromo* (robes); *tatsu* (to cut [string or fabric]); *asa* (hemp), which also means "morning," leading to *hi* (day), which suggests *himo* (thread); *ura* (bay), which also means the inner lining of a robe; and *haru* (to stretch [fabric]). In addition, *kasumi* (mist) is also related to *tatsu* (to rise); and *nami* (waves) is related to *awa* (spray, foam). *Engo* are more or less traditionally prescribed, and there are dictionaries of *engo* for *renga* poets. *Engo* is one of the essential rhetorical devices in Noh. In this volume, *engo* occur frequently in *Adachigahara,* an evil-fiend piece that is rich in poetic embellishment.

Another fifth-group play, *Yamanba,* a strange-apparition piece, is lavishly decorated with their use—indicating that the being was seen to be basically not demonic in nature. See also ***kakekotoba; yori-ai.***

first pine, the. See ***ichi no matsu.***

Fudō ("Immovable") A special type of mask used to portray Fudō Myō-ō (Acala) or other fierce Buddhist deities.

Fudō Myō-ō (Skt. Acala[nātha] Vidyārāja) A manifestation of Dainichi Nyorai, the main deity in Esoteric Buddhism, and the leader of the Five Wisdom Kings of the Matrix-Store Realm. Unmoved by any obstacles, he is a protector deity who defeats all those who hinder the practice of Buddhism.

fue-za ("the seat of the flute[-player]"). *See* Plan of a Noh Stage, p. xvi.

fukai ("deep") A type of mask for middle-aged women and goddesses, used primarily by the Kanze school; among fifth-group plays, it is worn by the *mae-shite* of *Adachigahara* and *Yamanba.* See also *Shakumi.*

fumi ("letter") A large folded sheet of white paper wrapped in white paper, a stage prop used not only as a letter, but also as a message, a statement, and so on, as in *Yuya, Jinen Koji,* and *Kurama Tengu.*

genzai-mono ("historical piece") A subgroup of the fourth-group Noh. The plays in this group are realistic, the *shite* is typically a maskless samurai, who either performs an *otoko-mai* (male dance) or engages himself in *kiriai* (sword fighting). *See* the introductions to the two *genzai-mono* in *Troubled Souls: Kogō* and *Eboshi-ori.*

Gikeiki (The Chronicle of Yoshitsune) A Muromachi-period *gunki monogatari* (*q.v.*) detailing the life of Minamoto no Yoshitsune (1159–89). Its author(s) unknown, it is seen by some to be a continuation of the *Heike Monogatari,* in that it takes one of the major characters and completes the tale up to his supposed death.

gobanme-mono (fifth-group Noh) A group of Noh that are performed fifth in the standard five-Noh program; the most spectacular of all five groups of Noh, it contains plays concerned with supernatural beings and has a few *deus ex machina* pieces.

gunki monogatari (" 'military-chronicle' tale") One of the principal genres of Heian and later literature, these stories gave details of activities in battle, often without any romance. Examples are the *Genpei Jōsuiki, Gikeiki, Heike Monogatari, Hogen Monogatari,* and *Soga Monogatari*—all of which served as the source for several Noh plays.

hachimaki (head band) Long and narrow white cloth worn as a head band over a *nashiuchi eboshi,* a military hat. It is also worn by bare-headed maskless characters in fighting. It is tied at the back in a knot, with the long ends hanging down the back. A *hachimaki* is usually white, but a *kokata* (child actor) or powerful *shite* sometimes wears a colored one.

hangire or ***hangiri*** A type of divided skirt made of gorgeous brocade with bold patterns, worn by powerful deities, demons, and warriors.

hannya Originally from the Sanskrit word for transcendent wisdom (*prajñā*), the word has come to be used for the demonic mask worn by a woman transformed into an evil demon. There are three types of *hannya* masks to indicate the nature of the *shite:* white (or half-red and half-white)—beginning transformation, elegant, *Aoi no Ue;* red—medium transformation, powerful, *Dōjōji;* and black—complete transformation, coarse, *Adachigahara.*

happi A long- and wide-sleeved brocade robe with large colorful patterns. Lined *happi* with bold patterns are worn by demons and mighty warrior ghosts; unlined ones with elegant patterns, by young warrior ghosts in place of *chōken.* A *happi* and *hangire* are often worn together.

hashi-gakari (bridgeway) The passage leading from the *kagami no ma* (mirror room) to the main stage, used as an extension of the main stage. *See* Plan of a Noh Stage, p. xvi.

hashihime ("bridge woman") A female mask with an angry expression, worn by a fiendish woman; *see also* demons, female.

hataraki-goto ("[dance-like] action movement") A general term for a series of energetic dance-like actions performed by the *shite* in various plays. There are seven types: *kakeri, iroe,* and *kirikumi* without the *taiko; mai-bataraki, uchiai-bataraki,* and *inori*[*-bataraki*] with the *taiko;* and *tachi-mawari,* both with and without the *taiko.* (*See under* separate entries.)

haya-fue (fast flute music) Quick-tempo entrance music played in the second act of a first- or fifth-category play for the appearance of a vigorous god or dragon deity.

haya-mai ("quick dance") Quick-tempo dance music similar in pattern to *chū-no-mai* but performed at a quicker pace and played in a different mode (*banshiki* mode). It is performed by characters who partake of a an elegant and joyful quality. In this volume, it is danced in Act 2 of *Matsuyama Tengu* by the ghost of a retired emperor.

haya-mai–mono ("quick-dance pieces") Plays in the fifth-group Noh, in which the *Nochi-shite* is a character of nobility or elegance. It is danced in Act 2 of *Ama* and *Taema* by female characters, and in *Matsuyama Tengu, Raiden-B, Suma Genji,* and *Tōru* by male characters.

hayashi (orchestra) The name given to the Noh orchestra, whose members are known as *hayashi-kata.* It can be appended to other terms as well; for example, *mai-bayashi* is a special performance of part of a

Noh, in which no costumes are worn and only the *shite* appears on stage, but that is sung in performance style with full instrumental accompaniment and chorus participation.

haya-tsuzumi ("quick drum") A quick-tempo type of entrance/exit music played only by the two *tsuzumi* drums, which creates an atmosphere of heightened anticipation. *See also* the introduction to *Eboshi-ori* (*Troubled Souls*), pp. 140–41.

hira-nori ("ordinary rhythm") In this rhythm, 12-syllable lines in a song are divided into eight beats. Example (from the Kanze-school text):

• 1	•	2	•	3	•	4	•	5	•	6	•	7	•	8
Fu -	*ne*	*hi -*	*ki*	-	*o -*	*ko -*	*shi*	–	*so -*	*n*	*ta -*	*i*	*no*	.
O -	*n*	*tsu -*	*tsu*	–	*ga*	*na -*	*ku*	–	*ka -*	*wa -*	*bu -*	*ne*	*no*	–
"Then	they	lift	the	–	boat	and	find	–	the	ro -	yal	be -	ing	,
With -	out	harm,	hid	–	den	un-	der-	–	neath	the	ri -	ver	boat	– "

Kuzu, lines 152–53.

hitamen This word, meaning "direct face," indicates that no mask is worn by the male *shite.* In this volume, there are three plays in which the *mae-shite* performs *hitamen: Kumasaka, Kurama Tengu,* and *Kurumazō.*

honka-dori A technique of allusive variation used by poets and playwrights that entailed using famous poems with slight changes. The use of the original poem lent their work a richness of association and produced a graceful elegance that was enhanced by their subtle yet innovative changes.

honzetsu The original work of Japanese or Chinese poetry of prose used as a source of allusion by Japanese poets and playwrights.

hora-eboshi A tall, upright hat worn by courtiers, made of thick, black paper, with the upper part pressed flat from front to back.

Huang-Shih Kung (Jpn. Kō-Seki Kō = Lord "Yellow Rock") A supernatural hermit met by Chang Liang (the hero of *Chōryō*), named after the yellow rock the general encountered thirteen years later at the foot of Mount Ku-cheng.

ichi no matsu Of the three pines standing by the *hashi-gakari,* the largest, and the one nearest to the main stage. Often a *shite* who has entered alone stands by the first pine and starts singing. When the *shite* enters with a *tsure,* the latter stands there, and the *shite* stands by the third pine. *See* Plan of a Noh Stage, p. xvi.

igyo-mono ("strange-apparition pieces") A type of fifth-group Noh in which the *Shite* is a non-human character. Plays without a dance include *Kappō, Nue* (in this volume), *Ryōko,* and *Sesshōseki;* those with a dance, *Shōjō, Taihei Shōjō,* and *Yamanba.*

imawaka A male mask, similar to a *chūjō* (*q.v.*), but less anguished and more lofty in expression; often worn in the second act by deities, as in *Takasago.*

inori (prayer) A dance-like action (*hataraki-goto*) performed by a fiendish woman and priests who try to placate her by prayer, accompanied by the flute in free rhythm, and the remaining three instruments in the *ō-nori* rhythm. *Inori* occurs in *Aoi no Ue, Dōjōji,* and *Kurozuka* (Kanze name: *Adachigahara*), and partially in *Funa-Benkei,* as well as in *Hiun* in the Hōshō and Kongō schools.

inori-bataraki See ***inori.***

iroe ("coloring") Written with the same characters as the word *saishoku/shikishoku*, this is a short dance-like sequence, accompanied by the flute and two hand drums, that indicates the feeling of some deep emotion—from joy to sorrow—within the *shite's* heart. A very slow and quiet circuit of the stage, it is usually found in *sanbanme* (woman) Noh, often before a *kuse* or *jo no mai,* as in *Kakitsubata* and *Sakura-gawa,* but is also found in plaintive pieces with male *shite,* such as *Yoroboshi* and *Koi no Omoni.*

issei

1. A type of music by the flute and *daishō,* played at the entrance of characters who first sing a song in free rhythm, such as *issei* or *sashi.* Example: at the entrance of the *Waki & Waki-tsure* in *Kuzu.*
2. A dignified brief song in free rhythm, typically consisting of five initial lines, two second-part lines, and two final lines. It is sung:
   a. By character(s) on entering the stage to *issei* or *shin-no-issei* music. When there are a *shite* and a *tsure,* they sing together, with the second part sung by the *tsure* alone. Example: at the entrance of the *nochi-shite* and *nochi-tsure* in *Eboshi-ori* in *Troubled Souls.* In this case, only the first part is sung and that, only by the *tsure.*
   b. Alternately by character(s) and the chorus before a *mai* or at a climactic point. Examples: In Act 2 of *Kuruma-zō,* between the *Shite* and the Chorus.

ji, also ***ji-utai*** 1. The parts in Noh texts sung by the chorus. 2. The chorus itself; it is led by the ***ji-gashira*** ("head of the chorus"), who serves as a sort of conductor.

jidori ("repetition by the chorus") After a *shidai* (an *age-uta*–type introductory song in three lines) is sung by actors or the chorus (*ji-shidai*), the chorus repeats it in free rhythm, omitting the second line, which is the same as the first line. This is called *jidori.* There is a variation to this: In a *waki*-Noh, in which the *waki* and *waki-tsure* enter accompanied by *shin no shidai* music, the actors sing the three lines, then the chorus sings the *jidori* in regular rhythm, and without omitting the second line, and after this, the actors sing the three lines once more.

ji-gashira The head of the chorus; he sits in the back row, either the second from the right (Kanze, Hōshō) or the second from the left (Kita, Kongō, Konparu).

ji-shidai See ***shidai.***

jo–ha–kyū Three development stages that govern all the phases of Noh, advocated by Ze-ami Motokiyo (*See* Part I of the general introduction to this volume.)

jo no mai ("introductory" [= slow] dance"). An elegant, quiet dance, usually performed in a *sanbanme-mono* by a female *shite.* See *Woman Noh,* Book 1, pp. 20–21, 143.

jōruri A name used for various types of performances involving the narrating (chanting) of tales to instrumental accompaniment. Although originally used broadly to include even street performers and the blind *biwa-Heike* (lute-playing *Heike* minstrels), it was later associated with the *shamisen* and the term came to be used exclusively for Bunraku puppet theatre and Kabuki.

Jō-za ("the fixed position") The place to the right of the *shite* pillar in the left rear corner of the stage (from the spectator's view; in normal stage directions, which are always given from the actor's viewpoint, it is upstage right), the *shite's* key position during the performance. The *shite,* as well as other characters on many occasions, stands there on first entering the main stage. For example, a *waki* often stands there at his entrance and tells his name. Hence, the position is also called *nanori-za* ("self-introduction/name-telling place"). *See* Plan of a Noh Stage, p. xvi.

kagura (Shinto dance) A long instrumental dance deriving from Shinto ceremonies in its melody and dance patterns. It is performed by shrine mediums and goddesses who dance with a purification wand. The stick drum always plays in the accompaniment.

kakaru In the Noh libretto, this designation is used where a speech in soliloquy or a conversation switches to singing in free rhythm, or when an actor starts singing in free rhythm after a pause in the music or action. Passages that should be marked *kakaru* according to this practice are sometimes marked *sashi* (singing in free rhythm). There are some cases of confusion in librettos in the use of the two terms.

kake-ai (exchange) Alternate singing in free rhythm between two characters, in most cases between the *shite* and *waki,* sometimes between two or more persons on either side, ending in a rhythmic song.

kake-kotoba (pivot-word) A rhetorical device akin to a pun in which a word or phrase carries multiple meanings, for example: in *kogarashi aki* *fukete,* while *kogarashi fukete* means "a cold wind blows," *aki fukete* means "autumn deepens"; and in *kuraki yori kuraki mi ni zo* from a famous poem by Izumi Shikibu, *kuraki yori* means "out of the darkness," but *yori kuraki michi ni zo* means "onto a yet darker path." See also ***engo; yori-ai.***

kakeri (literally, "flying")

1. A brief instrumental dance performed in some *shura*-Noh, fourth-group attachment pieces, and mad-person Noh, accompanied by the flute and two hand drums, coming at a climactic point to represent fighting, or, in contrast to the more subdued *iroe,* which it resembles, to express a very high-strung emotional state. During its brief duration, the tempo suddenly changes tempo twice from slow to quick, the quiet pacing accentuated by heavy stampings of the feet.
2. Different types of short instrumental dancing actions special to a few Noh, describing fighting, hunting, and so on. (Example: *kiri-kumi no kakeri* in *Eboshi-ori* in *Troubled Souls*)

kakko

1. A type of drum used in Gagaku (court music).
2. A type of dance in which the dancer dances, beating a small stage-prop drum representing a *kakko* tied to his waist.

Kan-ami (also: Kan'ami; Kannami) Yūzaki Saburō Kiyotsugu (1333–84). A great Noh actor and playwright of the Northern and Southern Courts (Namboku) period (1336–92), his greatest achievement was to transform Noh into a coherent, consistent art by enriching it with various techniques from other arts such as *sarugaku, dengaku, utamai, kusemai,* and so on. He was the father of Ze-ami (*q.v.*), who passed on his father's aesthetic theories in the *Fushi Kaden.* His troupe's name of Kanze derives from the priestly names given to him and his son by the shogun, the "Kan" and "Ze" of Kanzeon (Avalokiteśvara, *q.v.*). (Note that Ze-ami's successor, his adopted son, Motoshige (the son of his younger brother, was known as On-ami, completing the bodhisattva's name.)

Kanze The troupe name that was eventually taken as a family name by the descendants of **Kan**-ami and **Ze**-ami, formed from the first syllables of their artistic styles or priestly names.

karaori ("Chinese weave") A kimono-style robe with comparatively small sleeves that is made of rich brocade with colorful, elaborately woven and embroidered patterns, primarily used as ordinary attire for women.

kariginu A wide-sleeved robe, lined or unlined (its long front and back body parts, which are not sewn together, are tucked up around the waist when worn), a dignified type of attire for different types of characters including: *waki*-Noh deities and graceful spirits who perform *mai;*

Shinto priests and courtiers; mighty gods, demons, and goblins in fifth-group Noh.

kasshiki Mask worn by a young temple acolyte. *See* the introduction to *Jinen Koji* (*Troubled Souls*).

kata ("pattern") A prescribed gesture pattern with a specific name. It may be abstract or describe some action. Examples: *sashi-komi* (point and enter) is a gesture of pointing directly forward with the fan as you step forward (always in an even number of steps; *hiraki* (opening) is a gesture of spreading out both arms, and then dropping them as you take three steps backward—these *kata* have no special meaning. A *shiori* (weeping) gesture is made by lifting a hand up toward the eyes, palm turned upward. Both hands are raised to express very deep sorrow.

katari (narrative) Story-telling by a *shite* or a *waki* to other character(s), spoken throughout, or ending in singing. Almost always a *katari* begins with the narrator's introductory words such as, "Let me tell you the story," often in response to some other character's words of request to the effect, "Please tell us the story." In the Noh text, the section is marked with the word *katari.* Often, a *katari* is an important dramatic feature, such as the *katari* delivered by the *Ai-kyōgen.*

kazaori eboshi A type of tall hat folded down in a special way, worn by noblemen and courtiers, as well as by graceful spirits who perform *mai.*

kiriai (sword fighting) A sword-fighting sequence in a fourth-group Noh. *See* the introduction to *Eboshi-ori* (*Troubled Souls,* pp. 141–42).

kiriai-mono (sword-fighting piece) One of the two fourth-group subgroups of *genzai-mono* (historical pieces), in which sword fighting is performed.

kirikumi, also ***kirikumi no kakeri*** A type of *kiriai-mono* in which one character fights and defeats many. *See* the introduction to *Eboshi-ori* (*Troubled Souls,* pp. 141–42).

kitsuke A basic kimono usually worn under another robe, partially visible at the wide open front and from under the large sleeves of the upper robe. There are several kinds of *kitsuke* with different materials and patterns for different types of characters. Sometimes an upper robe, such as a *karaori,* is worn in the *kitsuke* style.

kogaki (lit., "written in small letters") Well over half of the Noh currently performed have one or more variations, or *kogaki,* so called because when a play is performed in variation, the name of the special version is printed in small letters in the program, beside the name of the play. In a *kogaki* performance, masks, costumes, *kata,* or *mai* will change from the standard ones. Often there are omissions, the *kuse* being the most often omitted section. The whole atmosphere may change under a *kogaki.* There will be greater accent on singing and action, with increased emphasis on the changing rhythm in performance, which Ze-ami refers to as *jo–ha–kyū* (*q.v.*).

kokata

1. A character, both adult and child, to be played by a child actor. In a number of Noh, an adult role is played by a child actor for an alienation effect, that is, so as not to attract attention away from the *shite,* or to de-emphasize the romantic relations between a man and a woman.
2. A boy or girl who plays a *kokata* role. A *kokata* never wears a mask, even when a boy is playing a female role, or vice versa.

kōken (stage assistant, lit., "watching from behind") During performance, two *kōken,* or three in a few special Noh, sit at the back of the stage. They are responsible primarily for the *shite*-group actors and take care of their costumes, accessories, and stage properties during performance, and also act as prompters. If the *shite,* or a *shite*-group actor, because of sudden illness or some other reason is unable to continue his performance, one of the *kōken* is expected to take his place immediately and to finish the performance.

kōken-za (*kōken's seat*) The place where the *kōken* sit, to the left of the *ato-za* at the back of the stage. *See* Plan of a Noh Stage, p. xvi.

Kongō-kai (Skt. *Vajra-dhātu*) In esoteric Vajrayāna Buddhism, one of the two great realms is known as the Diamond Realm, and it is a metaphysical space inhabited by the Five Wisdom Buddhas. The Diamond Realm Mandala, which Kūkai brought back from China, is based on an esoteric Buddhist tantra called the Vajrasekhara Sutra. Very important for its use in intiation rituals, the Diamond Realm Mandala is hung on the west wall, symbolizing the final realization of Mahā-Vairocana.

ko-omote The youngest (and best known) of female masks.

koshimaki ("draped about the waist") A way of wearing a *nuihaku* kimono around the waist like a skirt, over a *kitsuke* and usually under an upper robe, with the loose sleeves showing from under the robe. While the *koshimaki* style is very common among female characters, in rare cases a young male appears in this style without an upper robe.

kudoki (lament) *Sashi*-style singing in free rhythm, that, unlike a *sashi,* is keyed to the medium pitch at which it begins, and rises to a high pitch toward the end, sung throughout by character(s) with an appealing tone in a tragic situation.

Kūkai (774-835) The Japanese monk who traveled to China, where he was initiated into the esoteric lineages of both the *Taizo-kai* and *Kongo-kai* (*q.v.*). On his return to Japan he founded the Shingon sect, and was allowed by Emperor Saga in 816 to build his head temple on Mt. Kōya in Waka-yama Prefecture. In Kyoto, his sect took over Tōji, which fought his head temple (Kongōbuji) for dominion, and Ninnaji, whose abbot was often a retired Imperial prince. In 828, Kūkai open his School of Arts and Sciences (Shugei Shuchi-in, a private institution open to all regardless of social rank. High-ranking priests (*ajari*) of the sect were often called upon to put an end to plagues, for exorcisms, or to bring rain.

Kumasaka A grotesque mask worn exclusively by the *nochi-shite* of *Eboshi-ori,* the highwayman Kumasaka, and the *nochi-shite* of *Kumasaka,* the ghost of the same man. A similarly grotesque mask named *kuro-beshimi* is also used in these two plays. *See* the introductions to *Kumasaka* (in this volume, pp. 199–201) and *Eboshi-ori* (*Troubled Souls,* p. 143).

kuri A high-pitched melodious short song in free rhythm, sung alternately by an actor and the chorus. In the formal structure, both a *kuri* and *sashi* precede the *kuse.* The section referred to as *kuri–sashi–kuse* forms the core of a Noh.

kuri–sashi–kuse. *See* the separate entries for ***kuri, kuse,*** and ***sashi.***

kuro-beshimi ("black frown") A special type of *ō-beshimi* mask (*q.v.*).

kurui (mad scene) In some *kyōran-mono* (mad-person Noh), there is a section in which the *shite,* at the height of madness, dances with vigorous gestures and stamping of feet, accompanied by a song with a lively rhythm special to it. These sections are prized as *kurui* (mad scenes), and are as striking and well-loved as the mad scenes in famous operas, such as that in Donizetti's *Lucia di Lammermoor.* Examples: *Hanagatami, Hibari-yama.*

kurui-zasa ("mad bamboo") A bamboo branch, a symbol of madness, usually carried by the mad woman in a *kyōran-mono.* In ancient times, special Shinto prayer strips of folded white paper were hung from the bamboo, but this practice was stopped in the Kanze school in the Meiji era.

kuse A long thematic song in regular rhythm, beginning slowly at a low pitch, and ending in an *age-uta,* sung by the chorus, with the exception of a short passage in the middle, which is sung by the *shite,* sometimes by the *tsure* or *kokata* in solo or in duet. In the standard form, a *kuse* is preceded by a *kuri* and a *sashi.* The *kuse,* which used to be called *kuse-mai* (*kuse*-dance), is an adaptation of a popular song-and-dance form by the same name that Kan-ami first introduced into Noh with great success. Occurring in most Noh, the *kuse* forms the central part of the play. It is often accompanied by a dance. As a rule, a *kuse* that occurs in the first act of a visional Noh is not accompanied by a dance, but a *kuse* in the second act has a dance. A *kuse* without a dance is called *i-guse* (sitting *kuse*), and one with a dance is called *mai-guse* (dancing *kuse*). There is also a special type of *kuse* written in two parts, and this is called a *nidan-guse* (*kuse* in two parts).

"kyōgen kigo" ("wild words and decadent diction") This phrase comes from an important passage of prose that appears in the *Po-shih Wen-chi* (Anthology of the Works of Po) as well as in the *Hsiang-shan Po-shih Luo-chung Chi-chi* (An Account of the Collected Works of Master Po of Fragrant Mountain Temple while in Loyang) that is included in the *Wakan Rōei-shu* (588) by Po Chü-i (772–846): *Yuan i ching sheng su wen tzu chih yeh. K'uang yen ch'i yü chih wu. Fan wei tang lai shih. Tsan fo ch'eng chih yin chuan fa lun chih yuan.* (*Negawaku wa konjō sezoku mo monji no waza, kyōgen kigo no ayamachi o motte / Hiru-gaerite tōrai seisei no sanbutsujō no in, tenpōrin no en:* I vow to take the error of my "wild words and decadent diction" of my worldly literary enterprise in this life, and transform it into the karma of praising the Turning of the Wheel of the Vehicle of the Dharma), and it is from here that the word *kyōgen* is thought to have originated. The phrase is also used by the Kamakura-period Zen monk Mujū (1226–1312) in his *Shaseki-shū* (Anthology of Sand and Pebbles, p. 72), whose concern in writing this book was to "bring people into the marvelous Way of Buddha's teaching . . . through the wanton sport of wild words and decadent diction," in order "to illustrate the profound significance of this splendid doctrine." In his encounter with these "wild words and decadent diction," the reader is asked to "extract gold and jewels from sand and pebbles." The phrase appears just after the *tachi-mawari* in *Yamanba,* where its use seems to indicate that song-and-dance entertainments such as *kuse-mai* were also considered example of "wild words and decadent diction."

kyōgen kuchiake or ***kaikō*** (beginning with an *ai-kyōgen's* speech) This designation in a Noh text indicates that the play begins with the entrance of an *ai-kyōgen,* who makes some announcement as a sort of prologue.

kyōgen-za (kyōgen actor's place). *See* Plan of a Noh Stage, p. xvi.

kyōran-mono (mad-person Noh). A play about a mad person (usually a fourth-group play) that sometimes contains a special section known as *kurui* (*q.v.*). *See also* the introduction to *Semimaru* (*Troubled Souls,* pp. 46–47).

mae-shite The *shite* in the first act of a two-act Noh.

mai-bataraki A special type of *hataraki-goto* that is performed by dragons, *tengu,* and demons (examples: *Kasuga Ryūjin, Kurama Tengu*). It is performed by all four instruments and often depicts a threat or attack by the *shite,* though sometimes it indicates the joy of, and the bestowing of blessings by, the *shite.*

makura-kotoba ("pillow word") In a poetic language, there are some words and phrases, usually in five syllables, that are used before some specific words as a sort of modifier. Such words are called *makura-kotoba.* For example, *hisakata no,* which can mean "long lasting," is a pillow word for *sora* (heaven) or *hikari* (light), and *ashi-biki no,* "foot-dragging," which is a pillow word for mountains, or things at a distance, etc. Names of places are often preceded by their *makura-kotoba* (examples: *aoni yoshi* [green-soiled lovely] Nara; *sazanami no* [rippling-wave] Shiga). They are very similar in usage to the epithets found in ancient Greek poetry, as in the "wine-dark" sea (*οἴνοψ πόντος*) or the "rosy-fingered" dawn (*ἕως ῥοδοδακτυλος*) of Homer. See also *uta-makura.*

mantra A special word (e.g., Skt. *Oṁ*) or series of words or even prayers used in ceremony for specific purposes. Several of these appear in *Adachi-gahara,* when the priests attempt to overcome the demon with the power of their sacred words.

Mantrayāna A type of Buddhism that uses many mantras. *See* Vajrayāna.

masugami A young female mask, whose tense emotion is emphasized by a pair of incisions at the base of the eyebrows. Besides by the *Shite* of *Semimaru,* the mask is worn by some female deities.

metsuke-bashira (eye-setting pillar) The pillar at extreme downstage right; so named because the masked *shite* uses it to determine his position upon the stage. *See* Plan of a Noh Stage, p. xvi.

michiyuki (travel song)

1. A common type of *age-uta* describing a journey, sung by a character (and his companions) after he has announced his name and traveling intention. As a rule, this comes at the beginning of a play.
2. A travel song more elaborate and longer than the one explained above, forming an important part of a Noh. While the first type of *michiyuki* is indicated as such, this type is usually marked as an *age-uta, rongi,* etc., according to the occasion. Example: *Semimaru* (*Troubled Souls*), in which there are both types of *michiyuki,* the first describing the journey of the *Tsure,* Prince Semimaru, and the second, that of the *Shite,* Princess Sakagami.

mizu-goromo Most widely used as an informal upper robe for men and women. Of the two types of *mizu-goromo—shike* and *yori*—the latter, white as a rule, is thin and transparent and is worn by humble characters at work, by a *tsure* who accompanies the *shite,* and by a Shinto priest.

mondai, also ***mondō*** ("questions and answers") Dialogue spoken as a rule between the *shite* and *waki,* especially a dialogue that occurs in the early part of a Noh as part of the standardized dramatic structure, when the *waki* asks questions of the *shite,* a stranger, who has suddenly appeared before him. Similar in nature to the Zen *mondō.*

monogi In some Noh, during performance, the *shite* withdraws to the *kōken-za* to have a part of his costume changed, or to have a hat or some other accessory put on by the *kōken.* This is called *monogi.* In some Noh, *monogi* is done with the *shite* remaining where he happens to be. On rare occasions a change of costume of a non-*shite* character is also referred to as *monogi.* Example: *Semimaru.*

nakairi (interim exit) Exit of a major character who reappears later; typically, the exit of the *mae-shite* at the end of the first act.

namanari ("half-grown") A fiendish woman mask, with demonic horns just sprouting on her brow, about half as long as those on a *hannya* mask. *See* the introduction to *Kanawa* (*Troubled Souls,* p. 11).

nanori ("self-introduction," or "name-telling") Lines spoken by a character on his first entrance onto the stage, addressed to no specific person, telling who he is and what he is going to do. Usually this is done at the *jō-za* (fixed place), the key position on the stage for the *shite,* which is also called *nanori-za.* There is a special type of *nanori,* sung in a recitative style, known as *nanori-zashi.* In *Nue,* it appears after *Issei* entrance music.

nanori-bue ("self-introduction flute") Flute music that usually accompanies the entrance of a *waki* who, on entering the stage, immediately tells his name and intention without any preliminary song. Example: *Kogō.*

nanori-za ("name-telling place") See ***nanori.***

ni no matsu (the second pine) Of the three pines along the *hashi-gakari* (the bridgeway), the second one from the main stage. *See* Plan of a Noh Stage, p. xvi.

nochi-shite The *shite* in the second act of a two-act Noh. *Nochi-shite* is the Kanze pronunciation. The word is often pronounced *nochi-jite.*

nochi-tsure The *tsure* in the second act of a two-act Noh. *Nochi-tsure* is the Kanze pronunciation. The word is often pronounced *nochi-zure.*

noru A notation indicating that the rhythm switches to *ō-nori.*

nōshi A large-sleeved elegant robe worn as informal wear by a prince or a great lord.

noshime A *kitsuke* (kimono) made of a kind of silk of the same name. Plain dark blue *noshime* are robes for ordinary monks and common people (Example: the *Mae-shite* in *Kuzu,* the *Waki and Mae-shite* in *Matuyama Tengu*); *noshime* with bold horizontal stripes in white and blue, or yellow and brown, named *dan* (bar)-*noshime,* are used for more important maskless male characters, such as the *Shite* and *Waki* in *Eboshi-ori.*

notto (prayer to Shinto gods)

1. Chanting in free rhythm of a prayer to Shinto gods.

2. Music that accompanies *notto* chanting, performed by the flute and two hand drums.

nuihaku ("embroidered and gilt") A kimono-style silk dress with colorfully dyed, gilt, and embroidered elegant patterns, worn by a woman under an upper robe, or without a robe, wrapped about the waist like a skirt in the *koshimaki* style. Example: *Adachigahara,* in which the *Shite* wears the robe under some outer wear in the first act, and without outer wear in the second act. *Nuihaku* is also worn by certain types of young male characters as a *kitsuke,* such as the *Mae-kokata* in *Kurama Tengu.*

ō-beshi Entrance music played by the flute and three drums, for the energetic entrance of a *tengu* wearing an *ō-beshimi* mask.

ō-beshimi ("large frown") A type of mask with the mouth held tightly shut (*beshimi*), that is usually used for the *nochi-shite* in *tengu* plays, such as *Kurama Tengu.* See also *beshimi.*

ōkuchi ("large opening") A type of bulky divided skirt, made of thick silk, white or colored, with wide openings below. It is widely worn by men and women. A costume with an *ōkuchi* is more formal than one without. A smaller-sized *ōkuchi* is worn under a *sashinuki* or a *suō* skirt, to make the thin and soft outer skirt spread out bulkily.

Ōmi-onna ("woman of Ōmi") A type of mask showing the great determination or strong emotions of a mature woman, sometimes used for the *mae-shite* of *Ama* or *Dōjōji.* Originally used by the Ōmi Sarugaku troupe.

oni-mono ("demonic-apparition pieces") A type of fifth-group Noh in which the *Shite* appears as a demon. The two subgroups classify the *Shite* as demons who were formerly human (*Funa-Benkei, Raiden-A, Shōki, Shōkun*) and as true demons (*Nomori, Ukai*).

ō-nori ("large rhythm") In a song in *ō-nori,* there are six to eight syllables to eight beats, often one syllable to one beat, as in the example below (according to the Kanze school). Because of this, *ō-nori* is slower and more rhythmical than *hira-nori* (ordinary rhythm), which has twelve syllables distributed among eight beats, or *chū* (*shura*)*-nori,* which has more than twelve syllables to eight beats.

•	1	•	2	•	3	•	4	•	5	•	6	•	7	•	8
	U	–	*chi*	–	*mo*	–	*no*		*wa*	–	*za*		*ni*	–	*te*
–	*ka*	–	–	*no*	–	*u*	–	–	*ma*	–	–	*ji*	.		
	"If		I		fight		with		wea	–	pons		I		shall
–	ne	–	–	ver	–	beat	–	–	that	–	–	youth	."		

—*Kumasaka,* line 228

otoko-mai (male dance) An instrumental dance similar to *chū no mai, kami-mai,* and *jo no mai* in the musical and choreographic style, primarily performed by a maskless samurai in *otoko-mai-mono.*

otoko-mai–mono (male-dance pieces) A subgroup of *genzai-mono* (historical piece), in which the *shite,* a maskless samurai, performs an *otoko-mai.*

pillow word See ***makura kotoba.***

raijo A special type of solemn Noh music by all four instruments that sometimes accompanies the exit of deities, tengus, and other supernatural beings at the end of the first act.

ranjo A special type of Noh music by all four instruments that sometimes accompanies the entrance of supernatural beings at the beginning of the second act.

reiken-mono ("miracle pieces") A type of fifth-group Noh in which the *Shite* is a supernatural being who performs a miracle. There are two subgroups: in one, the play is similar to, and sometimes performed in the place of, a Waki-Noh (such as *Kasuga Ryūjin* and *Kuzu* [in this volume]); in the other, a deity appears as a *deus ex machina* to save the day (as in *Chōbuku Soga,* in which the god Acala appears as the *Nochi-shite*).

renga (linked verse) A type of linked poetry based upon the 31-syllable *waka* of 5-7-5-7-7 phrases. The 5-7-5 and 7-7 sections were written in a fashion linked by a number of special rules, either by a solo poet or a group of *renga* poets. They were characterized by the great use of *yori-ai* (*q.v.*) and other types of word and image play.

rongi ("discussion") Originally a Buddhist term meaning discussion about a sutra, this is an *age-uta* type song, sung alternately by the actors, or by the actor(s) and the chorus, ending in the chorus. A *rongi* is often sung toward the end of the first act of a visional Noh, where the *shite* makes an interim exit with a hint at his or her identity; at the end of a play describing a parting scene (Example: *Semimaru, Kogō*); or at a climactic place describing a journey or some work, such as drawing water, washing, or reaping. Example; the *Ito no Dan* (String Section) of *Adachigahara.*

sage-uta (low-pitched song) A brief song in *hira-nori* (ordinary rhythm) keyed to the low pitch, often preceding an *age-uta.*

sanbanme-mono ("third-on-the-program piece") So named because a Noh in this group is performed third in a standard five-Noh program. It is also referred to as *kazura-mono,* because its typical heroine, a graceful young woman, wears a gilt and embroidered colorful *kazura-obi* (wig band) on the wig (*kazura*). Young women in many other Noh also wear a colorful wig band, but as a rule it is not gilt.

Sankō-jō An old-man mask (named after its creator) worn by deities and ghosts of high-ranking nobles in the first act, where they appear as humble old men such as fishermen or rustics, as in *Kuzu, Matsuyama Tengu, Shōkun,* or *Tōru.*

san no matsu (the third pine) Of the three pines along the *hashi-gakari* (the bridgeway), the third one from the main stage. As a rule, when the *shite* and *tsure* enter together, the *shite* stands by the third pine, and the *tsure* by the first. *See* Plan of a Noh Stage, p. xvi.

saru-beshimi A *beshimi*-type mask with ape-like features used for evil creatures, such as the *nochi-shite* of *Nue.* (The Kanze school usually uses the *ko-tobide* or *saru-tobide* instead.)

saru-tobide A *tobide*-type mask with strong ape-like features and bulging eyes used for mischievous or evil creatures, such as the *nochi-shite* of *Nue* (in the Kanze school, while the others use the *saru-beshimi* instead.)

sashi A song in free rhythm, sung smoothly like a recitative, by actors in solo or in chorus, or alternately by actors and the chorus. It comes in various parts of a Noh. A section made up of a *kuri,* a *sashi,* and a *kuse,* referred to as *kuri–sashi–kuse,* forms the core of a Noh.

sashinuki A long divided silk skirt, worn over a small-sized *ōkuchi* divided skirt, and tucked up beneath the knees or at the ankles with a string. A *sashinuki* is worn by royalty and noblemen. Example: the *Kokata* (Emperor Tenmu) in *Kuzu.*

Semimaru A mask worn exclusively by the young blind Prince Semimaru in *Semimaru* (in *Troubled Souls).*

shakumi ("hollow-cheeked") A type of mask with concave, hollow cheeks that is worn for middle-aged women and goddesses, used primarily by all schools other than the Kanze school in place of a *fukai;* among fifth-group plays, it is often worn by the *mae-shite* of *Adachigahara* and *Yamanba.* See also *fukai.*

shidai

1. A brief introductory song in three lines (of 7–5, 7–5, and 7–4 syllables) in *hira-nori* (ordinary rhythm), sung by one or more characters on their entrance onto the stage, and repeated by the *ji-utai* (chorus) in free rhythm without the second line, which is the same as the first. This repetition by the *ji-utai* is called *jidori* (*q.v.*). Sometimes a *shidai* and *jidori* by the *ji-utai* come at a climactic point, or before a *kuri–sashi–kuse,* as a sort of prelude (as in *Adachigahara*).

   There is also a special type of *shidai* known as *ji-shidai,* which appears in a few plays, including *Shōkun* in this volume. For more details, see the introduction to that play.
2. Music by the flute and the two hand drums, played at the entrance of

those characters who sing a *shidai* on entering the stage. Examples: *Adachigahara, Kumasaka, Kuruma-zō, Matsuyama Tengu, Nue.*

shikami ("gnawing") A fierce mask worn by fierce demonic spirits, as the nochi-shite of *Ōeyama* or *Momiji-gari.*

Shingon sect The Shingon sect, a major schools of Japanese Buddhism, is one of the few surviving Esoteric Buddhist lineages that started in the 3rd to 4th century AD. The esoteric teachings would later flourish in Japan under a monk named Kūkai, who traveled to T'ang China to acquire transmission of the esoteric teachings. The word "Shingon" is the Japanese reading of Chinese word Chēn-yén, literally meaning "True Words," which in turn is the Chinese translation of the Sanskrit word mantra. Japanese Shingon Buddhism is unique in that it alone maintains he tradition of both the Diamond and Matrix-Store realms. These two mandalas are considered to be a compact expression of the entirety of the Dharma, and form the root of Buddhism. Shingon Buddhism teaches that through purification of body, speech, and mind, all can attain enlightenment within this lifetime.

shiori ("weeping") A *kata* (gesture or pattern) of weeping, made by lifting a hand toward the eyes, with the palm turned upside. Both hands are raised to express deep grief.

shishi ("lion") A special type of dance performed either by a human acting out a lion dance (as in *Mochizuki*), or by a real lion, as in *Shakkyō.* Note that it is called *shishi* in order to distinguish it from the more popular *shishi-mai* (lion dance) of folk festivals and street performers.

shishi-guchi ("lion mouth") A special type of mask used only for the lion-dog role in *Shakkyō.*

shite The leading role and the player of the role.

shite-bashira (*shite* pillar) The pillar on the left rear corner of the main stage (from the spectator's view; actually, at upstage right). *See* Plan of a Noh Stage, p. xvi.

shite-tsure (*shite's* companion) A role and its player, related to the *shite* as a brother, friend, servant, and so on, played by a *shite-kata* (*shite* actor). A *shite-tsure* can be male or female. *Shite-tsure* is the Kanze pronunciation and the word is often pronounced *shite-zure.* A shorter word, *tsure,* is more commonly in use now.

shura-nori (*shura* rhythm) Same as *chū-nori* (*q.v.*).

Six Realms (*rokudō*) The six categories of rebirths within Mahāyāna Buddhist cosmology. They include all the possibilities, advantageous and less advantageous, of lives in this world of illusion. The karma one accrues in a previous life determines which of the six realms one is reborn into. Birth into the six realms involves rebirth as: a *devā* (god), an *asura* (demi-god), a human being, an animal, a hungry ghost, or a being in hell. Note that in Theravada Buddhism there are only five realms, as the *asura* realm is regarded as part of the *devā* realm. It is also thought that our emotions cause us to live in these realms minute by minute.

sobatsugi A sleeveless upper robe worn by a soldier, as well as a Chinese man or woman.

sumi-bōshi A type of head gear worn by a Buddhist priest, it is a large piece of cloth that is worn like a cap and comes to a point (*sumi*) in the front, with another portion hanging down over the neck.

suō An unlined linen suit consisting of a finely patterned, large-sleeved robe and a pair of long trailing trousers of the same material. A *suō* suit is used for maskless males such as samurai of lower status, servants, merchants, and other types of commoners. Sometimes the upper robe is worn with an *ōkuchi* divided skirt or without any skirt.

surihaku A kimono-style robe of satin-type white silk, with patterns pressed in gold or silver, worn widely as a *kitsuke* (inner robe) by female characters.

Susano-o When the Lord of Heaven, Izanagi, returned from seeing his dead wife, Izanami, in the underworld, he washed his face. From washing his left eye, Amaterasu, the Sun Goddess, was born; from his right eye, Tsukiyomi, the Moon God; and from his nose, Susano-o, the Storm God. He appears in fifth-group Noh as the Shite of *Orochi.*

tachi-mawari ("circuiting around") A short dance-like circuit of the stage accompanied by the *hayashi,* either with or without the *taiko,* depending upon the play.

Taizō-kai (Skt. *Garbhakośa-dhātu*) In esoteric Vajrayāna Buddhism, one of the two great realms is known as the Matrix-Store Realm, and it is the metaphysical space inhabited by the Five Wisdom Kings. Often called the "Womb Realm," its name stems from a phrase in the Mahā-Vairocana Sutra, in which the Buddha revealed the mandala's secret teachings to his disciple Vajrasattva from his "womb of compassion." The Matrix-Store Mandala is used in several important initiatory rituals, and is usually hung on the east wall, symbolizing the youth of Mahā-Vairocana.

tengu (long-nosed goblin) A *tengu* is a mythical creature, thought to have magical powers, that comes in various types. For details, see the introduction to *Kurama Tengu.*

tengu-mono (goblin piece) A type of fifth-group Noh in which the *Shite* is a goblin. Usually, the goblin is intent on creating mischief or destroying Buddhism, as in *Dai-e, Dairoku-ten, Kuruma-zō* (in this volume), and *Zegai.* Only in *Kurama Tengu* (in this volume) is the goblin a benevolent creature who teaches Yoshitsune the military arts.

third pine, the See ***san no matsu.***

tobide ("bulging eyes"). A class of masks worn by powerful characters of a non-human (both semi-divine and animal) nature. The *ō-tobide* ("large bulging eyes") has a startled expression with eyes and mouth both wide open. It is often used for powerful deities who move rapidly and perform an active *hataraki* or *shimai,* such as Zaō Gongen in *Kuzu.* The *ko-tobide* ("small bulging eyes") has a slightly ferocious expression, and is like a small *ō-tobide* without ears. Used for fox spirits and demons, it is also often worn by the *nochi-shite* in *Nue.* The *saru-tobide* ("ape with bulging eyes") is a stronger, more ape-like version of the *ko-tobide,* and it is sometimes worn in place of it by the *nochi-shite* of *Nue.*

tokin ("helmet cloth") A special type of headgear that, despite the name, looks like a black box sitting on the head. A small version is worn by *yamabushi* (ascetic priests), as in *Adachigahara,* and a larger type, with wing-like extensions on each side, is worn by *tengu,* as in *Kurama Tengu* and *Matsuyama Tengu.*

tome-byōshi (end-stamping) Often a Noh comes to an end with the *shite's tome-byōshi,* that is, two slow stampings of his feet, which can be performed either at the *jōza* or on the *hashi-gakari* in rhythm with the chorus. Sometimes the *waki* stamps the *tome-byōshi* after the *shite's* exit. In *Eboshi-ori,* the *Kokata* stamps the *tome-byōshi.*

tomo (attendant) A minor role, typically a servant, male or female, performed by a *shite* actor.

tsubo-ori A manner of wearing a long upper robe, pulled up to the knees by a sash tied around the waist.

tsukizerifu (arrival announcement) A short speech announcing one's arrival at a particular place, usually by the *waki* and *waki-tsure.*

tsukurimono ("a fabricated object") A stage prop, so named because it is assembled every time it is used, to be dissembled afterward, a mere framework made of bamboo, wood, cloth, etc., representing all sorts of structures and smaller objects placed on the stage floor.

tsure See ***shite-tsure.***

tsure-men (*tsure* mask) A young female mask for a young *tsure* woman, similar to *ko-omote* (young woman mask worn by the *shite*), but of an inferior make.

uba ("old woman") A type of old-woman mask with the hair in a slightly deranged state; used for the *mae-tsure* of *Kuzu.*

uchiai-bataraki ("battle action") A type of *hataraki-goto* in which a *tengu* or demon appears, including a battle with a large number of warriors (examples: *Ōeyama, Ryōko*).

uchi-awase ("striking meeting") The special word used in the Noh world to mean what is called "stage rehearsal" in the West. It is the *only* time the actors and musicians get together, and usually occurs only once for each play. All are dressed in ordinary clothes, the drummers strike special hard wood blocks, the flute player either plays or just chants the melody, and the characters walk through the play. At this time, the *shite* makes any special requests he might have concerning how he wishes to perform to the play that might entail changes in the music or in the speeches and/or actions of the other actors.

uta-makura Though earlier used like epithets (*makura-kotoba*), in the time of the Noh playwrights, *uta-makura* were the names of famous places used to evoke a richness of poetic imagery; see also *makura-kotoba.*

Vajrayāna Vajrayāna is a complex and multifaceted system of Buddhist thought and practice that evolved over several centuries. Its main scriptures, even when called sutras, are actually Tantras. A distinctive feature of Vajrayāna is ritual, which is used as a substitute or alternative for abstract meditations. Based on the concept of "skillful means" (Skt. *upaya*), Vajrayāna is a system of lineages, whereby those who successfully receive an empowerment or initiation are seen to share in the mind-stream of the realization of a particular skillful means of the Vajra Master. In Vajrāyana these skillful means mainly relate to tantric, Mahāmudra, or Dzogchen practices. Vajrayāna teaches that its techniques provide an accelerated path to enlightenment.

waka A song in free rhythm, as a rule in the form of a *waka,* a poem of thirty-one syllables divided into five phrases of 5–7–5–7–7 syllables. It is sung by the dancer at the end of an instrumental *mai,* and taken over by the chorus. Often it is a quotation of a classical poem.

waki (supporting role/actor) The supporting role and actor, second to the *shite* in importance, always a male and a realistic person without a mask. In a visional Noh, he plays the part of a medium between the visional character and the spectator. The type of characters that a *waki* plays is limited: typically a Shinto priest or a courtier in a *waki*-Noh; a traveling priest in a *shura*-Noh and *sanbanme-mono.* In the fourth-category Noh, the *waki* plays a far wider range of roles. *Waki* and *waki-tsure* play the parts that belong to the *waki-kata* (*waki* players) and they never play the parts that belong to the *shite-kata* players. Many plays have only a *shite* and a *waki* (with or without *waki-tsure* as attendants). Plays without the *waki* are exceptionally few. Almost all of them are found among *genzai-mono* (historical pieces).

waki-za (supporting actor's place) Front right corner of the stage (from the spectator's view; actually, downstage left) where the *waki* sits most of the time during the play, especially after the *shite* has entered the stage.

waki-tsure (waki's companion) A minor role, as well as its player, typically an attendant of a *waki,* performed by a *waki*-group actor. *Waki-tsure* is the Kanze pronunciation. It is often pronounced *waki-zure.*

yamabushi Literally, "he who lies in the mountains," *yamabushi* were Japanese mountain ascetics with a long tradition as mighty warriors endowed with supernatural powers. Followers of the Shugendō doctrine founded by En no Gyōja, an integration of the esoteric Buddhism of the Shingon sect with Tendai and Shinto elements, they were well known for their mystical insight and supernatual powers.

yobanme-mono (fourth-group Noh) A group of Noh which are performed fourth in the standard five-Noh program; the largest of all five groups of Noh, it contains plays of great variety, including realistic, visional, and supernatural Noh.

yobikake ("calling to") Sometimes a character enters while calling out to another character on the main stage. This is called *yobikake.* Typically, the latter is a *waki* traveler, and the former, the *shite,* a supernatural being in the form of a local person. Exceptionally in *Eboshi-ori,* the boy Ushiwaka, a realistic person, enters calling out to the *Waki.*

yori-ai (word association) A canon of classical word associations used to link themes in *waka* poetry and *renga* (linked verse). The fifteenth-century *Renju Gappeki-shū* [Complete Compendium of Strung Gems] of Ichijō Kanera is a *yori-ai* manual. See also ***engo.***

yori-mizugoromo See ***mizugoromo.***

Yoroboshi A blind boy's mask, primarily worn by the blind boy in the title role of *Yoroboshi.*

Zaō A special mask worn only to depict the Buddhist deity Zaō Gongen in *Arashiyama* and *Kuzu.*

Zaō Gongen A mountain deity considered to be in between the inherent Shinto deities of Japan and the Buddhist deities imported from Mainland China, he is the avatar of the Diamond Realm and the protector of the *yamabushi* Shugendō sect. The protector deity of sacred Kimpusen (Mt. Kinpu) in Nara prefecture, Zaō is widely venerated in the entire mountain range stretching from Yoshino to Kumano (the cradle of Shugendō practice),

Ze-ami (also: Zeami; incorrectly, as Seami) Yūzaki Saburō Motokiyo (traditionally given as 1363–1443). The son of Kan-ami (*q.v.*), he transformed the entertainment known as *sarugaku*-Noh into the elegant art of Noh drama. Gaining the favor of Ashikaga shogun Yoshimitsu (1358–1428), Ze-ami was able to access the great corpus of court poetry and refinement of court circles. He is remembered as a brilliant playwright, as well as author of a number of extremely obscure but valuable dramatic treatises, the most important of which are considered to be *Kakyō* (The Mirror of the Flower), *Shikadō* (The Path Leading to the Flower), and *Sandō* (The Three Ways; also called *Nōsakusho* [Book of Composing Noh Plays]). He later took Kanze as his family name.

Zō, also ***Zō (no) onna*** A young female mask, used not only for young women, but also for female deities. The name originates from its creator, Zō-ami, a *dengaku* dancer and a contemporary of Ze-ami.

Selected Bibliography

Works in Japanese

Noh Texts Consulted

Haga, Yaichi, and Nobutsuna Sasaki, eds. *Kōchū Yōkyoku Sōsho* [Annotated Collection of Noh Texts]. 3 vols. Tokyo: Hakubunkan, 1913–15.

Itō, Masayoshi, ed. *Yōkyoku-shū* [Anthology of Noh Plays]. 3 vols. Shinchō Nihon Koten Shūsei, vols. 57, 73, 79. Tokyo: Shinchōsha, 1983–88. (Abbrev. as SNKS.)

Kanze, Ukon (XXIV), et al., eds. *Kanze-ryū yōkyoku zenshū* [Complete Anthology of Kanze School Noh Texts]. Tokyo: Hinoki Shoten, 1975.

Kongō, Iwao, ed. *Matsuyama Tengu.* An *utai-bon* of the Kongō school. Tokyo: Hinoki Shoten, 1961.

Koyama, Hiroshi, et al., eds. *Yōkyoku-shū* [Anthology of Noh Plays]. 2 vols. Nihon Koten Bungaku Zenshū, vols. 33, 34. Tokyo: Shōgakukan, 1973, 1975. (Abbrev. as NKBZ.)

Nishino, Haruo, ed. *Yōkyoku Hyakuban* [100 Noh Plays]. Shin NKBT, vol. 57. Tokyo: Iwanami Shoten, 1998.

Nogami, Toyoichirō, ed. *Kaichū Nōgaku zenshū* [The Complete Annotated Anthology of Noh Plays]. 6 vols. Tokyo: Chūō Kōronsha, 1935; rev. ed., 1961.

Nonomura, Kaizō, and Tsunejirō Andō, eds. *Kyōgen shūsei* [Complete Anthology of Kyogen]. Tokyo: Nōgaku Shorin, 1944.

Sanari, Kentarō, ed. *Yōkyoku Taikan* [Great Anthology of Noh Plays]. 7 vols. Tokyo: Meiji Shoin, 1964]; originally published in 7 vols., 1931–39.

Yokomichi, Mario, and Akira Omote, eds. *Yōkyoku-shū* [Anthology of Noh Plays]. 2 vols. Nihon Koten Bungaku Taikei, vols. 40, 41. Tokyo: Iwanami Shoten, 1967. (Abbrev. as NKBT.)

(*Note:* The published *utai-bon* (chanting texts) and performance texts for the various Noh and Ai-Kyōgen were also consulted.)

Other Works in Japanese

Aoki, Masao, ed. *Rihaku* [Li Po]. Kanshi Taikei, vol. 8. Tokyo: Shūeisha, 1965.

Chigiri, Kōsai. Tengu no Kenkyū [Research on Goblins]. Tokyo: Tairiku Shobō, 1975.

Dōmoto, Masaki. *Nō • Kyōgen no Gei* [The Arts of Noh and Kyogen]. Nihon no Gei series. Tokyo: Tokyo Shoseki, 1983.

———. *Zeami.* Tokyo: Geki Shobō, 1986.

———. *Zeami: Akutingu Mesōdo* [Zeami: Acting Method]. Tokyo: Geki Shobō, 1987.

———. *Zeami no Nō* [The Noh Plays of Zeami]. Shinchō Sensho. Tokyo: Shinchōsha, 1997.

Hanawa, Hokiichi, et al., eds. *Zoku Gunsho Ruiju* [Great Collection of Old Documents, II]. 34 vols. Tokyo: Zoku Gunsho Ruiju Kanseikai, 1929–33: 430.

Hayakawa, Jun'ichirō, ed. *Enkyoku 17-chō, Yōkyoku Mi-Hyaku-ban: Zen* [17 Books of Enkyoku, A New Group of 100 Noh Texts: Complete Edition]. Tokyo: Kokusho Kankō-kai, 1912.

Horie, Kyōko. *Ikyō ni Nemuru Higeki no Bijin: Ō Shōkun* [A Tragic Beauty Buried in a Foreign Land: Wang Chao-chün]. Tokyo: Hakuteisha, 2003.

Ichiko, Teiji, ed. *Heike Monogatari* [Tales of the Heike]. 2 vols. NKBZ, vols. 29, 30. Tokyo: Shogakukan, 1973, 1975.

Ishida, Jōji, and Yoshiko Shimizu, eds. & annot. *Genji Monogatari* (The Tale of Genji). 8 vols. SNKS, vols. 1, 13–19. Tokyo: Shinchosha, 1976–85.

Kaneko, Motoomi, and Seifū Emi, eds. *Wakan Rōei–shū Shin Shaku* [An Anthology of Chinese and Japanese Poems for Chanting: A New Interpretation]. Tokyo: Meiji Shoin, 1942.

Kanze, Hisao. *Kokoro yori Kokoro ni Tsutauru Hana* [The Flower Transmitted from Heart to Heart]. Tokyo: Hakusui-sha, 1979.

Kidō, Saizō, and Hiromi Shigematsu, eds. *Renju Gappeki–shū* [Complete Compendium of Strung Gems (a *yori-ai* manual)]. In: *Rengaron-shū 1.* Chūsei no Bungaku 1:2. Tokyo: Miyai Shoten, 1972.

Kokka Taikan. See Shinpen Kokka Taikan Henshū Iinkai, ed.

Kokumin Tosho Kabushiki Kaisha, eds. *Genpei Jōsuiki* [The Chronicle of the Rise and Fall of the Minamoto and Taira]. 2 vols. Nihon Bungaku Taikei, vols. 15, 16. Tokyo: Kokumin Tosho Kabushiki Kaisha, 1926.

Matsuda, Tamotsu. *Nō • Kyōgen* [Noh and Kyogen]. Dentō Geinō series, 5. Tokyo: Gyōsei, 1990.

Minemura, Fumito, ed. *Shin Kokin Waka–shū.* NKBZ, vol. 26. Tokyo: Shogakukan, 1974.

Nagazumi, Yasuaki, and Isao Shimada, eds. *Hogen Monogatari, Heiji Monogatari.* NKBT, vol. 31. Tokyo: Iwanami Shoten, 1978.

Nishino, Haruo, and Hisashi Hata, eds. *Nō • Kyōgen Jiten* [Dictionary of Noh and Kyogen]. Tokyo: Heibonsha, 1988.

Nishino, Haruo, and Yasushi Matsumoto. *Nō Genkō-kyoku Ichiran* [List of Currently Performed Noh]. In: Nogami, Toyoichirō, ed., with commentary and annotation by Haruo Nishino and Yasushi Matsumoto. *Nōgaku Zensho* [Compendium of Noh Drama], new ed. Vol. 6. Tokyo: Sōgensha, 1979.

Nogami, Toyoichirō. *Nō Nihyaku-yonju-ban: Shūdai to Kōsei* [240 Noh Plays: Their Themes and Structures]. Tokyo: Maruoka Publishing, 1943.

———. *Nogaku Zensho* [Compendium of Noh Drama]. 6 vols. Tokyo: Sōgensha, 1942–44; rev. ed., 7 vols., 1979.

Okami, Masao, ed. *Gikeiki* [The Chronicle of Yoshitsune]. NKBT, vol. 37. Tokyo: Iwanami Shoten, 1965.

Ōmachi, Keigetsu, and Tokiyori Hachiya. *Yōkyoku Jiten* [Dictionary of Noh Texts]. Tokyo: Tachikawa Bunmeidō, 1924.

Omote, Akira, and Shūichi Katō, eds. *Zeami, Zenchiku* [Zeami, Zenchiku]. Nihon Shisō Taikei, vol. 24. Tokyo: Iwanami Shoten, 1975.

Ōsone, Shōsuke, and Hideaki Horiuchi, eds. *Wakan Rōei–shū* [An Anthology of Chinese and Japanese Poems for Chanting]. SNKS, vol. 61. Tokyo: Shinchōsha, 1983.

Ōtsuka, Shin'ichi, ed. *Kyōgen no Sekai* (The World of Kyogen). Iwanami Kōza: Noh, Kyōgen V. Tokyo: Iwanami Shoten, 1987.

Ozawa, Masao, ed. *Kokin Waka–shū.* NKBZ, 7. Tokyo: Shōgakukan, 1971.

Saku, Misao, ed. *Kanshi Taikan* [Great Compendium of Chinese *Shih* Poetry]. 5 vols. Tokyo: Sekishoin, 1936–39.

Sakurama, Kinki. *Nō to Yoshitsune: Shite ga Kataru* [Noh and Yoshitsune: A *Shite* Actor Speaks]. Tokyo: Kōbōsha, 2000.

Shinpen Kokka Taikan Henshū Iinkai, ed. *Shinpen Kokka Taikan* [Great Compendium of Japanese *Waka* Poetry, new ed.]. 10 vols. (each consisting of 2 books). Tokyo: Kadokawa Shoten, 1983–92.

Takagi, Ichinosuke, ed. *Man'yōshū* [The Collection of Ten Thousand Leaves]. 4 vols. NKBT, vols. 4–7. Tokyo: Iwanami Shoten, 1960.

Takemoto, Mikio. "Tennyo no Mai no Kenkyū [A Study of the Angel's Dance]. *Nōgaku Kenkyū* 4:93–157 (1978).

Tanaka, Katsumi, ed. *Haku Rakuten* [Po Lo-t'ien (Po Chü-i)]. Kanshi Taikei, vol. 12. Tokyo: Shūeisha, 1964.

Tokue, Gensei. *Sakuhin Kenkyu:* Kuruma-zō (A Study of *Kuruma-zō*). *Kanze* (Nov. 1984)

Yashima, Masaharu. "'Tennyo-mai' no Kenkyū to Umewaka Makio to. ["A Study of *Tennyo-mai* and Makio Umewaka]. *Nōgaku Hyōron* 32:17–21 (1979).

Works in English

Reference Works

English Buddhist Dictionary Committee, eds. *The Soka Gakkai Dictinary of Buddhism.* Tokyo: Soka Gakkai, 2002.

Hayashima, Kyosho, et al., eds. Japanese-English Buddhist Dictionary (Based on: Ui, Hakuju, comp. *Konsaisu-bukkyo-jiten.* Tokyo: Daitō Publishing Co., 1935). Tokyo: Daitō, 1965.

Inagaki, Hisao, with P.G. O'Neill. *A Dictionary of Japanese Buddhist Terms (Based on References in Japanese Literature).* 4th ed., rev. ed. Kyoto: Nagata Bunshodō, 1992.

Mathews, R.H., comp. *A Chinese-English Dictionary, Compiled for the China Inland Mission.* Shanghai: China Inland Mission and Presbyterian Mission Press, 1931. Reprinted by Taipei: Caves Books, 1975 (Rev. American ed., with rev. English index, 13th printing).

Nichiren Shoshu International Center, ed. *A Dictionary of Buddhist terms and Concepts.* Tokyo: NSIC, 1983.

Other Works

Blofeld, John, trans. *The Book of Change.* London: George Allen and Unwin, 1965.

Eoyang, Eugene. "The Wang Chao-chun Legend: Configurations of the Classic." *Chinese Literature: Essays, Articles, Reviews* 4.1 (Jan. 1982), 3–22.

Goff, Janet. *Noh Drama and* The Tale of Genji: *The Art of Allusion in Fifteen Classical Plays.* Princeton Library of Asian Translations. Princeton: Princeton University Press, 1991.

Hare, Tom. *Zeami: Performance Notes.* Translations from the Asian Classics. New York: Columbia University Press, 2008.

Katō, Bunnō, et al., trans. "The Sutra of the Lotus Flower of the Wonderful Law." In: *The Threefold Lotus Sutra.* New York and Tokyo: Weatherhill/Kosei, 1975.

Komparu, Kunio. *The Noh Theater: Principles and Perspectives.* Trans. by Jane Corddry and Stephen Comee. Weatherhill/Tankosha, 1983.

McCullough, Helen Craig, trans. *Tales of Ise: Lyrical Episodes from Tenth-Century Japan.* Tokyo: The University of Tokyo Press, 1968.

———. *Yoshitsune: A Fifteenth-Century Japanese Chronicle.* Tokyo: The University of Tokyo Press, 1966.

Miner, Earl, et al. *The Princeton Companion to Classical Japanese Literature.* Princeton: Princeton University Press, 1985.

Morrell, Robert E. *Sand & Pebbles: The Tales of Mujū Ichien, A Voice for*

Pluralism in Kamakura Buddhism. Albany, New York: State University of New York Press, 1985.

Munro, Stanley R. "The Evolution of the Wang Chao-Chun Legend." *Chung Chi Journal* 9:2 (May 1970), pp. 202–9.

Papinot, E. *Historical and Geographical Dictionary of Japan.* 4th printing. Tokyo: Charles E. Tuttle, 1976. A reprint of Yokohama: Kelly & Walsh, Ltd., 1910.

Oyler, Elizabeth. "The *Nue* and Other Monsters in *Heike Monogatari.*" *Harvard Journal of Asiatic Studies* 68:2 (Dec. 2008), pp. 1–32.

Shimazaki, Chifumi. (All previous published translations, as listed in the preface.)

Soothill, William Edward, trans. *The Analects, or The Conversations of Confucius with His Disciples and Certain Others.* Oxford: Oxford University Press, 1910; reprinted in The World's Classics, 1937

Stiskin, Nahum. *The Looking-Glass God: Shinto, Yin-Yang, and a Cosmology for Today.* An Autumn Press Book. Tokyo: Weatherhill, 1971. Rev. ed., 1972.

Szu-ma Ch'ien (Ssu-ma Ch'ien). *Records of the Historian.* Trans. by Yang Hsien-yi and Gladys Yang. Hong Kong: The Commercial Press, 1985.

Thera, Nyoniponika. *The Heart of Buddhist Meditation.* London: Rider & Co., 1962.

Twitchett, Denis C., et al. *Cambridge History of China, Vol. 1: The Ch'in and Han Empires, 221 BC–AD 200.* Cambridge: Cambridge University Press, 1986 (esp. 235–36).

Wang, Rongpei, and Ren, Xiuhua, trans. and annot. *The Book of Poetry* [*Shih-ching*]. Beijing: Liaoning Education Press, 1995.

Wild Bird Society of Japan. *A Field Guide to the Birds of Japan.* Tokyo: Kodansha International, 1982.

de Wisser, M.W. "The Tengu." *Transactions of the Asiatic Society of Japan* 36.2 (1908).

Index

Ch. = *Chinese; Jpn.* = *Japanese; Skt.* = *Sanskrit*

CORNELL EAST ASIA SERIES

4 Fredrick Teiwes, *Provincial Leadership in China: The Cultural Revolution and Its Aftermath*
8 Cornelius C. Kubler, *Vocabulary and Notes to Ba Jin's Jia: An Aid for Reading the Novel*
16 Monica Bethe & Karen Brazell, *Nō as Performance: An Analysis of the Kuse Scene of Yamamba*. Available for purchase: DVD by Monica Bethe & Karen Brazell, "Yamanba: The Old Woman of the Mountains"
18 Royall Tyler, tr., *Granny Mountains: A Second Cycle of Nō Plays*
23 Knight Biggerstaff, *Nanking Letters, 1949*
28 Diane E. Perushek, ed., *The Griffis Collection of Japanese Books: An Annotated Bibliography*
37 J. Victor Koschmann, Ōiwa Keibō & Yamashita Shinji, eds., *International Perspectives on Yanagita Kunio and Japanese Folklore Studies*
38 James O'Brien, tr., *Murō Saisei: Three Works*
40 Kubo Sakae, *Land of Volcanic Ash: A Play in Two Parts*, revised edition, tr. David G. Goodman
44 Susan Orpett Long, *Family Change and the Life Course in Japan*
48 Helen Craig McCullough, *Bungo Manual: Selected Reference Materials for Students of Classical Japanese*
49 Susan Blakeley Klein, *Ankoku Butō: The Premodern and Postmodern Influences on the Dance of Utter Darkness*
50 Karen Brazell, ed., *Twelve Plays of the Noh and Kyōgen Theaters*
51 David G. Goodman, ed., *Five Plays by Kishida Kunio*
52 Shirō Hara, *Ode to Stone*, tr. James Morita
53 Peter J. Katzenstein & Yutaka Tsujinaka, *Defending the Japanese State: Structures, Norms and the Political Responses to Terrorism and Violent Social Protest in the 1970s and 1980s*
54 Su Xiaokang & Wang Luxiang, *Deathsong of the River: A Reader's Guide to the Chinese TV Series* Heshang, trs. Richard Bodman & Pin P. Wan
55 Jingyuan Zhang, *Psychoanalysis in China: Literary Transformations, 1919–1949*
56 Jane Kate Leonard & John R. Watt, eds., *To Achieve Security and Wealth: The Qing Imperial State and the Economy, 1644–1911*
57 Andrew F. Jones, *Like a Knife: Ideology and Genre in Contemporary Chinese Popular Music*
58 Peter J. Katzenstein & Nobuo Okawara, *Japan's National Security: Structures, Norms and Policy Responses in a Changing World*
59 Carsten Holz, *The Role of Central Banking in China's Economic Reforms*
60 Chifumi Shimazaki, *Warrior Ghost Plays from the Japanese Noh Theater: Parallel Translations with Running Commentary*
61 Emily Groszos Ooms, *Women and Millenarian Protest in Meiji Japan: Deguchi Nao and Ōmotokyō*

62 Carolyn Anne Morley, *Transformation, Miracles, and Mischief: The Mountain Priest Plays of Kōygen*
63 David R. McCann & Hyunjae Yee Sallee, tr., *Selected Poems of Kim Namjo*, afterword by Kim Yunsik
64 Hua Qingzhao, *From Yalta to Panmunjom: Truman's Diplomacy and the Four Powers, 1945-1953*
65 Margaret Benton Fukasawa, *Kitahara Hakushū: His Life and Poetry*
66 Kam Louie, ed., *Strange Tales from Strange Lands: Stories by Zheng Wanlong*, with introduction
67 Wang Wen-hsing, *Backed Against the Sea*, tr. Edward Gunn
69 Brian Myers, *Han Sōrya and North Korean Literature: The Failure of Socialist Realism in the DPRK*
70 Thomas P. Lyons & Victor Nee, eds., *The Economic Transformation of South China: Reform and Development in the Post-Mao Era*
71 David G. Goodman, tr., *After Apocalypse: Four Japanese Plays of Hiroshima and Nagasaki*, with introduction
72 Thomas Lyons, *Poverty and Growth in a South China County: Anxi, Fujian, 1949–1992*
74 Martyn Atkins, *Informal Empire in Crisis: British Diplomacy and the Chinese Customs Succession, 1927-1929*
76 Chifumi Shimazaki, *Restless Spirits from Japanese Noh Plays of the Fourth Group: Parallel Translations with Running Commentary*
77 Brother Anthony of Taizé & Young-Moo Kim, trs., *Back to Heaven: Selected Poems of Ch'ŏn Sang Pyŏng*
78 Kevin O'Rourke, tr., *Singing Like a Cricket, Hooting Like an Owl: Selected Poems by Yi Kyu-bo*
79 Irit Averbuch, *The Gods Come Dancing: A Study of the Japanese Ritual Dance of Yamabushi Kagura*
80 Mark Peterson, *Korean Adoption and Inheritance: Case Studies in the Creation of a Classic Confucian Society*
81 Yenna Wu, tr., *The Lioness Roars: Shrew Stories from Late Imperial China*
82 Thomas Lyons, *The Economic Geography of Fujian: A Sourcebook*, Vol. 1
83 Pak Wan-so, *The Naked Tree*, tr. Yu Young-nan
84 C.T. Hsia, *The Classic Chinese Novel: A Critical Introduction*
85 Cho Chong-Rae, *Playing With Fire*, tr. Chun Kyung-Ja
86 Hayashi Fumiko, *I Saw a Pale Horse and Selections from Diary of a Vagabond*, tr. Janice Brown
87 Motoori Norinaga, *Kojiki-den, Book 1*, tr. Ann Wehmeyer
88 Chang Soo Ko, tr., *Sending the Ship Out to the Stars: Poems of Park Je-chun*
89 Thomas Lyons, *The Economic Geography of Fujian: A Sourcebook*, Vol. 2
90 Brother Anthony of Taizé, tr., Midang: *Early Lyrics of So Chong-Ju*
92 Janice Matsumura, *More Than a Momentary Nightmare: The Yokohama Incident and Wartime Japan*
93 Kim Jong-Gil tr., *The Snow Falling on Chagall's Village: Selected Poems of Kim Ch'un-Su*

94 Wolhee Choe & Peter Fusco, trs., *Day-Shine: Poetry by Hyon-jong Chong*
95 Chifumi Shimazaki, *Troubled Souls from Japanese Noh Plays of the Fourth Group*
96 Hagiwara Sakutarō, *Principles of Poetry (Shi no Genri)*, tr. Chester Wang
97 Mae J. Smethurst, *Dramatic Representations of Filial Piety: Five Noh in Translation*
98 Ross King, ed., *Description and Explanation in Korean Linguistics*
99 William Wilson, *Hōgen Monogatari: Tale of the Disorder in Hōgen*
100 Yasushi Yamanouchi, J. Victor Koschmann and Ryūichi Narita, eds., *Total War and 'Modernization'*
101 Yi Ch'ŏng-jun, *The Prophet and Other Stories*, tr. Julie Pickering
102 S.A. Thornton, *Charisma and Community Formation in Medieval Japan: The Case of the Yugyō-ha (1300-1700)*
103 Sherman Cochran, ed., *Inventing Nanjing Road: Commercial Culture in Shanghai, 1900-1945*
104 Harold M. Tanner, *Strike Hard! Anti-Crime Campaigns and Chinese Criminal Justice, 1979-1985*
105 Brother Anthony of Taizé & Young-Moo Kim, trs., *Farmers' Dance: Poems by Shin Kyŏng-nim*
106 Susan Orpett Long, ed., *Lives in Motion: Composing Circles of Self and Community in Japan*
107 Peter J. Katzenstein, Natasha Hamilton-Hart, Kozo Kato, & Ming Yue, *Asian Regionalism*
108 Kenneth Alan Grossberg, *Japan's Renaissance: The Politics of the Muromachi Bakufu*
109 John W. Hall & Toyoda Takeshi, eds., *Japan in the Muromachi Age*
110 Kim Su-Young, Shin Kyong-Nim, Lee Si-Young; *Variations: Three Korean Poets*; trs. Brother Anthony of Taizé & Young-Moo Kim
111 Samuel Leiter, *Frozen Moments: Writings on* Kabuki, *1966–2001*
112 Pilwun Shih Wang & Sarah Wang, *Early One Spring: A Learning Guide to Accompany the Film Video* February
113 Thomas Conlan, *In Little Need of Divine Intervention: Scrolls of the Mongol Invasions of Japan*
114 Jane Kate Leonard & Robert Antony, eds., *Dragons, Tigers, and Dogs: Qing Crisis Management and the Boundaries of State Power in Late Imperial China*
115 Shu-ning Sciban & Fred Edwards, eds., *Dragonflies: Fiction by Chinese Women in the Twentieth Century*
116 David G. Goodman, ed., *The Return of the Gods: Japanese Drama and Culture in the 1960s*
117 Yang Hi Choe-Wall, *Vision of a Phoenix: The Poems of Hŏ Nansŏrhŏn*
118 Mae J. Smethurst and Christina Laffin, eds., *The Noh* Ominameshi*: A Flower Viewed from Many Directions*
119 Joseph A. Murphy, *Metaphorical Circuit: Negotiations Between Literature and Science in Twentieth-Century Japan*
120 Richard F. Calichman, *Takeuchi Yoshimi: Displacing the West*

121 Fan Pen Li Chen, *Visions for the Masses: Chinese Shadow Plays from Shaanxi and Shanxi*
122 S. Yumiko Hulvey, *Sacred Rites in Moonlight: Ben no Naishi Nikki*
123 Tetsuo Najita and J. Victor Koschmann, *Conflict in Modern Japanese History: The Neglected Tradition*
124 Naoki Sakai, Brett de Bary, & Iyotani Toshio, eds., *Deconstructing Nationality*
125 Judith N. Rabinovitch and Timothy R. Bradstock, *Dance of the Butterflies: Chinese Poetry from the Japanese Court Tradition*
126 Yang Gui-ja, *Contradictions*, trs. Stephen Epstein and Kim Mi-Young
127 Ann Sung-hi Lee, *Yi Kwang-su and Modern Korean Literature:* Mujŏng
128 Pang Kie-chung & Michael D. Shin, eds., *Landlords, Peasants, & Intellectuals in Modern Korea*
129 Joan R. Piggott, ed., *Capital and Countryside in Japan, 300–1180: Japanese Historians Interpreted in English*
130 Kyoko Selden and Jolisa Gracewood, eds., *Annotated Japanese Literary Gems: Stories by Tawada Yōko, Nakagami Kenji, and Hayashi Kyōko* (Vol. 1)
131 Michael G. Murdock, *Disarming the Allies of Imperialism: The State, Agitation, and Manipulation during China's Nationalist Revolution, 1922–1929*
132 Noel J. Pinnington, *Traces in the Way: Michi and the Writings of Komparu Zenchiku*
133 Charlotte von Verschuer, *Across the Perilous Sea: Japanese Trade with China and Korea from the Seventh to the Sixteenth Centuries*, Kristen Lee Hunter, tr.
134 John Timothy Wixted, *A Handbook to Classical Japanese*
135 Kyoko Selden and Jolisa Gracewoord, with Lili Selden, eds., *Annotated Japanese Literary Gems: Stories by Natsume Sōseki, Tomioka Taeko, and Inoue Yasushi* (Vol. 2)
136 Yi Tae-Jin, *The Dynamics of Confucianism and Modernization in Korean History*
137 Jennifer Rudolph, *Negotiated Power in Late Imperial China: The Zongli Yamen and the Politics of Reform*
138 Thomas D. Loooser, *Visioning Eternity: Aesthetics, Politics, and History in the Early Modern Noh Theater*
139 Gustav Heldt, *The Pursuit of Harmony: Poetry and Power in Late Heian Japan*
140 Joan R. Piggott and Yoshida Sanae, *Teishinkōki: The Year 939 in the Journal of Regent Fujiwara no Tadahira*
141 Robert Bagley, *Max Loehr and the Study of Chinese Bronzes: Style and Classification in the History of Art*
142 Edwin A. Cranston, *The Secret Island and the Enticing Flame: Worlds of Memory, Discovery, and Loss in Japanese Poetry*
143 Hugh de Ferranti, *The Last Biwa Singer: A Blind Musician in History, Imagination and Performance*
144 Roger des Forges, Minglu Gao, Liu Chiao-mei, haun Saussy, with Thomas Burkman, eds., *Chinese Walls in Time and Space: A Multidisciplinary Perspective*
145 Hye-jin Juhn Sidney & George Sidney, trs., *I Heard Life Calling Me: Poems of Yi Sŏng-bok*
146 Sherman Cochran & Paul G. Pickowicz, eds., *China on the Margins*

147 Wang Lingzhen & Mary Ann O' Donnell, trs., *Years of Sadness: Autobiographical Writings of Wang Anyi*

148 John Holstein, tr., *A Moment's Grace: Stories from Korea in Transition*

149 Sunyoung Park in collaboration with Jefferson J.A. Gatrall, trs., *On the Eve of the Uprising and Other Stories from Colonial Korea*

150 Brother Anthony of Taizé & Lee Hyung-jin, trs., *Walking on a Washing Line: Poems of Kim Seung-Hee*

151 Matthew Fraleigh, trs., with introduction, *New Chronicles of Yanagibashi and Diary of a Journey to the West: Narushima Ryūhoku Reports from Home and Abroad*

152 Pei Huang, *Reorienting the Manchus: A Study of Sinicization, 1583–1795*

153 Karen Gernant & Chen Zeping, *White Poppies and Other Stories by Zhang Kangkang*

154 Mattias Burell & Marina Svensson, eds., *Making Law Work: Chinese Laws in Context*

155 Tomoko Aoyama & Barbara Hartley, trs., *Indian Summer by Kanai Mieko*

156 Lynne Kutsukake, tr., *Single Sickness and Other Stories by Masuda Mizuko*

157 Takako U. Lento, tr. with introduction, *Tanikawa Shuntarō: The Art of Being Alone, Poems 1952–2009*

158 Shu-ning Sciban & Fred Edwards, eds., *Endless War: Fiction & Essays by Wang Wen-hsing*

159 Elizabeth Oyler & Michael Watson, eds., *Like Clouds and Mists: Studies and Translations of Nō Plays of the Genpei War*

160 Michiko N. Wilson & Michael K. Wilson, trs., *Of Birds Crying by Minako Ōba*

161 Chifumi Shimazaki & Stephen Comee *Supernatural Beings from Japanese Noh Plays of the Fifth Group: Parallel Translations with Running Commentary*

162 Petrus Liu, *Stateless Subjects: Chinese Martial Arts Literature and Postcolonial History*

163 Lim Beng Choo, *Another Stage: Kanze Nobumitsu and the Late Muromachi Noh Theater*

eap.einaudi.cornell.edu/publications